Second Grade Math with Confidence

Student Workbook

Second Grade Math with Confidence

Student Workbook

KATE SNOW

WELL-TRAINED MIND PRESS

Reprinted May 2023 by Bradford & Bigelow

5 6 7 8 9 10 11 12 B&B 31 30 29 28 27 26 25 24 23

Table of Contents

This Student Workbook is only one component of *Second Grade Math with Confidence,* and it is not meant to be used as a stand-alone workbook. The hands-on teaching activities in the Instructor Guide are an essential part of the program.

See the Instructor Guide for how to play.
Save this game board for future lessons.

Addition Climb and Slide

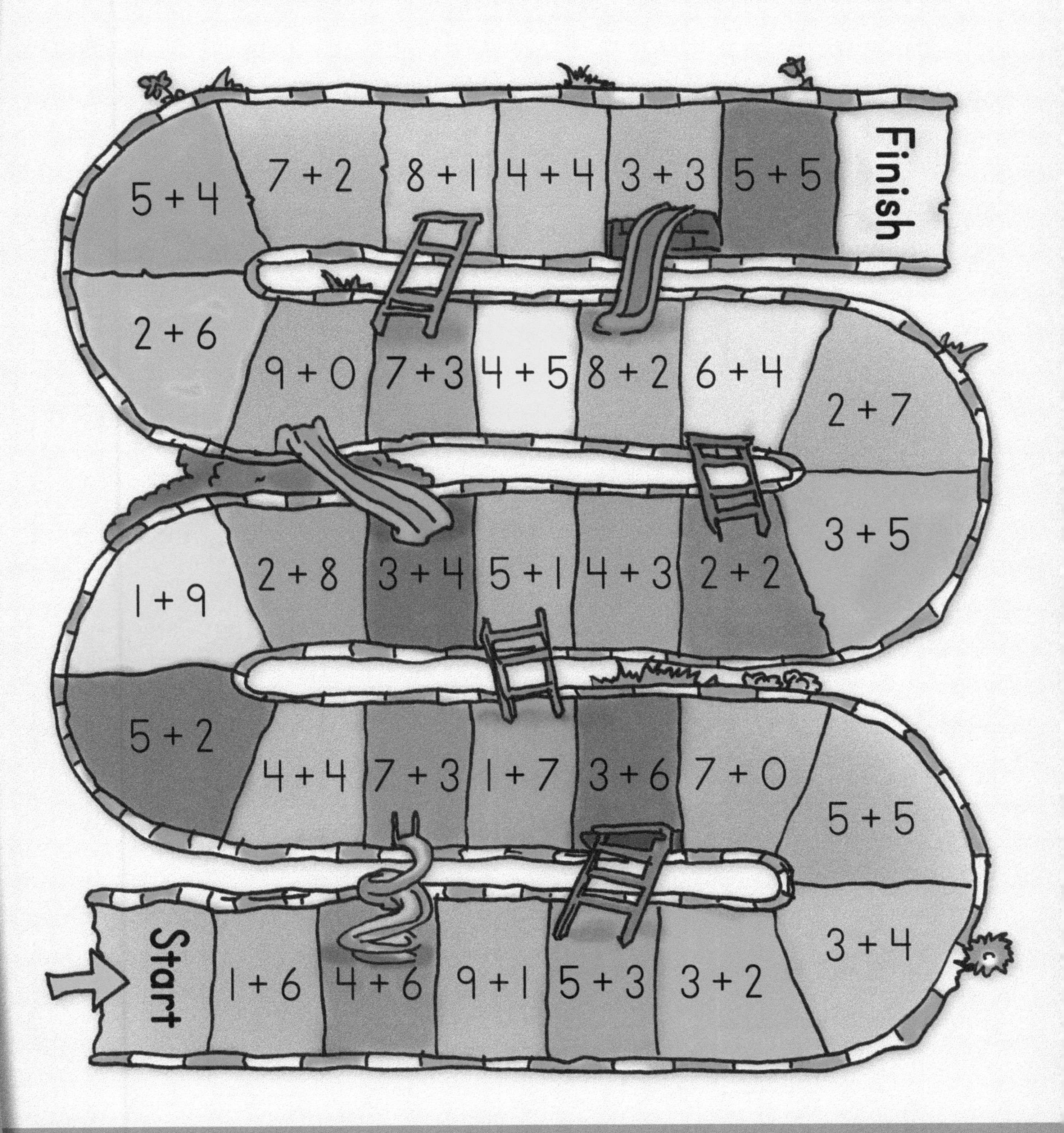

Trace and copy.

0 1 2 3 4

0

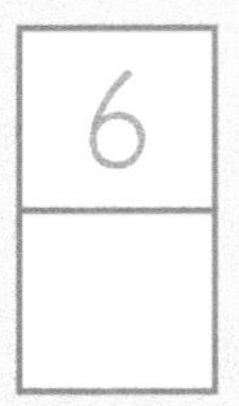

5 6 7 8 9

Complete.

4 + 2 = ☐   2 + 3 = ☐   6 + 2 = ☐

1 + 5 = ☐   4 + 1 = ☐   3 + 2 = ☐

1 + 6 = ☐   2 + 2 = ☐   0 + 4 = ☐

Complete.

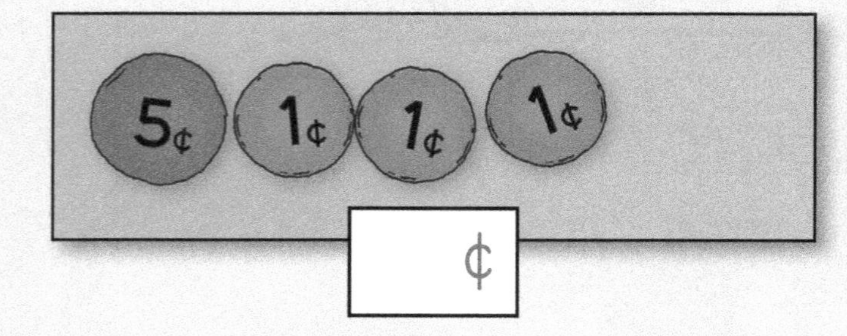

☐ ¢

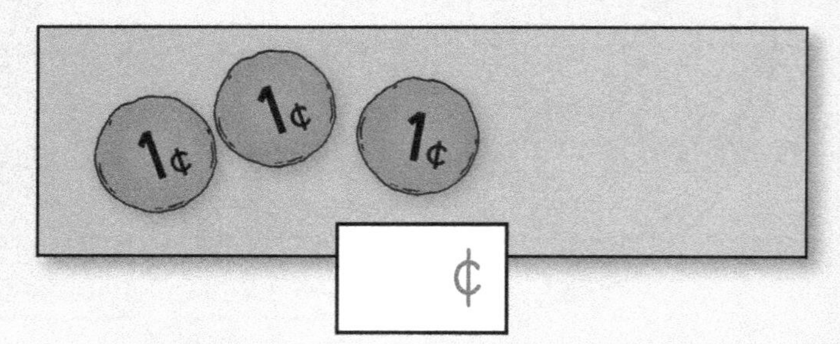

☐ ¢

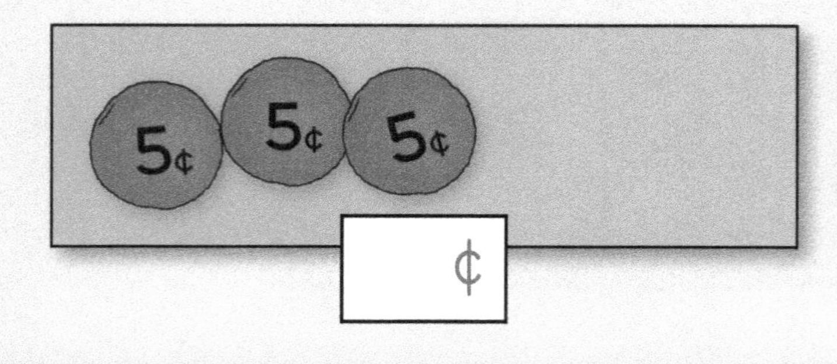

☐ ¢

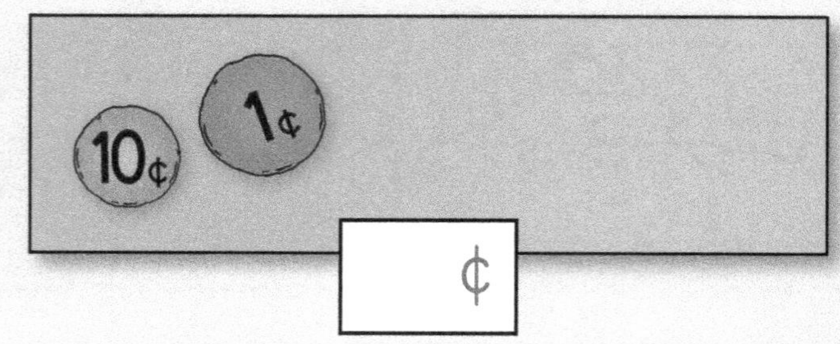

☐ ¢

Complete.

$7 + 2 = \square$

$17 + 2 = \square$

$4 + 5 = \square$

$14 + 5 = \square$

$3 + 6 = \square$

$13 + 6 = \square$

$1 + 6 = \square$

$11 + 6 = \square$

$4 + 4 = \square$

$14 + 4 = \square$

$5 + 5 = \square$

$15 + 5 = \square$

Write the sum of each row of cards.

Sum: ☐

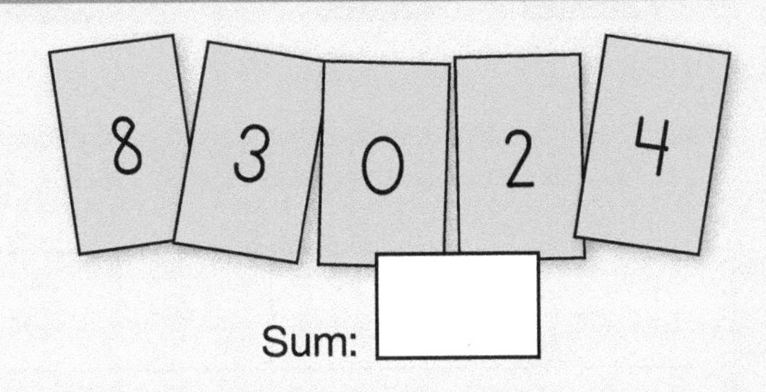

Sum: ☐

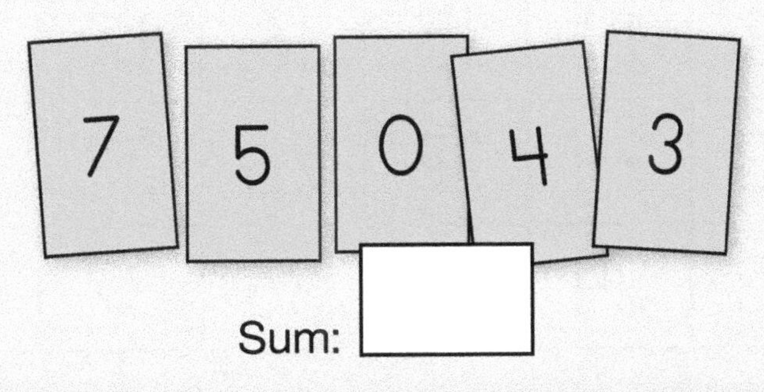

Sum: ☐

Ava made a tally chart of the weather each day. Use the chart to answer the questions.

How many days were cloudy? ☐

How many days were sunny? ☐

How many days were rainy? ☐

Weather Tally Chart

Cloudy Days	~~||||~~ ||
Sunny Days	~~||||~~ ||||
Rainy Days	|||

Circle the greater number in each pair.

7 5	4 8	10 11
20 2	11 15	12 18

Color the numbers you say when you count by 2s.

1	2	3	4	5	6	7	8	9	10
11	12	13	14	15	16	17	18	19	20
21	22	23	24	25	26	27	28	29	30
31	32	33	34	35	36	37	38	39	40

See the Instructor Guide for how to play.
Save this game board for future lessons.

Subtraction Climb and Slide

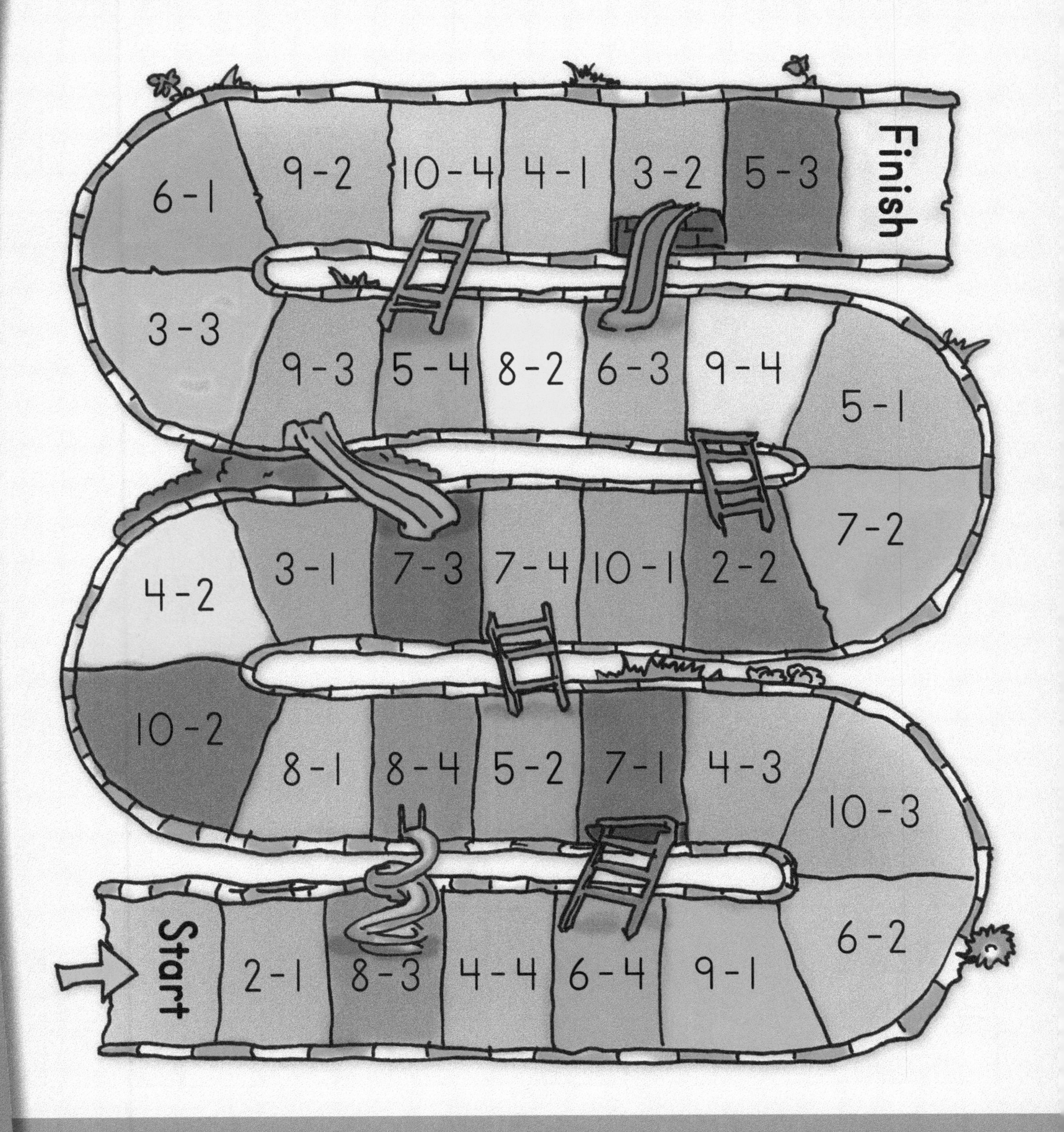

Complete.

$5 - 1 =$ ☐ $4 - 4 =$ ☐ $10 - 2 =$ ☐

$8 - 0 =$ ☐ $8 - 1 =$ ☐ $5 - 2 =$ ☐

$10 - 3 =$ ☐ $4 - 3 =$ ☐ $8 - 3 =$ ☐

Color the triangles. X the shapes that are not triangles.

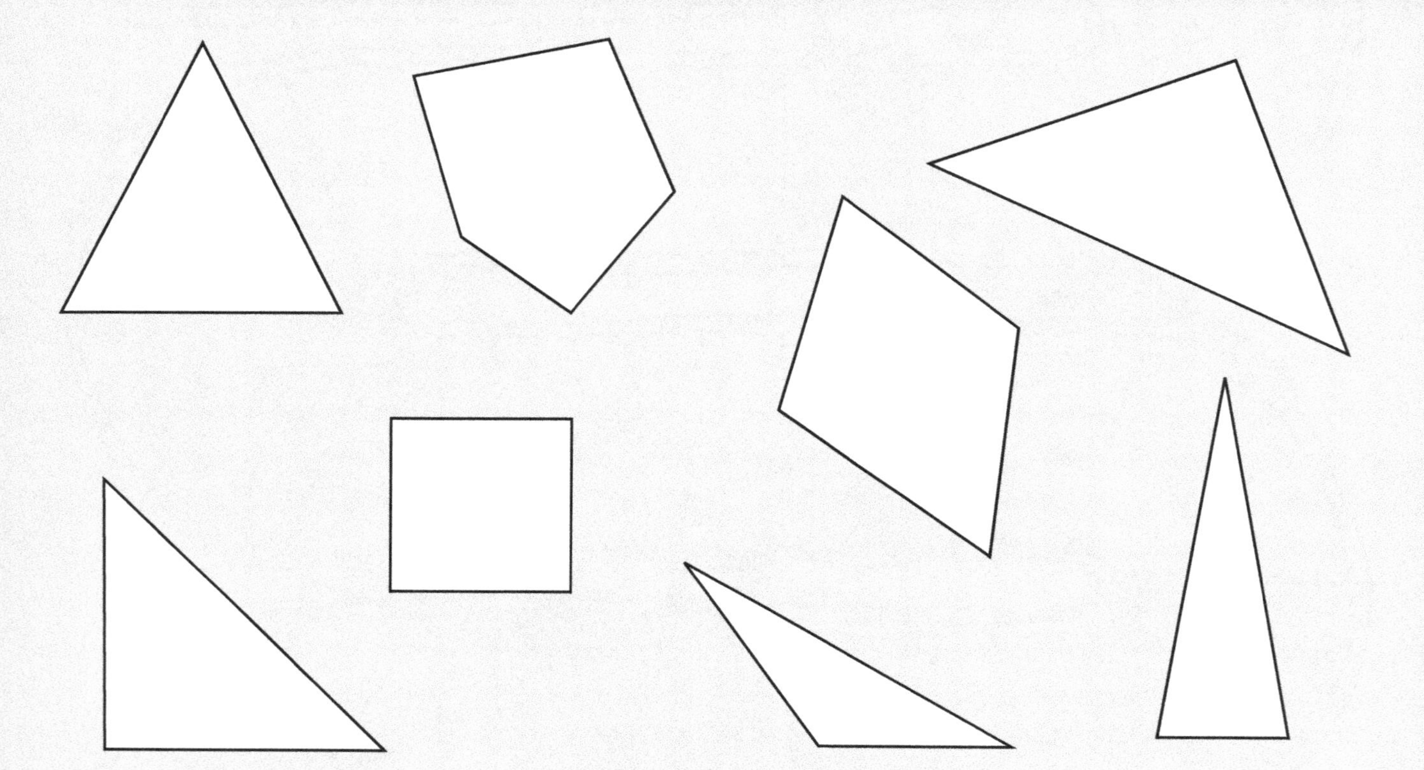

Write the number that comes before and after.

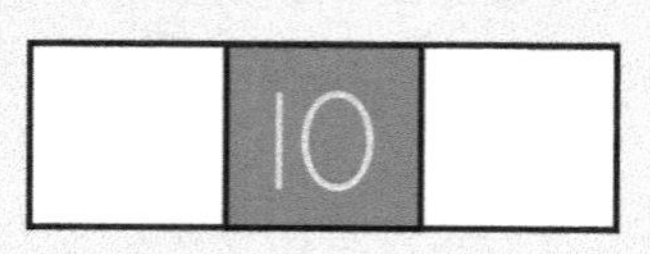

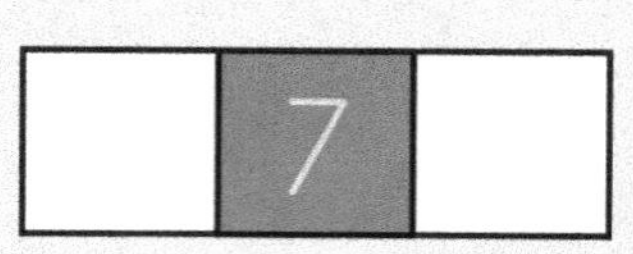

	16	

Complete.

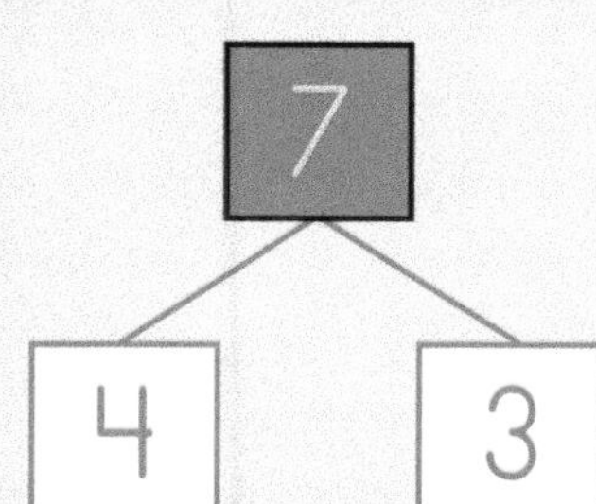

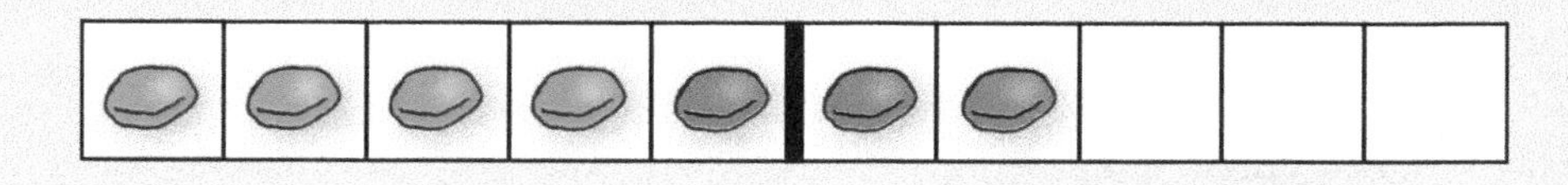

4 + 3 = 7

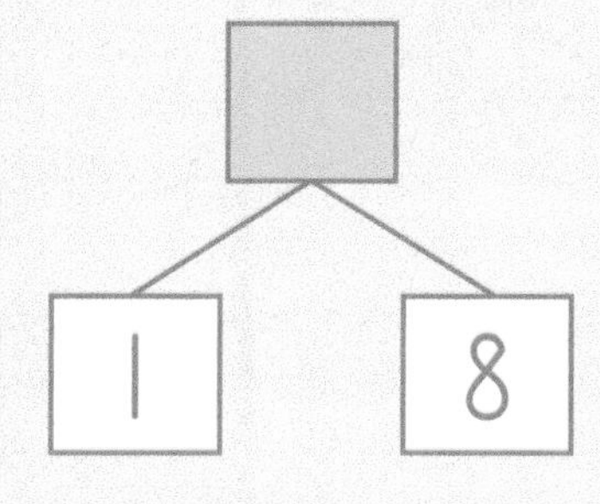

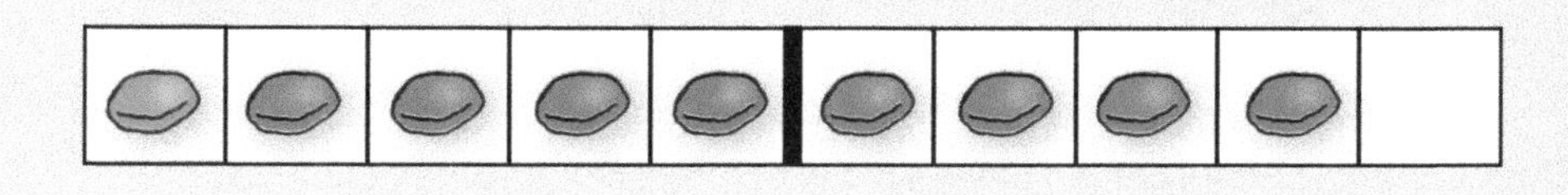

☐ + ☐ = ☐

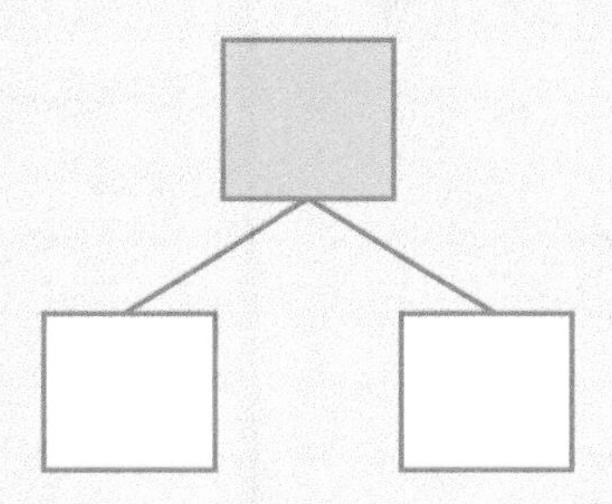

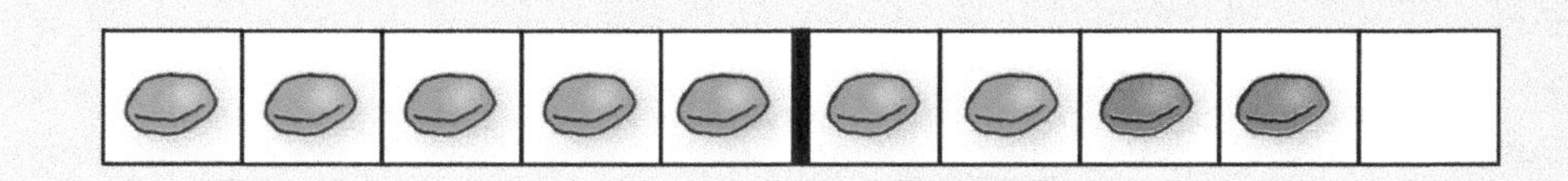

☐ + ☐ = ☐

Complete the fact families to match the Part-Total Diagrams.

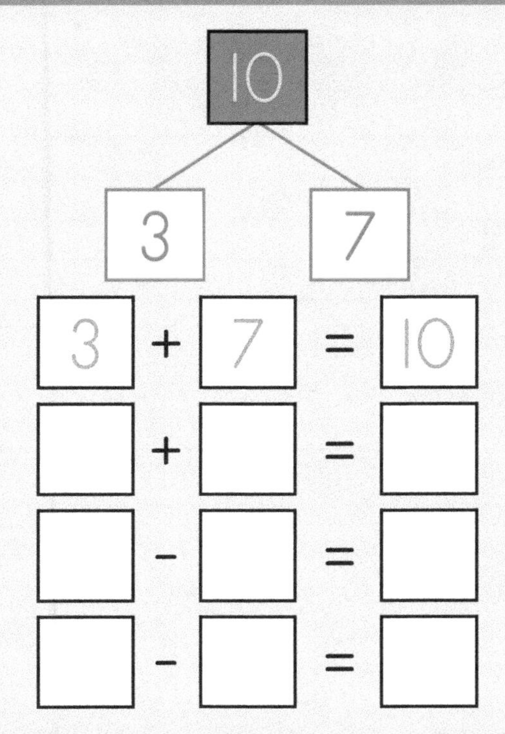

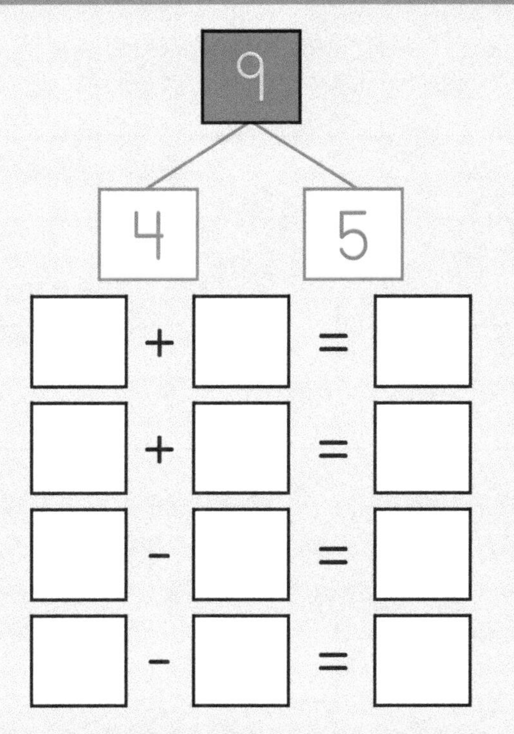

Draw a line that splits each cookie in half.

Complete.

9 - 1 = ☐   6 - 2 = ☐   9 - 4 = ☐

10 - 4 = ☐   5 - 4 = ☐   3 - 1 = ☐

7 - 2 = ☐   5 - 3 = ☐   9 - 0 = ☐

Complete.

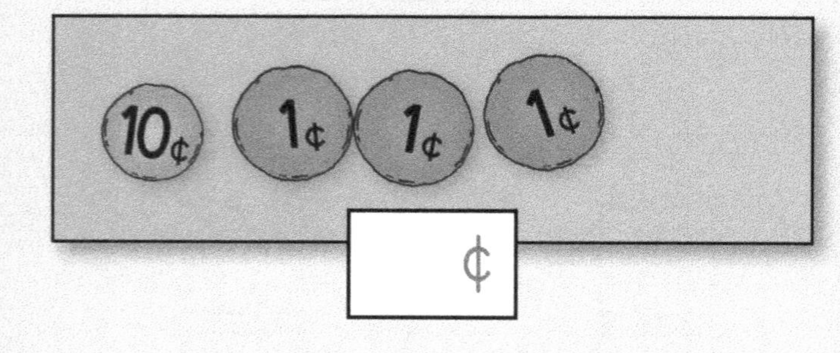

☐ ¢

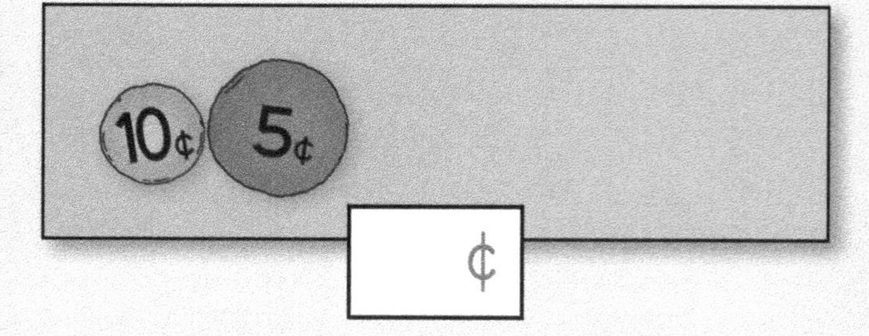

☐ ¢

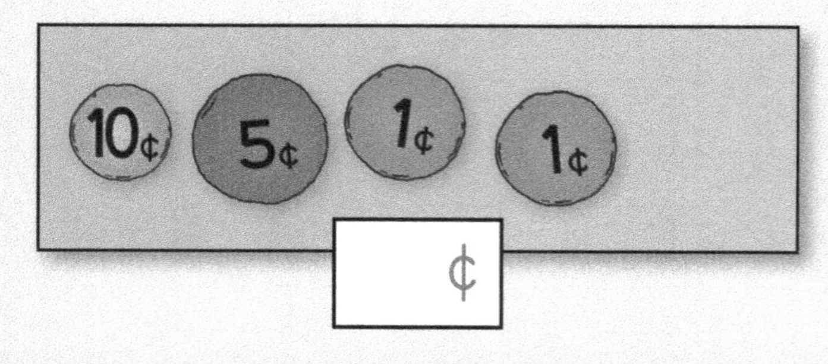

☐ ¢

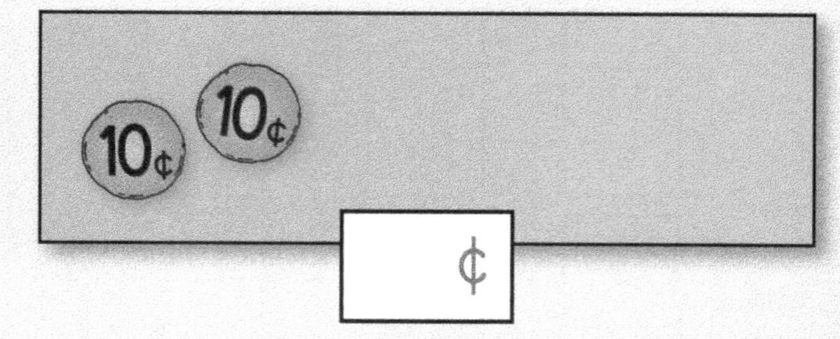

☐ ¢

Complete the circles with <, >, or =

4 < 5	8 > 2	6 = 6
7 ◯ 7	6 ◯ 5	10 ◯ 9
17 ◯ 16	8 ◯ 18	80 ◯ 18
36 ◯ 63	40 ◯ 42	50 ◯ 50
64 ◯ 67	95 ◯ 95	83 ◯ 82

Complete the missing numbers on the 100 Chart.

51	52	53	54		56	57	58	59	
61		63	64	65	66	67	68	69	70
71	72		74	75	76	77		79	80
	82	83	84	85	86		88	89	
91	92	93		95	96	97	98		100

Complete the fact family to match the Part-Total Diagram.

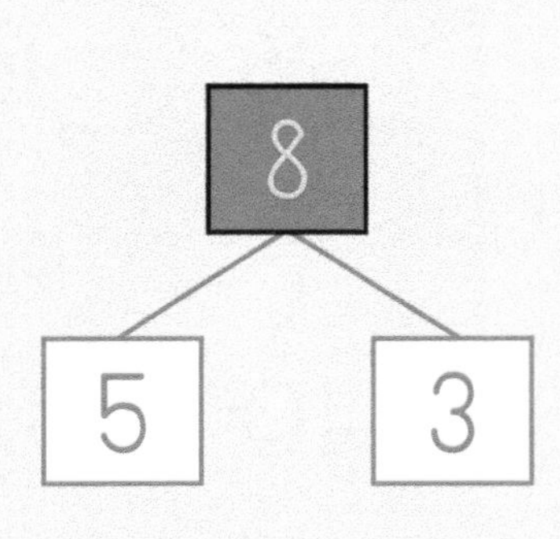

☐ + ☐ = ☐

☐ + ☐ = ☐

☐ - ☐ = ☐

☐ - ☐ = ☐

Complete. Use the ten-frame to help.

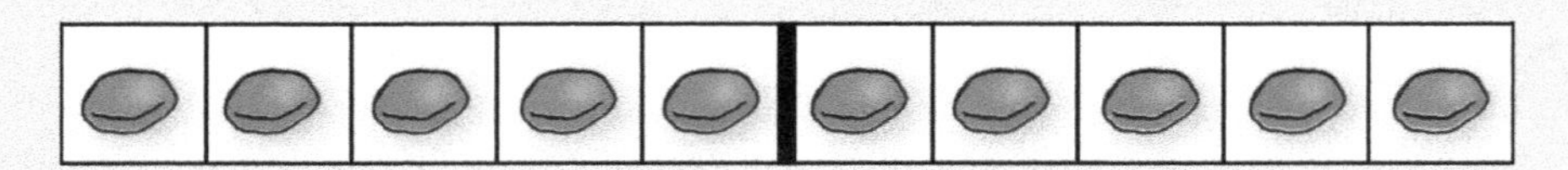

10 - 1 = ☐

10 - 4 = ☐

10 - 2 = ☐

10 - 3 = ☐

10 - 5 = ☐

10 - 9 = ☐

10 - 6 = ☐

10 - 8 = ☐

10 - 7 = ☐

10 - 0 = ☐

Draw lines that split each cookie into fourths.

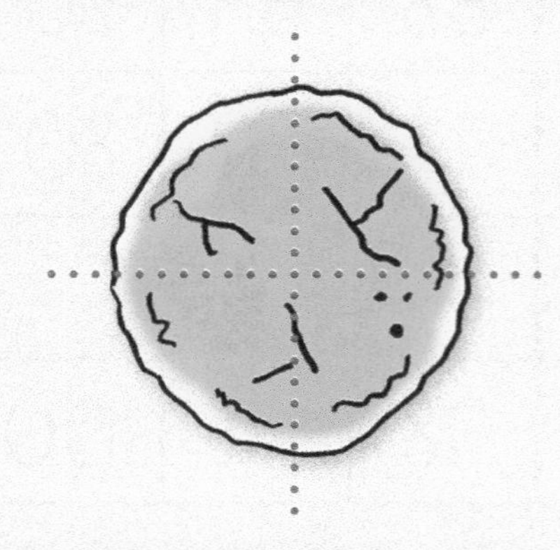

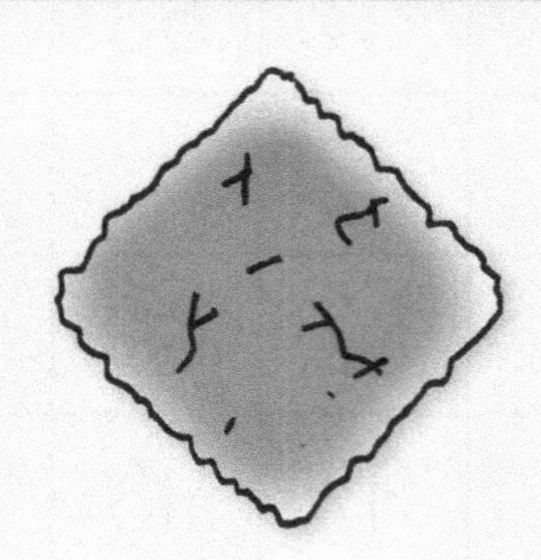

Complete the circles with <, >, or =.

42 (>) 41	35 (<) 36	40 (=) 40
7 ( ) 17	38 ( ) 20	43 ( ) 40
55 ( ) 60	100 ( ) 99	82 ( ) 83
6 ( ) 60	50 ( ) 50	100 ( ) 10
11 ( ) 10	17 ( ) 71	74 ( ) 54

Complete each box with a number that makes the statement true.

6 > ☐	4 < ☐	5 = ☐
3 > ☐	10 < ☐	19 < ☐
26 < ☐	48 > ☐	73 = ☐
☐ > 40	☐ < 75	☐ > 82
99 < ☐	99 > ☐	99 = ☐

Match.

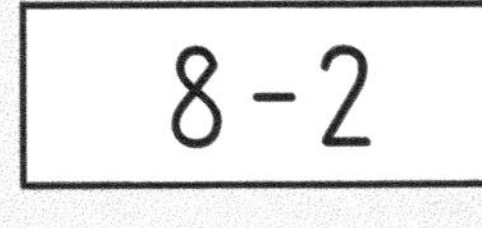

8 - 2		8 - 4
	4	
9 - 4		7 - 2
	5	
7 - 3		10 - 5
	6	
9 - 5		9 - 3

Liam flipped a coin. He made a bar graph to show how many times he flipped heads and how many times he flipped tails. Use the bar graph to answer the questions.

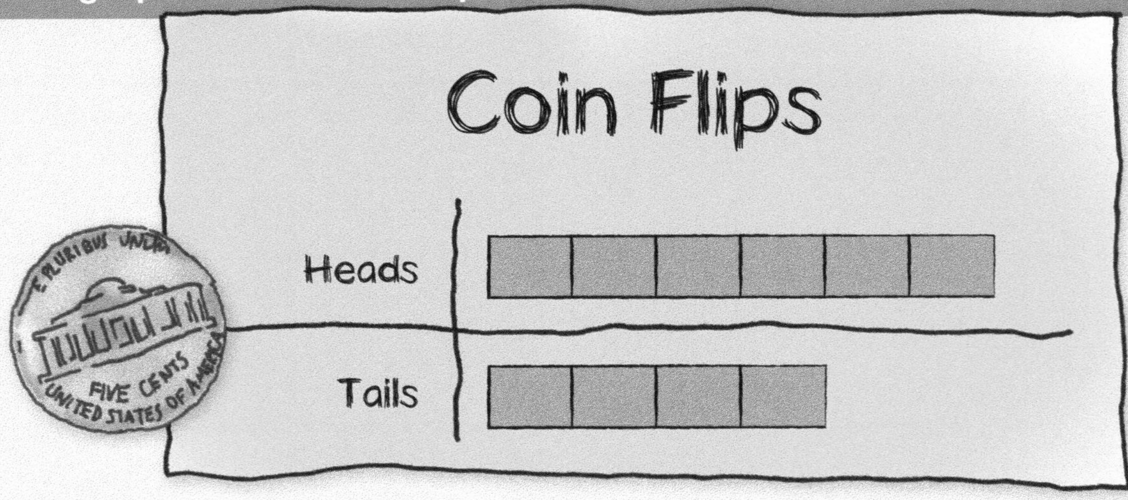

How many heads did he flip? 

How many tails did he flip?

How many more heads than tails did he flip?

How many times did he flip the coin in all?

Connect each number to its spot on the number line.

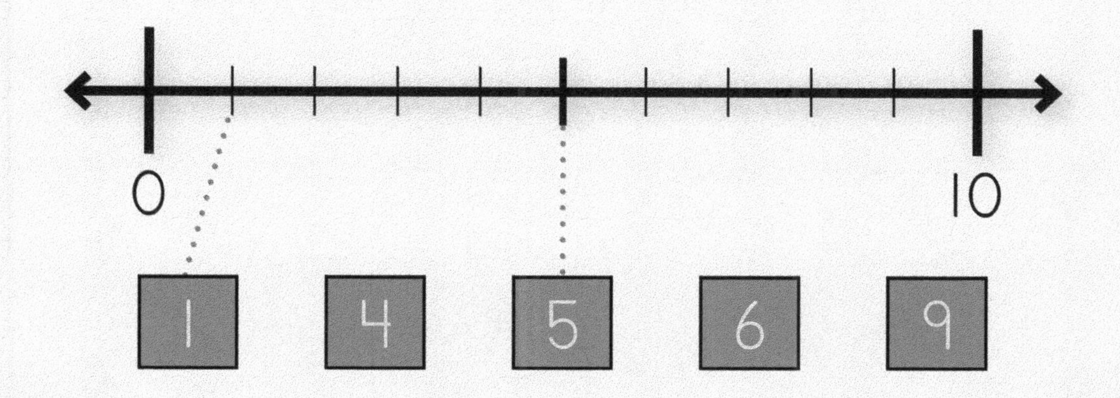

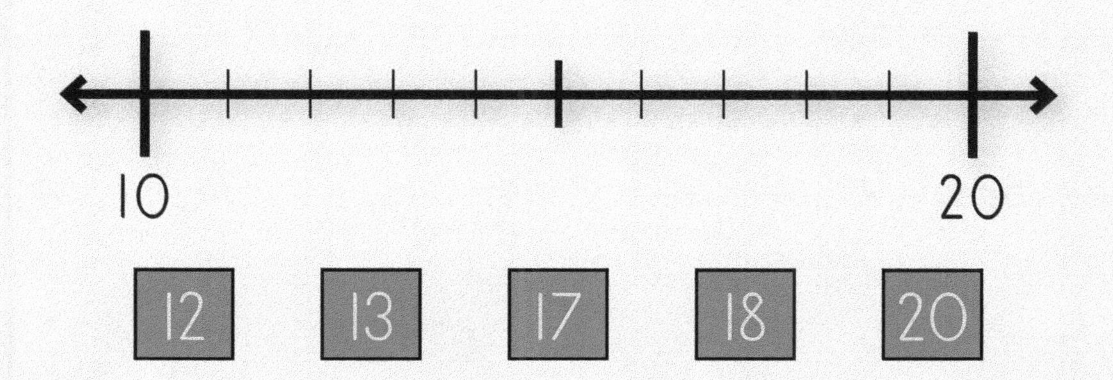

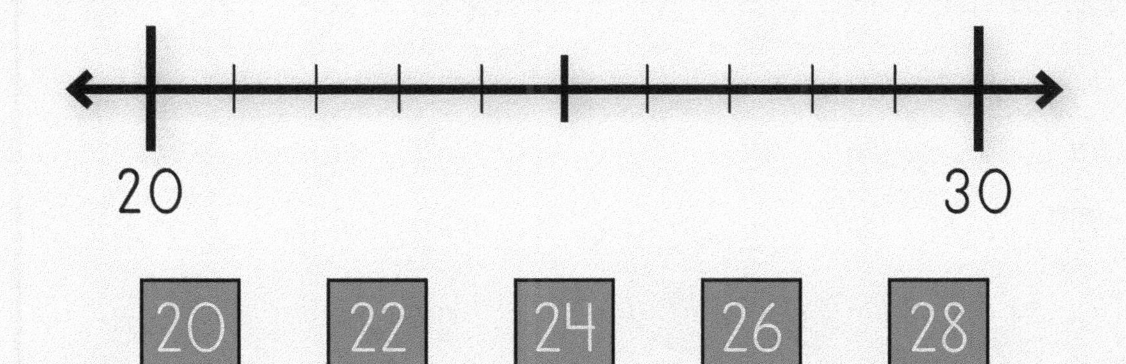

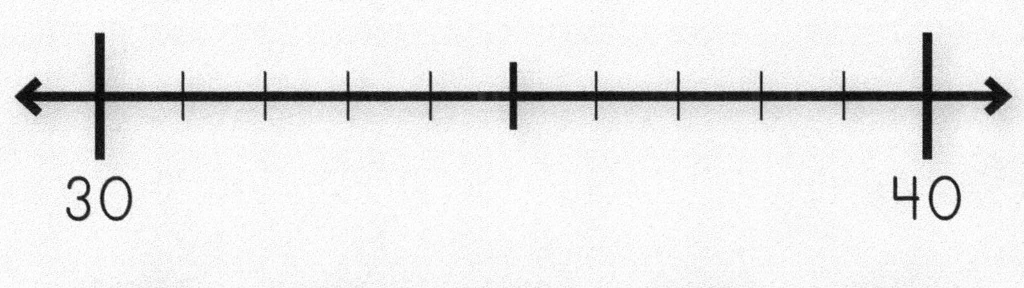

Complete.

$6 + 3 = \square$ $3 + 1 = \square$ $1 + 7 = \square$

$2 + 6 = \square$ $4 + 4 = \square$ $3 + 2 = \square$

$3 + 7 = \square$ $2 + 5 = \square$ $0 + 6 = \square$

$5 + 4 = \square$ $2 + 8 = \square$ $1 + 9 = \square$

X the shape that doesn't belong in each row.

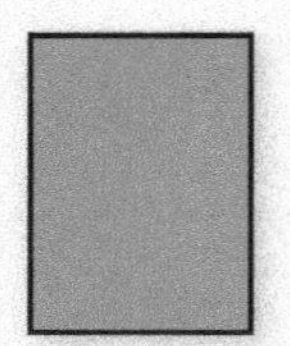

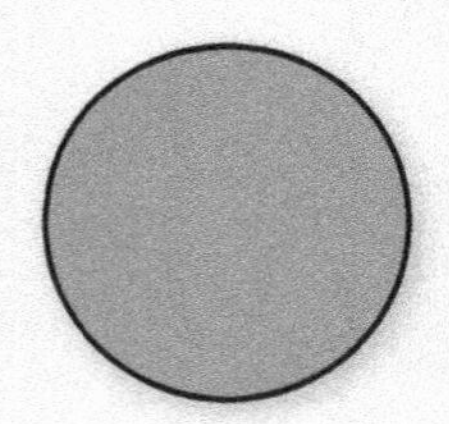
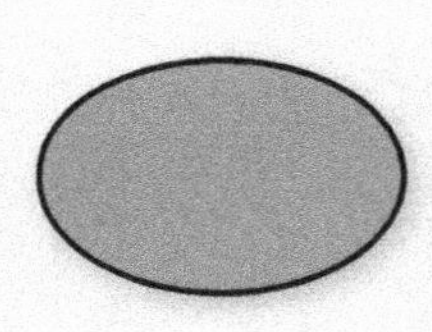
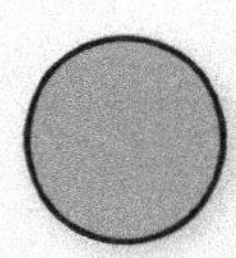

Complete.

$ [ ]

$ [ ]

Complete the missing numbers in the sequences.

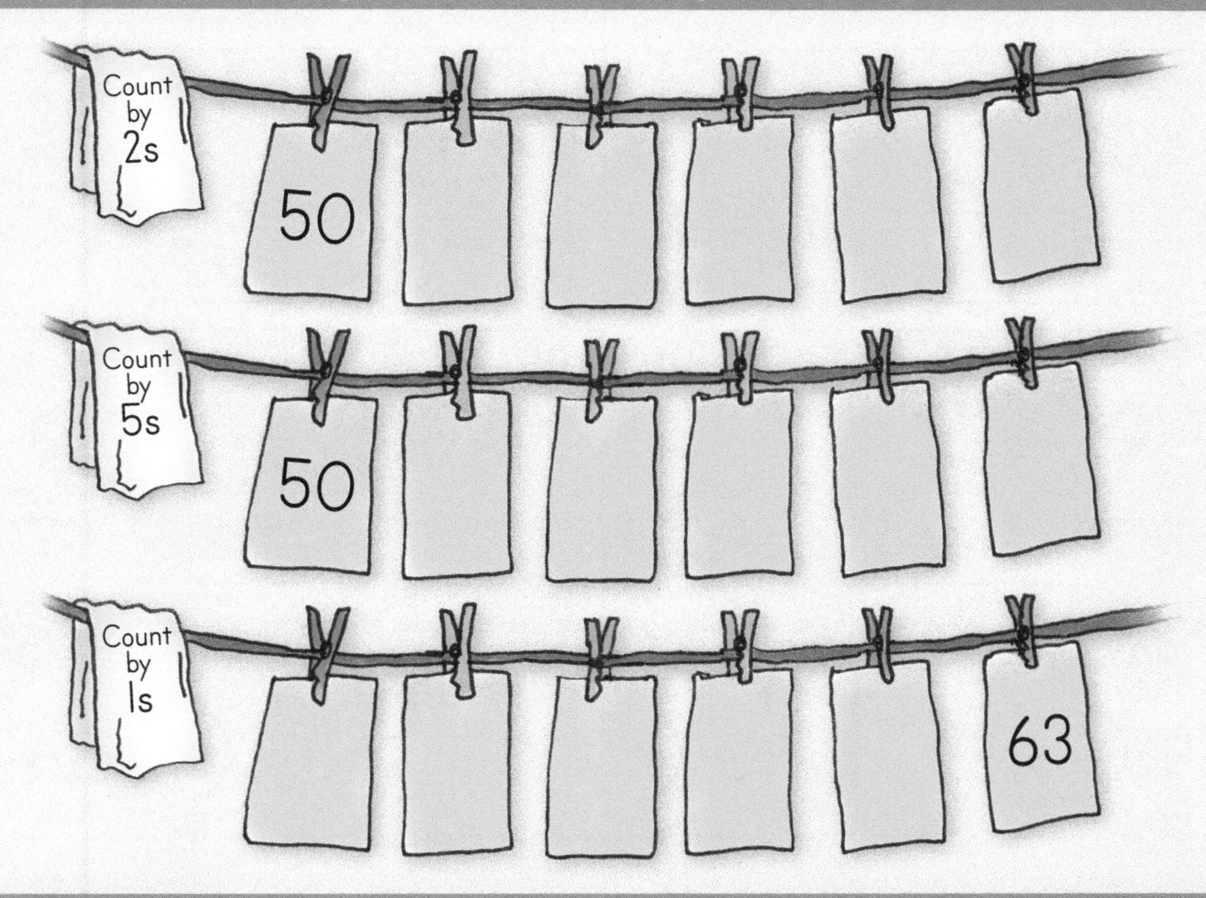

Use the number line to complete.

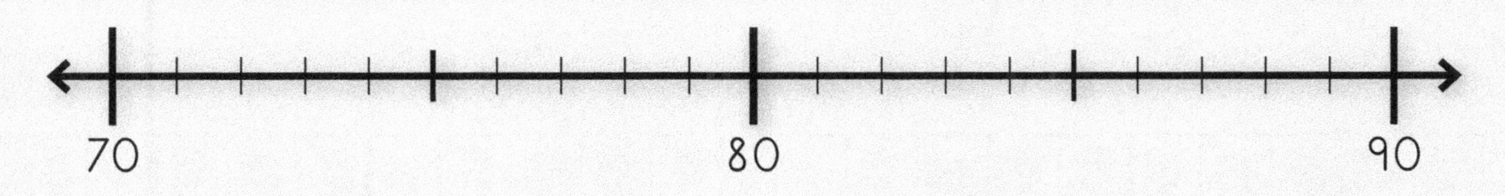

What number is 1 more than 80? ☐	What number is 1 less than 80? ☐
What number is 3 more than 75? ☐	What number is 3 less than 84? ☐
What number is 5 more than 70? ☐	What number is 5 less than 80? ☐

Complete.

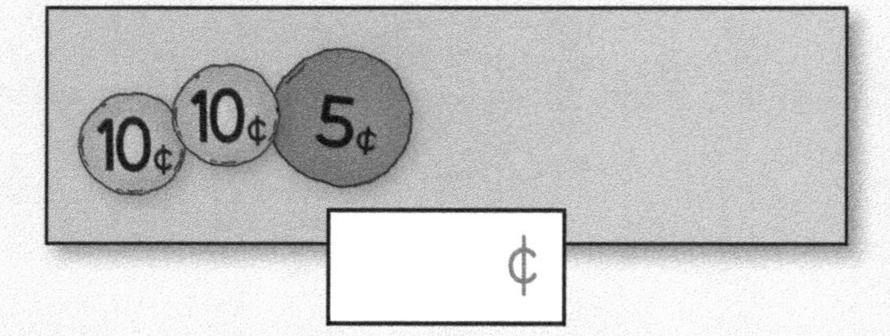

☐ ¢

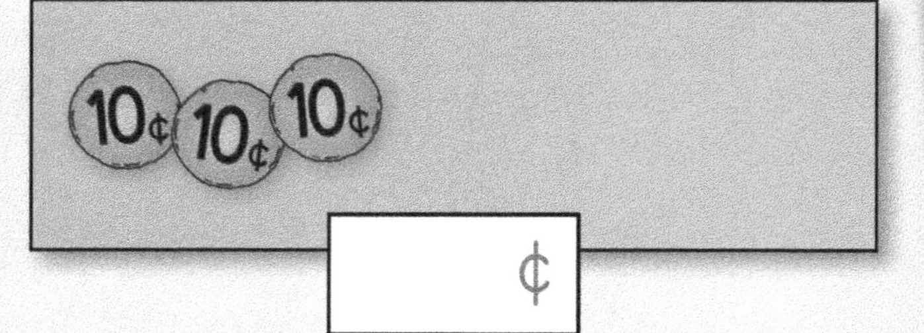

☐ ¢

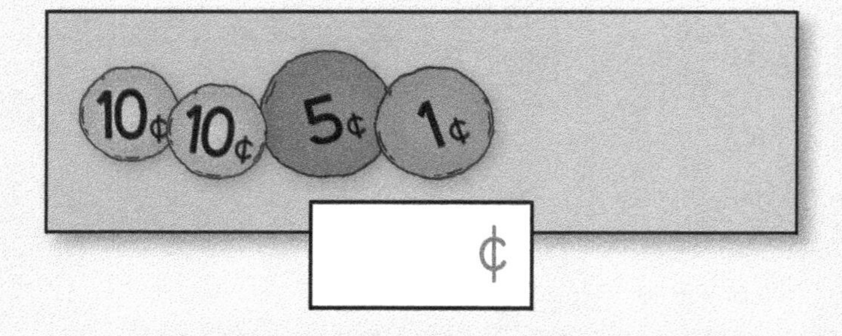

☐ ¢

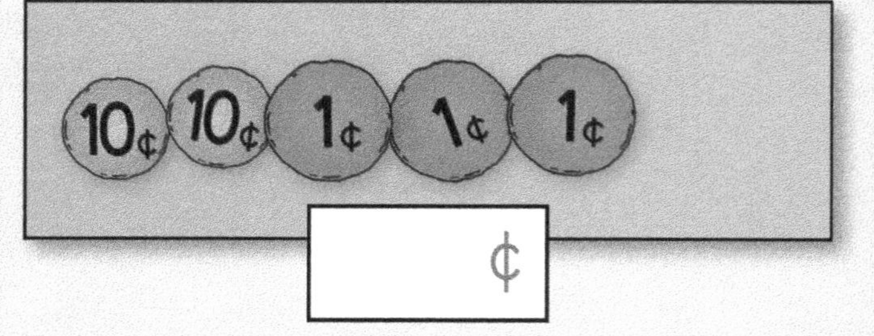

☐ ¢

Complete the circles with <, >, or =.

14 ◯ 12	90 ◯ 100	37 ◯ 36
85 ◯ 75	75 ◯ 85	75 ◯ 75

Complete.

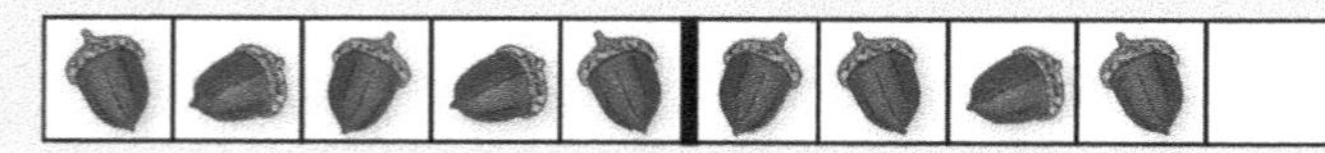

$6 + \square = 9$

$\square + 8 = 9$

$0 + \square = 9$

$7 + \square = 9$

$5 + \square = 9$

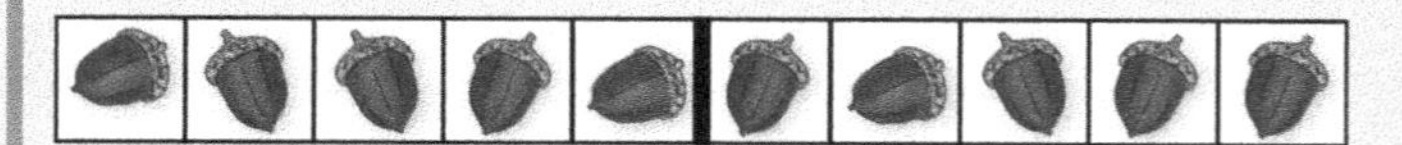

$5 + \square = 10$

$9 + \square = 10$

$\square + 3 = 10$

$\square + 6 = 10$

$8 + \square = 10$

Match.

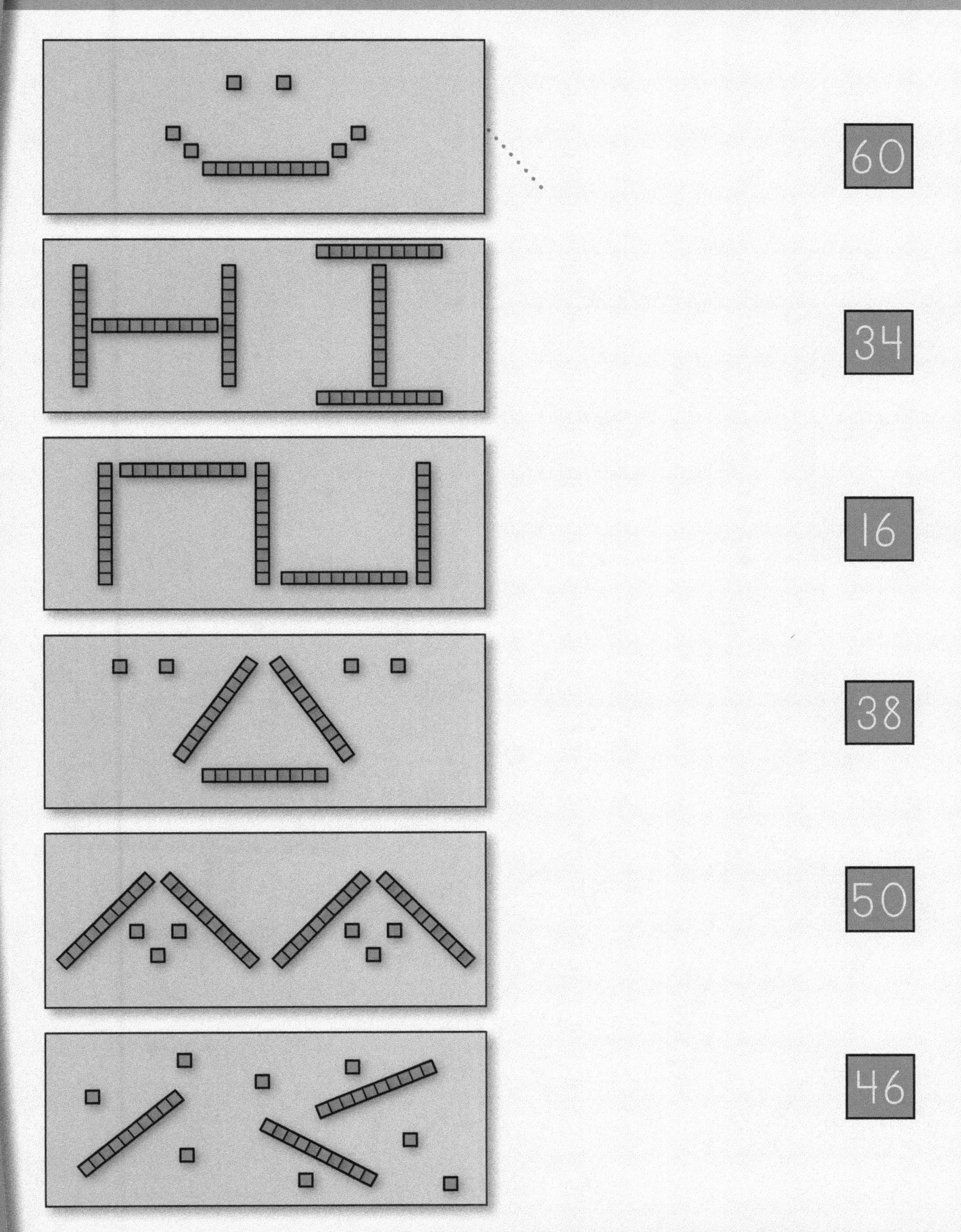

Complete.

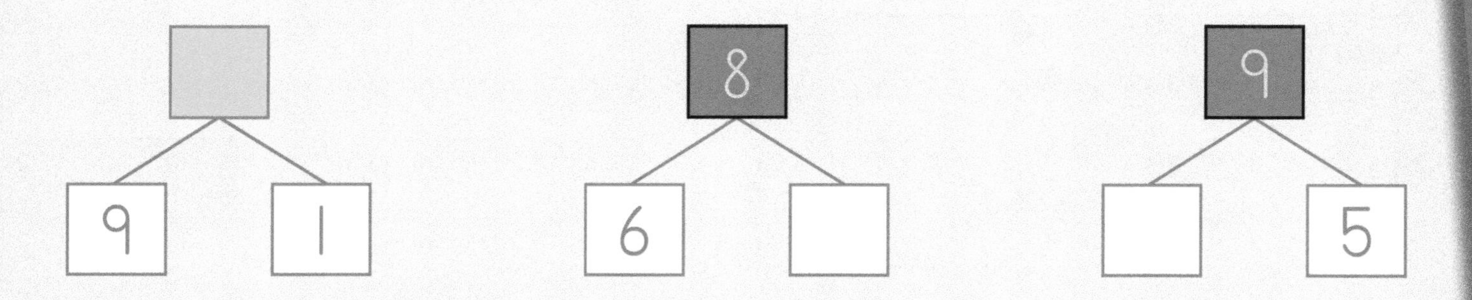

Copy the shape.

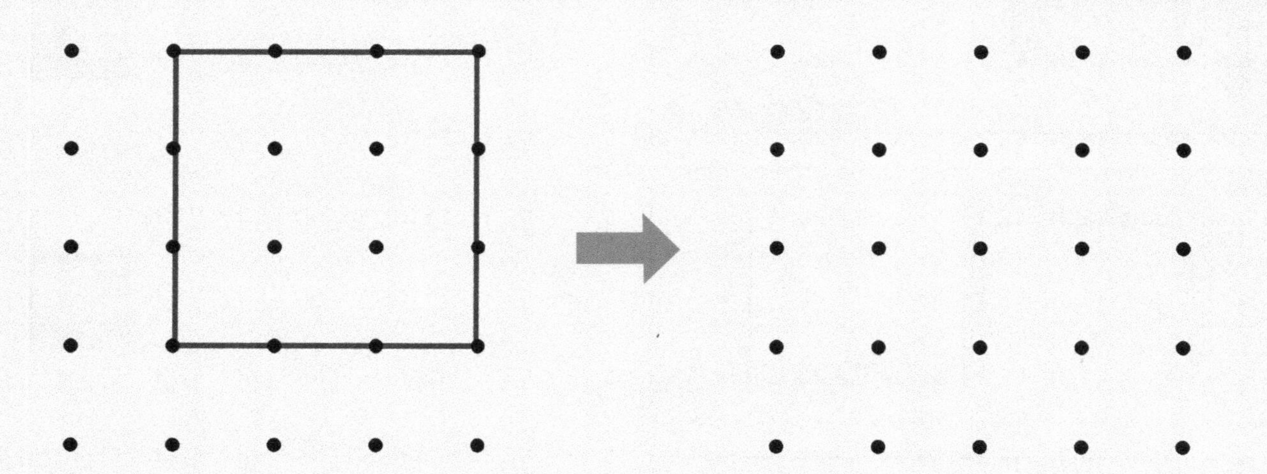

Use the key to color the leaves.

Write the value of each set of base-ten blocks.

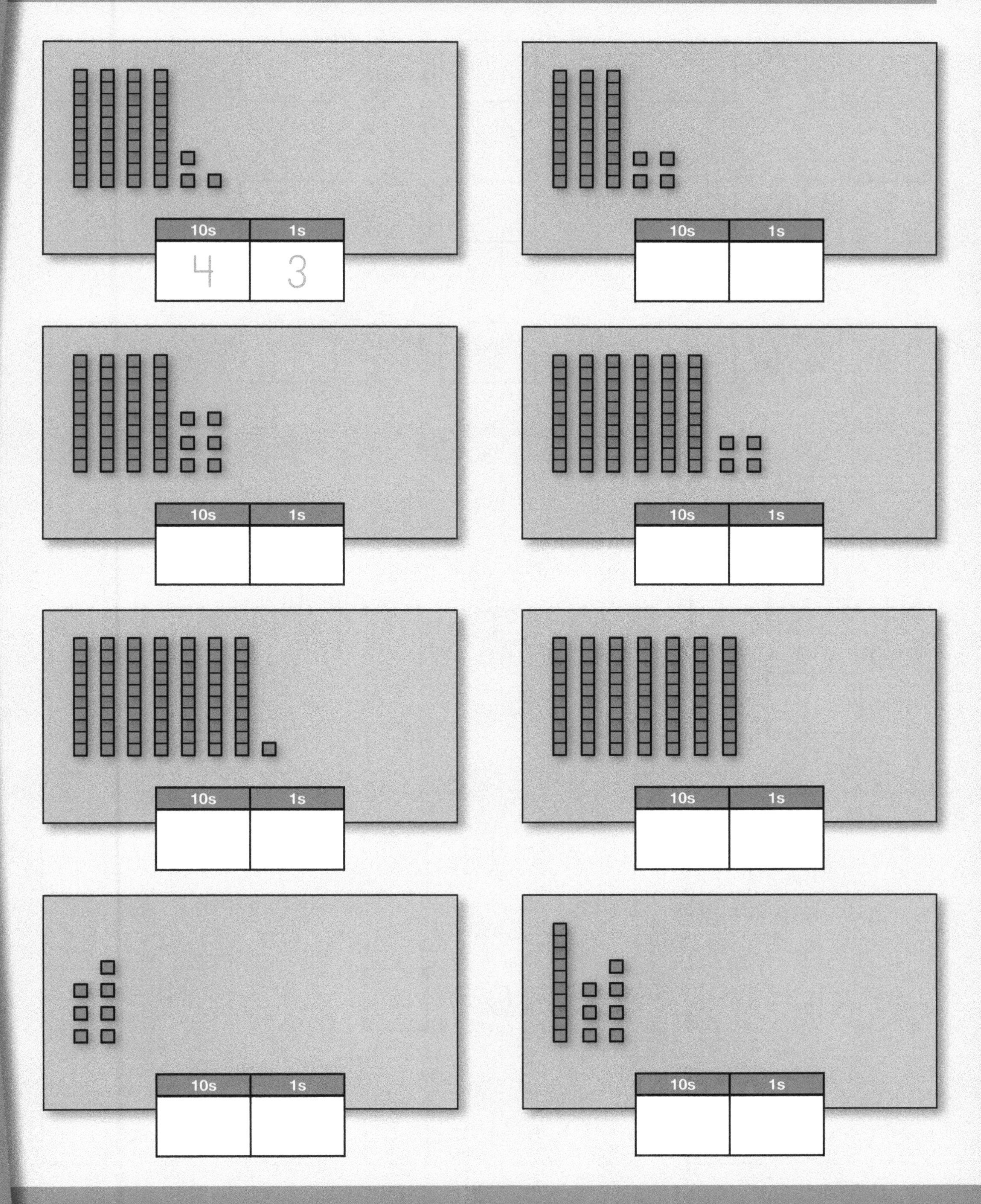

Complete.

2 → +2 → ☐ → +2 → ☐ → +2 → ☐ → +2 → 10

5 → +5 → ☐ → +5 → ☐ → +5 → ☐ → +5 → 25

3 → +3 → ☐ → +1 → ☐ → +3 → ☐ → +6 → 16

Label the numbers on the number line.

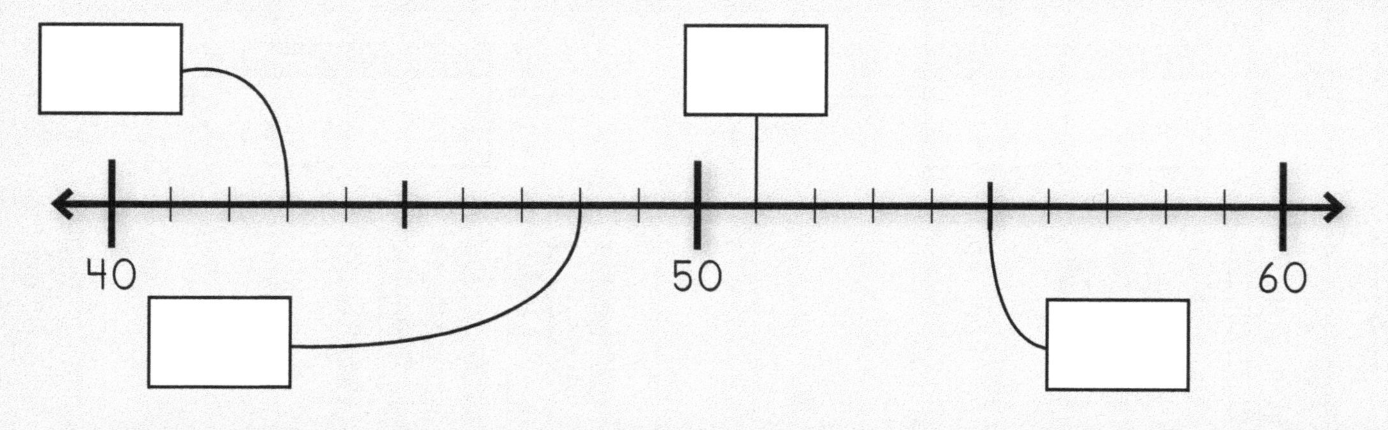

Complete.

7 - 4 = ☐ 6 - 3 = ☐ 7 - 1 = ☐

6 - 1 = ☐ 8 - 0 = ☐ 6 - 4 = ☐

9 - 3 = ☐ 10 - 4 = ☐ 8 - 2 = ☐

Complete.

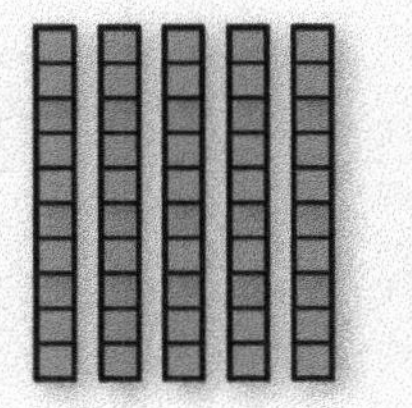

$50 + 3 = \square$

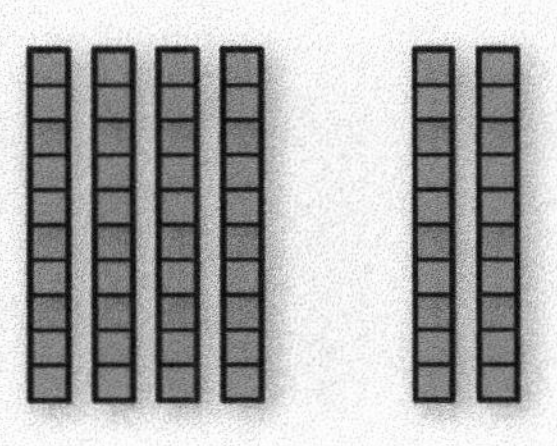

$40 + 20 = \square$

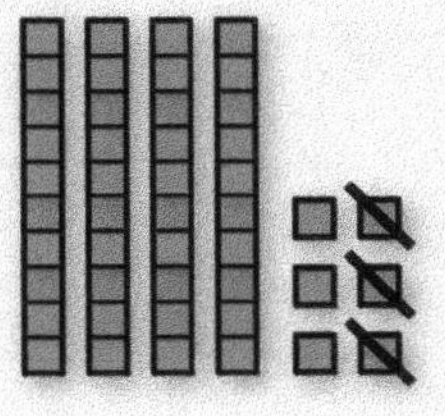

$35 + 30 = \square$

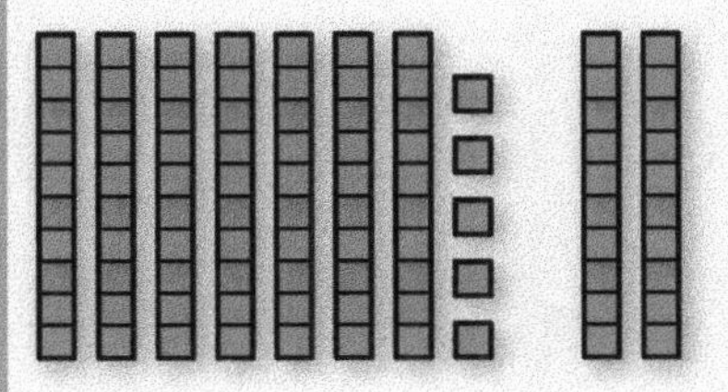

$75 + 20 = \square$

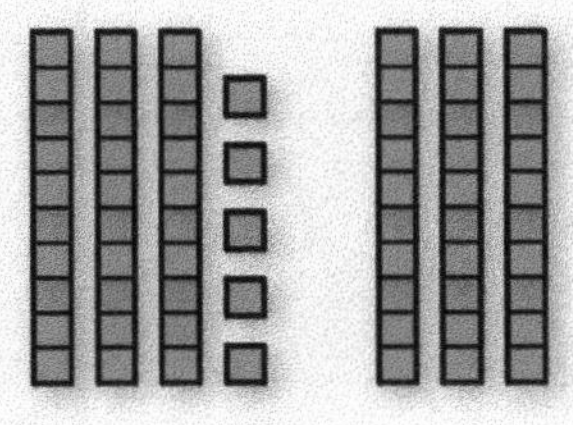

$46 - 3 = \square$

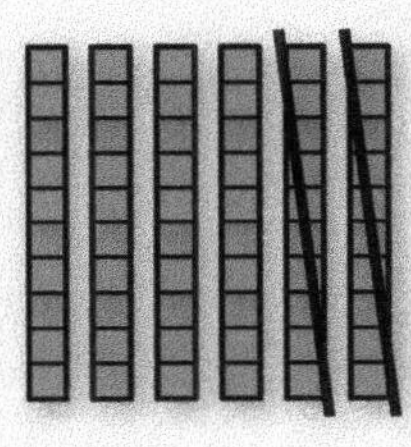

$60 - 20 = \square$

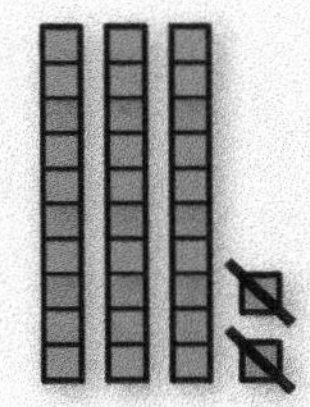

$32 - 2 = \square$

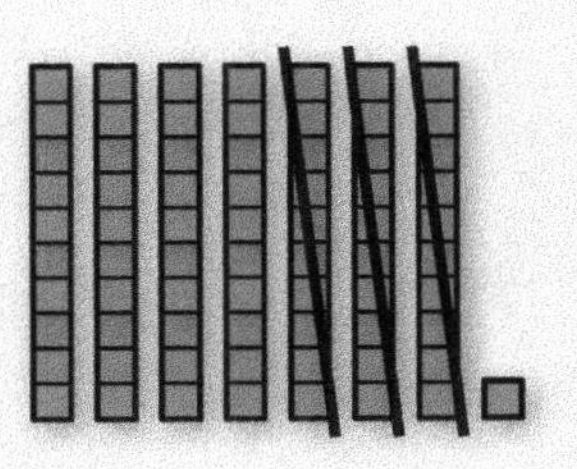

$71 - 30 = \square$

Color the addition facts that equal the number in the star.

7	8	9	10
4 + 3	7 + 2	3 + 6	3 + 7
6 + 2	4 + 4	9 + 0	9 + 1
2 + 5	6 + 1	5 + 4	6 + 5
7 + 0	3 + 5	1 + 8	8 + 2

Complete the missing numbers in the sequences.

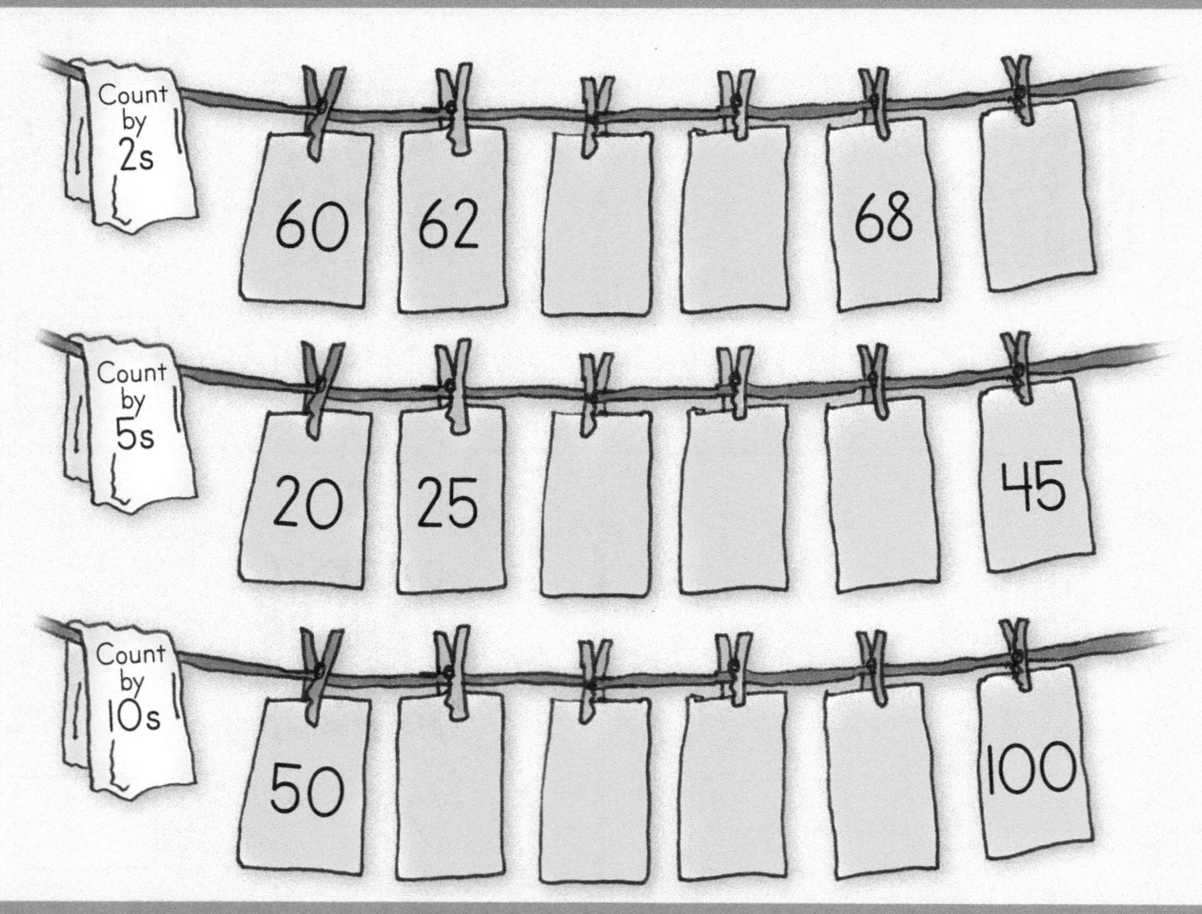

Complete.

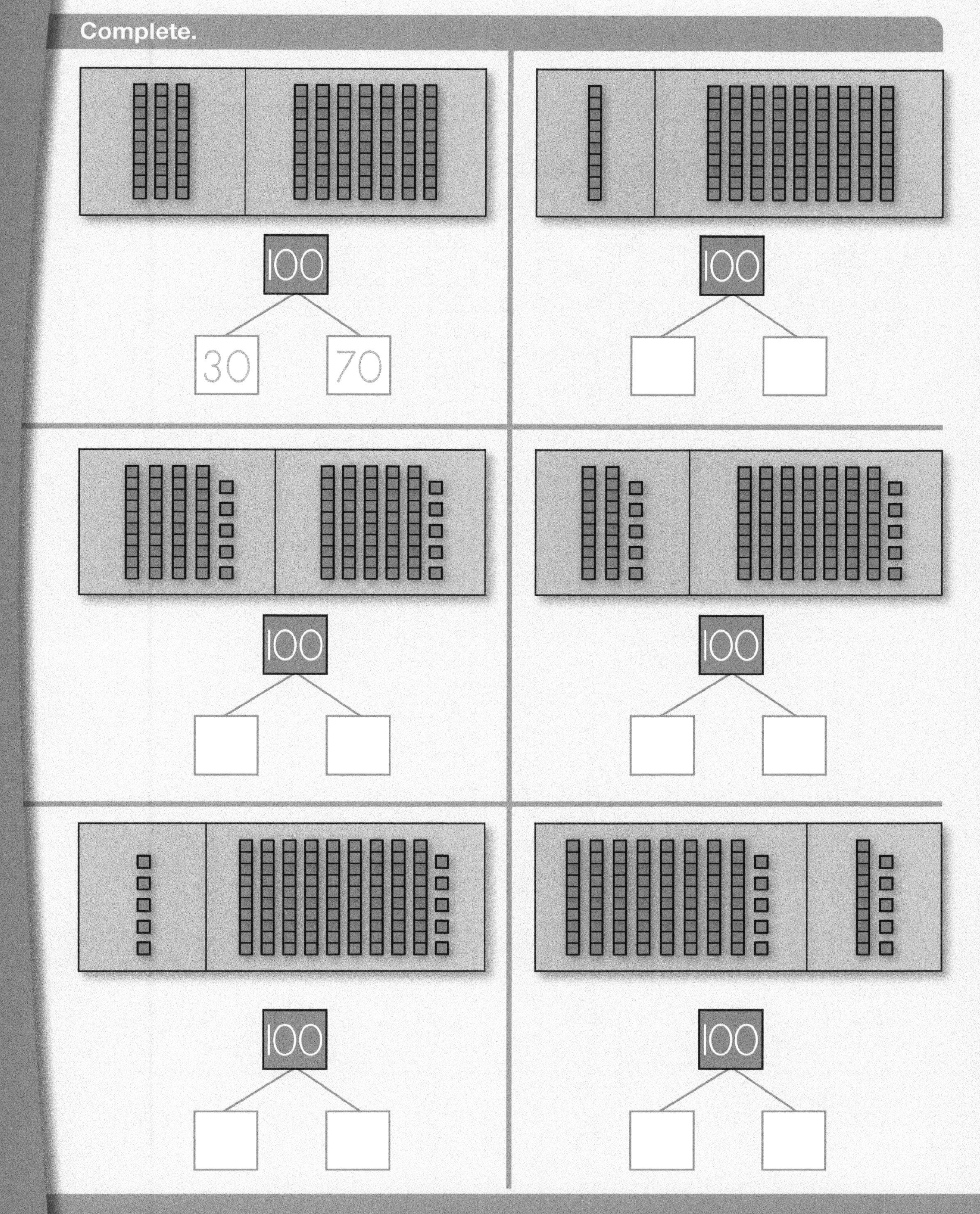

Sarah made a bar graph about the children in her swim class.
Use the bar graph to answer the questions.

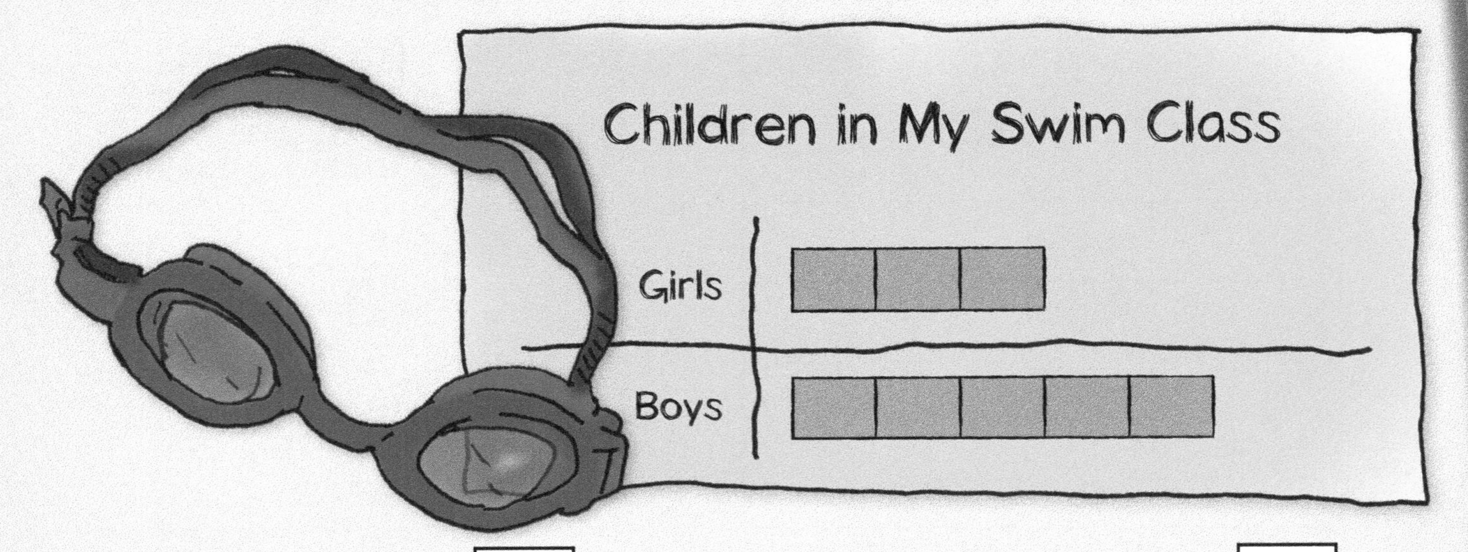

How many girls are in the class? ☐

How many more boys than girls are in the class? ☐

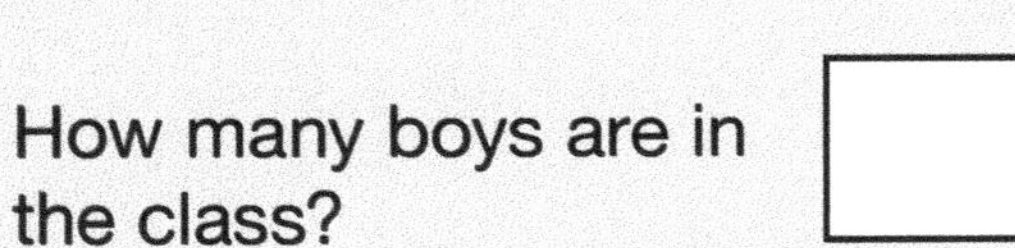

How many boys are in the class? ☐

How many children are in the class? ☐

Complete.

4 - 1 = ☐	7 - 3 = ☐	8 - 4 = ☐
9 - 2 = ☐	10 - 2 = ☐	4 - 2 = ☐
3 - 3 = ☐	10 - 1 = ☐	5 - 0 = ☐

Complete the circles with <, >, or =.

42 ○ 36	87 ○ 85	39 ○ 79
7 ○ 70	15 ○ 50	94 ○ 94

See the Instructor Guide for how to play.
Save this game board for future lessons.

Addition Crash

Game Board

15	13	16	12
18	14	11	17
11	16	18	13
14	12	15	17

Complete.

$9 + 3 =$ ☐ $9 + 1 =$ ☐ $9 + 6 =$ ☐

$9 + 8 =$ ☐ $9 + 2 =$ ☐ $9 + 5 =$ ☐

$9 + 4 =$ ☐ $9 + 9 =$ ☐ $9 + 7 =$ ☐

Complete.

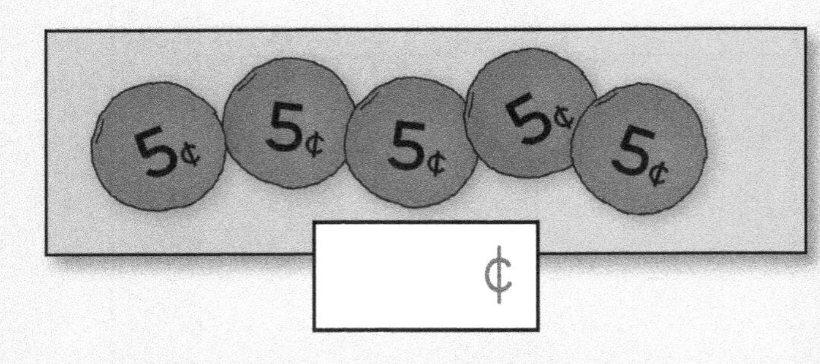

☐ ¢

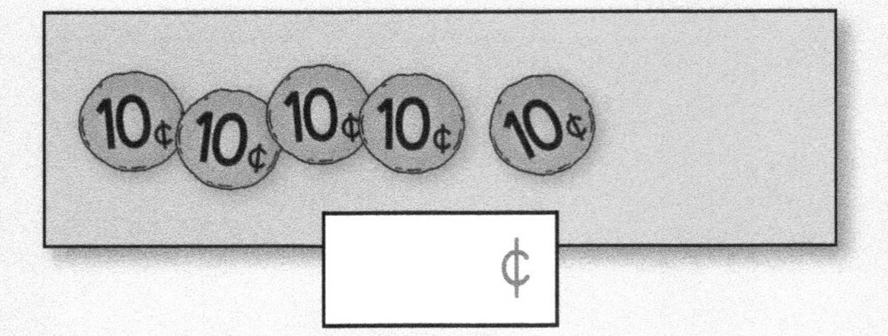

☐ ¢

Complete.

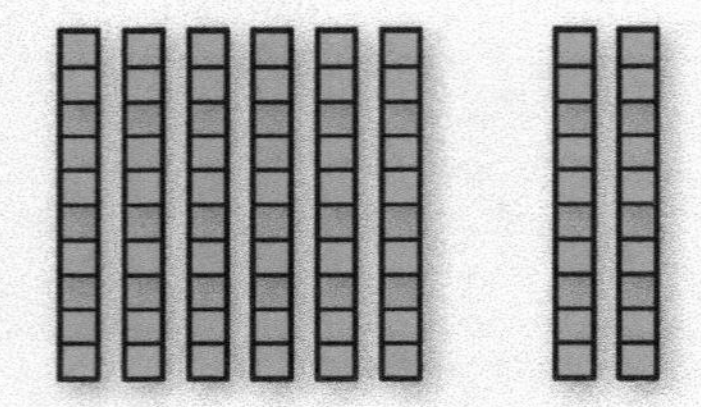

$60 + 20 =$ ☐

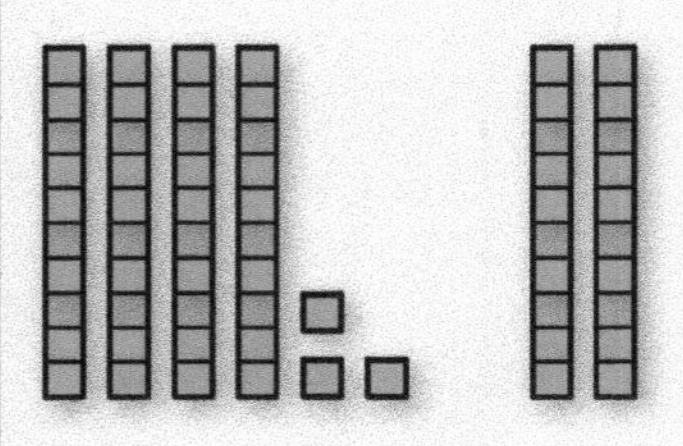

$43 + 20 =$ ☐

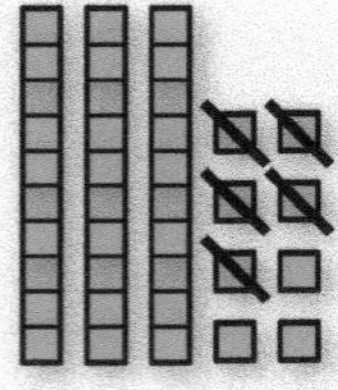

$38 - 5 =$ ☐

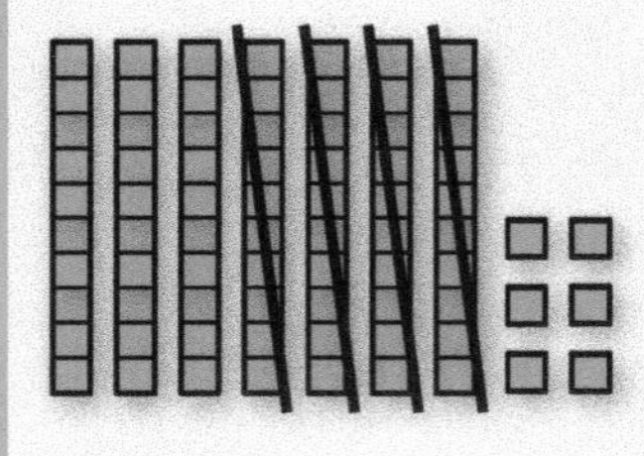

$76 - 40 =$ ☐

Solve.

You put 4 red lollipops and 3 purple lollipops in the treat bag.

How many lollipops are in the bag?

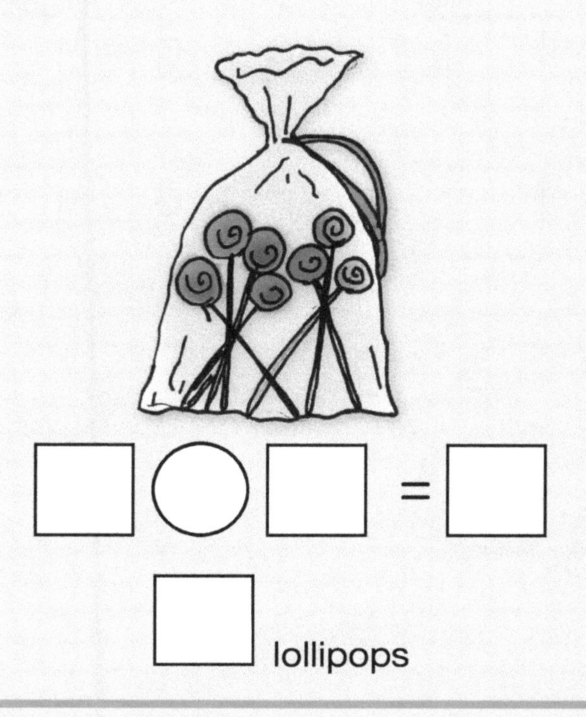

☐ ◯ ☐ = ☐

☐ lollipops

You put 9 bouncy balls in the treat bag. Then, you take out 5.

How many bouncy balls are left?

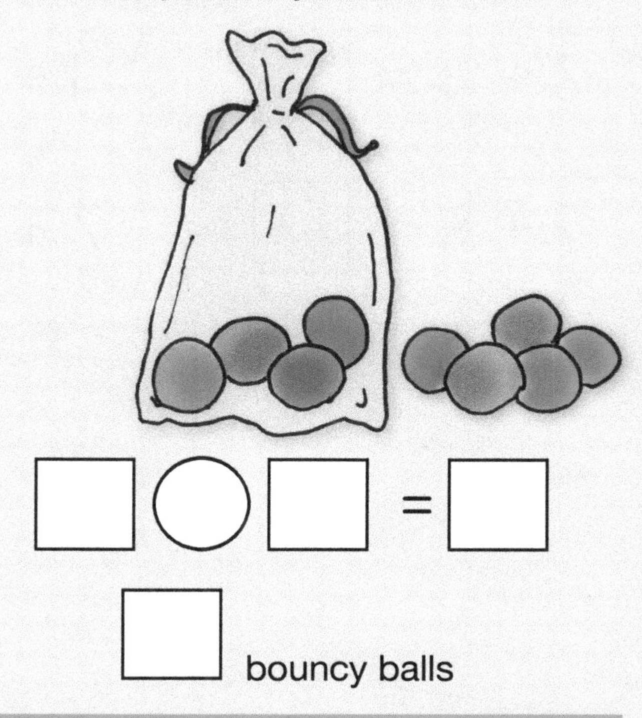

☐ ◯ ☐ = ☐

☐ bouncy balls

You put 6 erasers and 3 pencils in the treat bag.

How many things are in the bag?

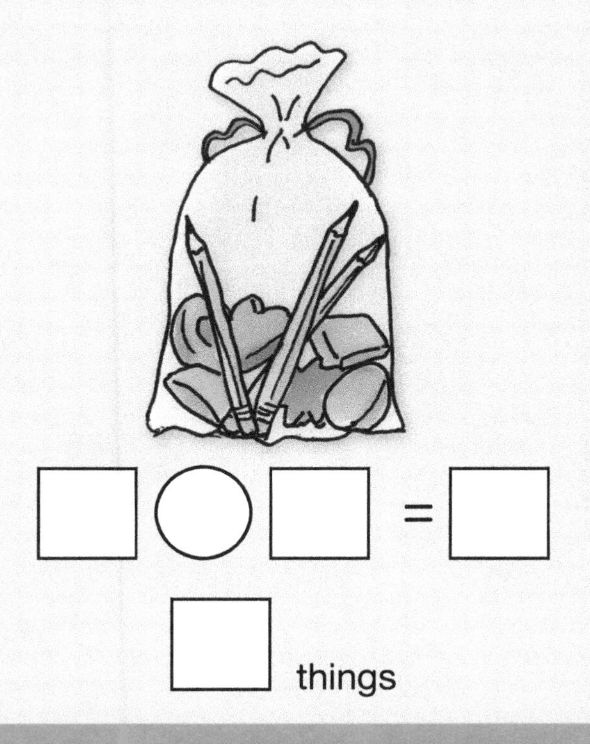

☐ ◯ ☐ = ☐

☐ things

You have 8 lollipops in the treat bag. Then, you eat 2.

How many are left?

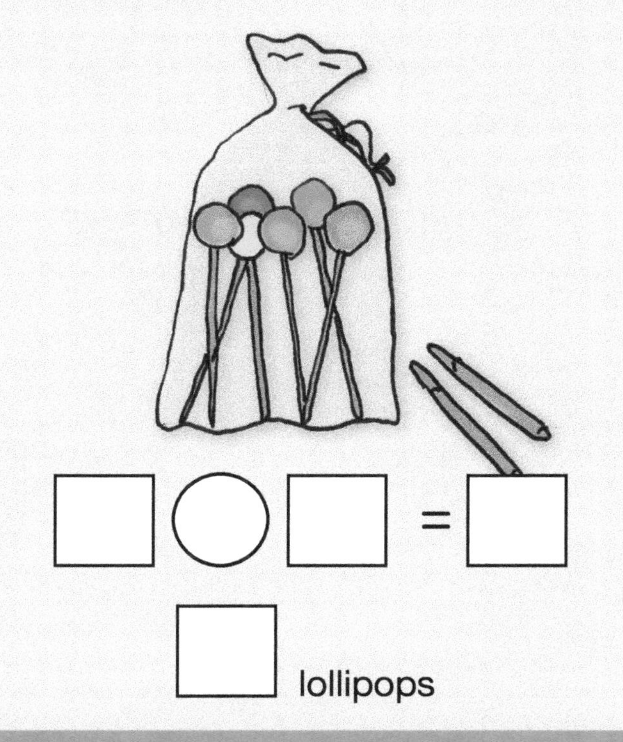

☐ ◯ ☐ = ☐

☐ lollipops

Complete.

$4 + 9 = \square$ $\quad$ $6 + 9 = \square$ $\quad$ $3 + 9 = \square$

$8 + 9 = \square$ $\quad$ $1 + 9 = \square$ $\quad$ $9 + 9 = \square$

$2 + 9 = \square$ $\quad$ $7 + 9 = \square$ $\quad$ $5 + 9 = \square$

X the shape that doesn't belong in each row.

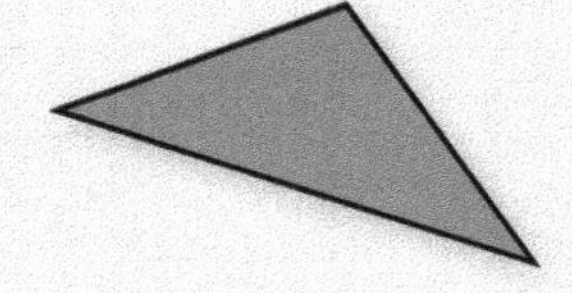
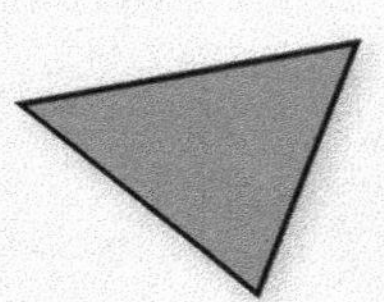

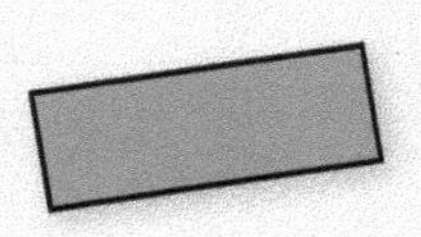

Complete.

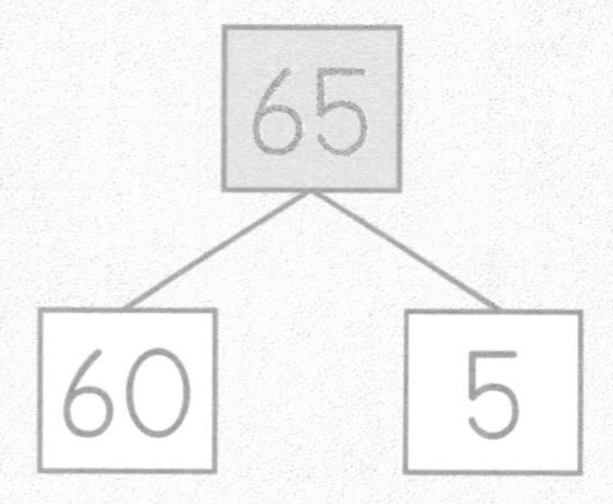

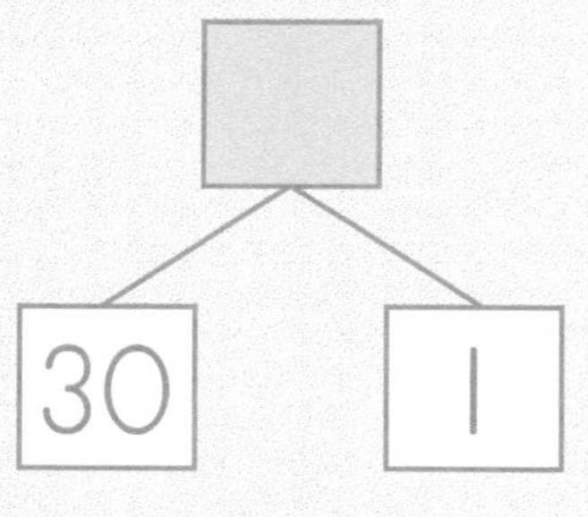

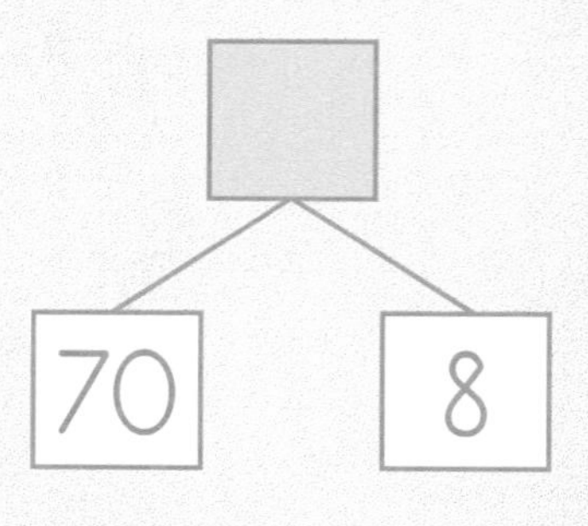

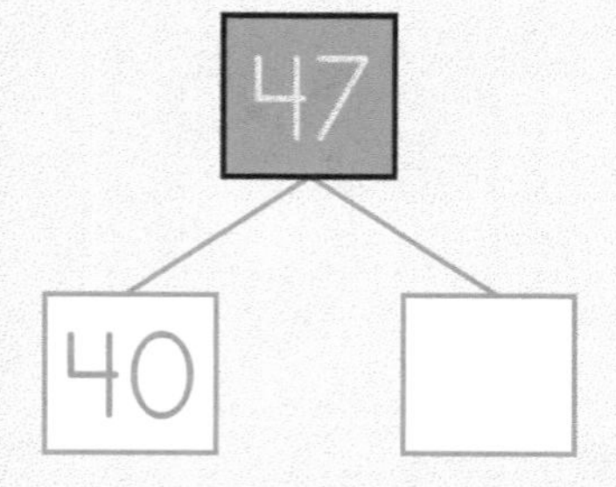

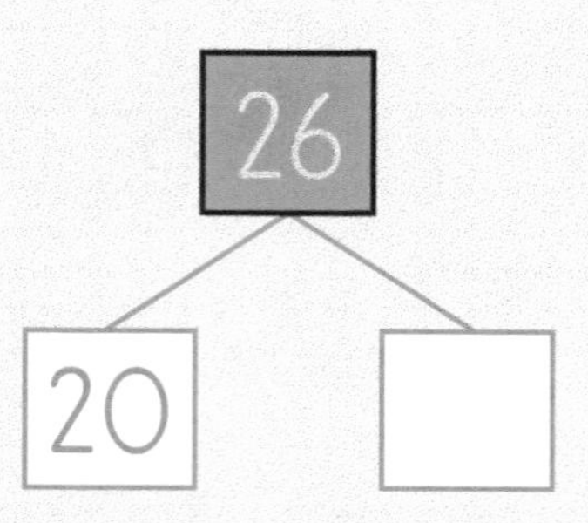

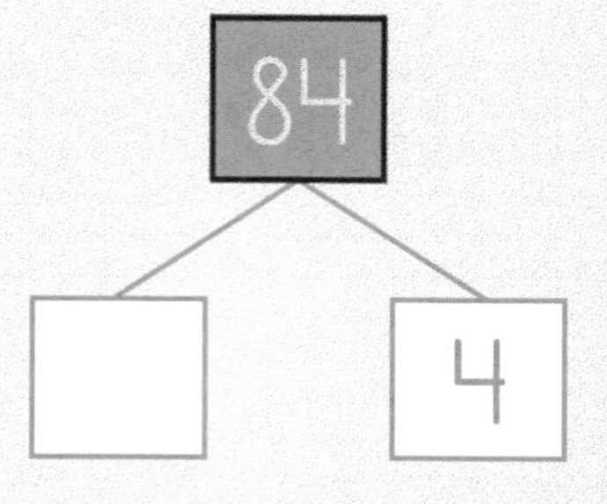

Match.

8 + 4	11	9 + 2
8 + 3	12	9 + 4
8 + 7	13	9 + 6
8 + 5	14	9 + 3
8 + 9	15	9 + 7
8 + 6	16	9 + 8
8 + 8	17	9 + 5

Complete the equations to match the base-ten blocks.

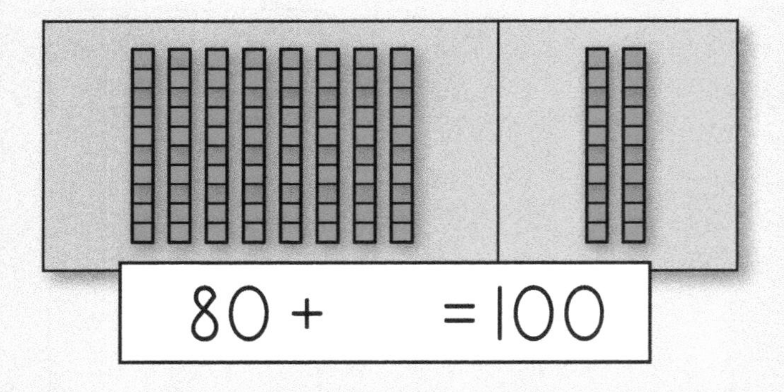

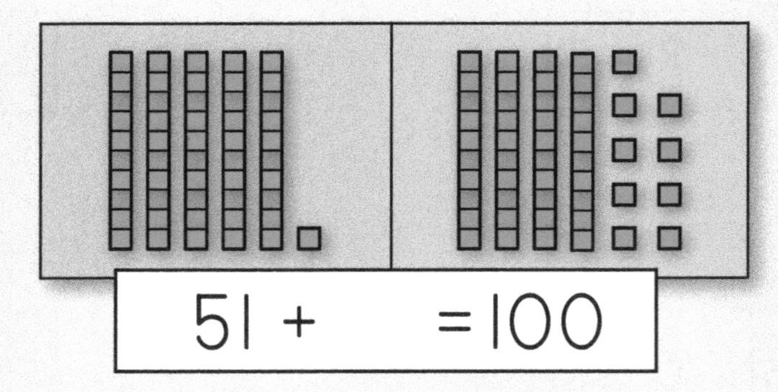

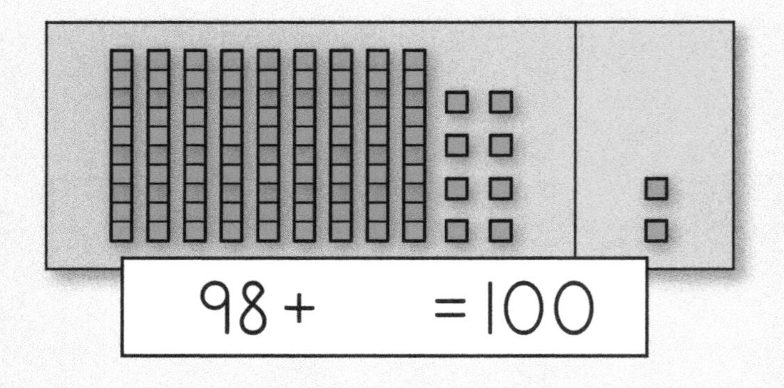

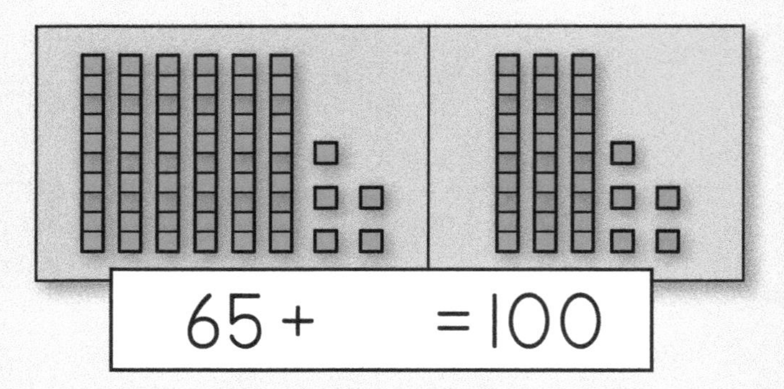

Complete.

Label the numbers on the number line.

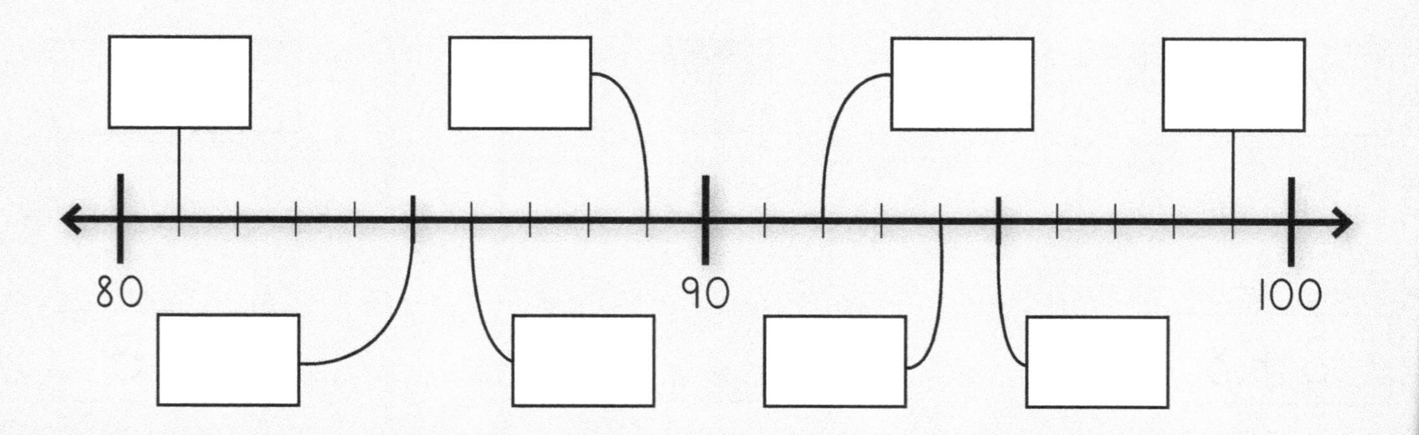

Complete.

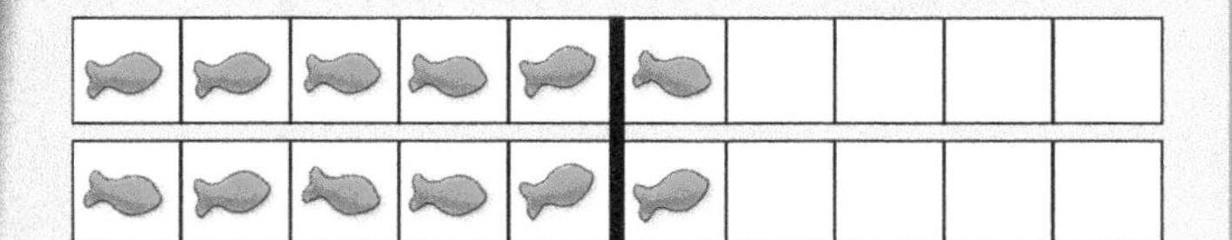

6 double

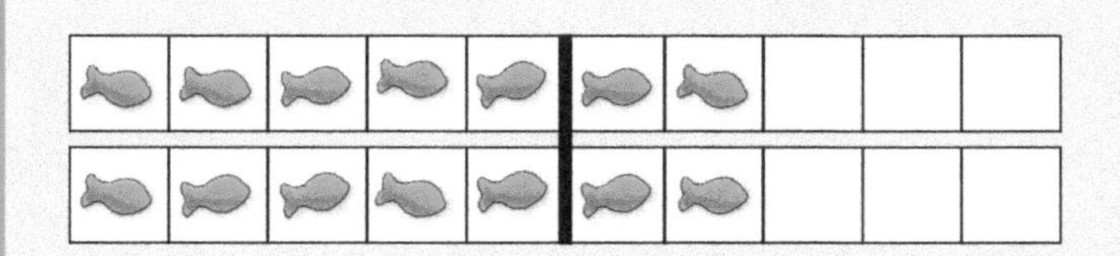

7 double

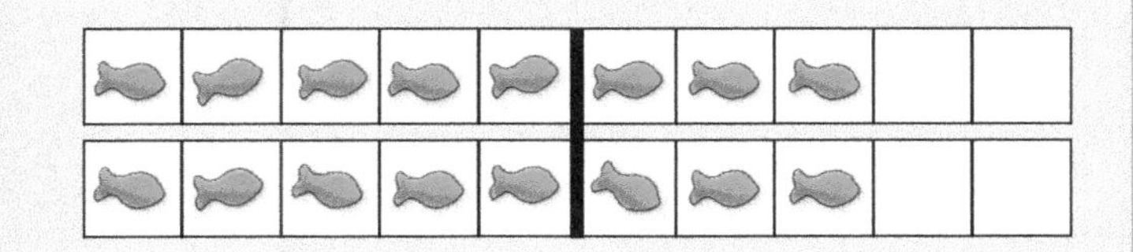

8 double

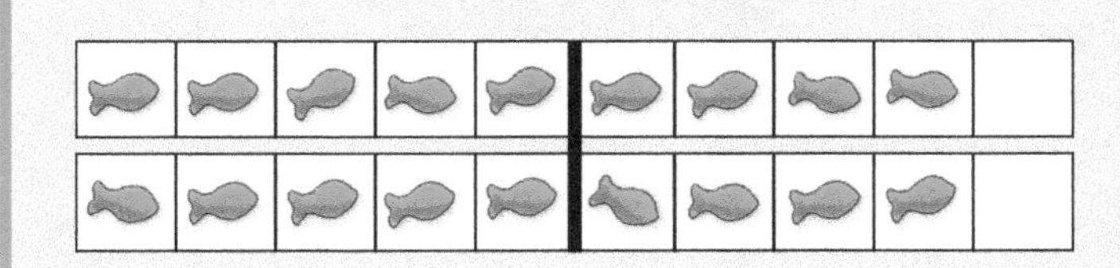

9 double

Complete.

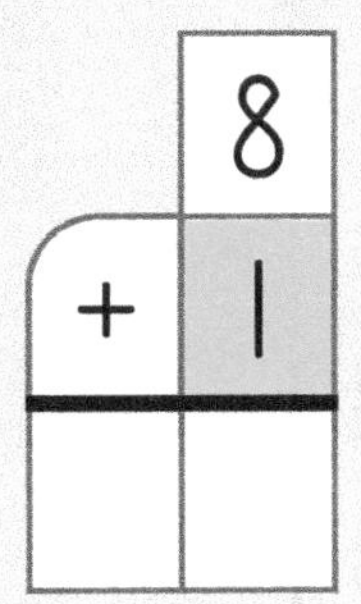

$8 + 1 = \square$

$8 + 4 = \square$

$8 + 8 = \square$

$8 + 5 = \square$

$8 + 6 = \square$

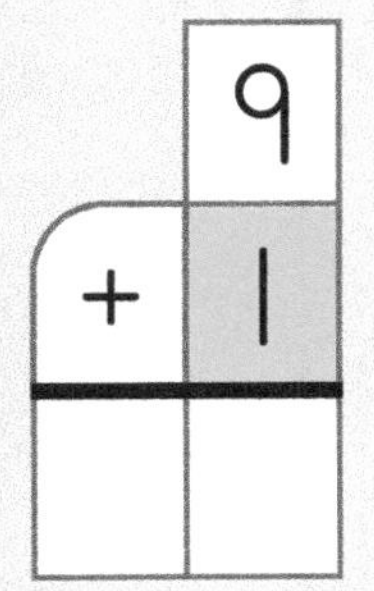

$9 + 1 = \square$

$9 + 9 = \square$

$9 + 5 = \square$

$9 + 8 = \square$

$9 + 6 = \square$

Solve.

You pick 8 yellow apples and
5 green apples.

How many apples do you pick?

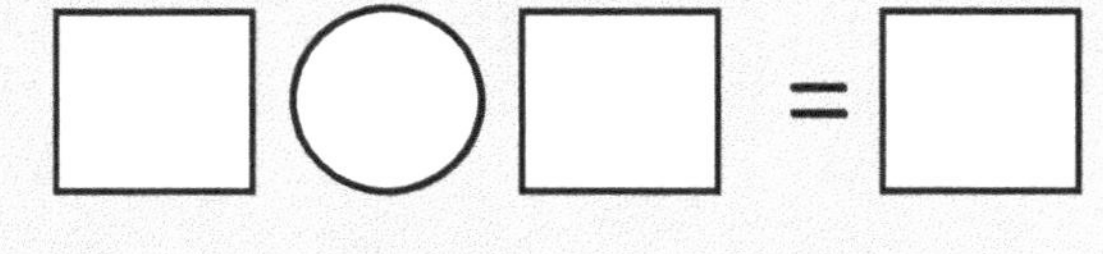

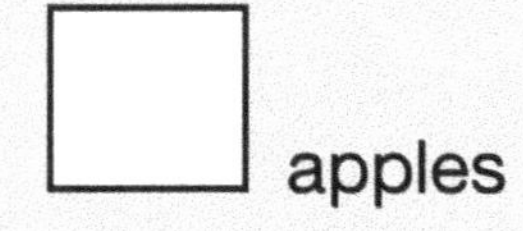

apples

You pick 9 apples.
Then, you pick 7 more.

How many apples do you pick?

apples

Write the value of each set of base-ten blocks.

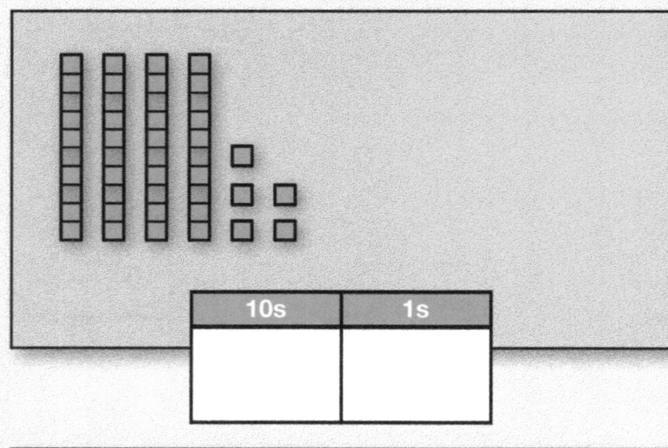

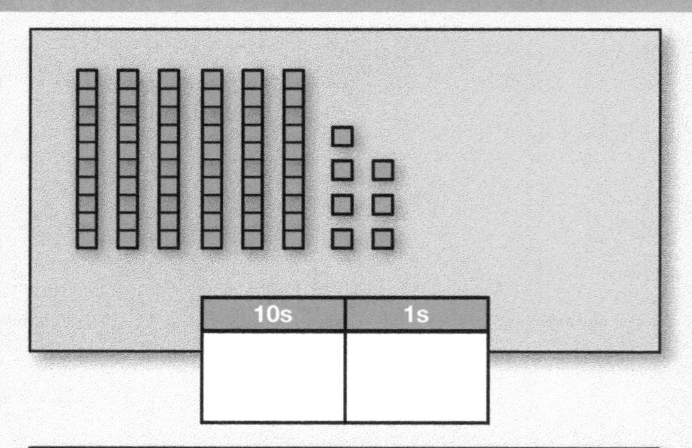

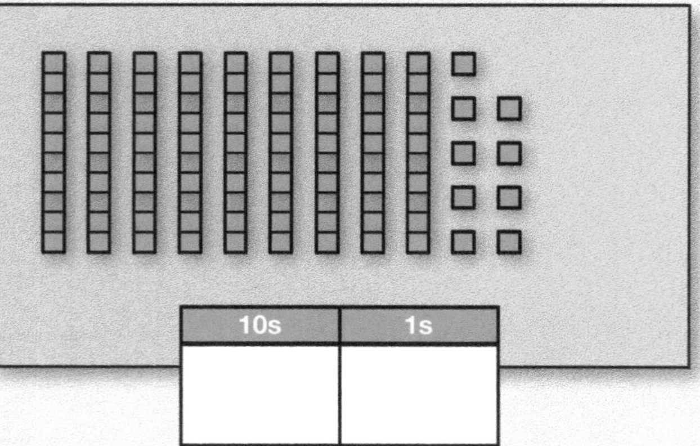

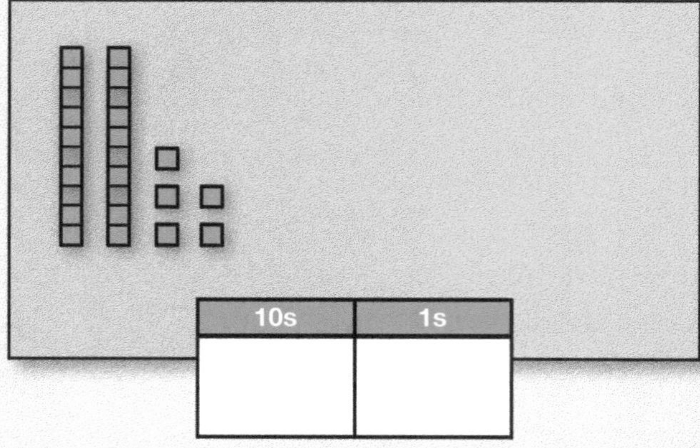

See the Instructor Guide for how to play.
Save these game boards for future lessons.

Addition Bingo

B	I	N	G	O
13	14	15	16	12
16	11	15	12	11
13	15	FREE	11	14
11	16	12	14	13
14	12	13	16	15

B	I	N	G	O
12	13	11	16	12
15	11	16	11	14
13	14	FREE	12	15
11	15	13	14	16
16	12	15	13	14

Complete.

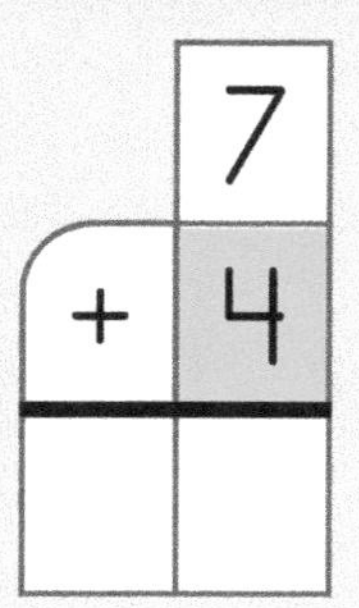

$7 + 4 =$ ___

$7 + 7 =$ ___

$7 + 5 =$ ___

$7 + 8 =$ ___

$7 + 6 =$ ___

$3 + 8 =$ ___

$8 + 8 =$ ___

$8 + 4 =$ ___

$6 + 8 =$ ___

$5 + 8 =$ ___

Complete.

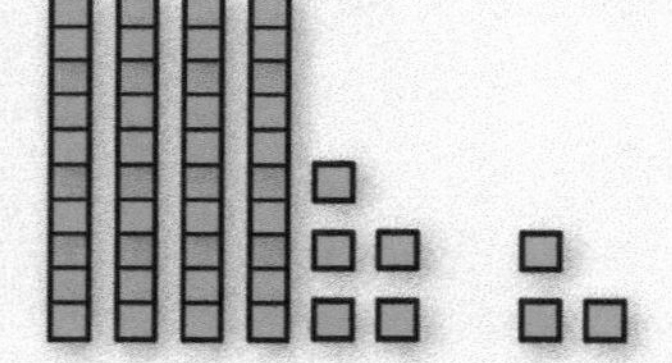

$45 + 3 =$ ☐

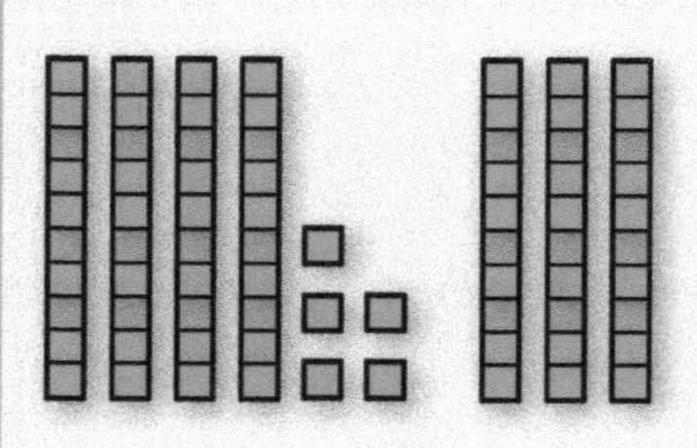

$45 + 30 =$ ☐

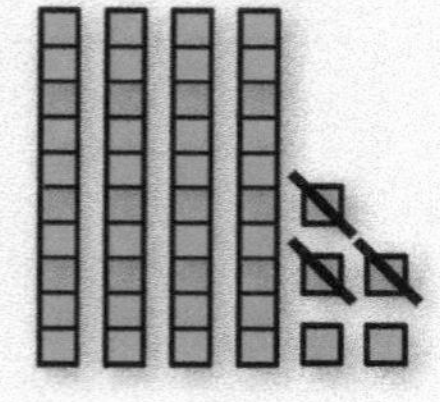

$45 - 3 =$ ☐

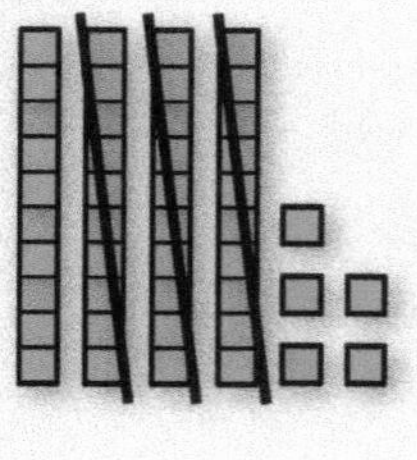

$45 - 30 =$ ☐

Solve.

You pick 5 sunflowers. You want 10 sunflowers to make a bouquet.

How many more sunflowers do you need?

☐ ◯ ☐ = ☐

☐ sunflowers

You pick 9 sunflowers. You want 14 to make a bouquet.

How many more sunflowers do you need?

☐ ◯ ☐ = ☐

☐ sunflowers

Complete.

	7
+	4

	7
+	6

	7
+	5

	7
+	7

	7
+	8

	9
+	7

	8
+	8

	6
+	8

	9
+	4

	5
+	8

Complete.

5 double

4 double

10 double

6 double

Color the rectangles. X the shapes that are not rectangles.

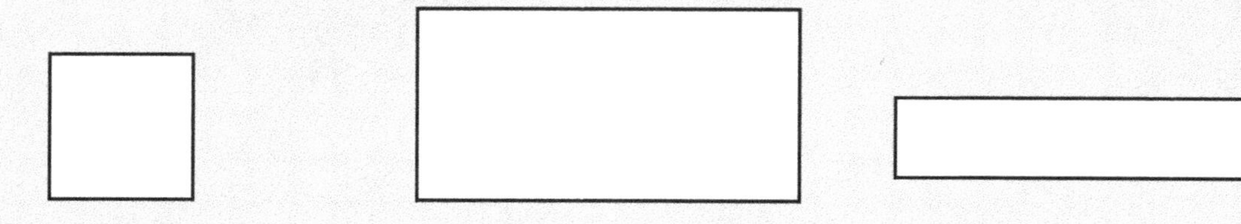

Match the pairs that make 100.

10

30

Complete.

	6
+	6

	6
+	4

	6
+	5

	6
+	7

	6
+	8

	7
+	5

	7
+	8

	7
+	7

	7
+	4

	7
+	6

Color the addition facts that equal the number in the star.

5 + 8

9 + 3

7 + 7

7 + 6

7 + 7

9 + 4

6 + 8

5 + 7

9 + 6

8 + 7

4 + 8

8 + 8

9 + 9

8 + 8

6 + 5

7 + 9

Ethan made a bar graph about the animals he saw at the zoo. Use the bar graph to answer the questions.

Animals at the zoo

Giraffes	▭▭▭▭▭▭▭
Elephants	▭▭▭▭
Lions	▭▭

How many giraffes did he see? ☐

How many elephants did he see? ☐

How many lions did he see? ☐

How many more giraffes than elephants did he see? ☐

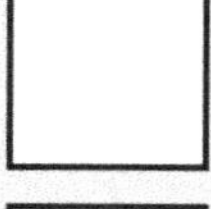

How many more giraffes than lions did he see? ☐

Complete the circles with <, >, or =.

35 ◯ 36	34 ◯ 35	30 ◯ 30
76 ◯ 46	92 ◯ 27	50 ◯ 83

Complete the fact family to match the Part-Total Diagram.

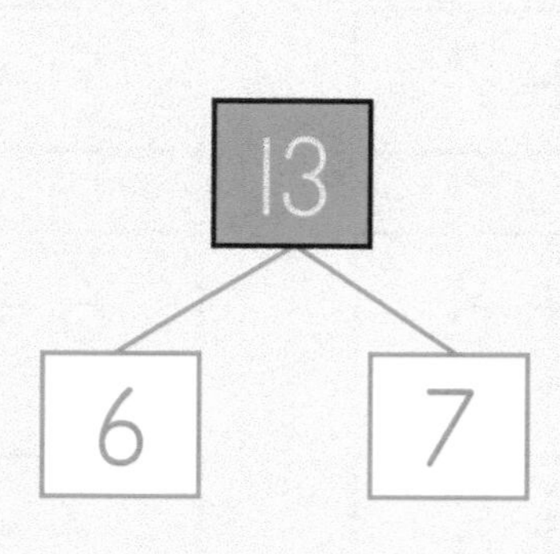

☐ + ☐ = ☐

☐ + ☐ = ☐

☐ - ☐ = ☐

☐ - ☐ = ☐

Solve.

You have 4 round crackers,
5 square crackers, and 4 triangle crackers.
How many crackers do you have?

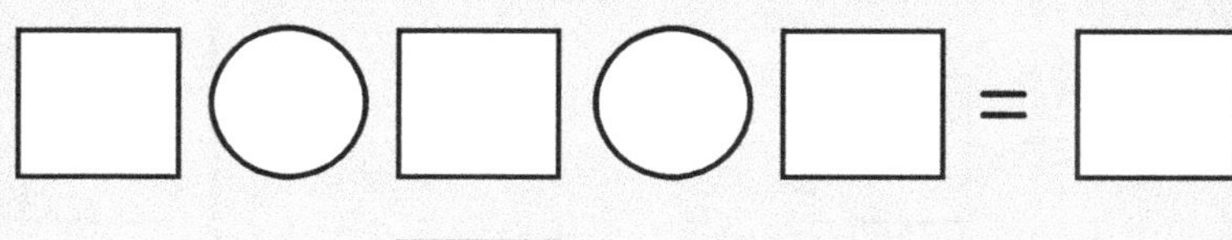

crackers

You see 3 cardinals, 5 blue jays,
and 7 robins.
How many birds do you see?

birds

You buy 3 packs of pencils.
Each pack has 6 pencils.
How many pencils do you buy?

pencils

Complete.

5 + 6 = ☐	7 + 4 = ☐	6 + 7 = ☐
6 + 9 = ☐	6 + 6 = ☐	9 + 9 = ☐
4 + 7 = ☐	9 + 5 = ☐	7 + 7 = ☐
8 + 8 = ☐	6 + 5 = ☐	8 + 6 = ☐

Color the squares. X the shapes that are not squares.

Complete the missing numbers in the sequences.

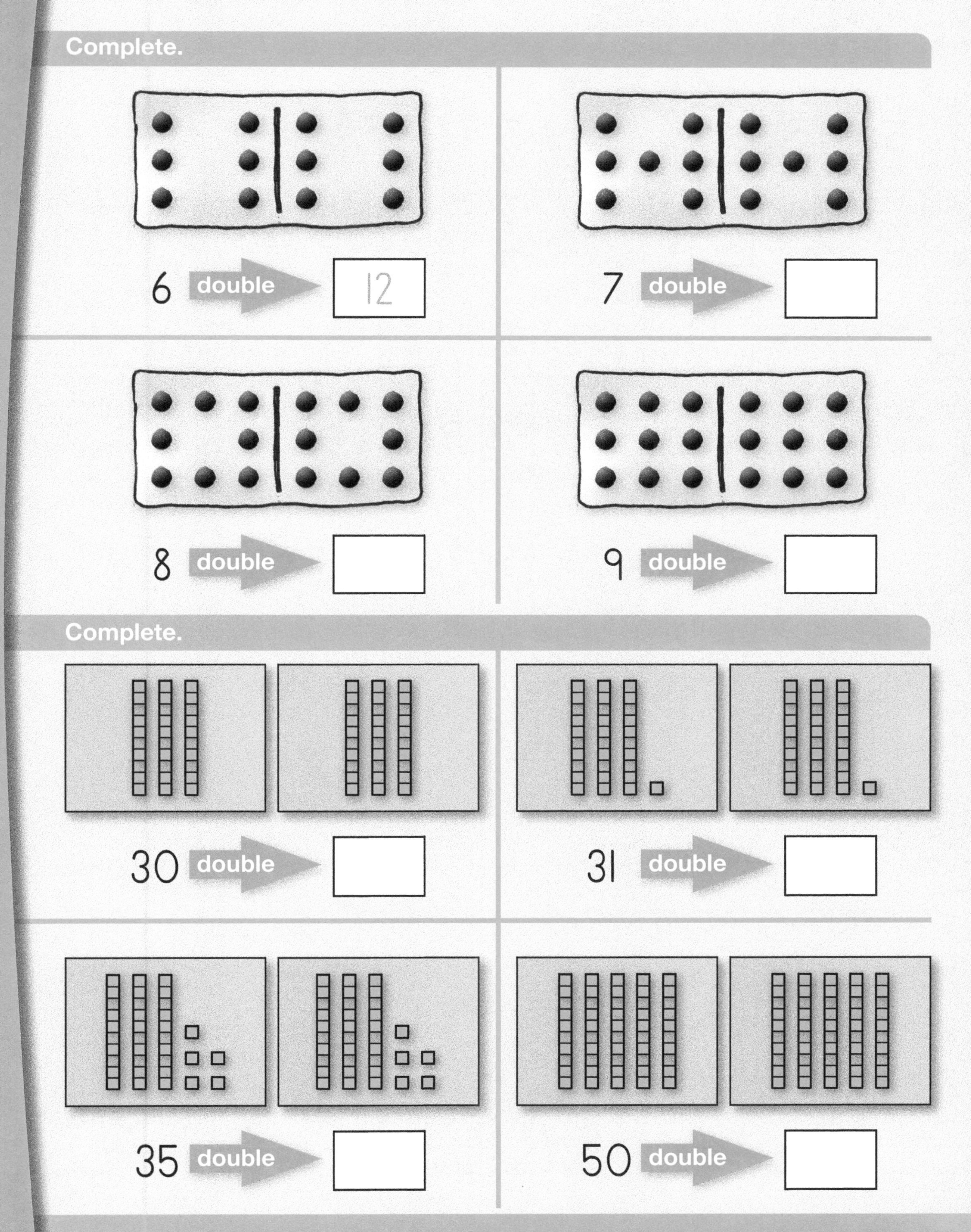
Complete.
6 double 12
7 double
8 double
9 double
Complete.
30 double
31 double
35 double
50 double

Complete.

$5 + 1 = \square$ $7 + 5 = \square$ $4 + 9 = \square$

$6 + 7 = \square$ $4 + 2 = \square$ $8 + 8 = \square$

$5 + 4 = \square$ $9 + 6 = \square$ $1 + 6 = \square$

Complete.

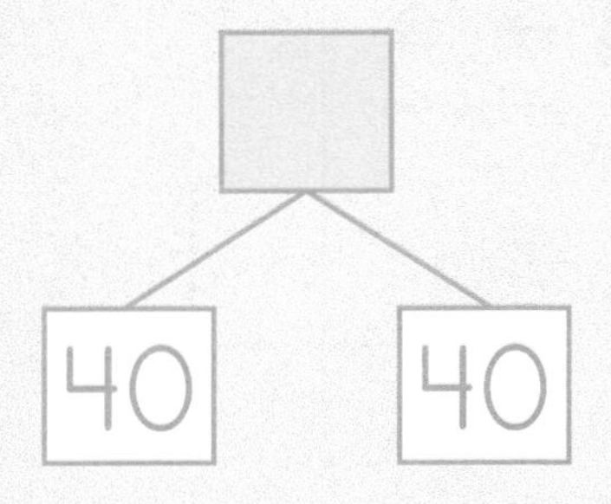

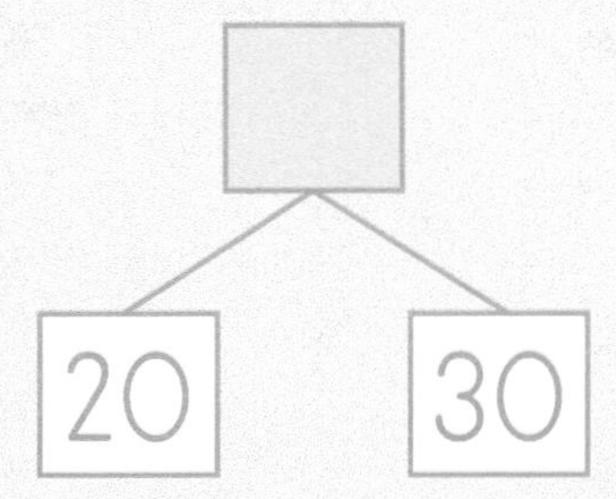

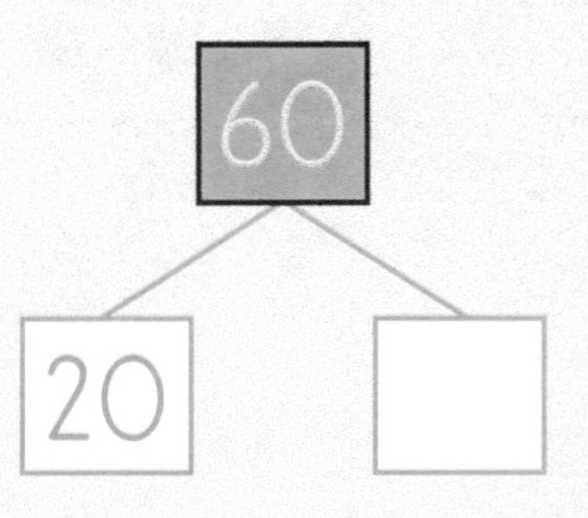

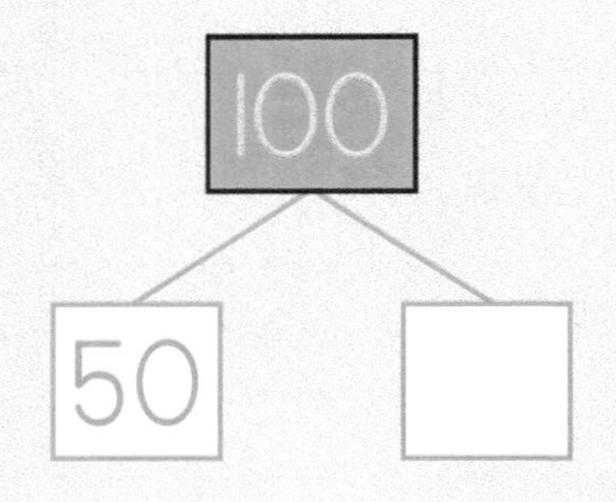

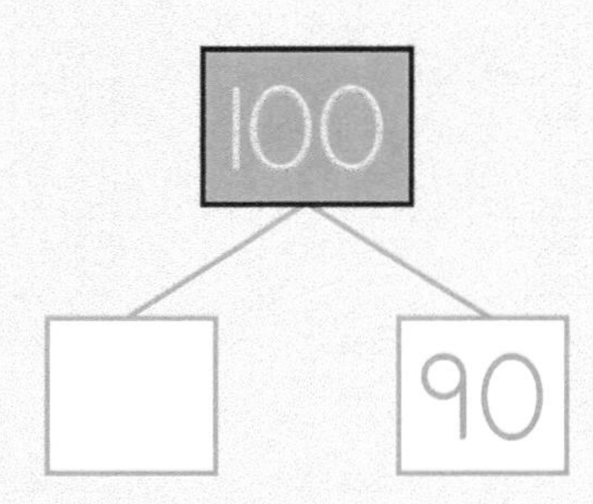

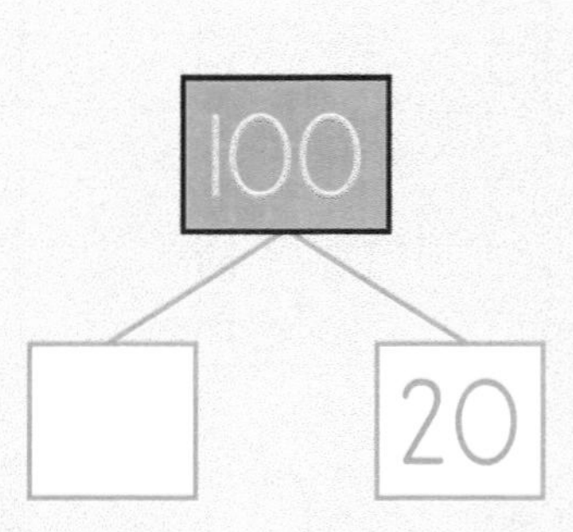

Draw lines to cut each pizza into halves.

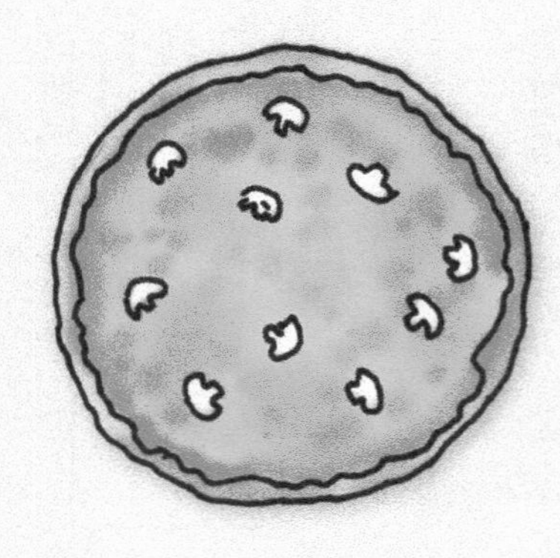

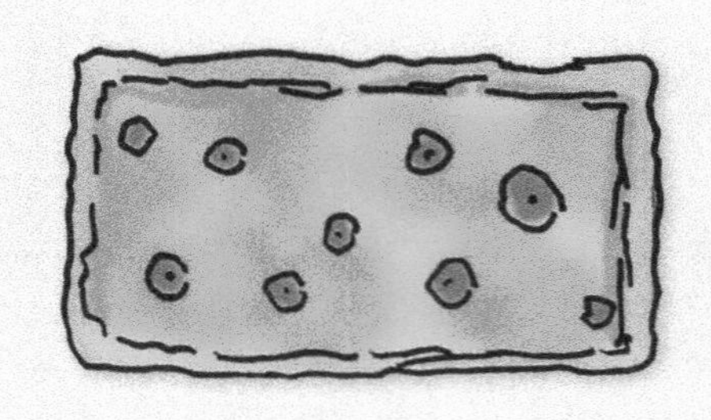

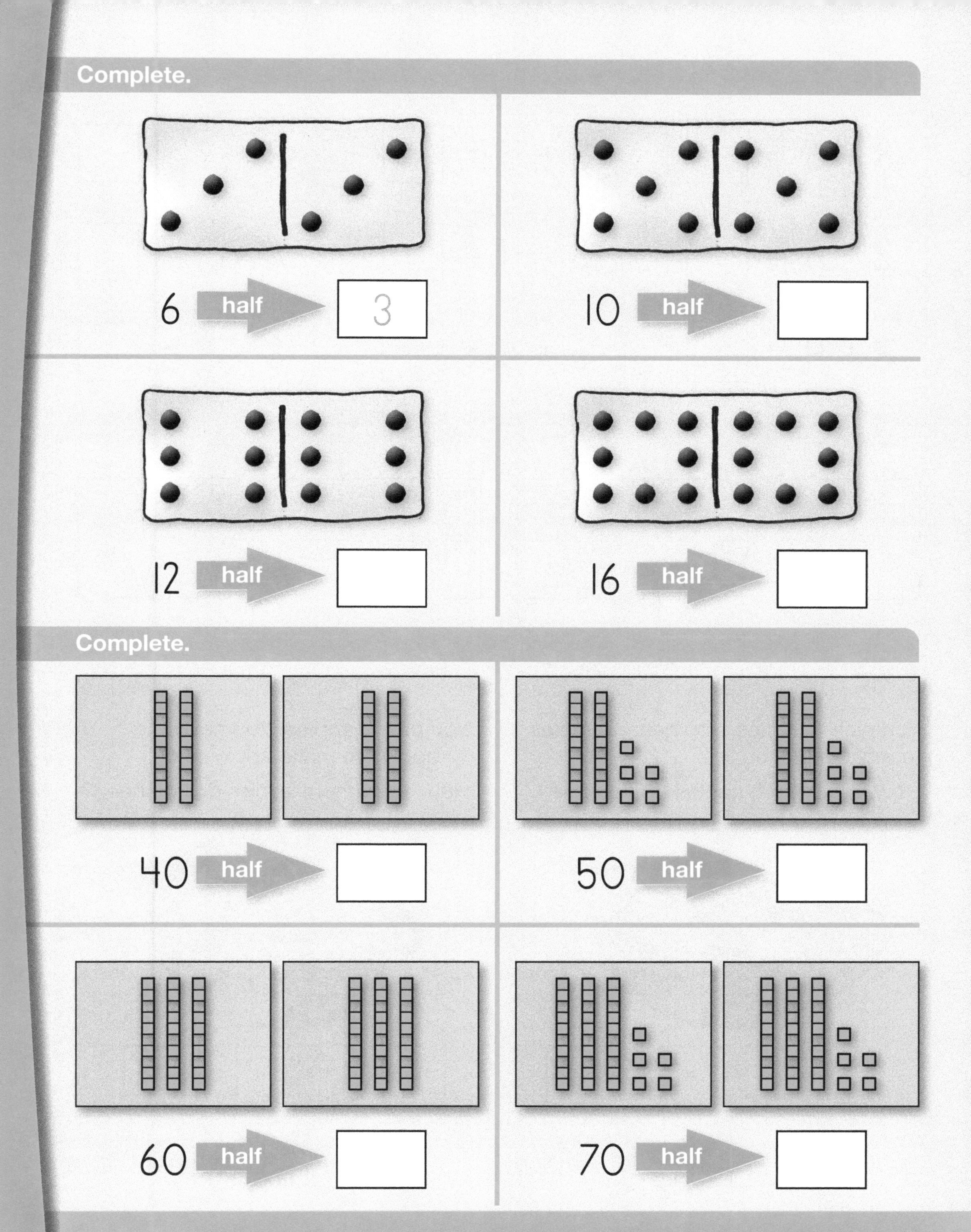
Complete.
6 half 3
10 half
12 half
16 half
Complete.
40 half
50 half
60 half
70 half

Complete.

$8 + 6 = \square$ $3 + 5 = \square$ $9 + 2 = \square$

$2 + 8 = \square$ $8 + 4 = \square$ $7 + 9 = \square$

$7 + 4 = \square$ $6 + 6 = \square$ $8 + 7 = \square$

Complete.

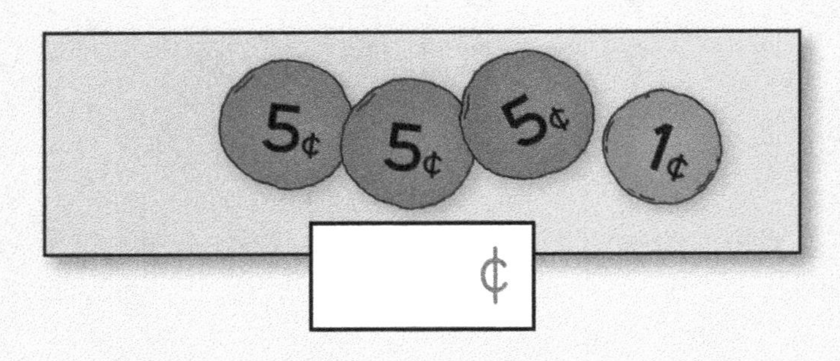

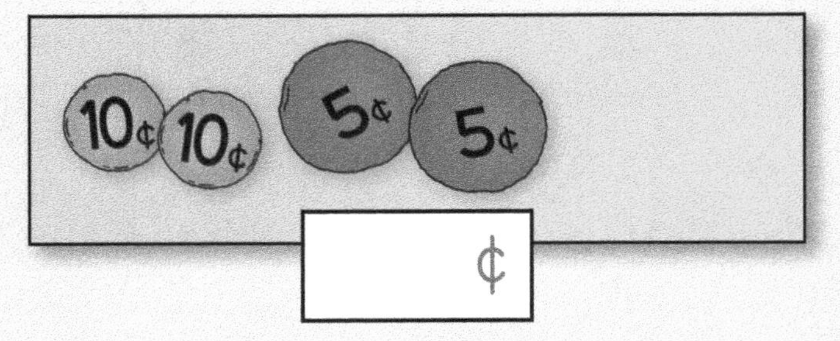

Solve.

You pick 4 apples. You need 8 apples to make a pie.

How many more apples do you need?

☐ ◯ ☐ = ☐

☐ apples

You pick 9 apples. You need 12 apples to make applesauce.

How many more apples do you need?

☐ ◯ ☐ = ☐

☐ apples

Color the odd numbers purple. Color the even numbers green.

1	2	3	4	5	6	7	8	9	10
11	12	13	14	15	16	17	18	19	20
21	22	23	24	25	26	27	28	29	30
31	32	33	34	35	36	37	38	39	40
41	42	43	44	45	46	47	48	49	50
51	52	53	54	55	56	57	58	59	60
61	62	63	64	65	66	67	68	69	70
71	72	73	74	75	76	77	78	79	80
81	82	83	84	85	86	87	88	89	90
91	92	93	94	95	96	97	98	99	100

Match.

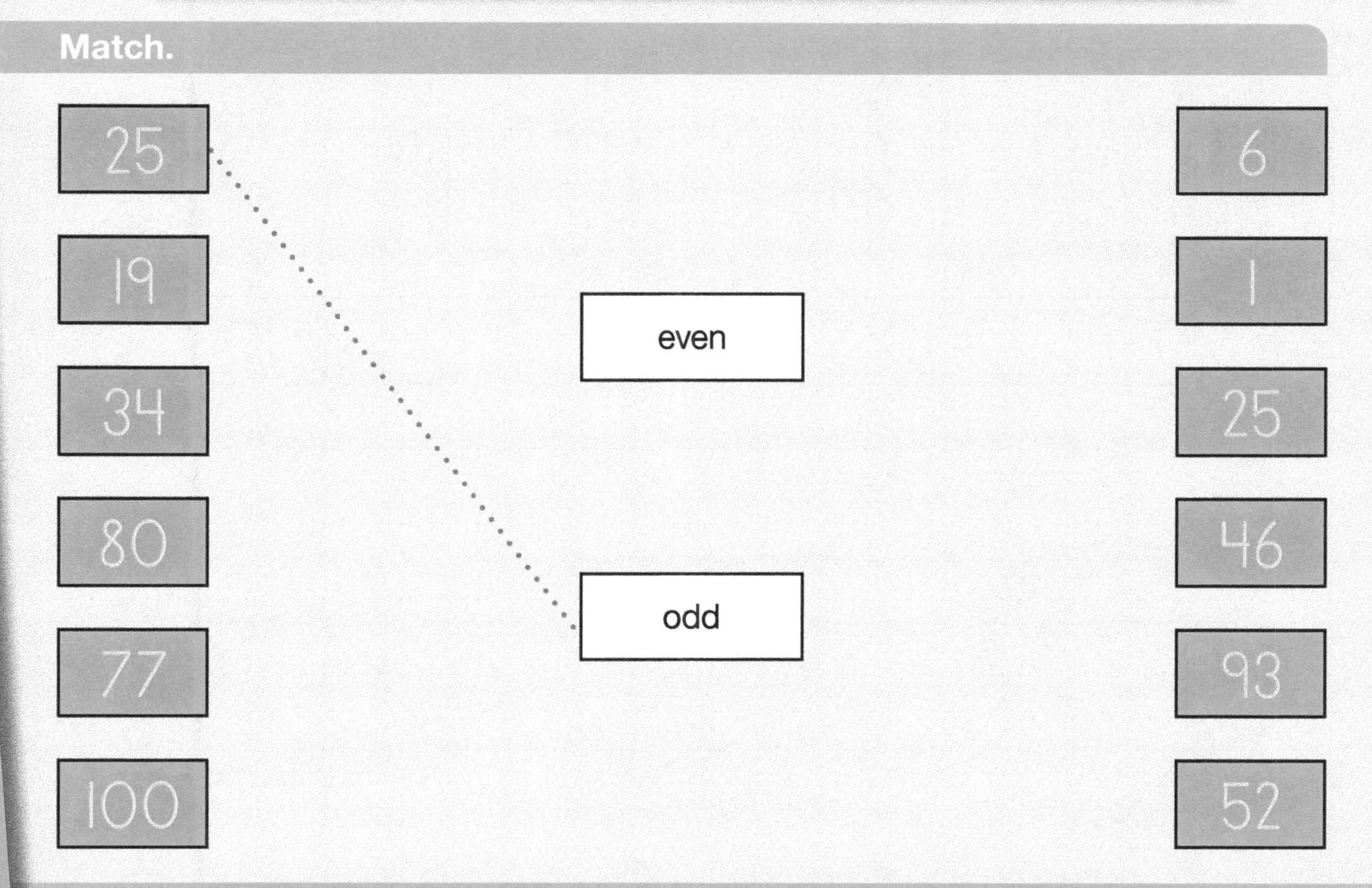

Complete.

$6 + 2$

$8 + 3$

$5 + 8$

$3 + 7$

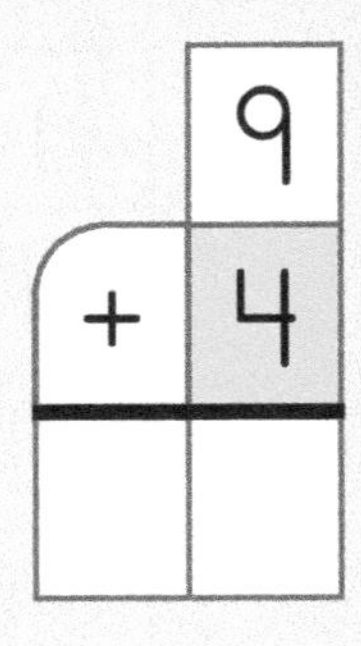

$6 + 6$

$8 + 9$

$4 + 5$

$7 + 7$

$6 + 9$

Complete.

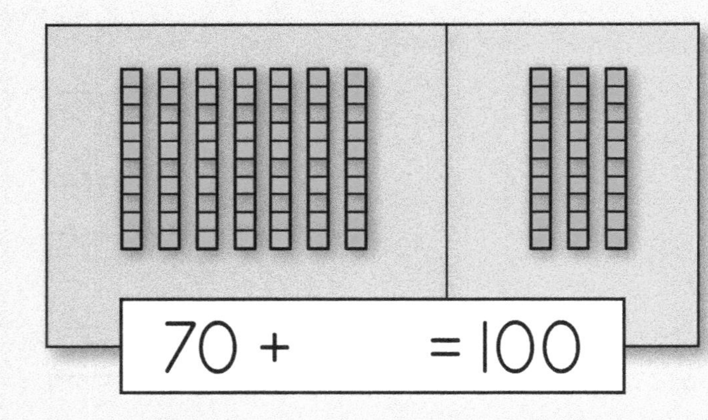

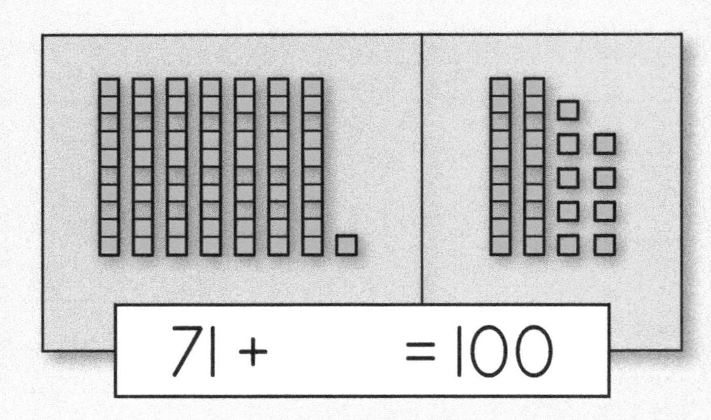

Draw lines to cut each pizza into fourths.

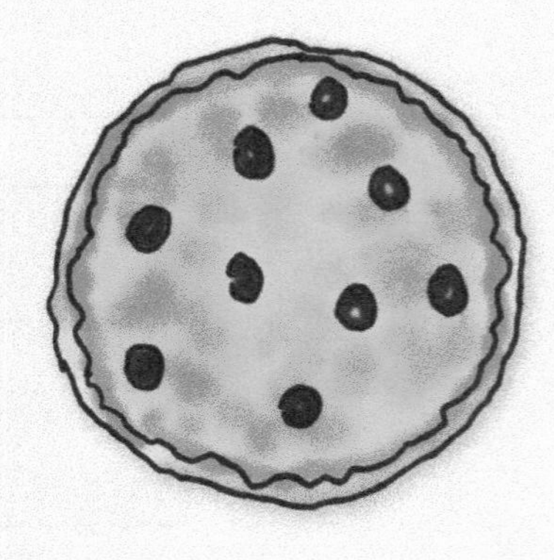

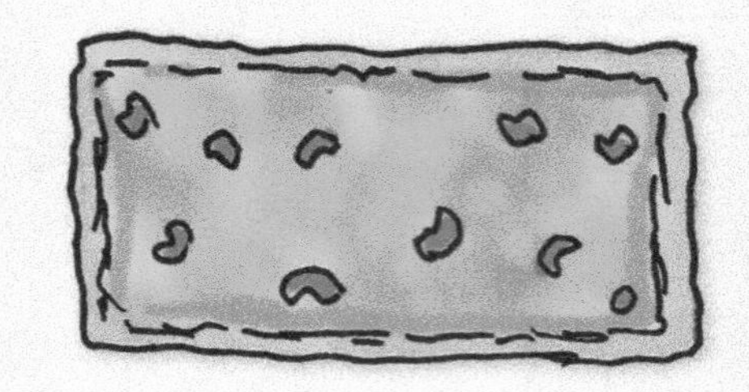

Complete.

BAKE
SALE
brownies
brownies
brownies
brownies
brownies
brownies
brownies
brownies

Match.

7 + 6		6 + 6
7 + 4	12	6 + 8
7 + 7	13	6 + 7
7 + 5	14	6 + 5

Complete.

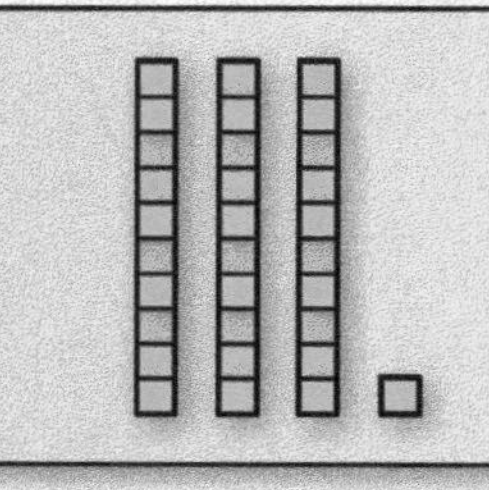

31 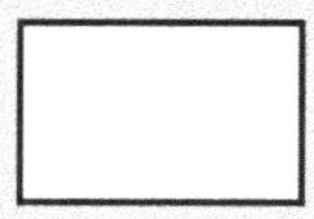

☐

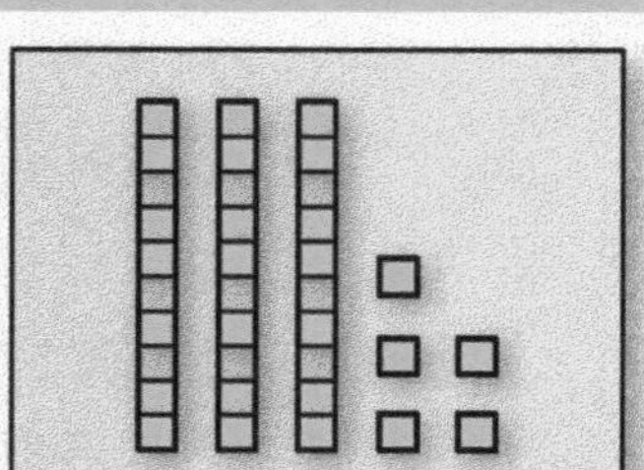
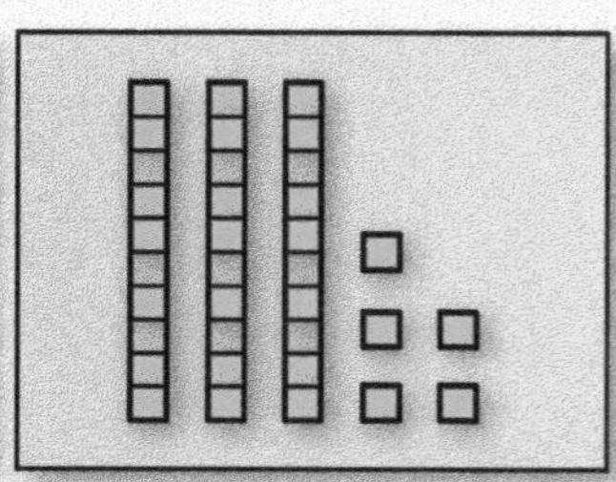

35 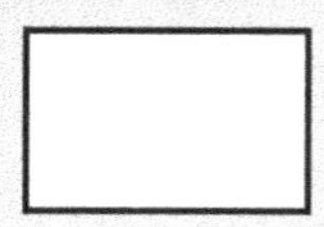

☐

Solve.

How much does it cost to buy all three toys?

Match.

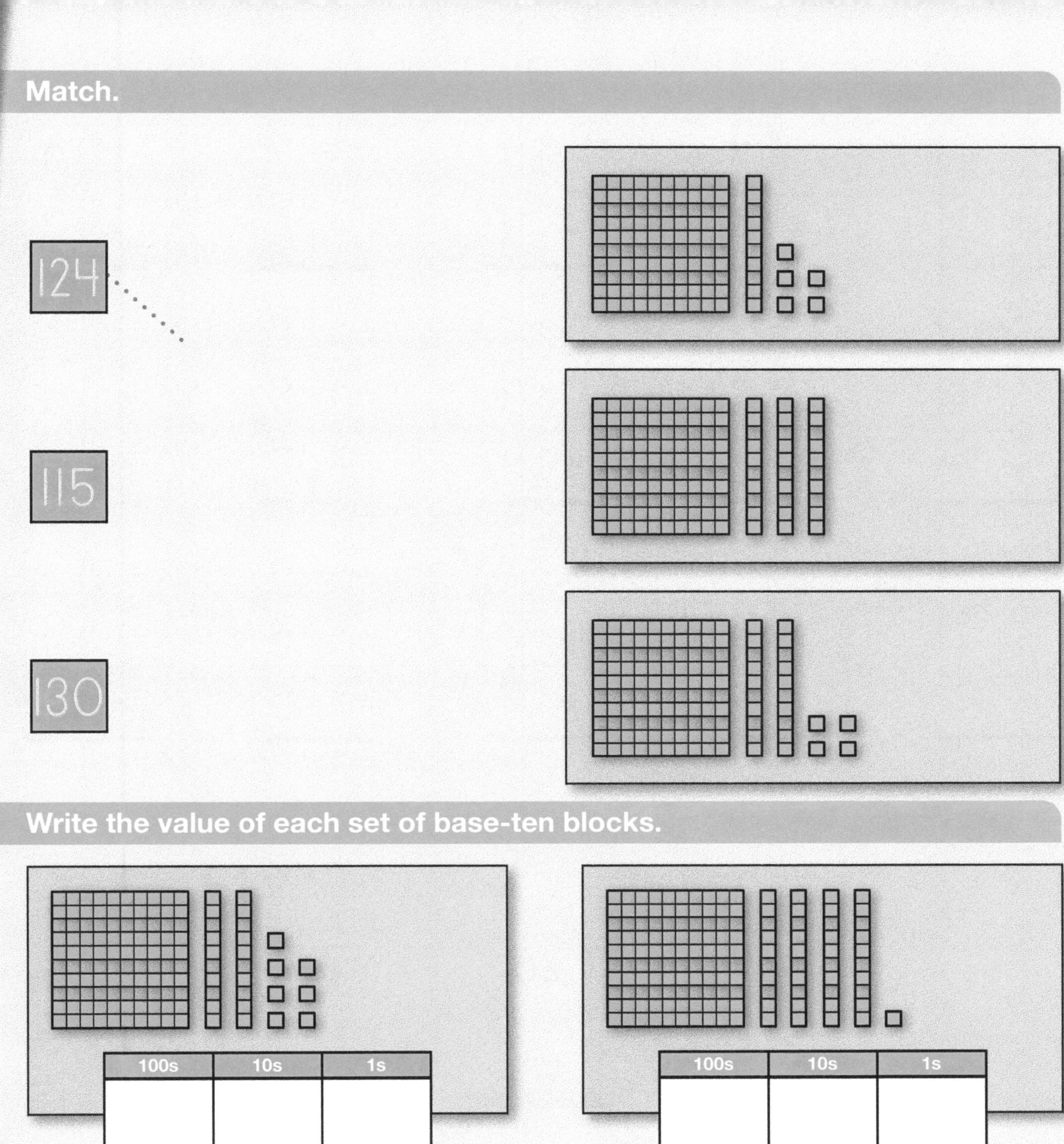

Write the value of each set of base-ten blocks.

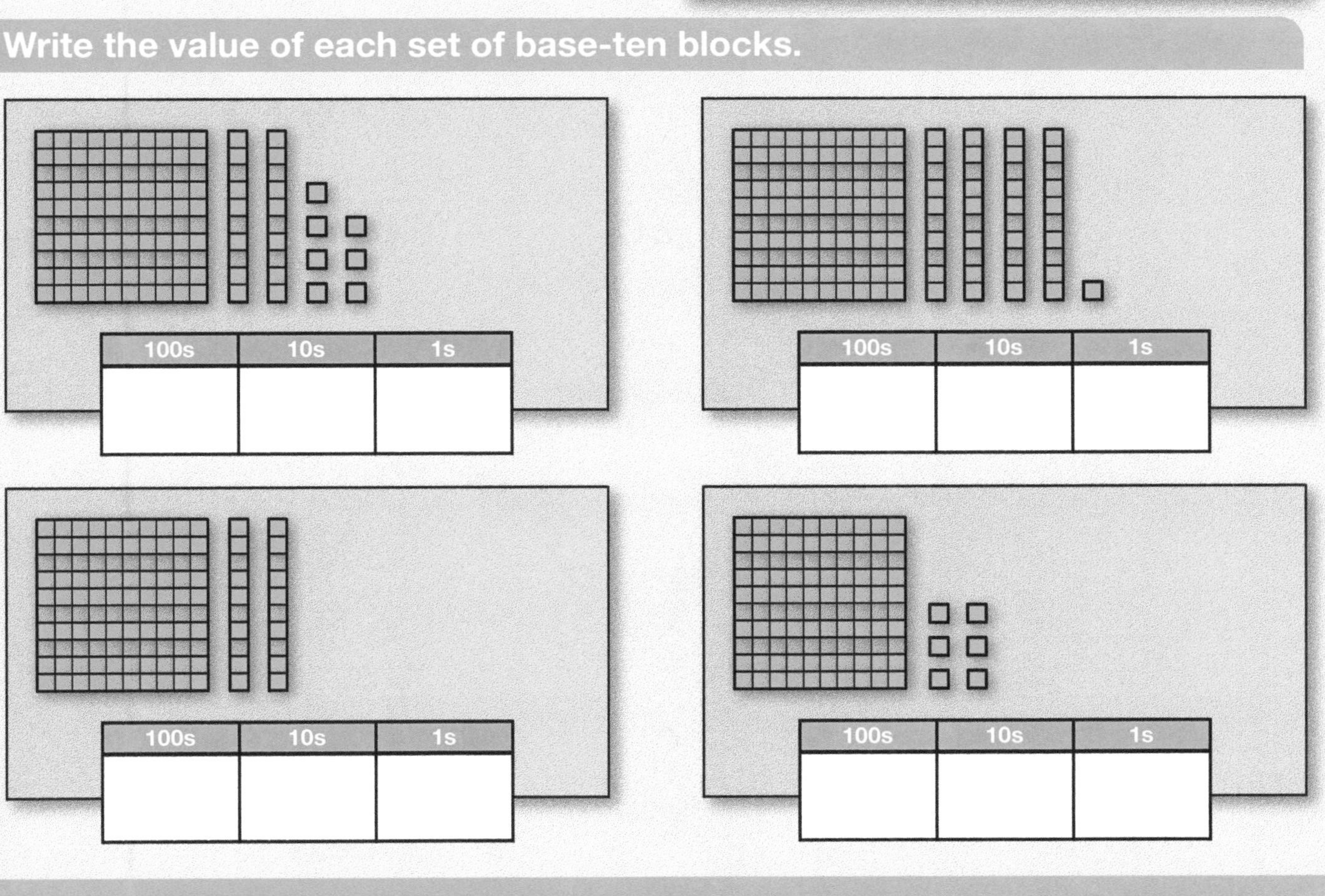

Complete.

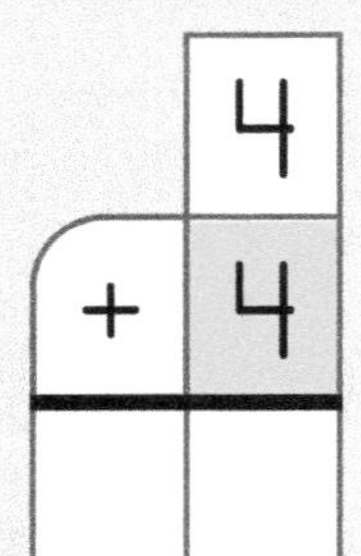

$7 + 6 =$ ___

$9 + 4 =$ ___

$2 + 6 =$ ___

$9 + 7 =$ ___

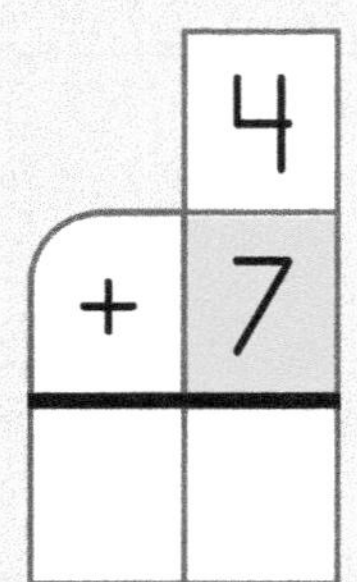

$8 + 2 =$ ___

$9 + 9 =$ ___

$8 + 5 =$ ___

$3 + 9 =$ ___

$5 + 5 =$ ___

$6 + 6 =$ ___

$7 + 7 =$ ___

$8 + 8 =$ ___

$9 + 9 =$ ___

Color the even numbers yellow. Color the odd numbers red.

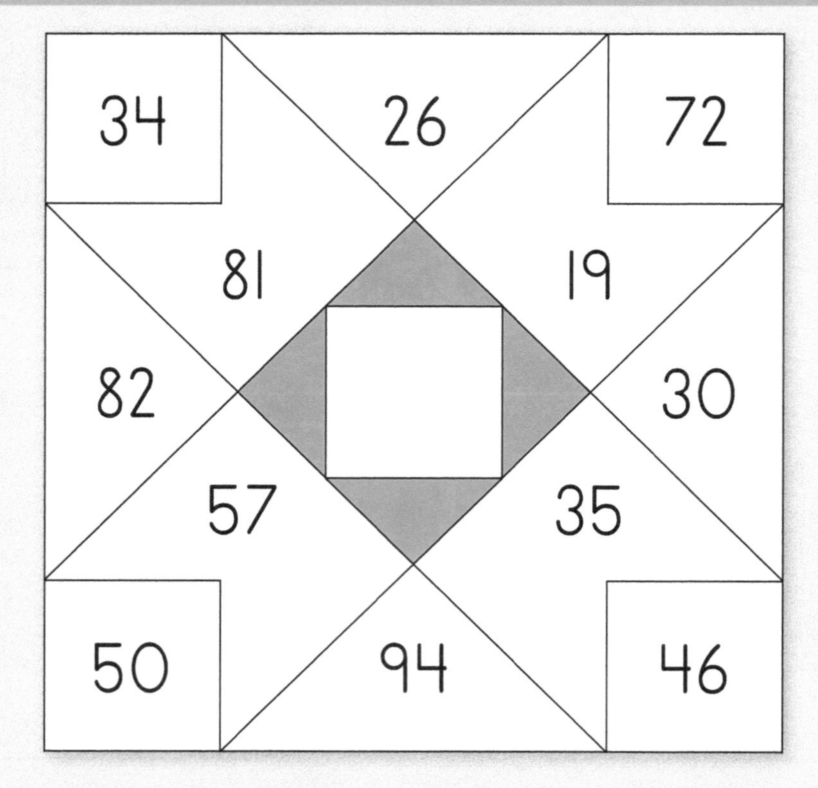

Complete the circles with <, >, or =.

148 ◯ 149	196 ◯ 112	134 ◯ 175
146 ◯ 142	177 ◯ 187	140 ◯ 140
163 ◯ 136	148 ◯ 149	185 ◯ 118
107 ◯ 105	97 ◯ 101	199 ◯ 200
29 ◯ 129	100 ◯ 200	86 ◯ 142

Complete the missing numbers on the 200 Chart.

101	102	103	104	105		107	108	109	110
111	112	113	114		116	117	118		120
121		123	124	125	126	127	128	129	
131	132	133			136	137	138	139	140
141	142		144	145	146		148	149	150

Complete.

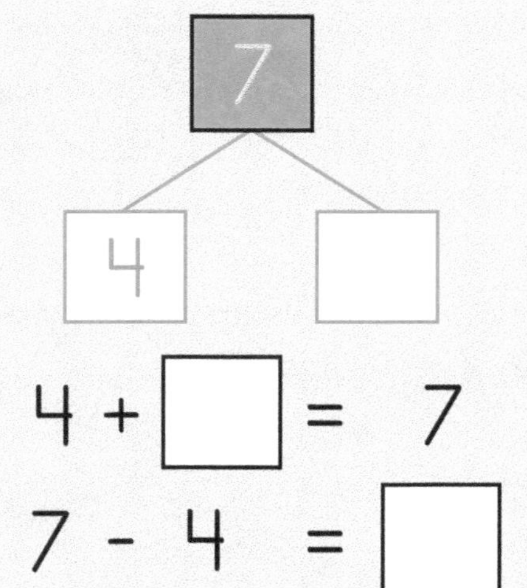

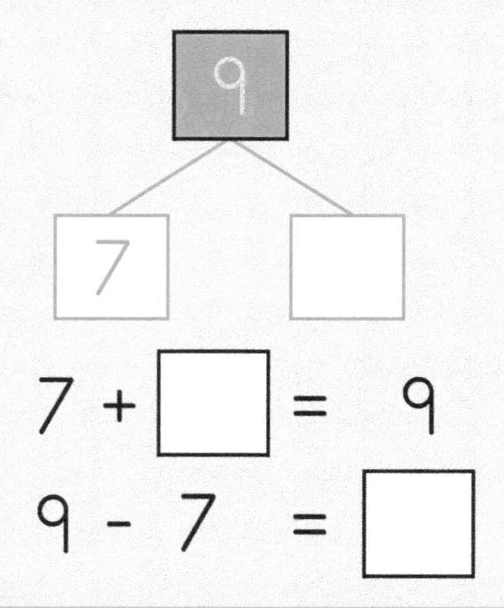

Complete.

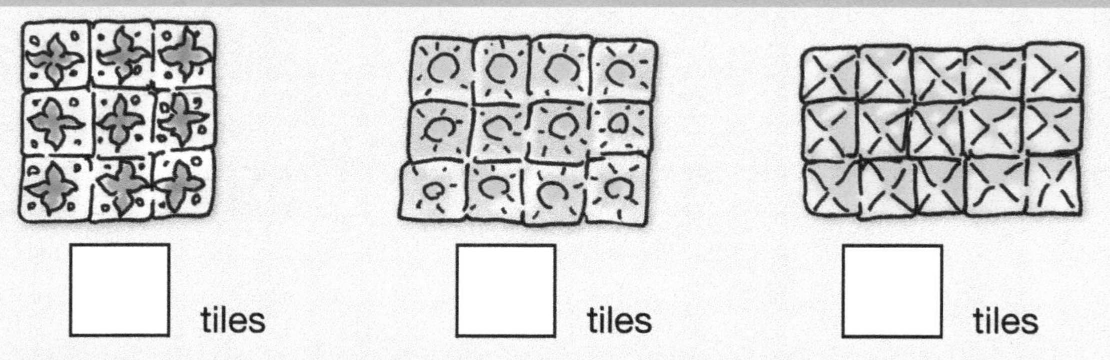

Color the subtraction facts that equal the number in the star.

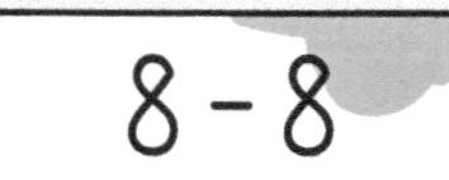

0	1	2	3
8 - 8	7 - 6	10 - 5	6 - 3
9 - 5	8 - 7	9 - 6	10 - 7
6 - 6	9 - 8	10 - 8	8 - 4
10 - 3	10 - 7	8 - 6	9 - 5

Complete.

55 + 3 = ☐	48 + 30 = ☐
155 + 3 = ☐	148 + 30 = ☐
68 - 2 = ☐	39 - 20 = ☐
168 - 2 = ☐	139 - 20 = ☐
20 + 17 = ☐	34 - 4 = ☐
120 + 17 = ☐	134 - 4 = ☐

Complete the missing numbers in the sequences.

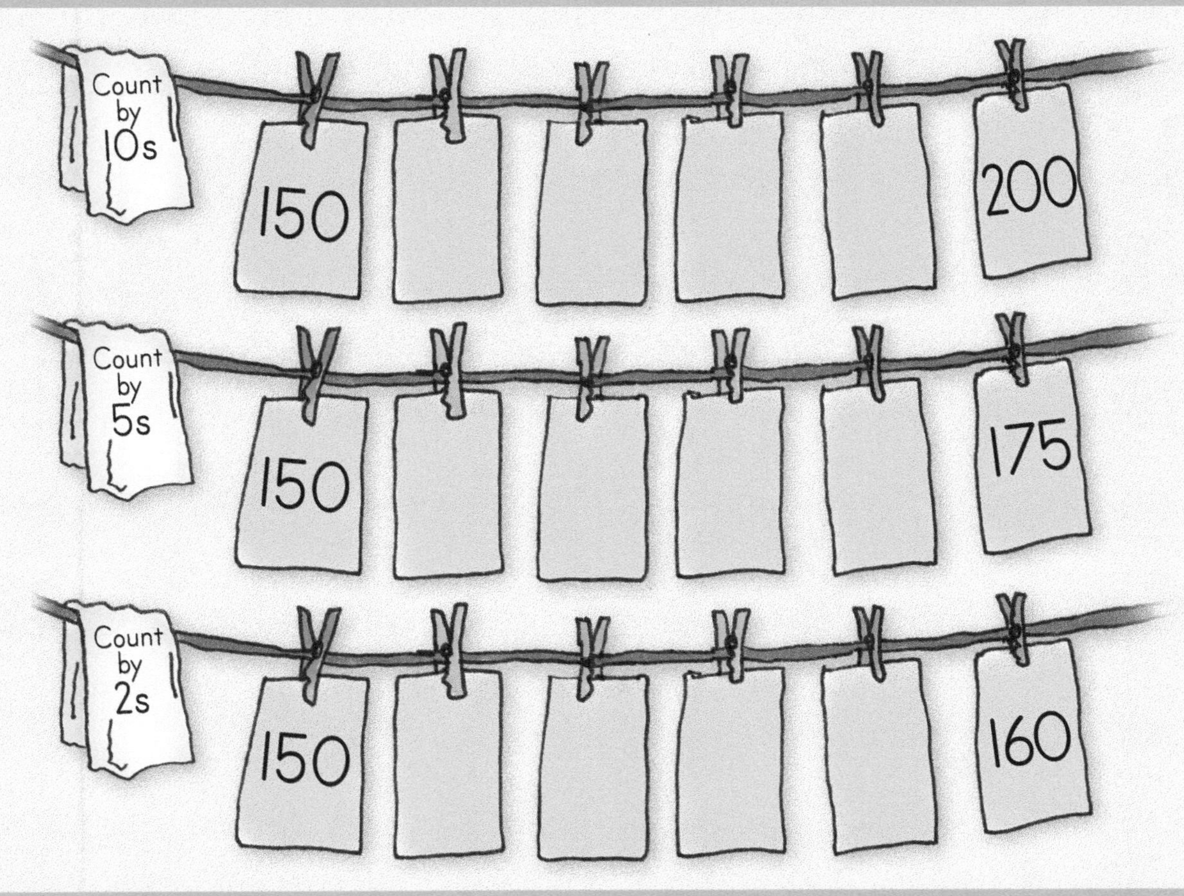

Use the key to color the apples.

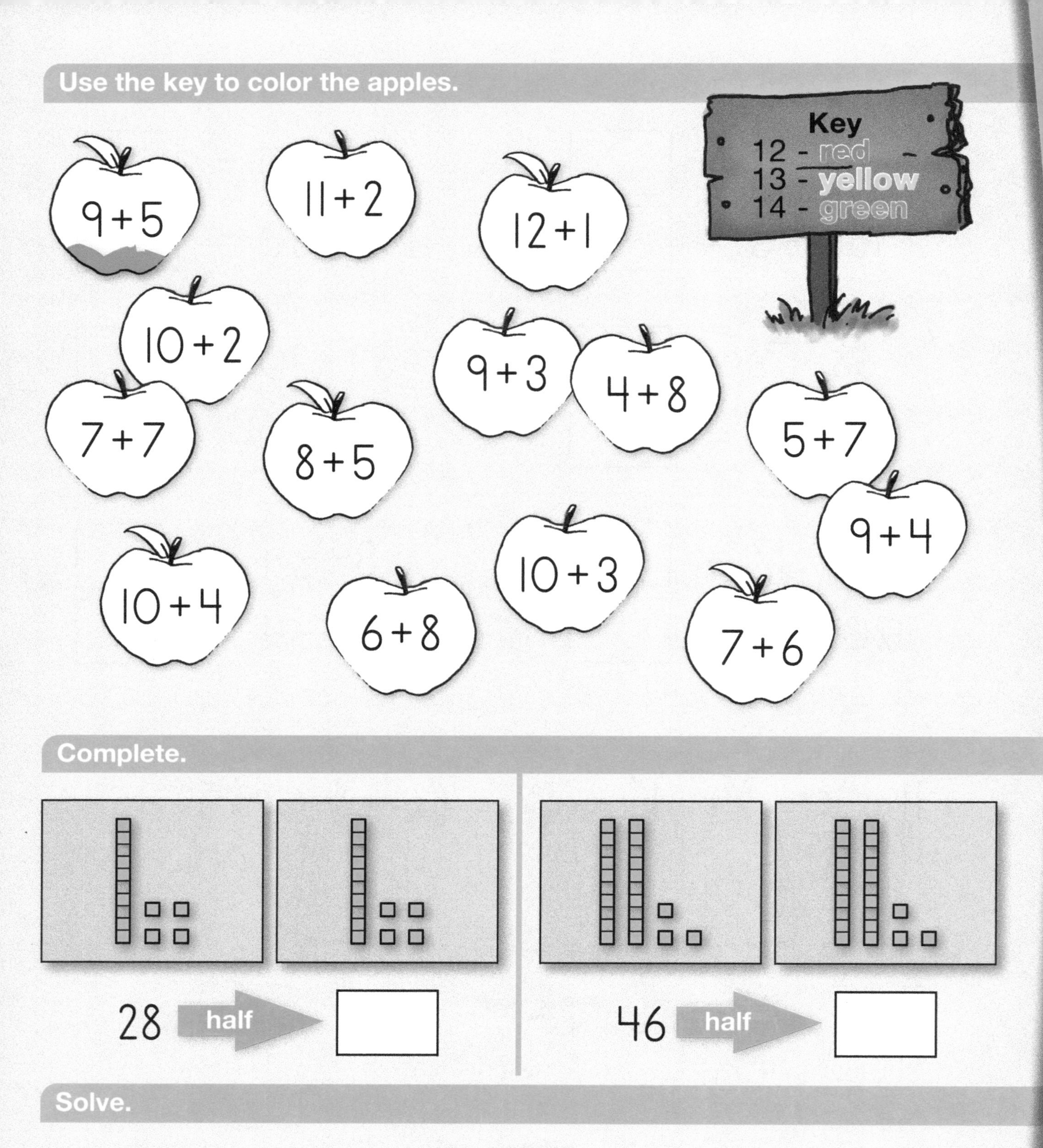

Complete.

Solve.

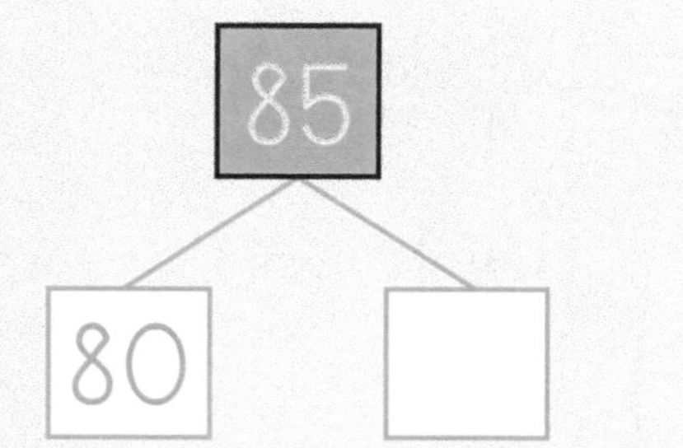

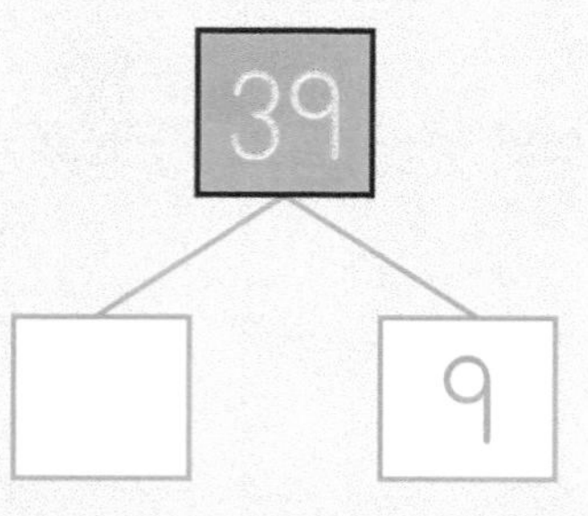

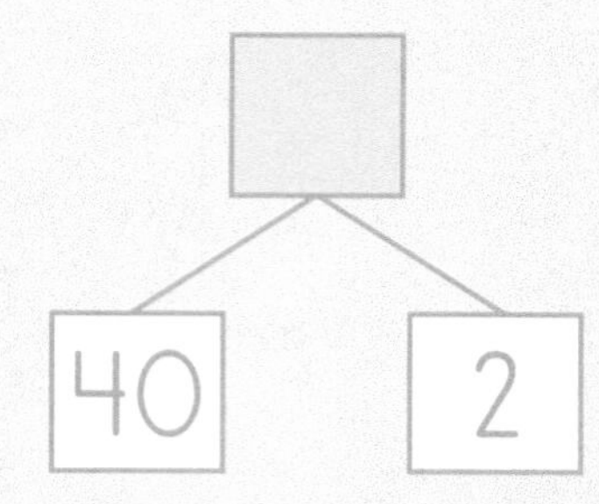

Write the expanded form of each number.

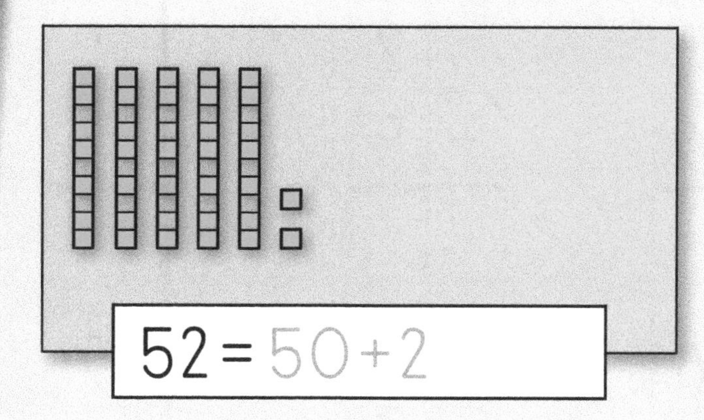

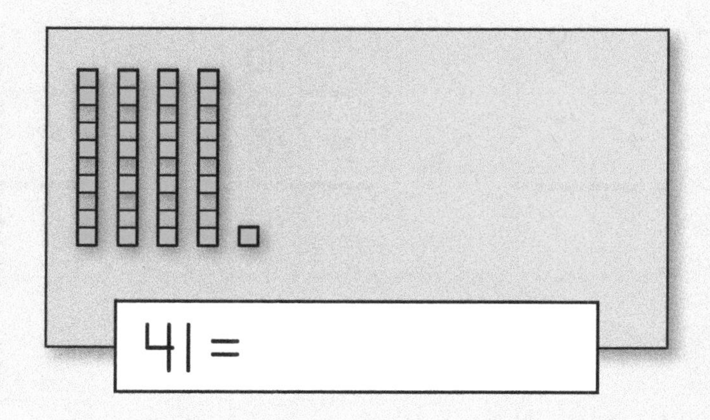

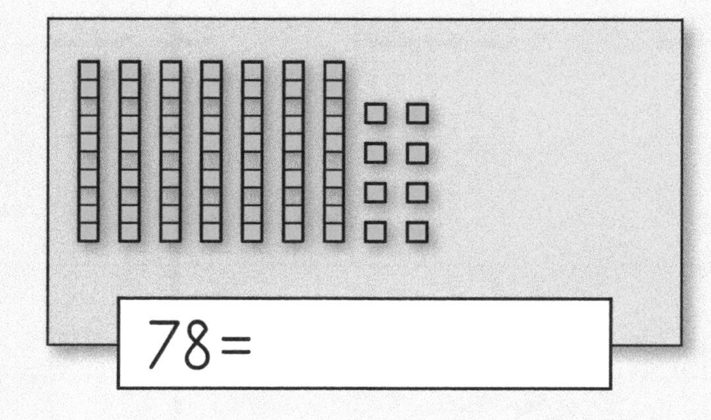

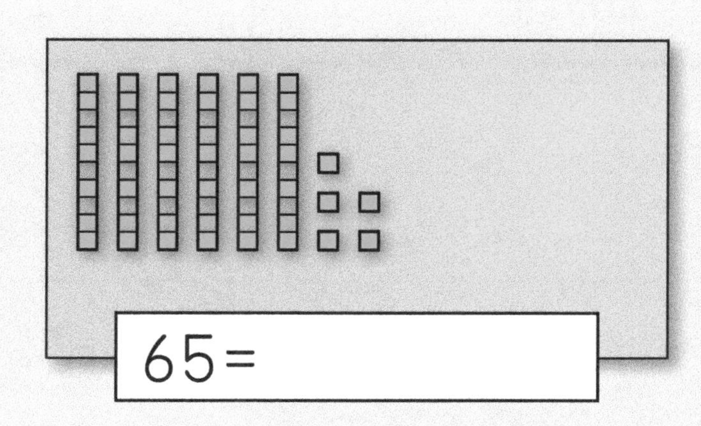

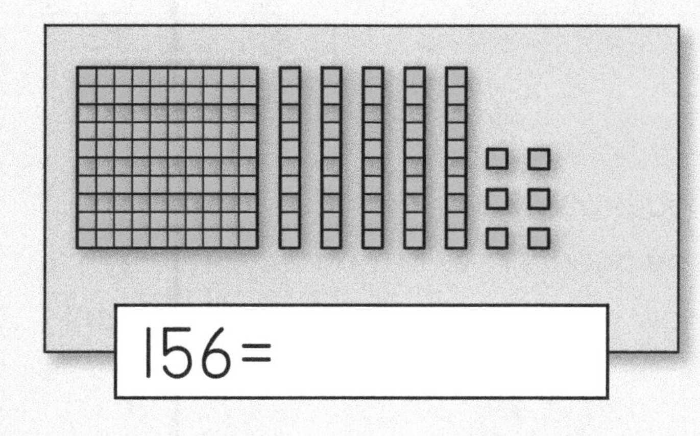

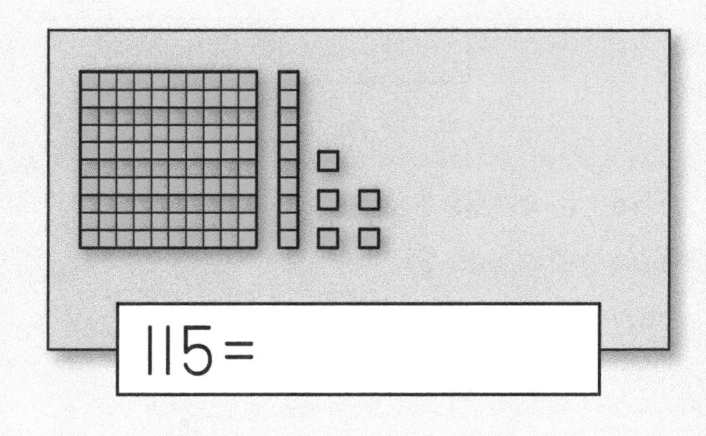

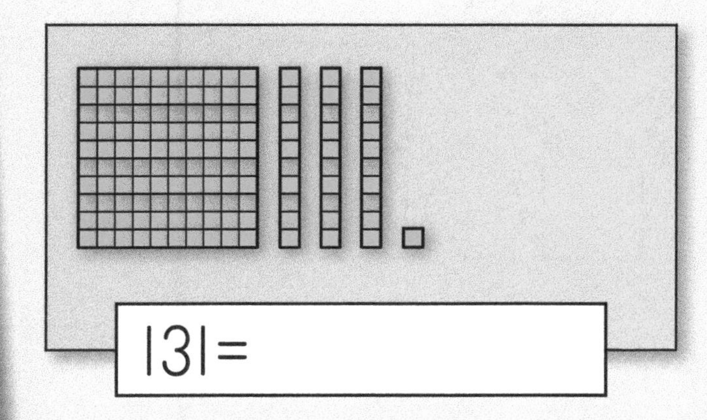

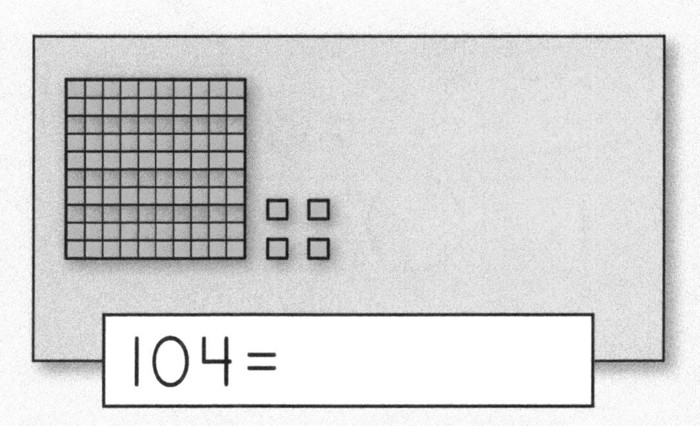

Complete.

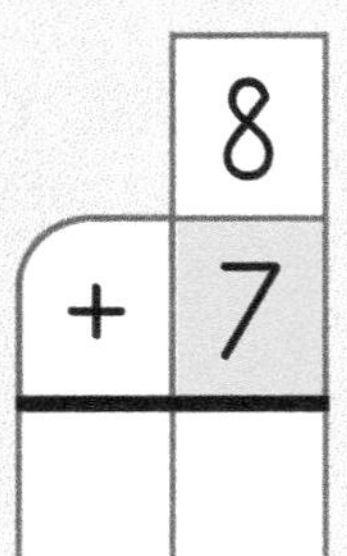

$$\begin{array}{r} 6 \\ +\,8 \\ \hline \end{array} \quad \begin{array}{r} 9 \\ +\,6 \\ \hline \end{array} \quad \begin{array}{r} 2 \\ +\,9 \\ \hline \end{array} \quad \begin{array}{r} 9 \\ +\,4 \\ \hline \end{array}$$

$$\begin{array}{r} 7 \\ +\,4 \\ \hline \end{array} \quad \begin{array}{r} 3 \\ +\,8 \\ \hline \end{array} \quad \begin{array}{r} 6 \\ +\,5 \\ \hline \end{array} \quad \begin{array}{r} 9 \\ +\,1 \\ \hline \end{array} \quad \begin{array}{r} 7 \\ +\,8 \\ \hline \end{array}$$

Complete.

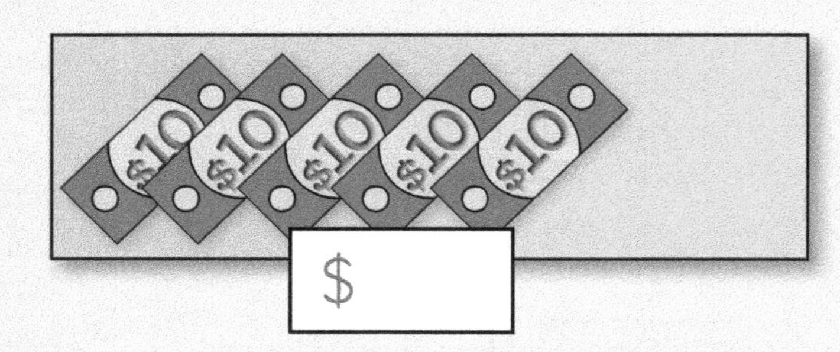

Solve.

The ball costs $5.

The bat costs $7.

How much does it cost to buy both the ball and the bat?

You have $8.

You need $11 to buy the toy.

How much more money do you need?

☐ ◯ ☐ = ☐

$ ☐

Write how much money is in each coin purse.
Use a dollar sign and decimal point.

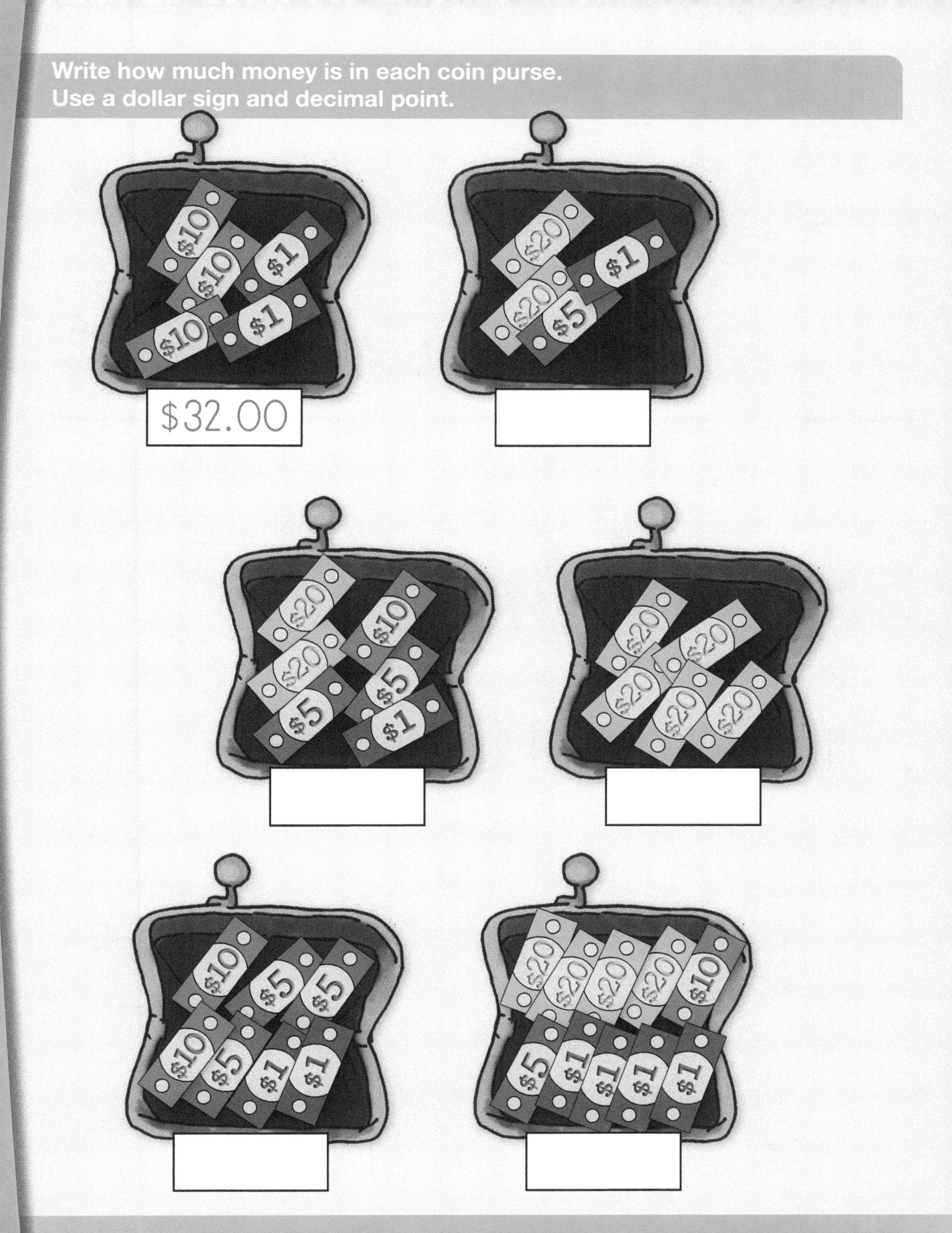

Complete.

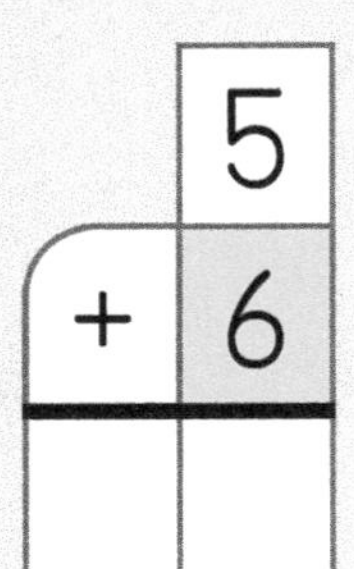

5 + 6	7 + 6	7 + 3	9 + 8	7 + 7
4 + 6	8 + 7	2 + 9	8 + 6	5 + 9

Complete the circles with <, >, or =.

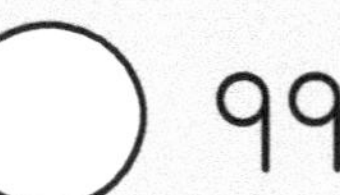

139 ◯ 155	146 ◯ 146	150 ◯ 99
111 ◯ 110	101 ◯ 100	193 ◯ 194

Complete.

35 + 4 = ☐

135 + 4 = ☐

62 + 20 = ☐

162 + 20 = ☐

58 - 4 = ☐

158 - 4 = ☐

71 - 30 = ☐

171 - 30 = ☐

Match.

45¢		$0.27
5¢		$0.45
27¢		$0.09
9¢		$0.50
50¢		$0.05

Write how much money is in each coin purse two ways.

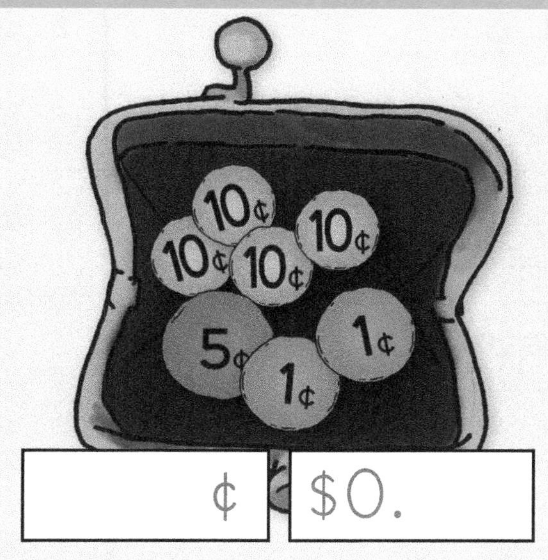

___ ¢ $0.___

___ ¢ $0.___

Complete.

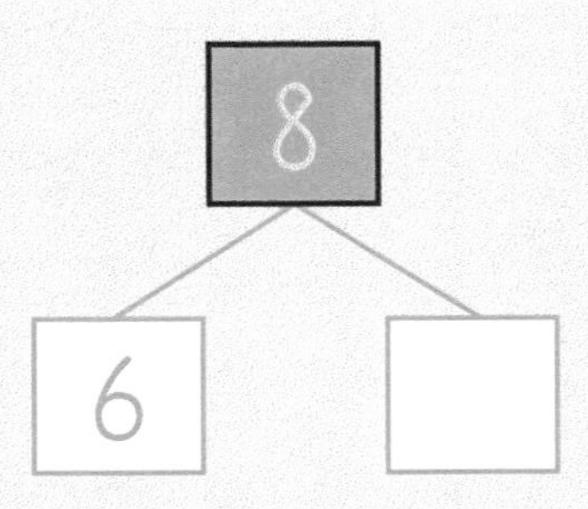

$6 + \square = 8$

$8 - 6 = \square$

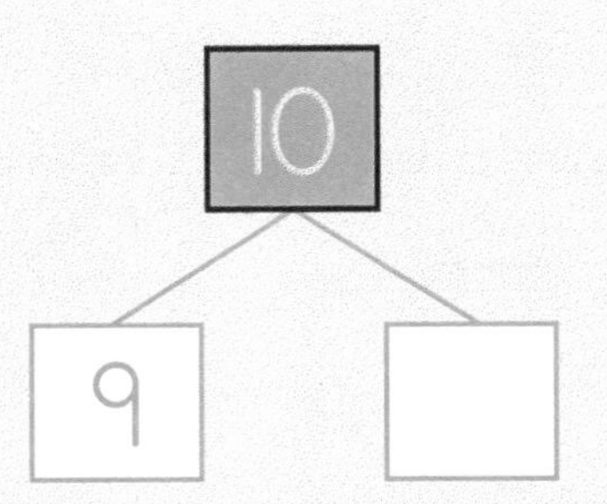

$9 + \square = 10$

$10 - 9 = \square$

Complete.

$9 - 4 = \square$ $7 - 2 = \square$ $10 - 3 = \square$

$8 - 1 = \square$ $9 - 6 = \square$ $7 - 4 = \square$

$10 - 5 = \square$ $8 - 4 = \square$ $10 - 8 = \square$

Write the expanded form of each number.

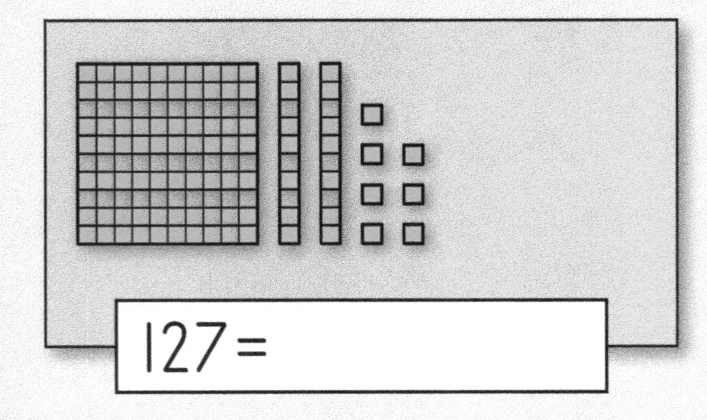

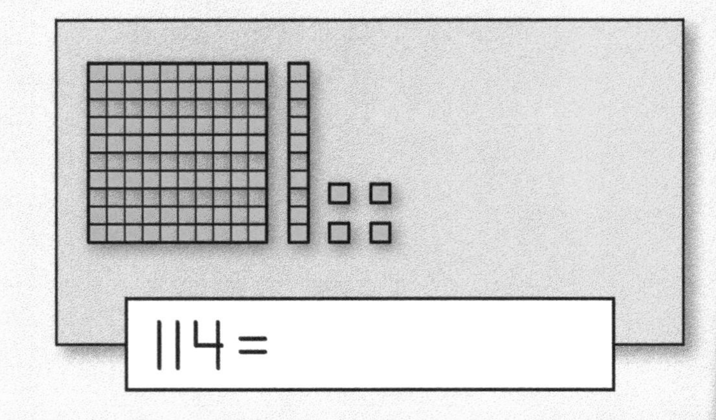

Write how much money is in each coin purse.
Use a dollar sign and decimal point.

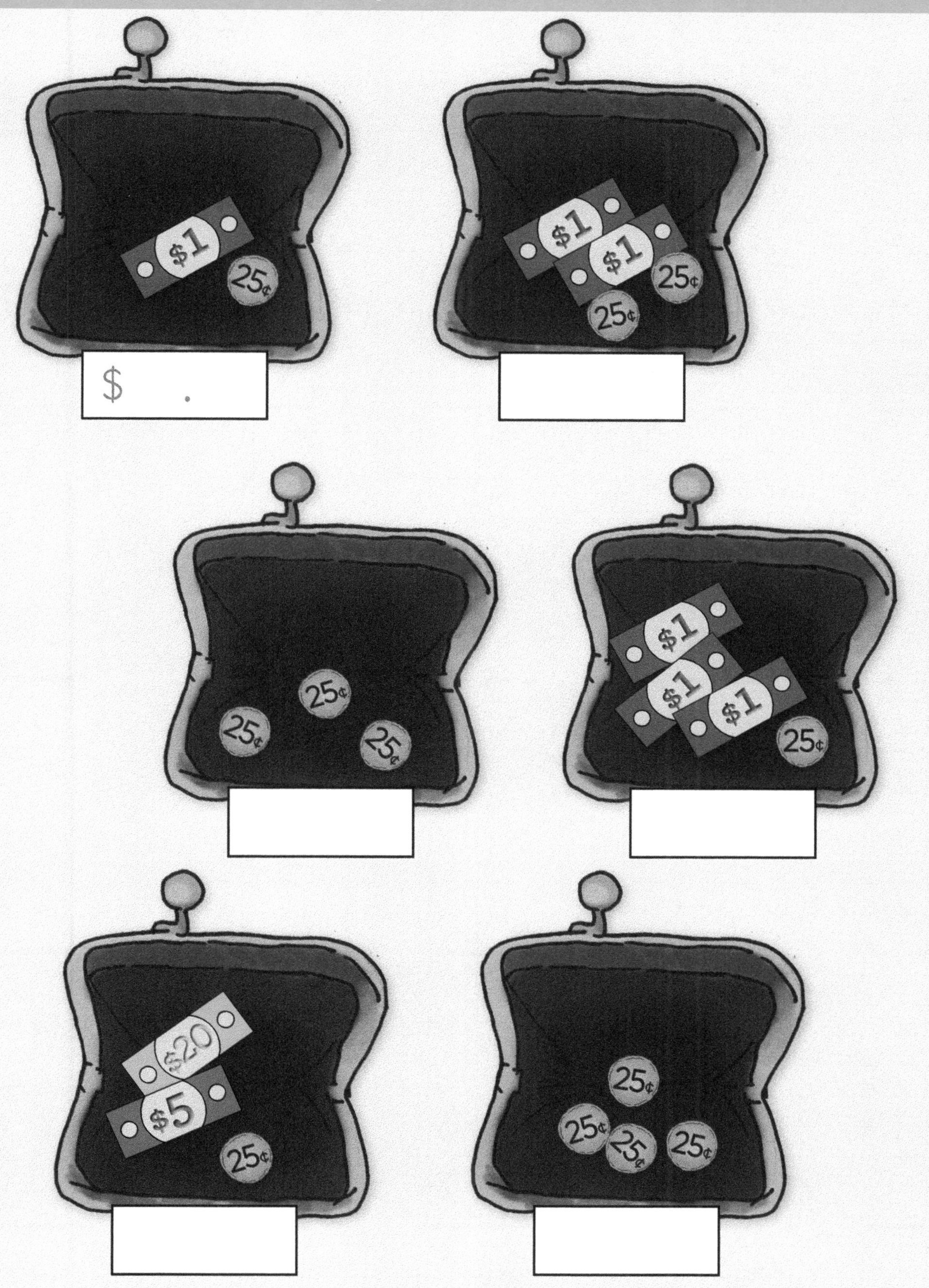

Complete.

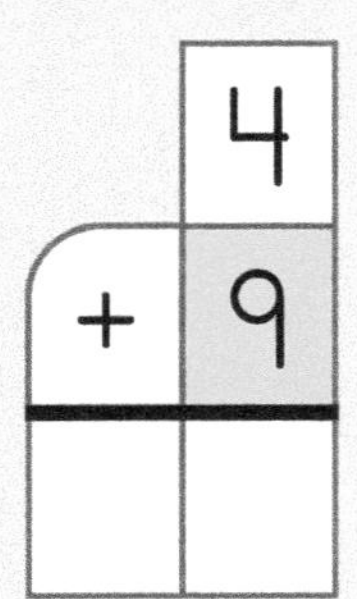

$4 + 9 =$ ___	$8 + 2 =$ ___	$9 + 7 =$ ___	$6 + 2 =$ ___	$9 + 5 =$ ___
$9 + 9 =$ ___	$1 + 8 =$ ___	$7 + 7 =$ ___	$5 + 6 =$ ___	$5 + 1 =$ ___
$0 + 9 =$ ___	$8 + 6 =$ ___	$2 + 7 =$ ___	$6 + 7 =$ ___	$3 + 5 =$ ___
$9 + 6 =$ ___	$7 + 8 =$ ___	$7 + 5 =$ ___	$1 + 6 =$ ___	$5 + 5 =$ ___
$1 + 9 =$ ___	$8 + 0 =$ ___	$3 + 7 =$ ___	$6 + 8 =$ ___	$6 + 5 =$ ___

See the Instructor Guide for how to play.
Save this game board for future lessons.

Complete.

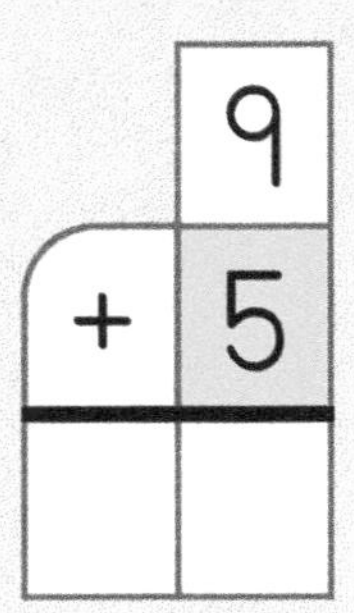 9 + 5	3 + 8	7 + 1	6 + 6	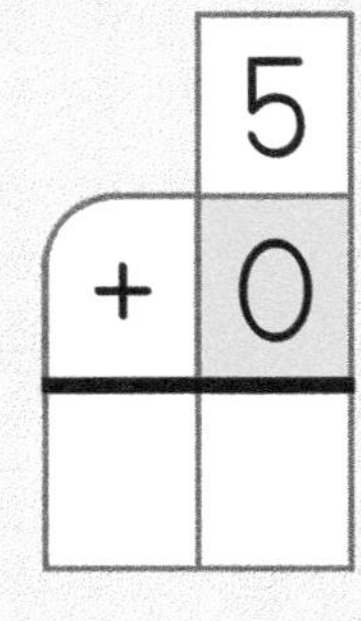 5 + 0
7 + 9	8 + 8	8 + 7	6 + 9	4 + 5
9 + 2	9 + 8	7 + 6	3 + 6	5 + 8
8 + 9	8 + 4	0 + 7	6 + 4	2 + 5
9 + 3	5 + 8	7 + 4	0 + 6	5 + 7

Match.

10 - 7		7 - 6
	0	
9 - 8		10 - 8
8 - 5	1	10 - 6
9 - 7		7 - 7
	2	
7 - 5		9 - 5
8 - 7	3	10 - 9
8 - 8	4	8 - 6
9 - 6		6 - 5

Write how much money is in each coin purse.
Use a dollar sign and decimal point.

Complete the circles with <, >, or =.

48 ◯ 84	72 ◯ 27	172 ◯ 170
60 ◯ 60	60 ◯ 160	200 ◯ 120
117 ◯ 71	99 ◯ 105	106 ◯ 104

See the Instructor Guide for how to play.
Save this game board for future lessons.

Use the ten-frames to complete the equations.

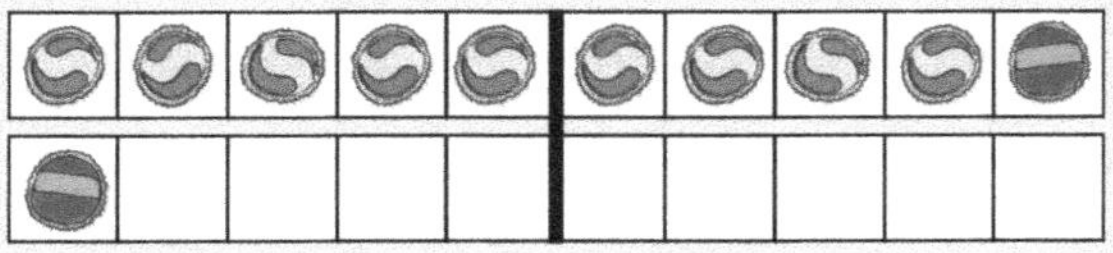

$9 + \square = 11$

$11 - 9 = \square$

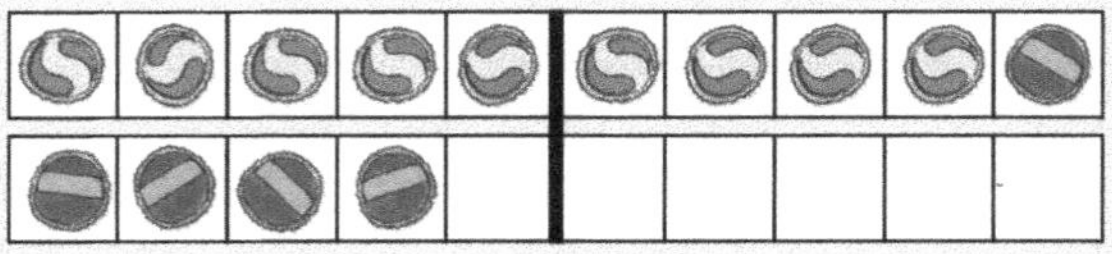

$9 + \square = 14$

$14 - 9 = \square$

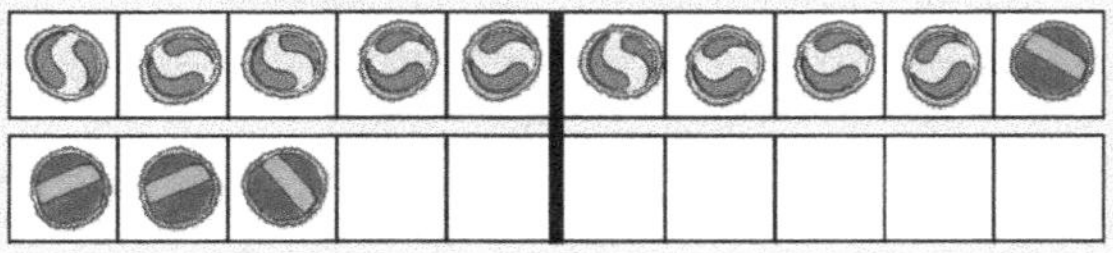

$9 + \square = 13$

$13 - 9 = \square$

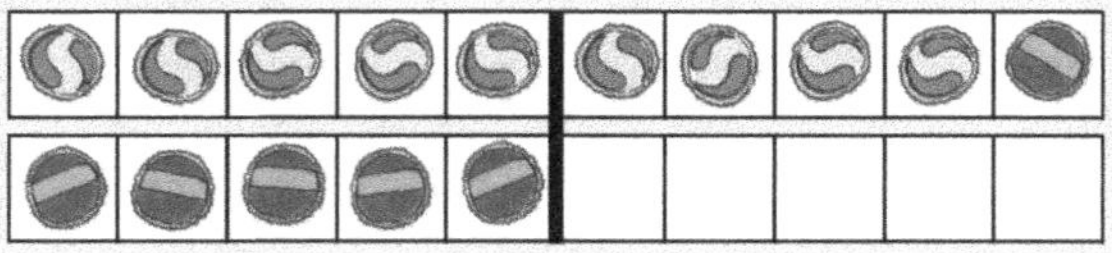

$9 + \square = 15$

$15 - 9 = \square$

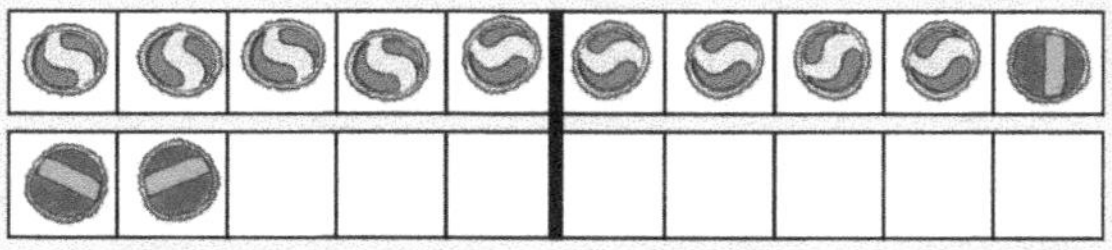

$9 + \square = 12$

$12 - 9 = \square$

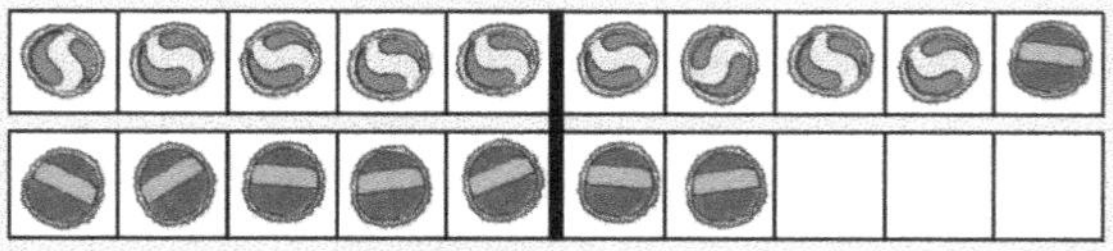

$9 + \square = 17$

$17 - 9 = \square$

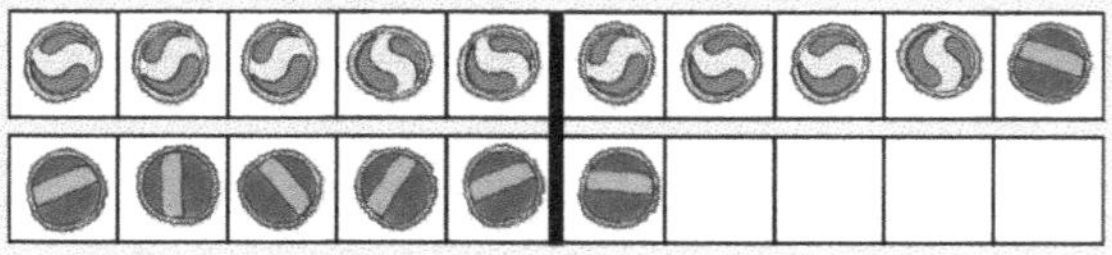

$9 + \square = 16$

$16 - 9 = \square$

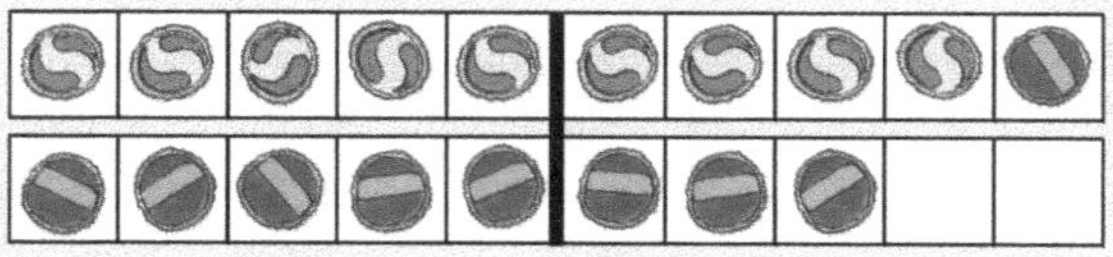

$9 + \square = 18$

$18 - 9 = \square$

Solve.

You have 8 apples.

You eat 5.

How many are left?

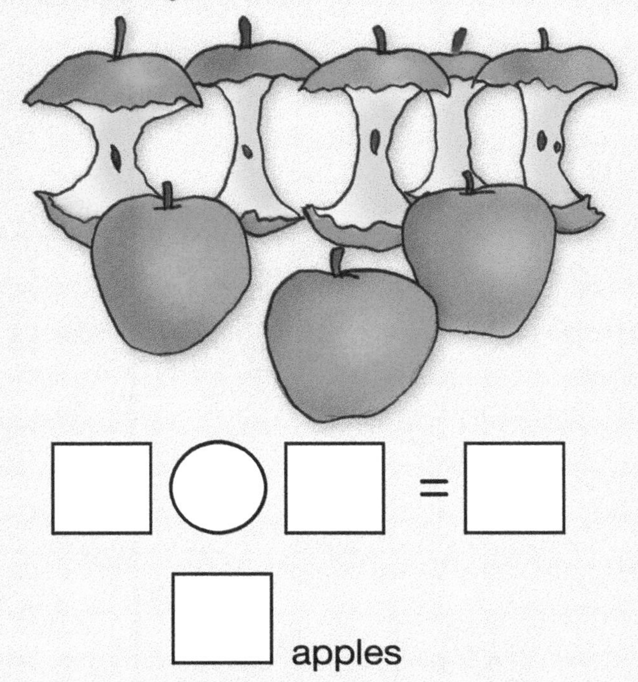

☐ ○ ☐ = ☐

☐ apples

You have 7 lollipops.

You eat 2.

How many are left?

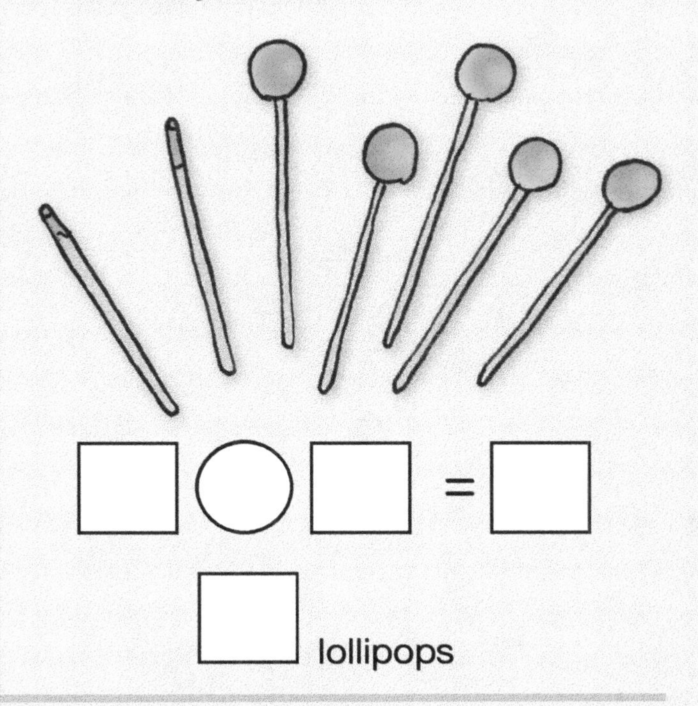

☐ ○ ☐ = ☐

☐ lollipops

You have 10 pencils.

1 pencil breaks.

How many whole pencils are left?

☐ ○ ☐ = ☐

☐ pencils

You have 10 stickers.

You use 3.

How many do you have left?

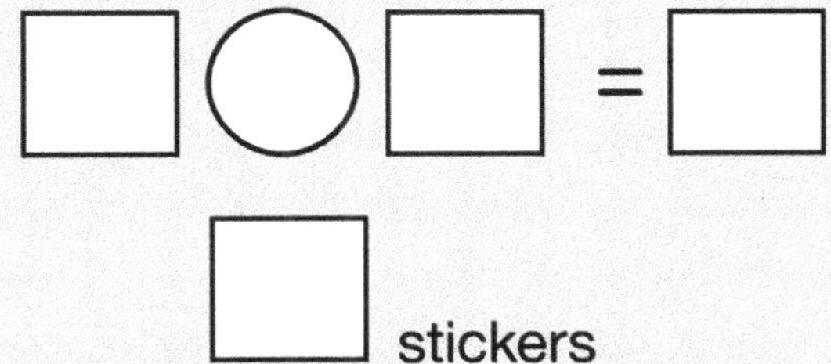

☐ ○ ☐ = ☐

☐ stickers

Complete. Look at the ten-frame to help find the answers.

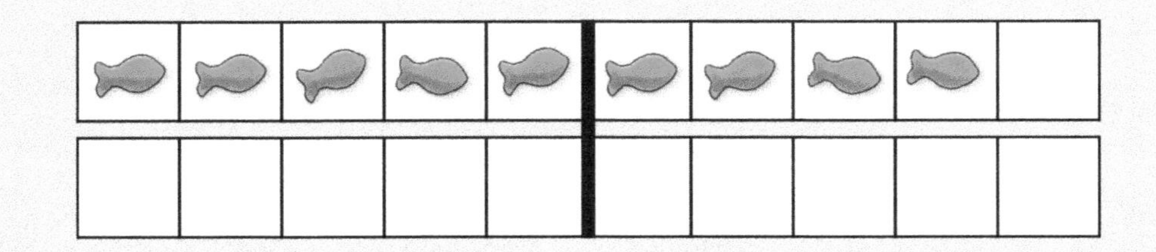

$9 + \square = 12$

$12 - 9 = \square$

$9 + \square = 14$

$14 - 9 = \square$

$9 + \square = 18$

$18 - 9 = \square$

$9 + \square = 11$

$11 - 9 = \square$

$9 + \square = 17$

$17 - 9 = \square$

$9 + \square = 16$

$16 - 9 = \square$

$9 + \square = 15$

$15 - 9 = \square$

$9 + \square = 13$

$13 - 9 = \square$

Use the ten-frames to complete the equations.

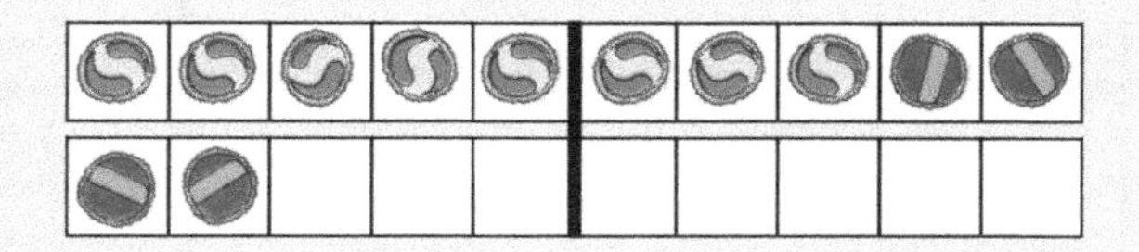

$8 + \square = 12$

$12 - 8 = \square$

$8 + \square = 14$

$14 - 8 = \square$

$8 + \square = 16$

$16 - 8 = \square$

$8 + \square = 11$

$11 - 8 = \square$

$8 + \square = 13$

$13 - 8 = \square$

$8 + \square = 17$

$17 - 8 = \square$

$8 + \square = 15$

$15 - 8 = \square$

$8 + \square = 18$

$18 - 8 = \square$

Write the expanded form for each number.

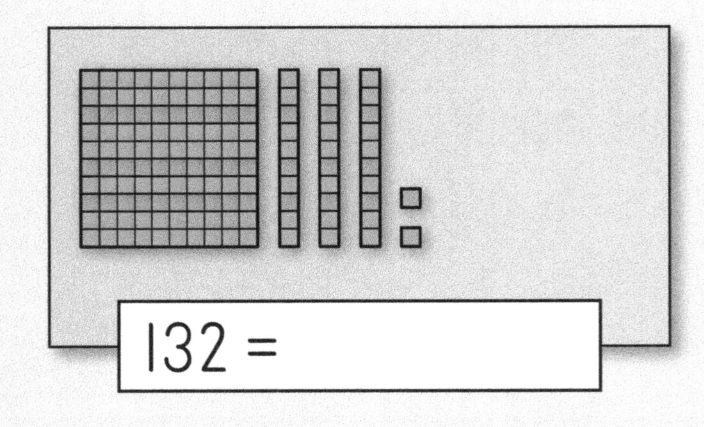

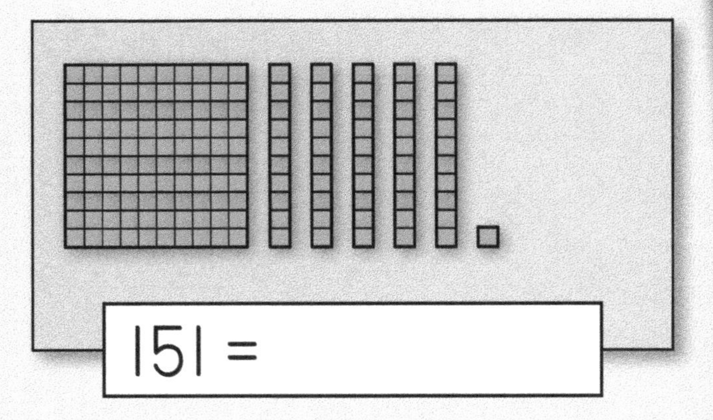

Lucia made a bar graph about the animals she saw at the pet store. Use the bar graph to answer the questions.

Animals at the Pet Store

Animal	Count
Guinea pigs	■■■■■■■■■
Hamsters	■■■
Gerbils	■■■■■

How many guinea pigs did she see? ☐

How many hamsters did she see? ☐

How many gerbils did she see? ☐

How many more guinea pigs than gerbils did she see? ☐

How many more gerbils than hamsters did she see? ☐

How many guinea pigs, gerbils, and hamsters did she see in all? ☐

Color the pictures to match the word problems and solve.

You have 8 apples.
5 are green, and the rest are red.
How many are red?

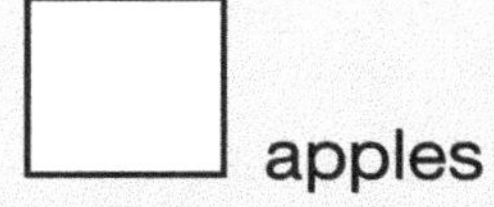
apples

You have 7 lollipops.
6 are purple, and the rest are yellow.
How many are yellow?

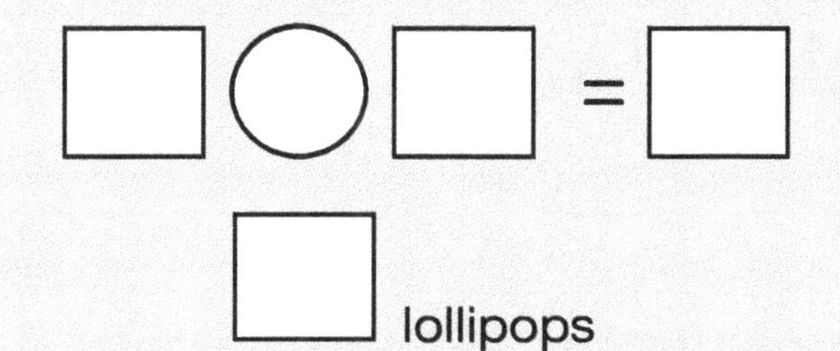

lollipops

You have 10 pencils.
7 are yellow, and the rest are green.
How many are green?

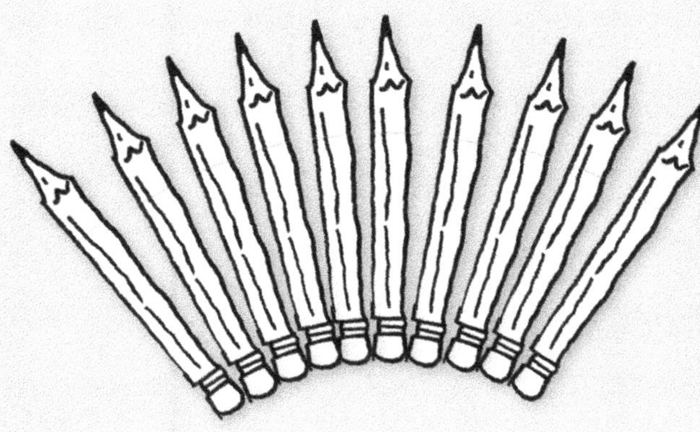

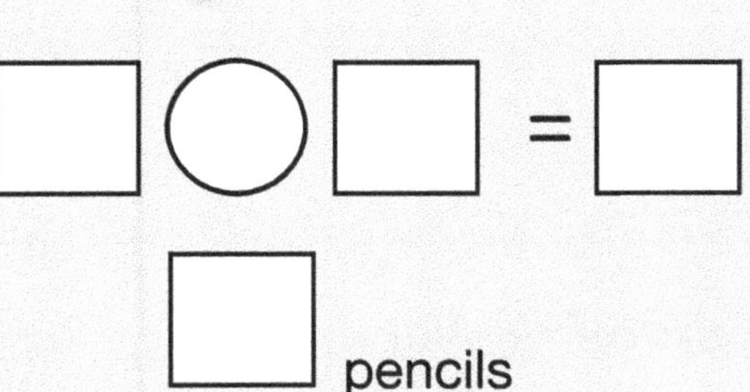
pencils

You have 9 pompoms.
1 is blue, and the rest are orange.
How many are orange?

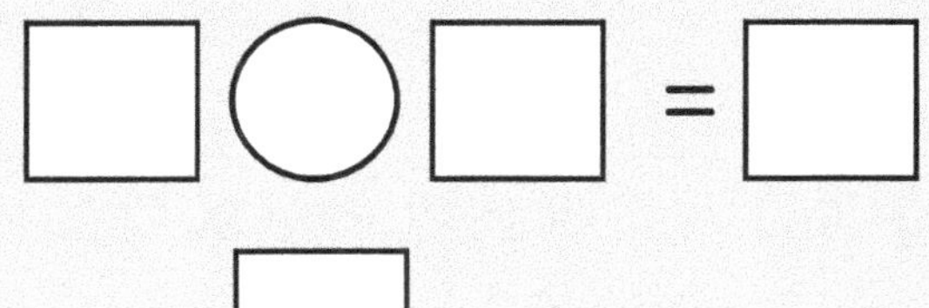

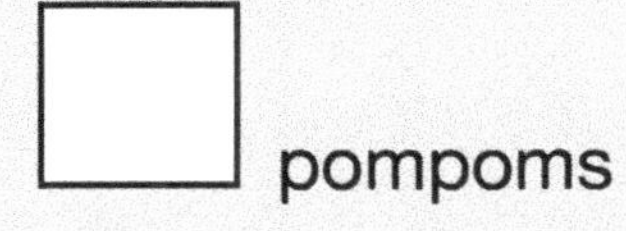
pompoms

Match.

17 - 9	4	15 - 8
13 - 9	5	16 - 8
14 - 9	6	12 - 8
16 - 9	7	14 - 8
15 - 9	8	13 - 8

Match.

155

150

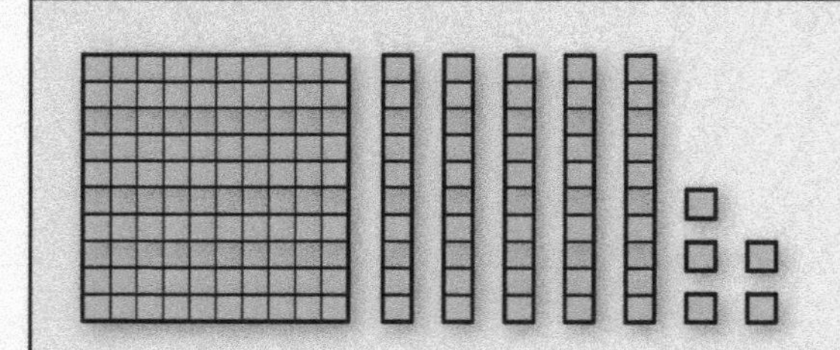

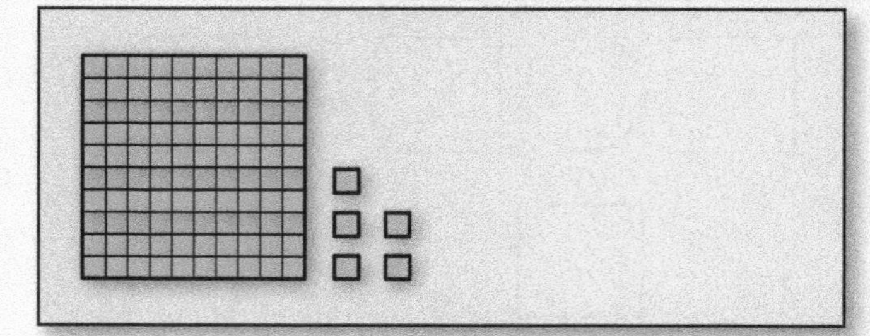

See the Instructor Guide for how to play.
Save this game board for future lessons.

Treasure Hunt

Player 1 Start

14 - 6

14 - 7

13 - 7

Take 3 pieces of treasure

12 - 6

15 - 6

Lose 1 piece of treasure

11 - 7

Player 2 Start

16 - 7

13 - 6

14 - 7

Take 2 pieces of treasure

12 - 7

11 - 6

Lose all your treasure

15 - 7

Use the ten-frames to complete.

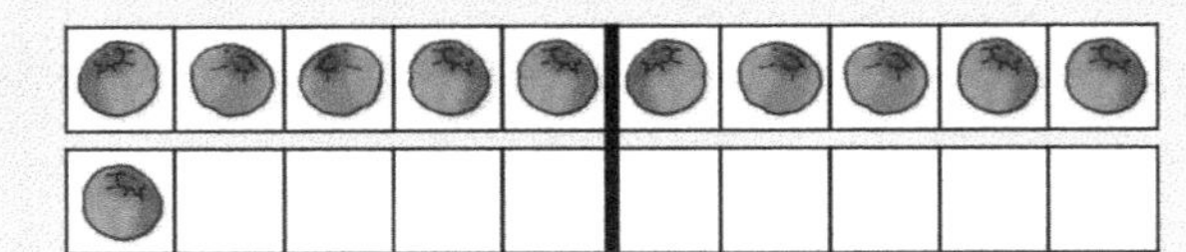

11 - 6 = ☐

11 - 7 = ☐

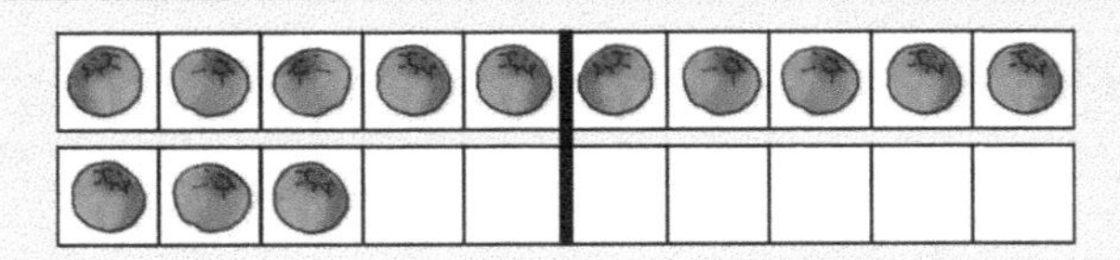

13 - 6 = ☐

13 - 7 = ☐

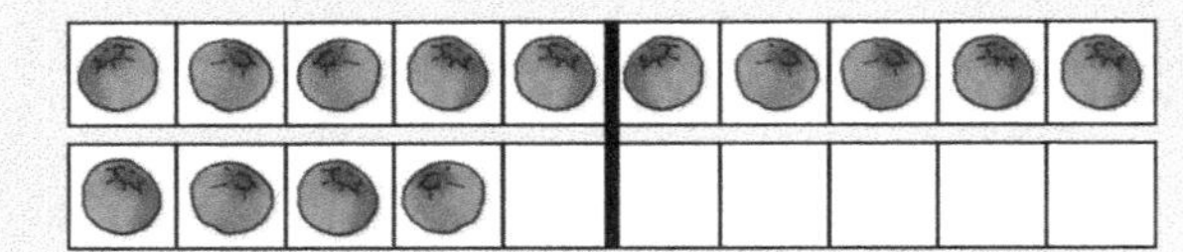

14 - 6 = ☐

14 - 7 = ☐

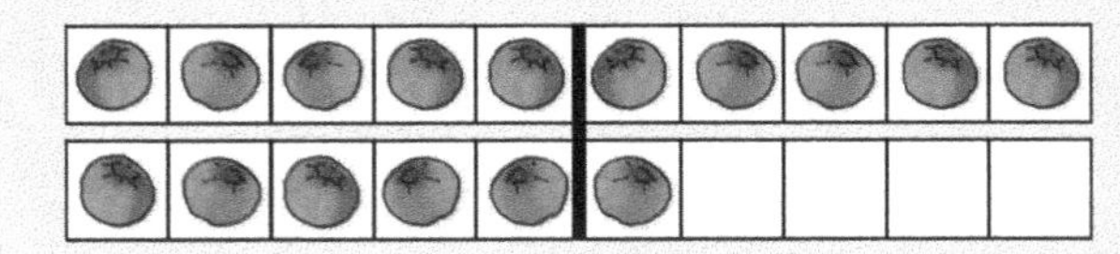

16 - 6 = ☐

16 - 7 = ☐

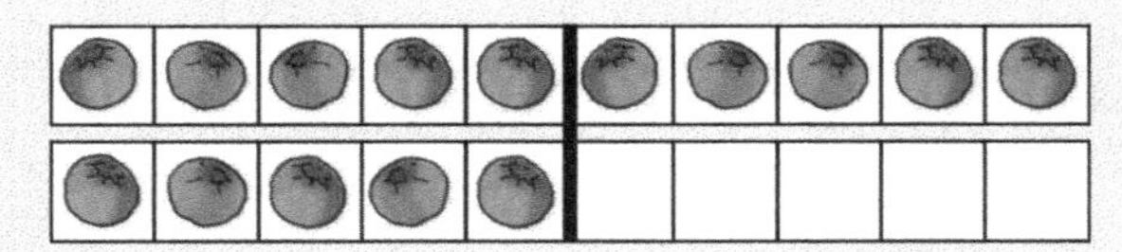

15 - 6 = ☐

15 - 7 = ☐

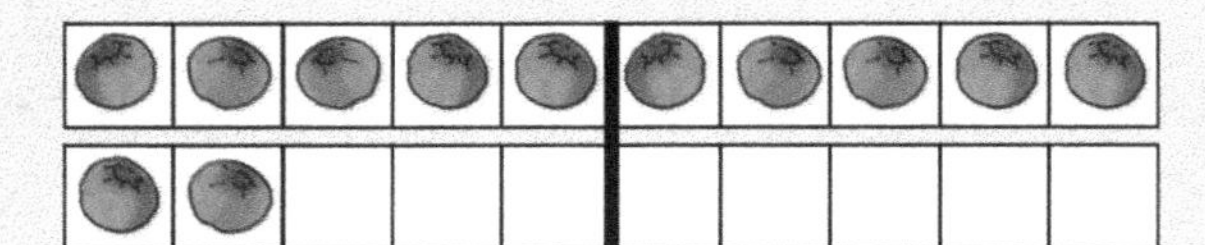

12 - 6 = ☐

12 - 7 = ☐

Use the key to color the leaves.

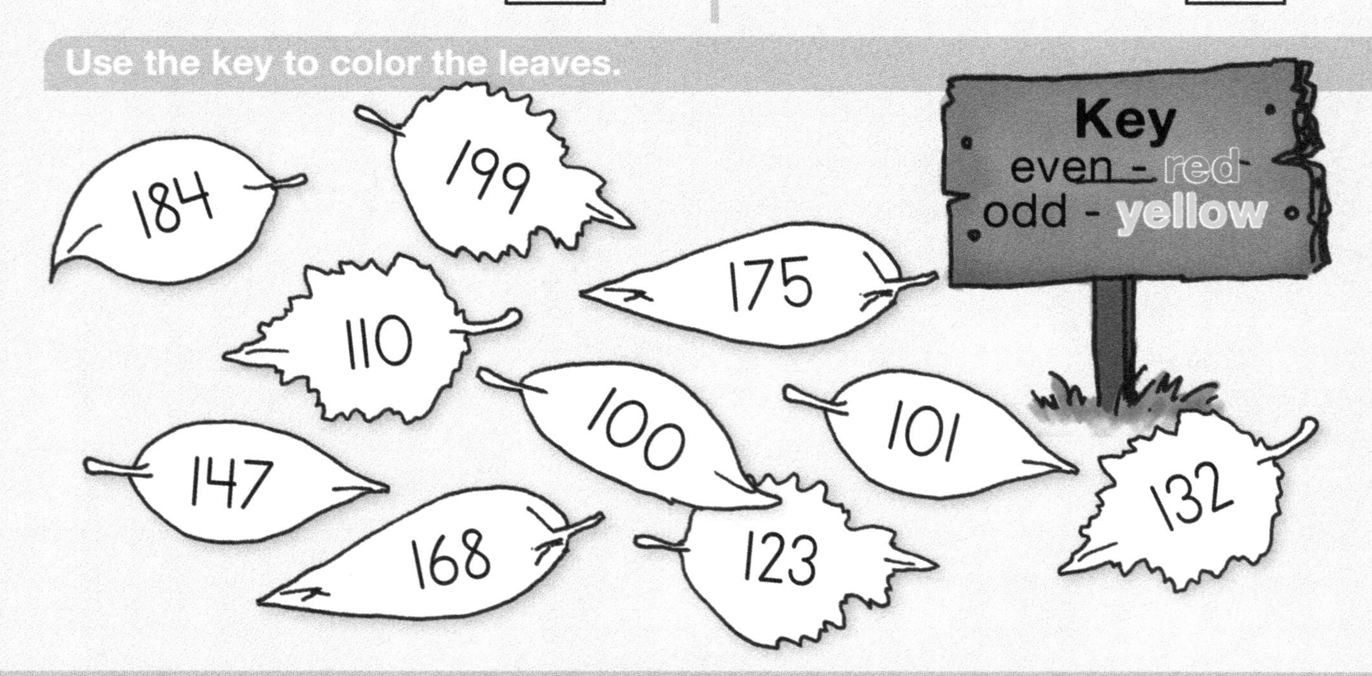

Solve.

You have 10 blue marbles and 8 green marbles.

How many more blue marbles than green marbles do you have?

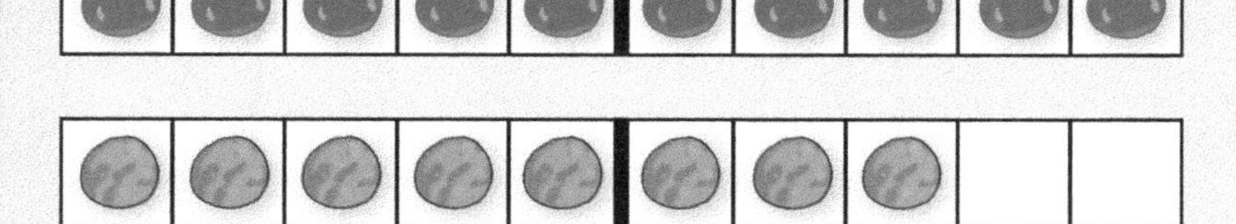

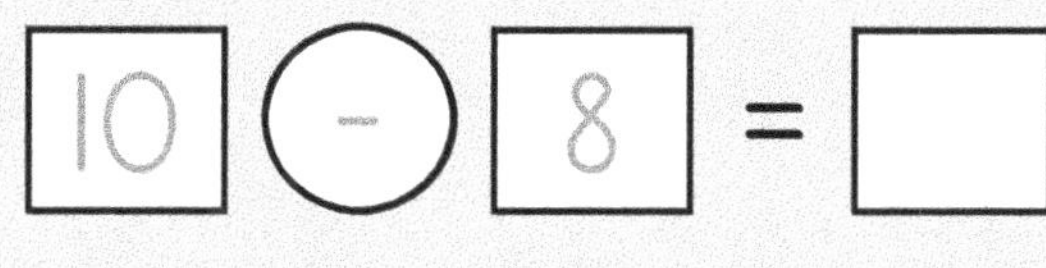

marbles

You have 6 purple marbles and 9 orange marbles.

How many fewer purple marbles than orange marbles do you have?

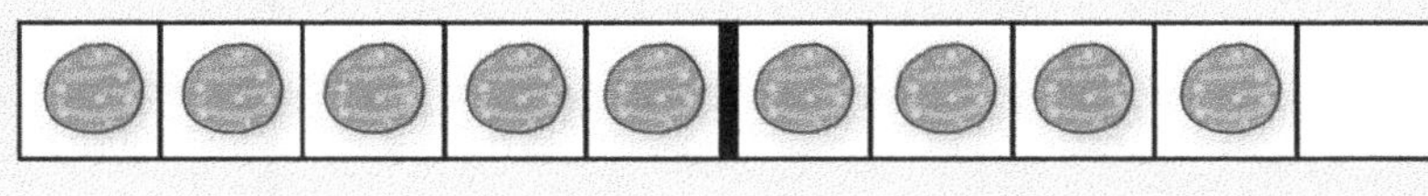

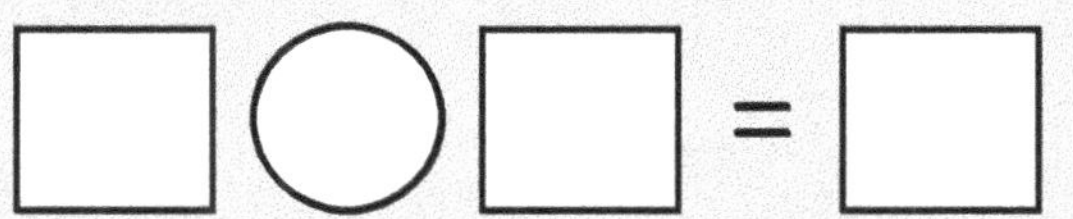

marbles

You have 12 red marbles and 7 rainbow marbles.

How many more red marbles than rainbow marbles do you have?

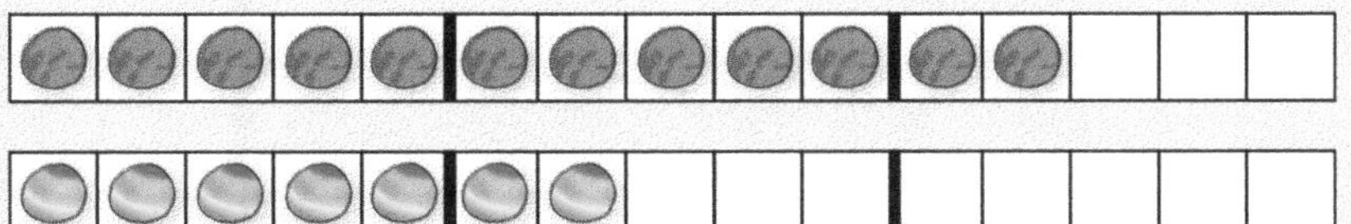

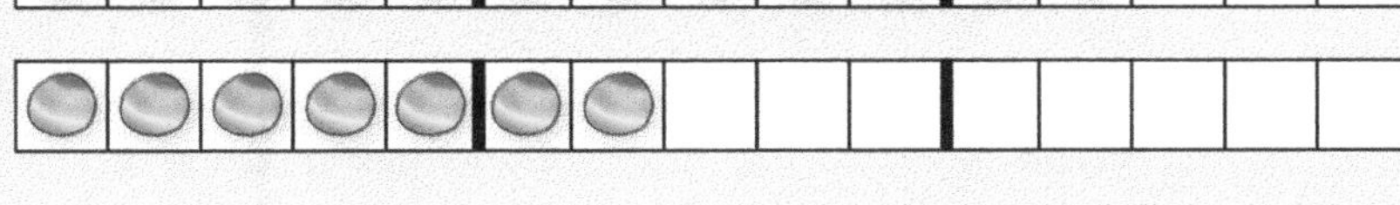

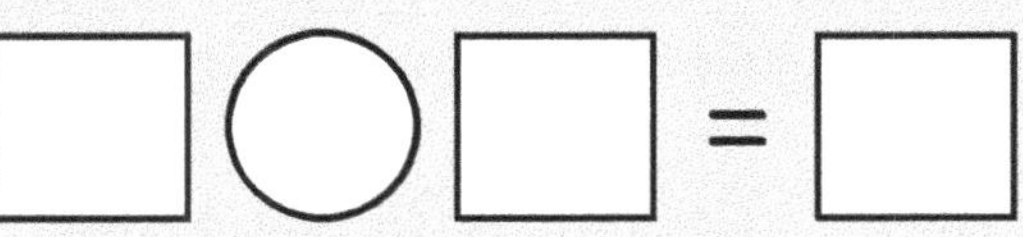

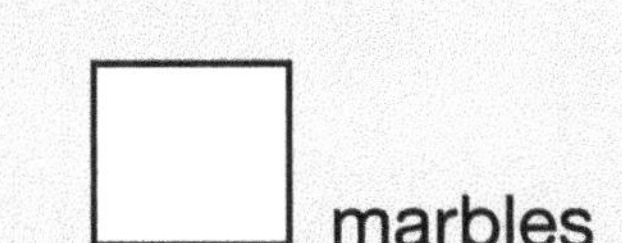

marbles

You have 15 yellow marbles and 9 striped marbles.

How many fewer striped marbles than yellow marbles do you have?

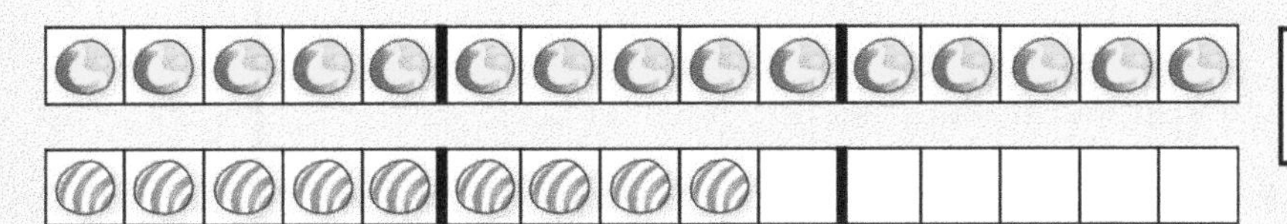

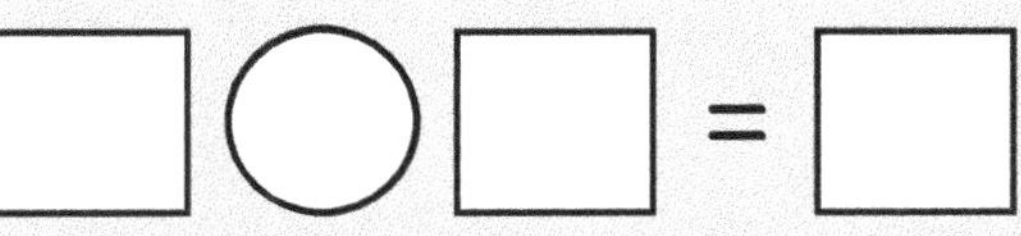

marbles

Complete.

$11 - 6 = \square$ $15 - 6 = \square$ $14 - 6 = \square$

$16 - 7 = \square$ $13 - 6 = \square$ $12 - 7 = \square$

$12 - 6 = \square$ $11 - 7 = \square$ $13 - 7 = \square$

$14 - 7 = \square$ $10 - 6 = \square$ $15 - 7 = \square$

X the shape that doesn't belong.

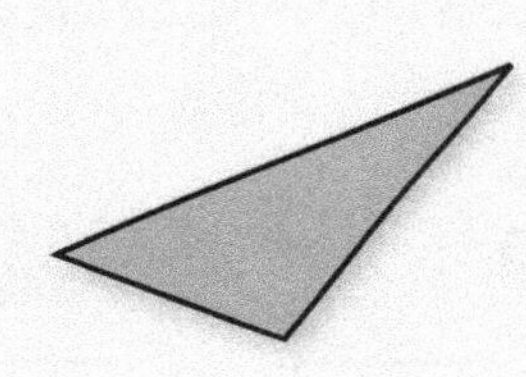 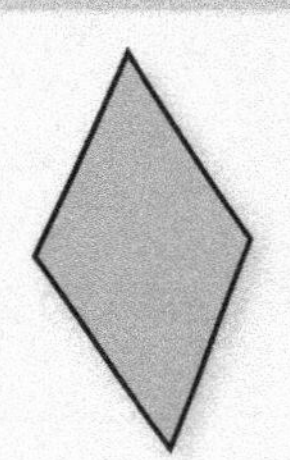 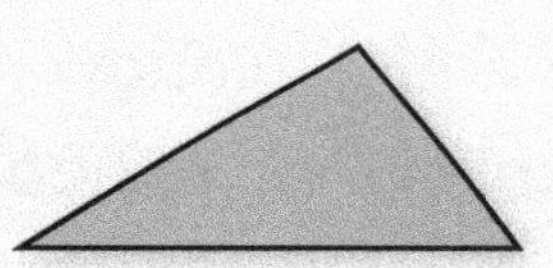 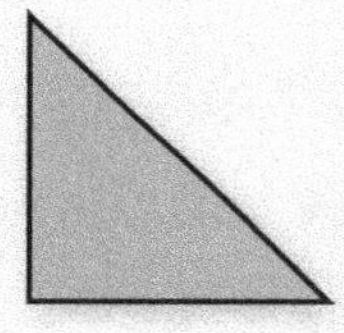

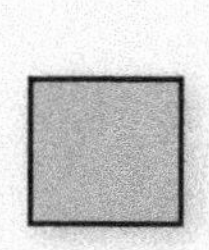 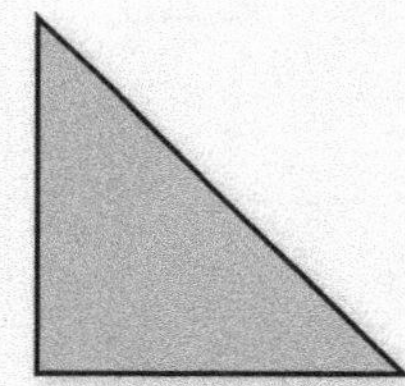  

Complete.

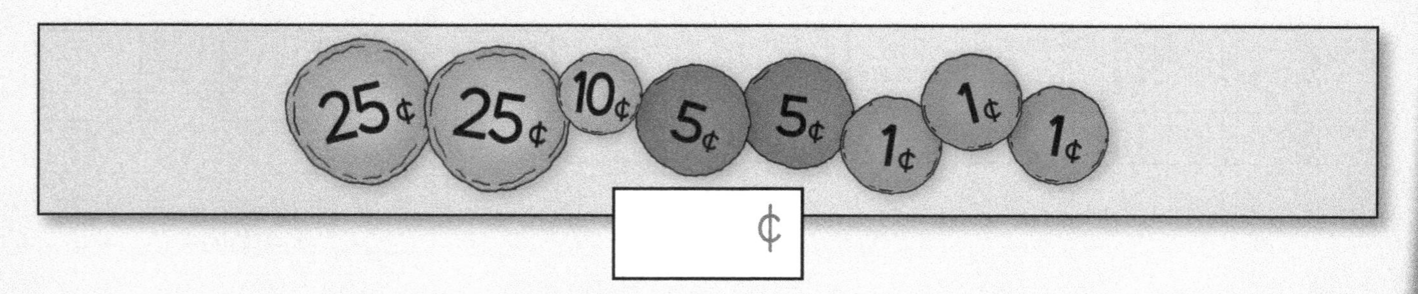

Use the chart to solve.

Name	Age
Dylan	5
Jasmine	11
Titus	14

How much older is Jasmine than Dylan?

☐ ◯ ☐ = ☐

☐ years

How much younger is Dylan than Titus?

☐ ◯ ☐ = ☐

☐ years

How much older is Titus than Jasmine?

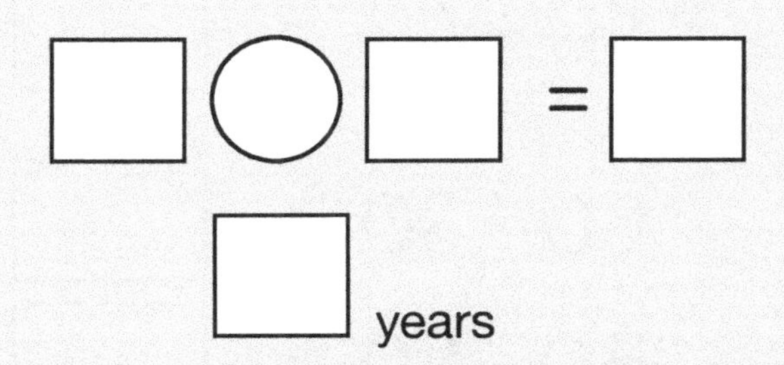

☐ years

Color the subtraction facts that equal the number in the star.

11 - 7
12 - 8
14 - 8
13 - 9

12 - 9
13 - 8
11 - 6
14 - 9

12 - 6
14 - 7
13 - 7
15 - 9

Label the numbers on the number line.

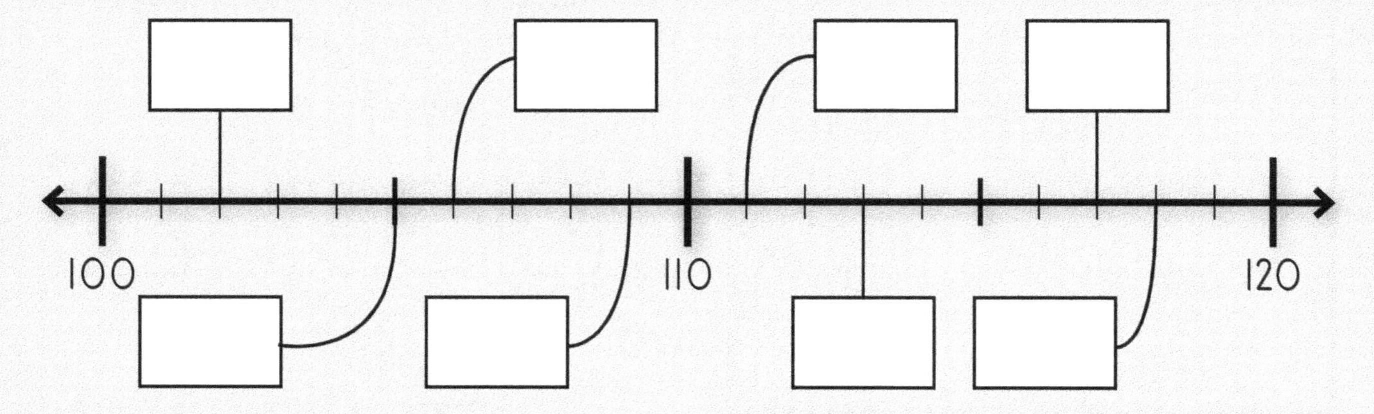

Complete.

10 + 60 = ☐	76 + 2 = ☐
110 + 60 = ☐	176 + 2 = ☐
50 - 30 = ☐	97 - 5 = ☐
150 - 30 = ☐	197 - 5 = ☐
24 + 40 = ☐	28 - 20 = ☐
124 + 40 = ☐	128 - 20 = ☐

Complete.

☐ muffins

☐ muffins

☐ muffins

See the Instructor Guide for how to play.
Save this game board for future lessons.

Four in a Row

12 - 3	11 - 4	14 - 5	13 - 4	11 - 5
13 - 5	12 - 4	11 - 5	11 - 4	13 - 5
11 - 3	11 - 3	12 - 3	11 - 2	11 - 3
11 - 2	12 - 4	12 - 5	13 - 5	13 - 4
12 - 5	11 - 5	13 - 4	14 - 5	12 - 4

Complete.

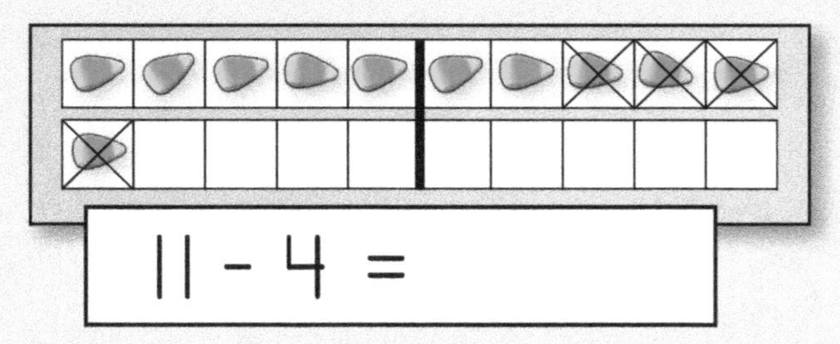

$11 - 4 =$

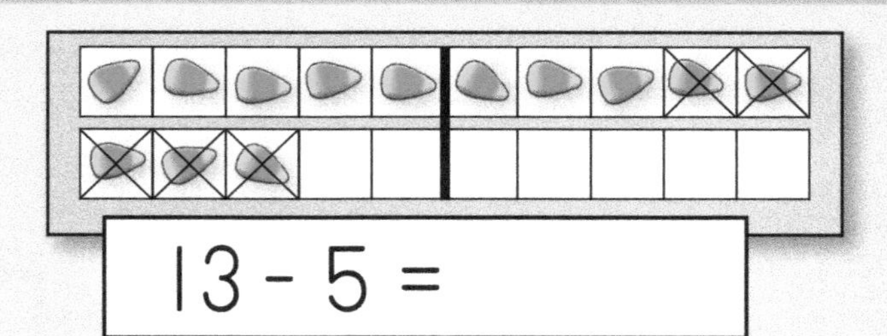

$13 - 5 =$

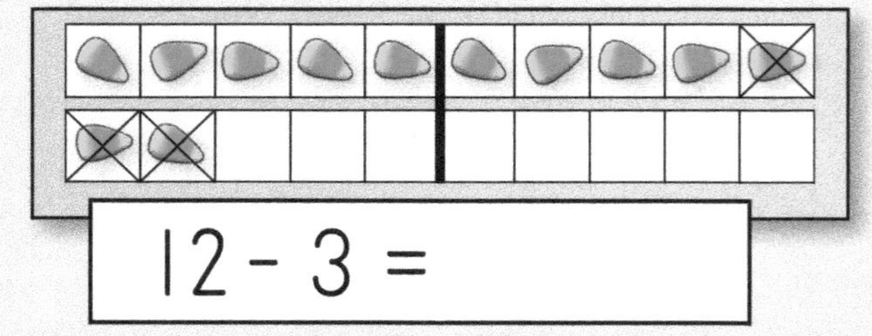

$12 - 3 =$

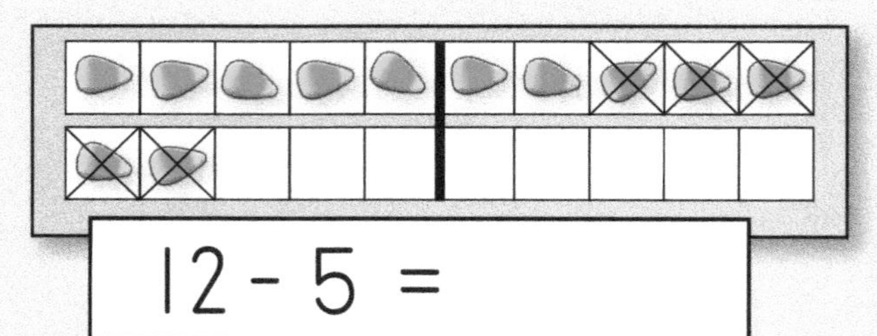

$12 - 5 =$

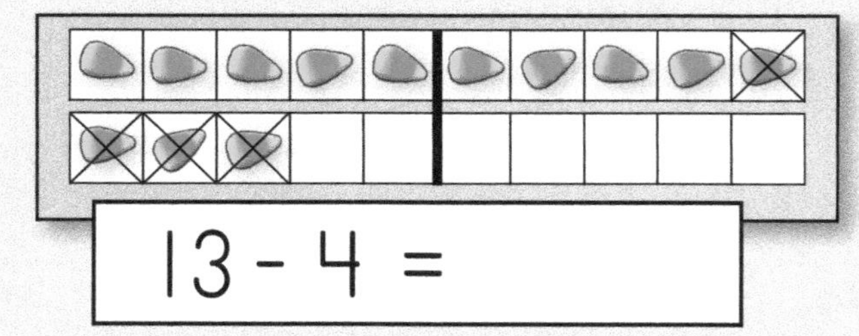

$13 - 4 =$

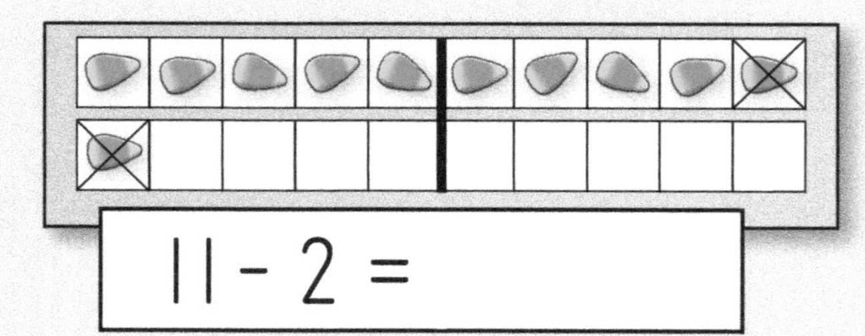

$11 - 2 =$

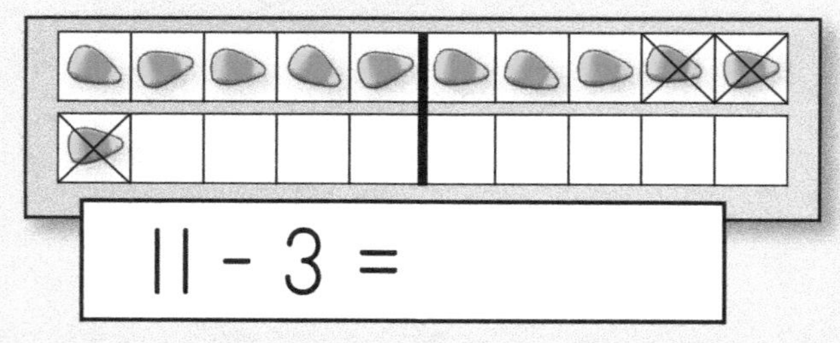

$11 - 3 =$

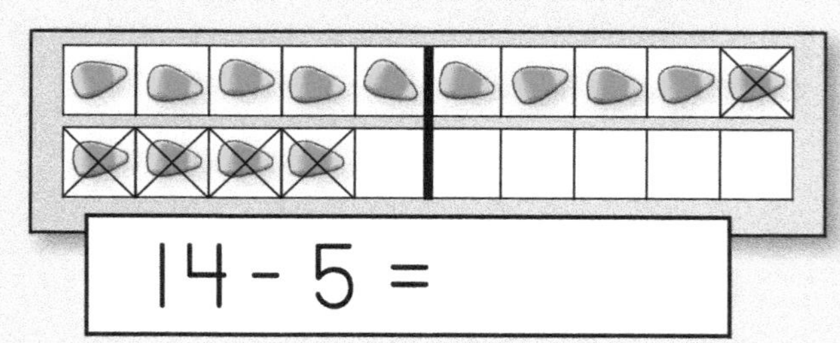

$14 - 5 =$

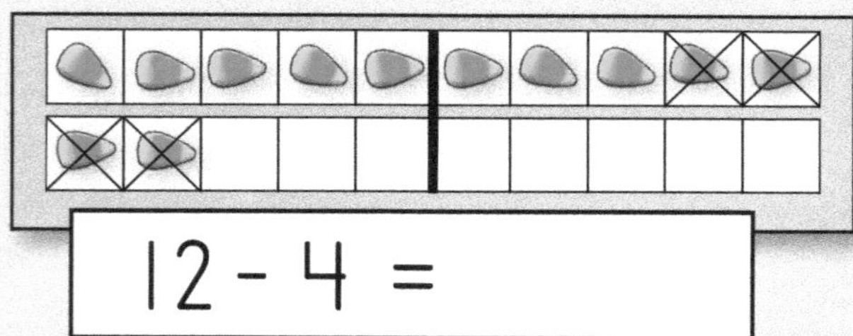

$12 - 4 =$

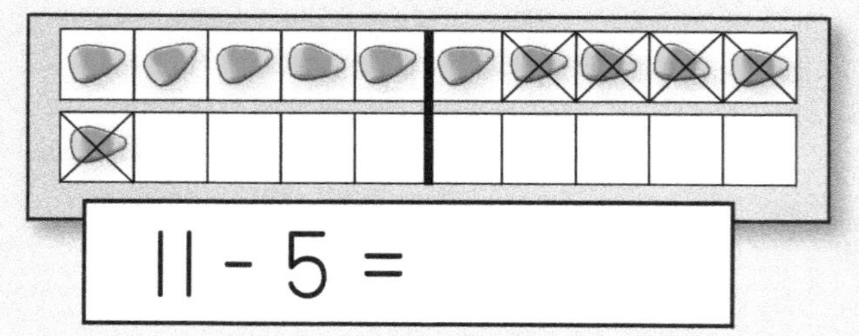

$11 - 5 =$

Complete the missing numbers in the sequence.

Complete. Use the ten-frames to help.

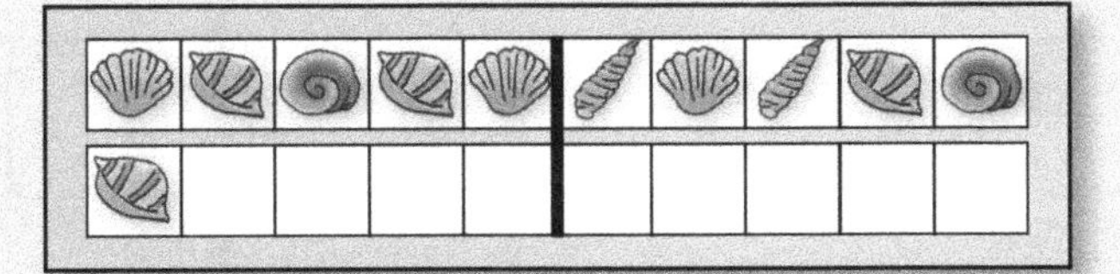

$$\begin{array}{r} 11 \\ -\ \ 2 \\ \hline \end{array} \qquad \begin{array}{r} 11 \\ -\ \ 3 \\ \hline \end{array} \qquad \begin{array}{r} 11 \\ -\ \ 4 \\ \hline \end{array} \qquad \begin{array}{r} 11 \\ -\ \ 5 \\ \hline \end{array}$$

$$\begin{array}{r} 12 \\ -\ \ 2 \\ \hline \end{array} \qquad \begin{array}{r} 12 \\ -\ \ 3 \\ \hline \end{array} \qquad \begin{array}{r} 12 \\ -\ \ 4 \\ \hline \end{array} \qquad \begin{array}{r} 12 \\ -\ \ 5 \\ \hline \end{array}$$

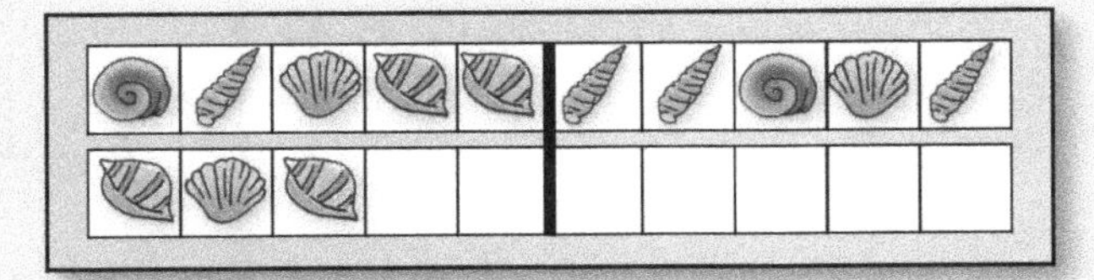

$$\begin{array}{r} 13 \\ -\ \ 2 \\ \hline \end{array} \qquad \begin{array}{r} 13 \\ -\ \ 3 \\ \hline \end{array} \qquad \begin{array}{r} 13 \\ -\ \ 4 \\ \hline \end{array} \qquad \begin{array}{r} 13 \\ -\ \ 5 \\ \hline \end{array}$$

$$\begin{array}{r} 14 \\ -\ \ 2 \\ \hline \end{array} \qquad \begin{array}{r} 14 \\ -\ \ 3 \\ \hline \end{array} \qquad \begin{array}{r} 14 \\ -\ \ 4 \\ \hline \end{array} \qquad \begin{array}{r} 14 \\ -\ \ 5 \\ \hline \end{array}$$

Complete.

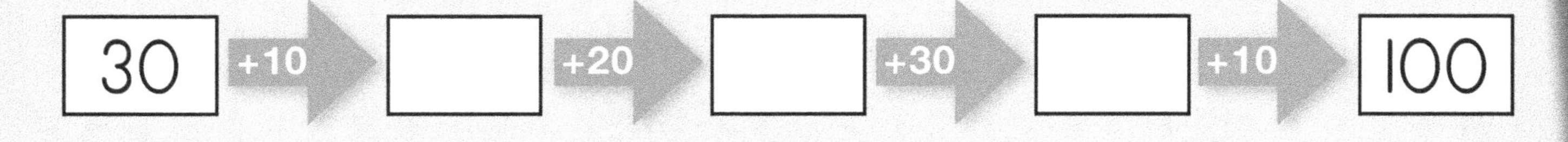

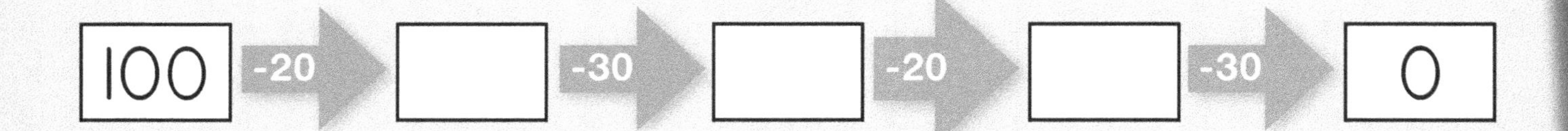

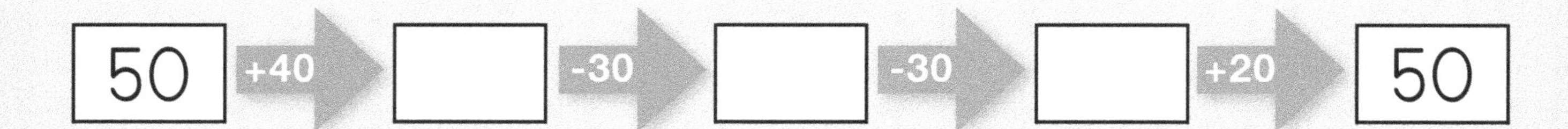

Write the expanded form for each number.

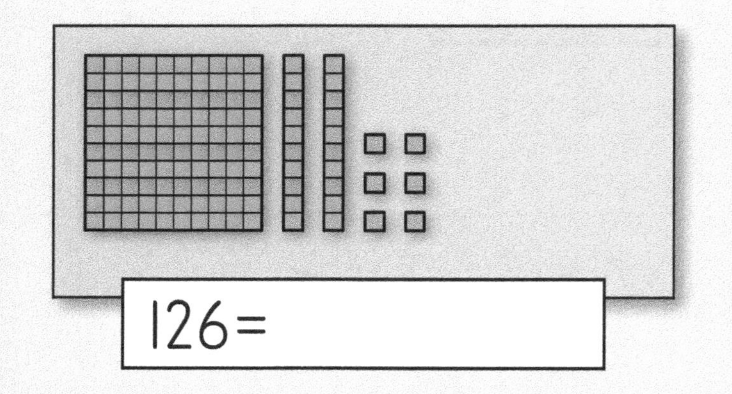

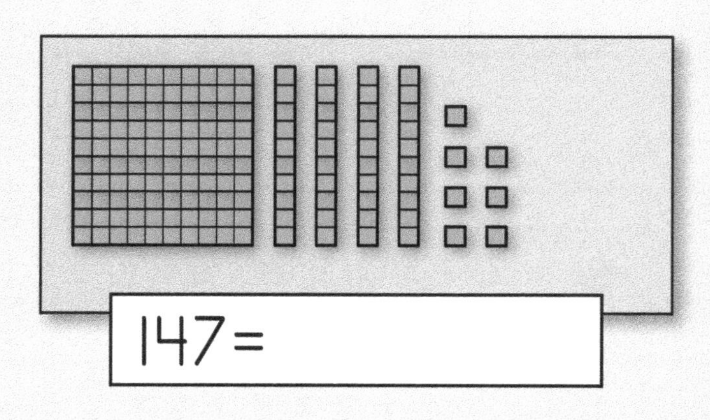

Write how much money is in each coin purse in two ways.

Use the clues to complete the chart.

The Eagles won 3 more games than the Hornets.

The Comets won 6 games fewer than the Eagles.

The Rockets won 2 games more than the Comets.

Team	Number of Games Won
Hornets	12
Eagles	
Comets	
Rockets	

Solve.

Ruby went down the slide 8 times.

Kayla went down the slide 6 more times than Ruby.

How many times did Kayla go down the slide?

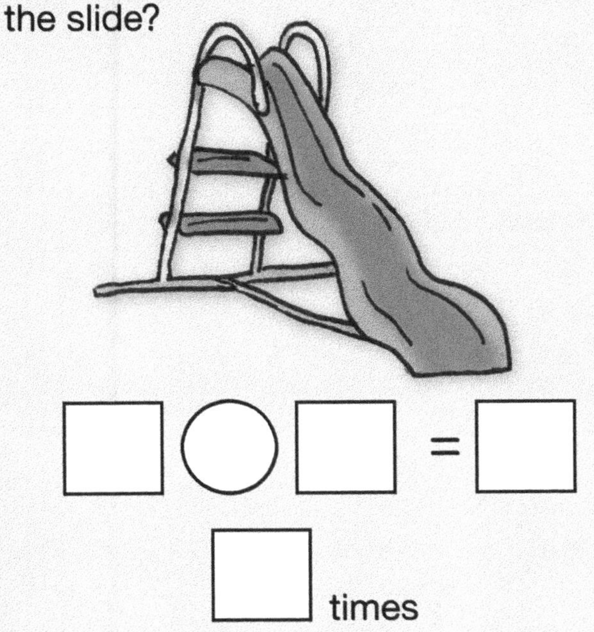

☐ ◯ ☐ = ☐

☐ times

Julian climbed the monkey bars 13 times.

Evan climbed the bars 4 fewer times than Julian.

How many times did Evan climb the monkey bars?

☐ ◯ ☐ = ☐

☐ times

Match.

11 - 2	6	11 - 5
13 - 6		13 - 4
12 - 4	7	11 - 3
13 - 5	8	14 - 5
11 - 4		12 - 3
12 - 5	9	12 - 6

Count by 2s to connect the dots in order.

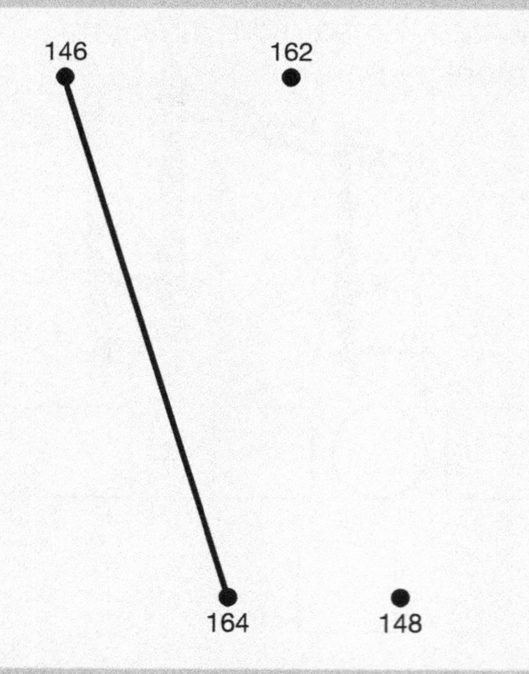

150 158 154

160 152 156

Solve.

How much more does the teddy bear cost than the soccer ball?

$

How much does it cost to buy both the markers and the soccer ball?

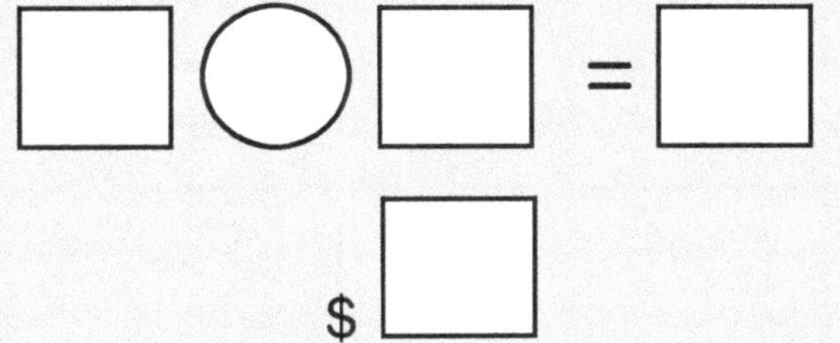

$

The robot costs $2 less than the race car. How much does the robot cost?

$

You have $15. Then, you buy the airplane for $9. How much money do you have left?

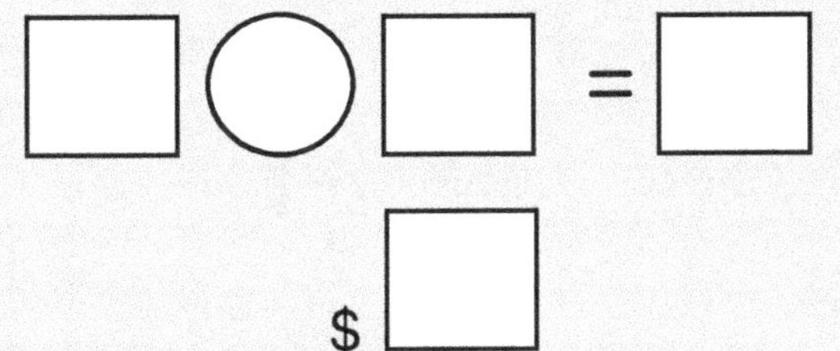

$

Complete.

13 - 6

11 - 5

14 - 8

16 - 9

15 - 8

17 - 9

14 - 7

12 - 4

16 - 8

13 - 7

11 - 2

15 - 6

14 - 5

13 - 8

12 - 6

Complete the missing numbers in the sequences.

See the Instructor Guide for directions.

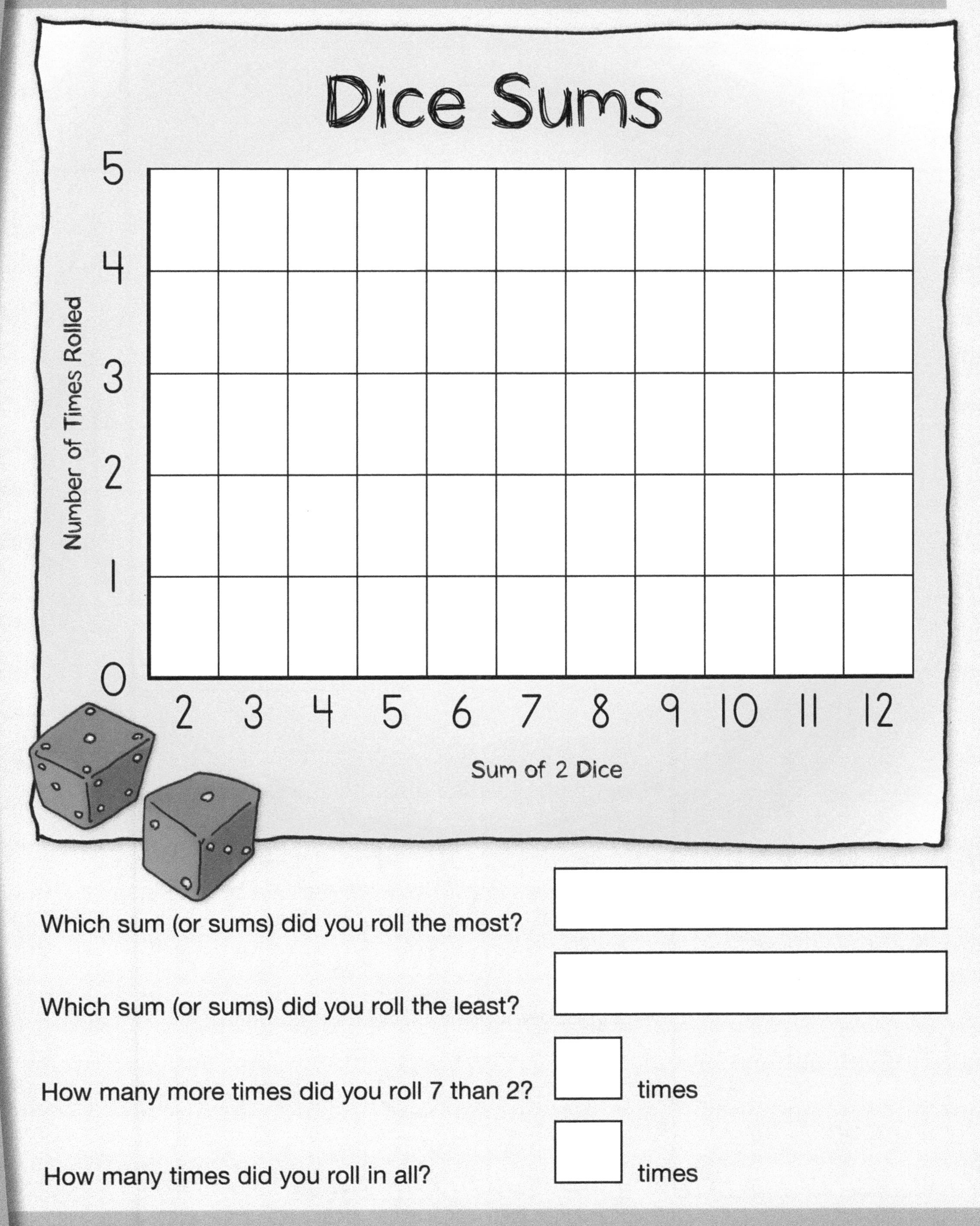

Which sum (or sums) did you roll the most?

Which sum (or sums) did you roll the least?

How many more times did you roll 7 than 2? ____ times

How many times did you roll in all? ____ times

Complete.

1	2	1	3	1	1	1	3	1	1
−	5	−	4	−	2	−	5	−	4

1	1	1	4	1	1	1	2	1	2
−	3	−	5	−	5	−	4	−	3

Use the chart to answer the questions.

Name	Age
Isabella	12
Alex	14
Mia	7
Jacob	9

Who is the oldest? ______

Who is the youngest? ______

How much older is Alex than Jacob?

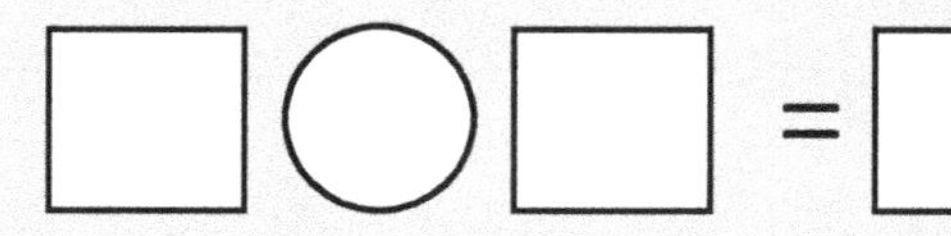

______ years

How much younger is Mia than Isabella?

☐ ○ ☐ = ☐

______ years

See the Instructor Guide for directions.

Number of Tails Recording Sheet

Number of Tails Flipped

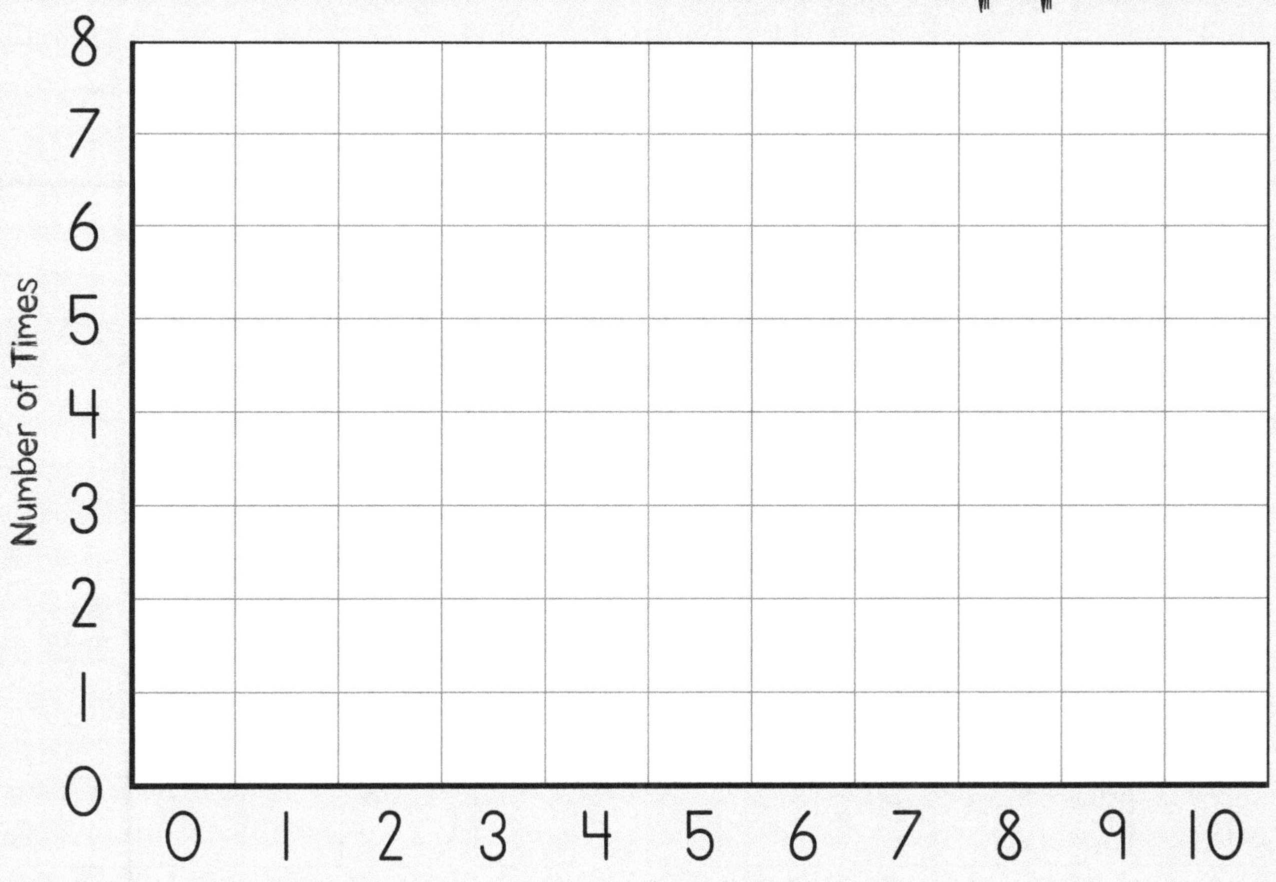

Number of Tails

Complete.

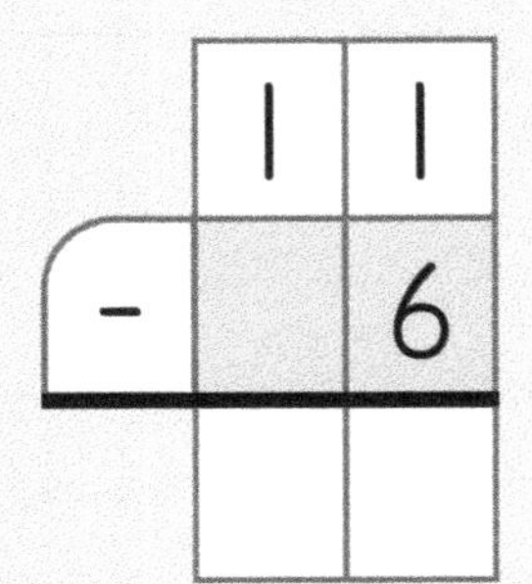

$11 - 6 =$	$12 - 7 =$	$14 - 6 =$	$14 - 5 =$
$13 - 7 =$	$12 - 6 =$	$16 - 7 =$	$15 - 6 =$
$14 - 7 =$	$11 - 7 =$	$13 - 6 =$	$15 - 7 =$

Solve.

You earn $12 on Monday and
$5 on Tuesday.

How much do you earn in all?

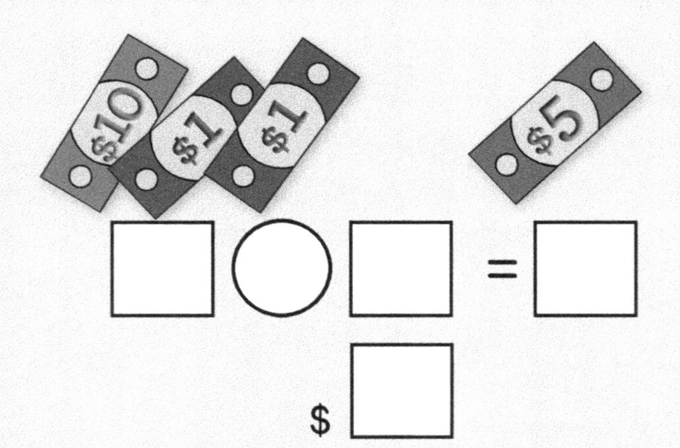

You earn $12 on Monday and
$5 on Tuesday.

How much less do you earn
on Tuesday than Monday?

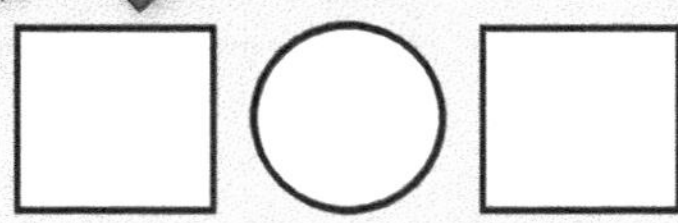

=

$

Rebecca surveyed her family and friends about their favorite season. She made a bar graph of the results. Use the bar graph to complete the chart.

Season	Spring	Summer	Fall	Winter
Number of people				

Use the bar graph and chart to complete.

How many people chose spring or summer?

☐ ◯ ☐ = ☐

☐ people

How many more people chose summer than spring?

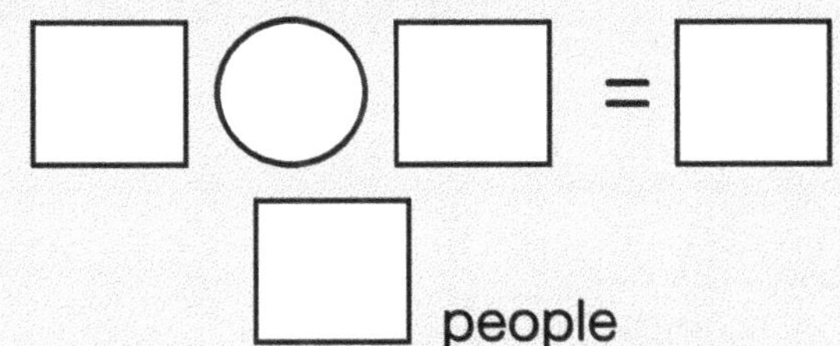

☐ people

How many fewer people chose winter than fall?

☐ ◯ ☐ = ☐

☐ people

How many people did Rebecca survey? Write your own equation.

☐ people

Complete.

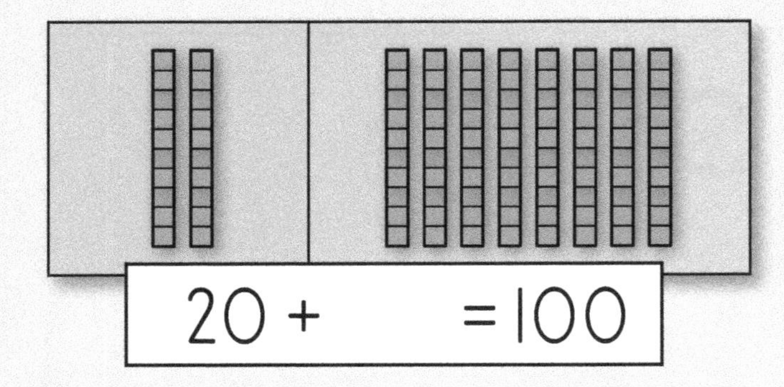

20 + ___ = 100

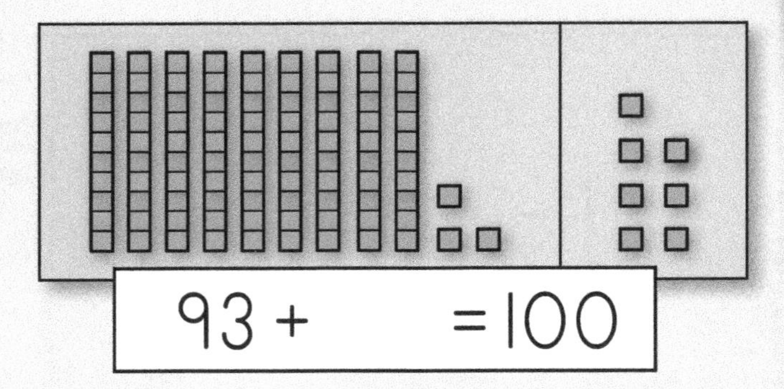

93 + ___ = 100

Complete.

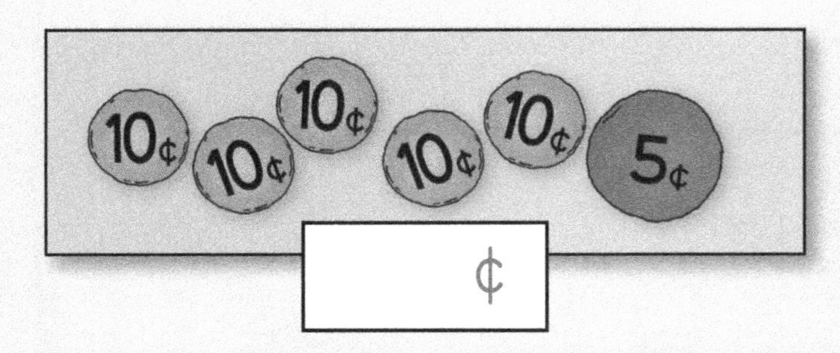

___ ¢

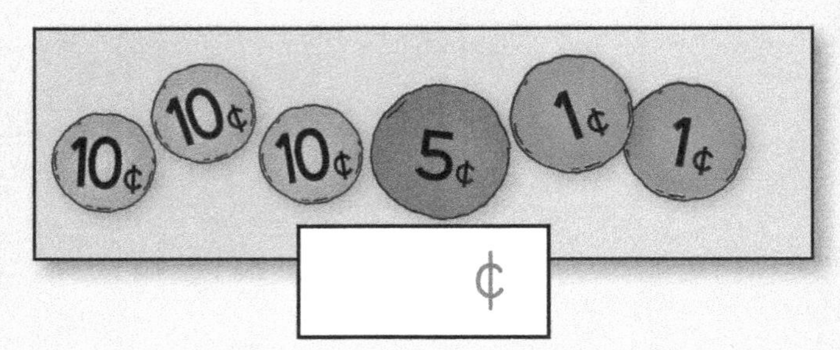

___ ¢

Match.

12 - 4		11 - 2
17 - 8	7	12 - 5
13 - 5		16 - 8
11 - 3	8	12 - 3
18 - 9	9	11 - 4
13 - 4		17 - 9

Use this page to make a bar graph based on your survey results. See the Instructor Guide for directions.

Use your bar graph to answer the questions.

What was the most popular answer? ☐

What was the least popular answer? ☐

How many more people chose the most-popular answer than the least-popular answer? ☐ people

How many people did you survey? ☐ people

Complete.

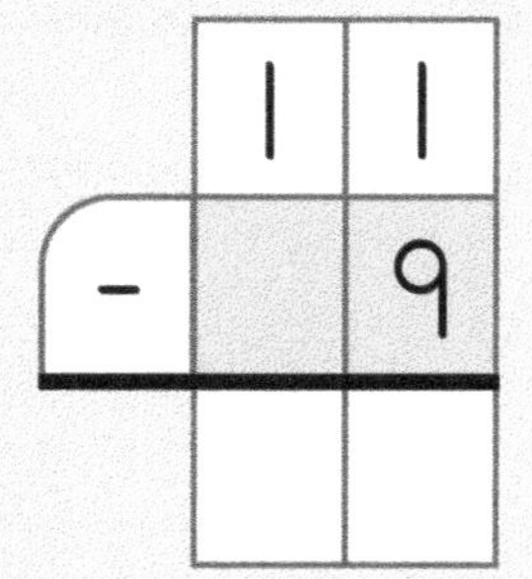

	1	1
-		9

	1	2
-		8

	1	1
-		5

	1	3
-		9

	1	3
-		8

	1	2
-		9

	1	1
-		8

	1	4
-		9

Complete.

$6 + 3 = \square$

$96 + 3 = \square$

$106 + 3 = \square$

$196 + 3 = \square$

$8 - 4 = \square$

$38 - 4 = \square$

$108 - 4 = \square$

$138 - 4 = \square$

Circle the sandwiches that are split in half. X the sandwiches that are not split in half.

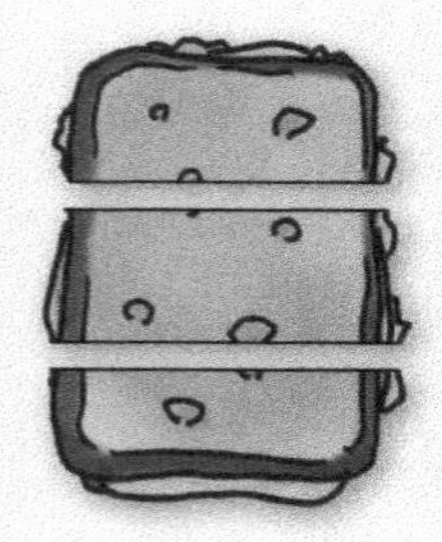

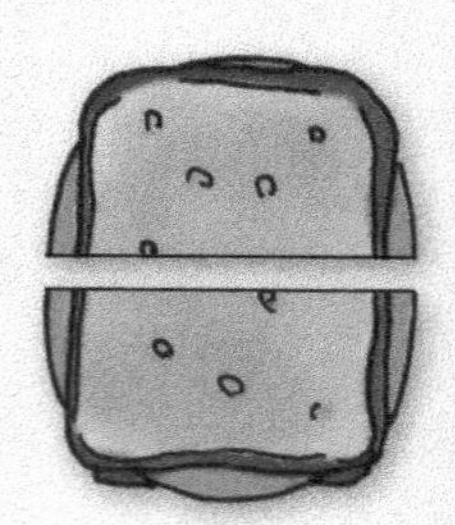

Riley helped her parents wrap gifts. She made a pictograph of how many gifts she wrapped. Use the pictograph to complete the chart.

Gifts I Wrapped

Monday   

Tuesday  

Wednesday      

= 2 gifts

Day	Monday	Tuesday	Wednesday
Number of Gifts			

Use the pictograph and chart to complete.

How many different gifts did she wrap on Monday and Tuesday?

☐ ◯ ☐ = ☐

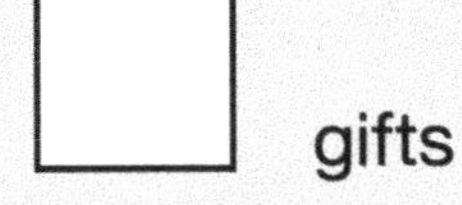

☐ gifts

How many more gifts did she wrap on Monday than Tuesday?

☐ ◯ ☐ = ☐

☐ gifts

How many fewer gifts did she wrap on Tuesday than Wednesday?

☐ ◯ ☐ = ☐

☐ gifts

How many gifts did she wrap in all? Write your own equation.

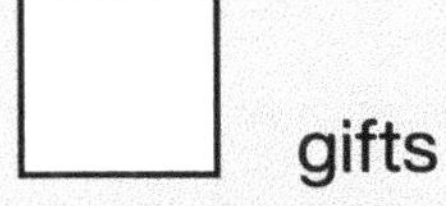

☐ gifts

Color the subtraction facts that equal the number in the star.

14 - 7

16 - 9

12 - 5

15 - 7

12 - 3

14 - 6

13 - 4

15 - 7

13 - 4

14 - 6

18 - 9

15 - 6

Write the value of each set of base-ten blocks.

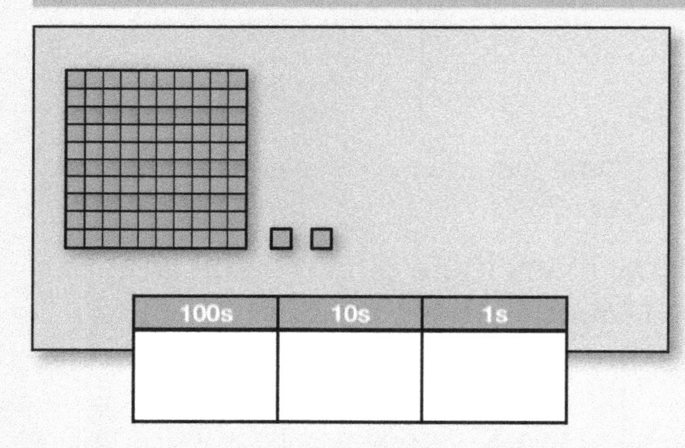

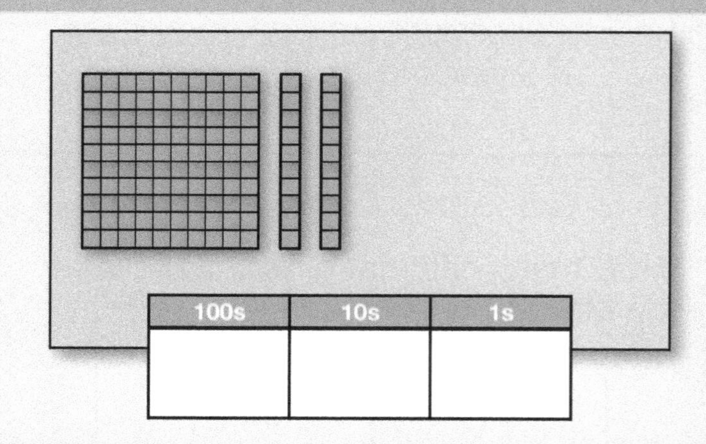

Copy the shape.

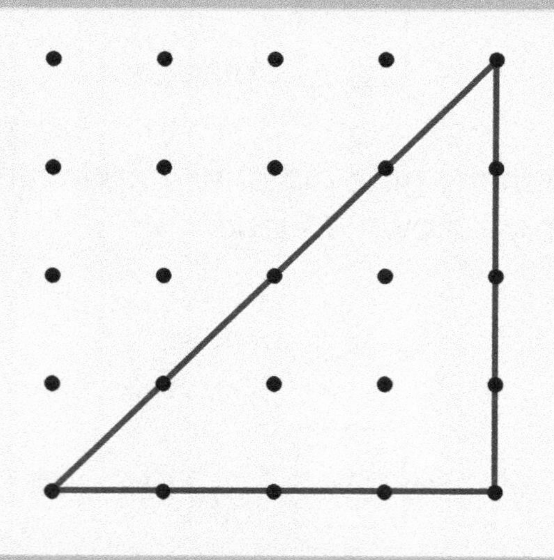

Tommy made a pictograph about how much time he spent playing soccer each day. Use the pictograph to complete the chart.

Time Spent Playing Soccer

Monday	⚽⚽⚽
Tuesday	⚽⚽
Wednesday	⚽⚽⚽⚽⚽

⚽ = 10 minutes

Day	Minutes
Monday	
Tuesday	
Wednesday	

Then, Tommy also made a bar graph about how much time he spent playing soccer the rest of the week. Use the bar graph to complete the chart.

Time Spent Playing Soccer

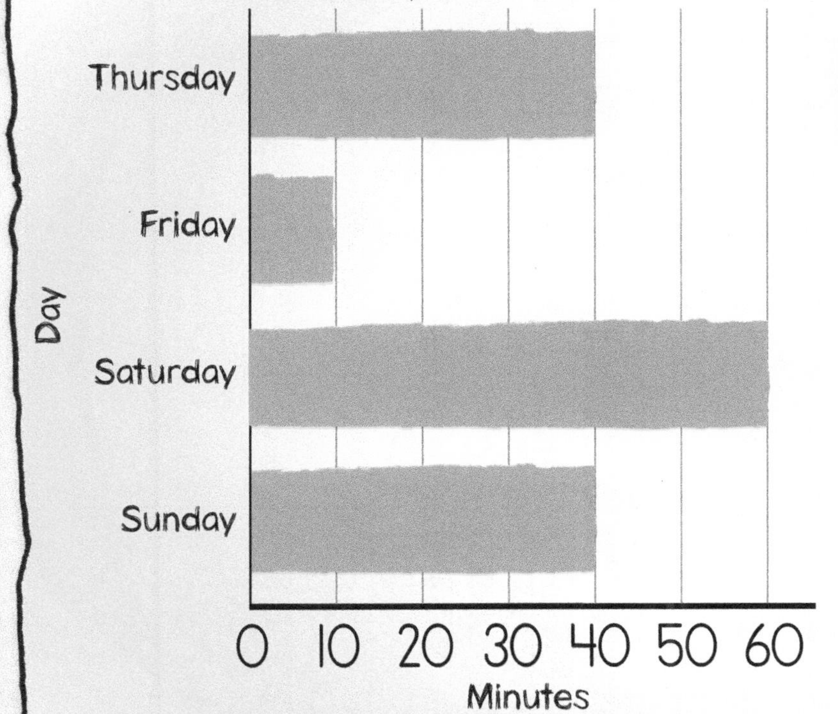

Day	Minutes
Thursday	
Friday	
Saturday	
Sunday	

Complete.

11 - 3 = ☐ | 12 - 8 = ☐ | 14 - 5 = ☐

12 - 7 = ☐ | 13 - 9 = ☐ | 12 - 6 = ☐

15 - 9 = ☐ | 12 - 3 = ☐ | 14 - 9 = ☐

14 - 8 = ☐ | 13 - 5 = ☐ | 16 - 7 = ☐

Complete.

$ ☐

$ ☐

Match.

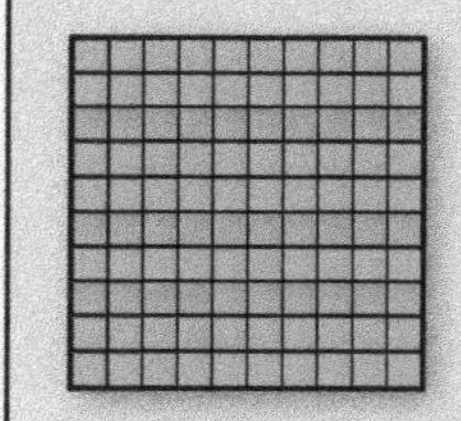

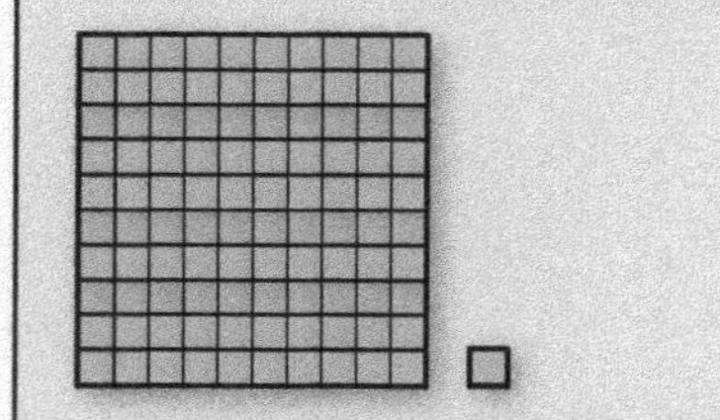

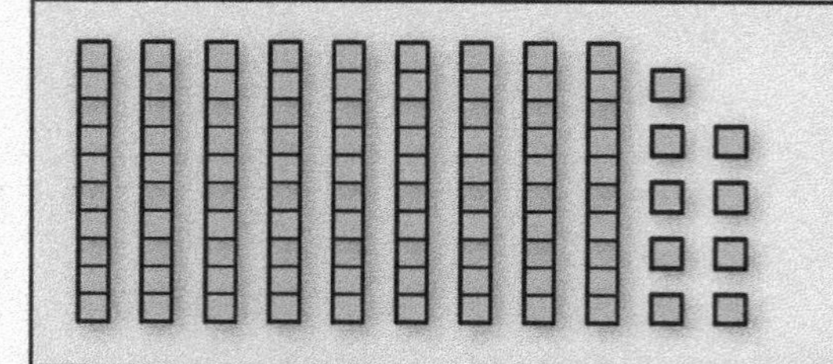

Alejandro planted a bean seed. He made a line graph to show how his plant grew. Use his line graph to complete the chart.

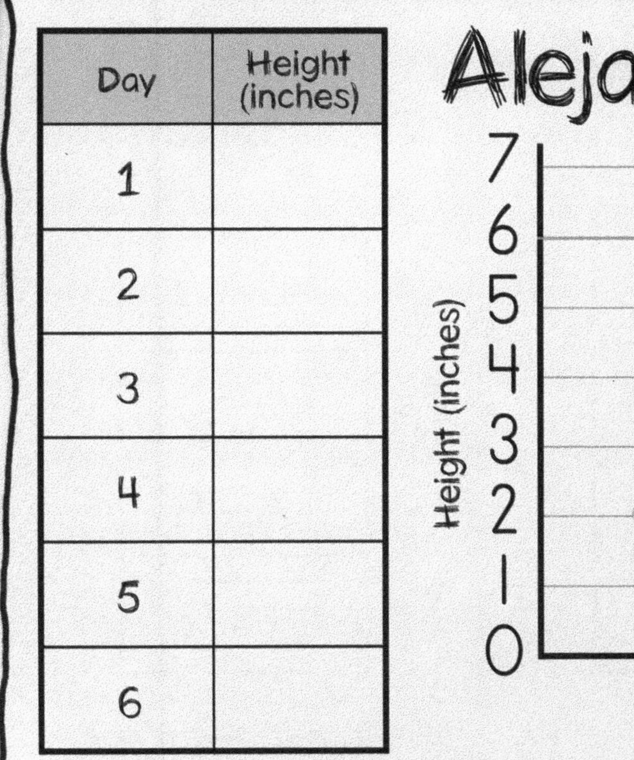

Day	Height (inches)
1	
2	
3	
4	
5	
6	

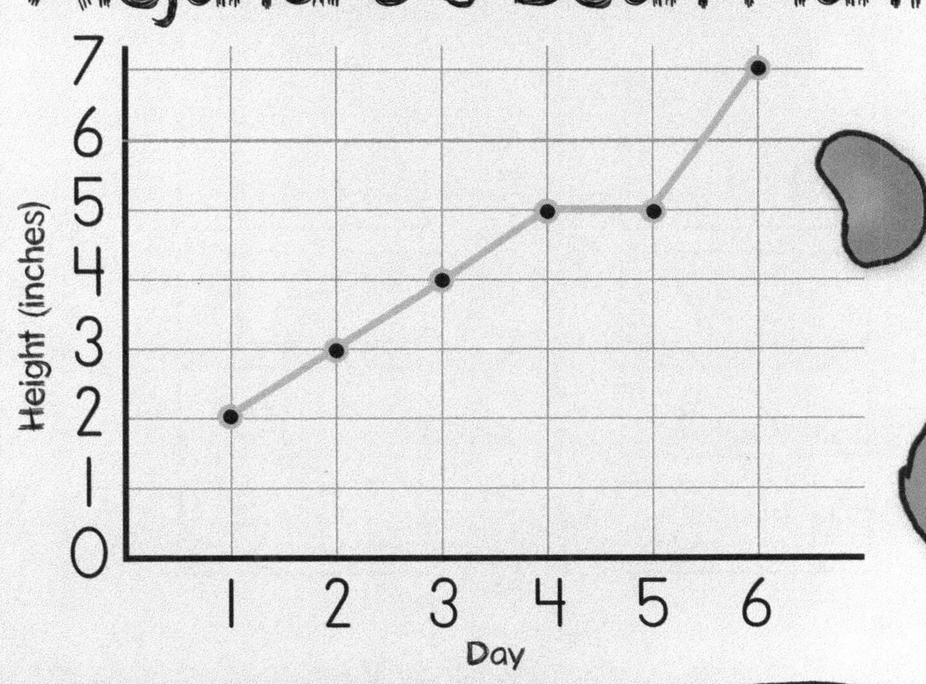

Sofia planted a bean seed, too. Once it sprouted, she measured its height every day. Use her chart to complete the line graph.

Day	Height (inches)
1	1
2	2
3	3
4	5
5	7
6	7

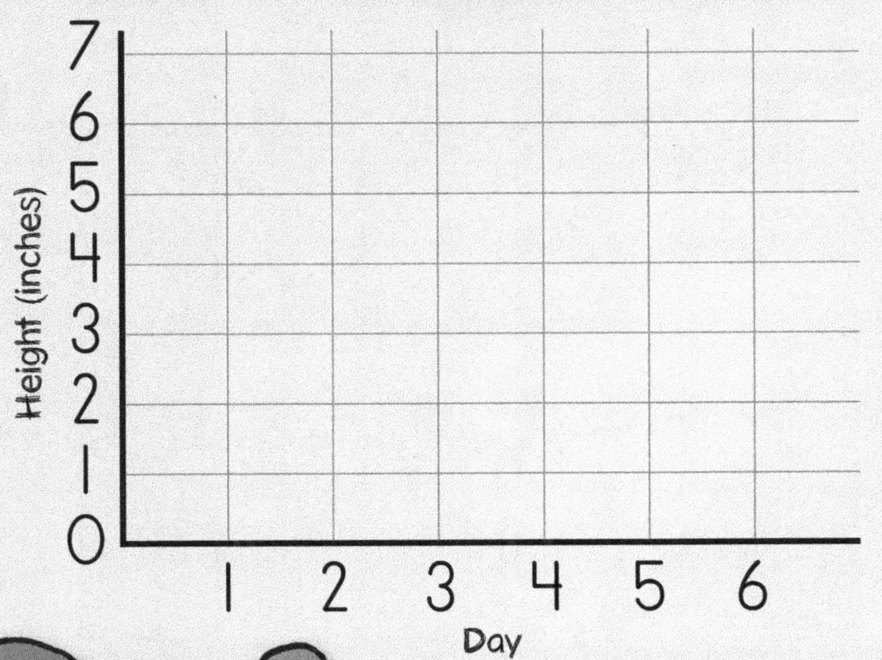

Color the subtraction facts that equal the number in the star.

9	8	7
11 - 2	16 - 9	13 - 6
15 - 7	12 - 4	15 - 8
17 - 8	14 - 6	16 - 9
14 - 5	13 - 5	11 - 5

Complete the missing numbers in the sequences.

James helps his parents at their bakery. He made a chart of how many pies the bakery sold each week in November. Use the chart to complete the graphs.

November Pie Sales

Week	Pies Sold
1	10
2	30
3	20
4	70

November Pie Sales Pictograph

Week 1	
Week 2	
Week 3	
Week 4	

◎ = 10 pies

November Pie Sales Bar Graph

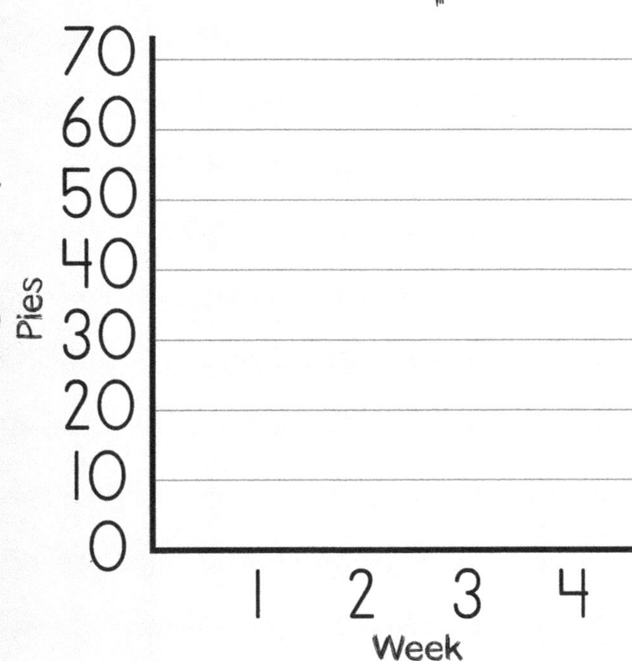

November Pie Sales Line Graph

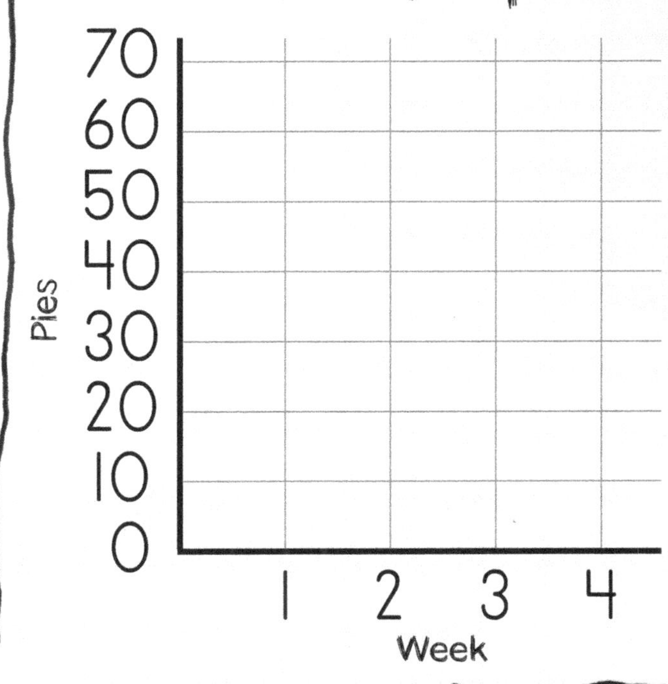

Complete.

$17 - 9 = \square$	$14 - 7 = \square$	$12 - 9 = \square$
$11 - 5 = \square$	$15 - 8 = \square$	$12 - 6 = \square$
$13 - 7 = \square$	$11 - 2 = \square$	$13 - 8 = \square$
$8 + 4 = \square$	$6 + 7 = \square$	$5 + 9 = \square$

Complete the circles with <, >, or =.

48 ◯ 58	148 ◯ 158	148 ◯ 148
58 ◯ 48	158 ◯ 148	158 ◯ 158

Count by 10s to connect the dots in order.

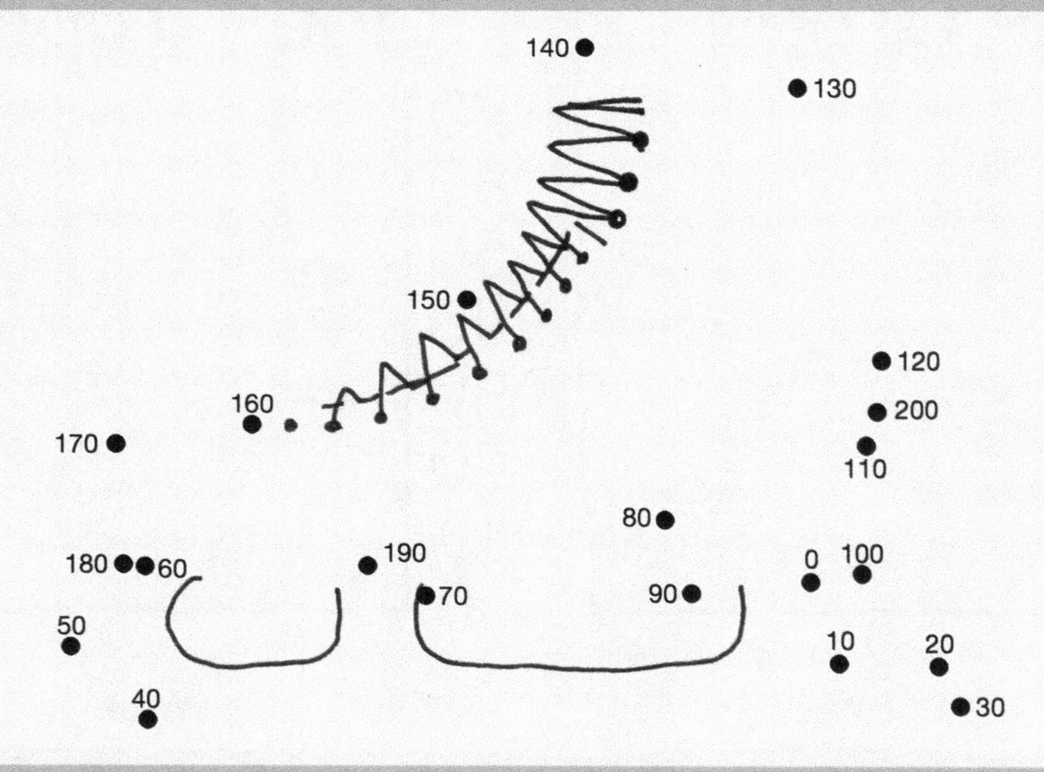

See the Instructor Guide for directions.

37 + 4 = ☐	59 + 6 = ☐
48 + 2 = ☐	47 + 5 = ☐

Roll and Add

Player 1	Player 2
29 + ☐ = ☐	29 + ☐ = ☐
38 + ☐ = ☐	38 + ☐ = ☐
47 + ☐ = ☐	47 + ☐ = ☐
56 + ☐ = ☐	56 + ☐ = ☐
79 + ☐ = ☐	79 + ☐ = ☐

Tiana made a graph of the money she earned at the craft fair.
Use the graph to complete the chart and answer the questions.

My Earnings

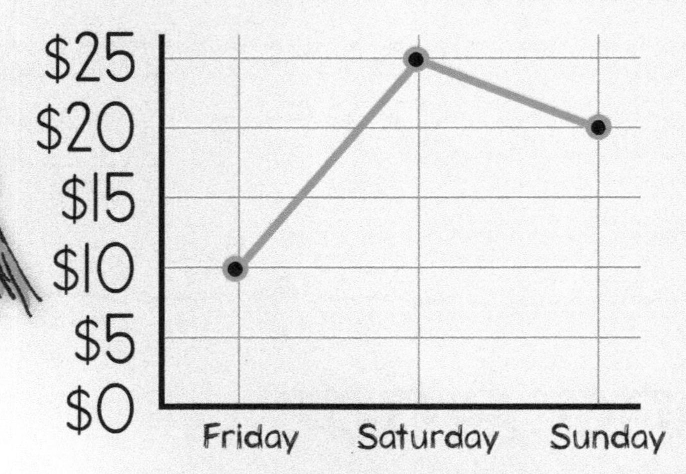

Day	Money
Friday	
Saturday	
Sunday	

Which day did she earn the most?

Which day did she earn the least?

How much more did she earn on Saturday than Friday?

☐ ◯ ☐ = ☐

$ ☐

How much money did Tiana earn in all? Write your own equation.

Complete.

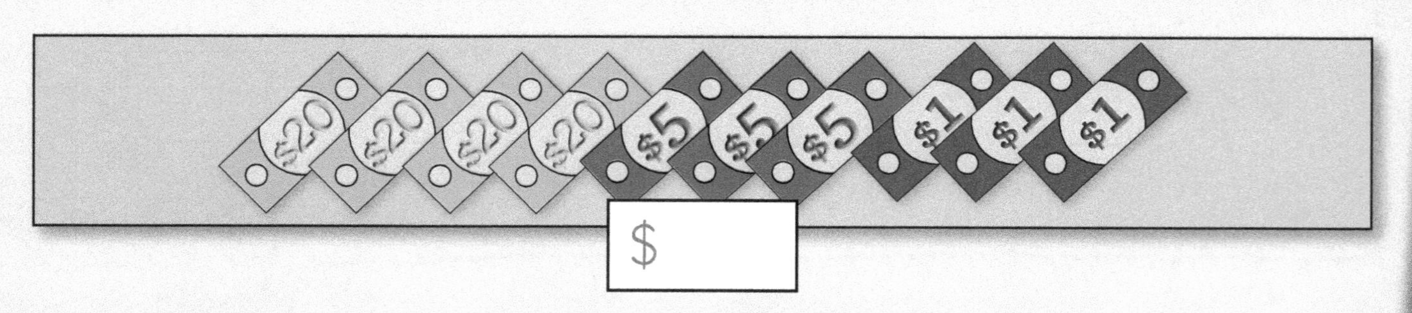

See the Instructor Guide for directions.

39 + 6 = ☐	48 + 7 = ☐
76 + 5 = ☐	87 + 4 = ☐

SPIN TO WIN!

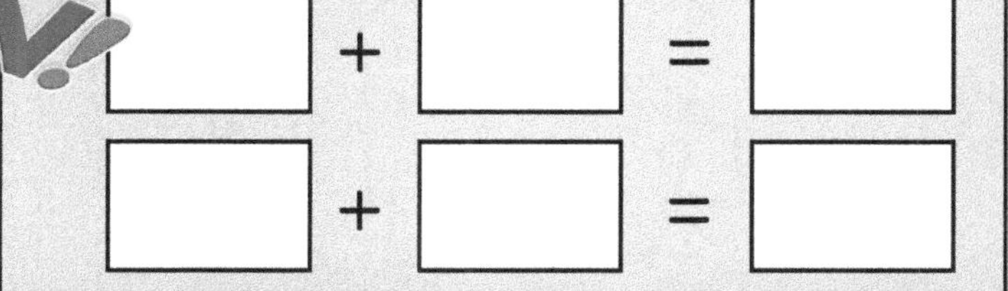

56 59 55 54 57 58

☐ + ☐ = ☐

☐ + ☐ = ☐

☐ + ☐ = ☐

☐ + ☐ = ☐

☐ + ☐ = ☐

☐ + ☐ = ☐

☐ + ☐ = ☐

☐ + ☐ = ☐

☐ + ☐ = ☐

☐ + ☐ = ☐

Complete the missing numbers in the sequences.

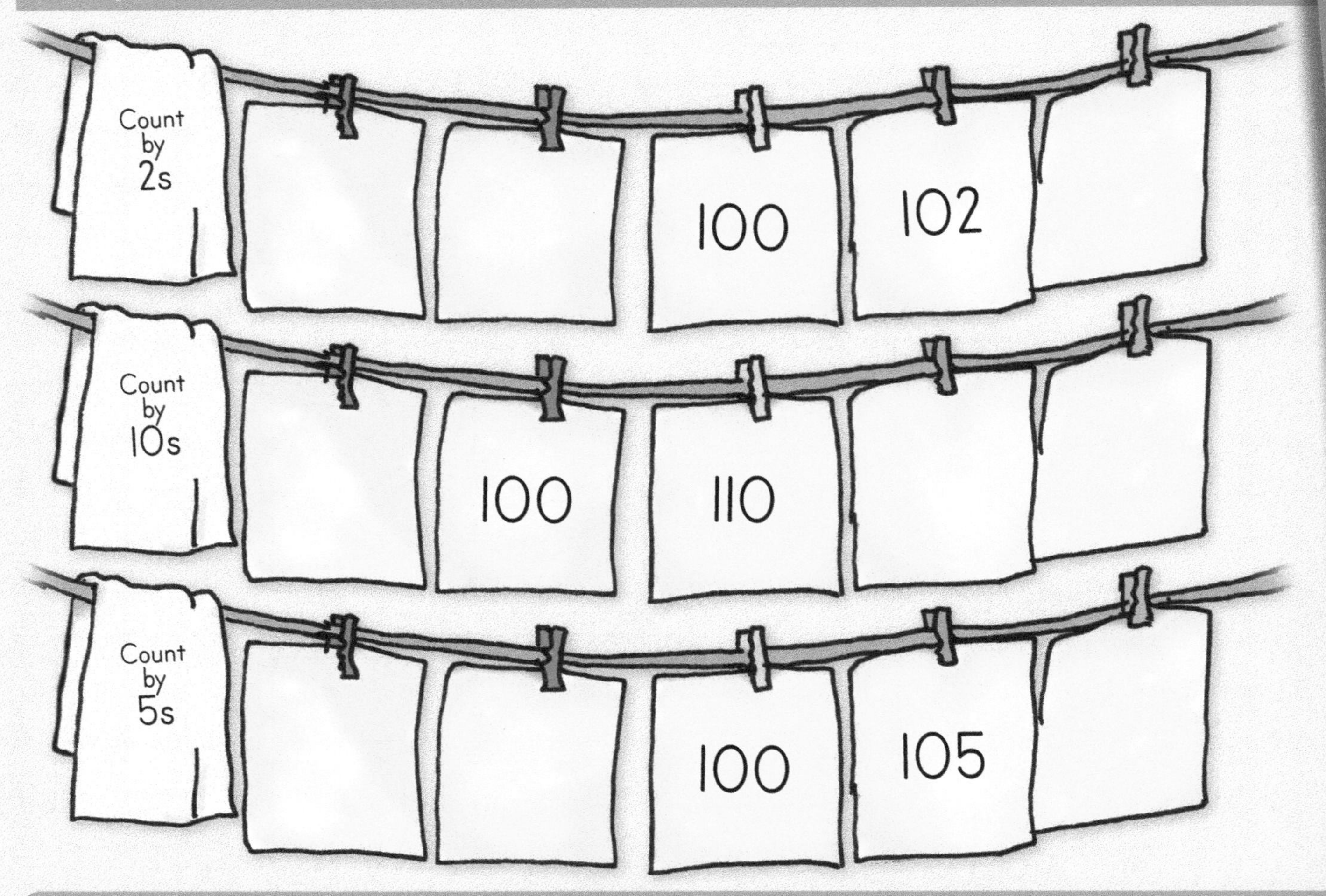

Solve. For the second problem, color the picture to match.

You have 15 stickers.

You use 7.

How many do you have left?

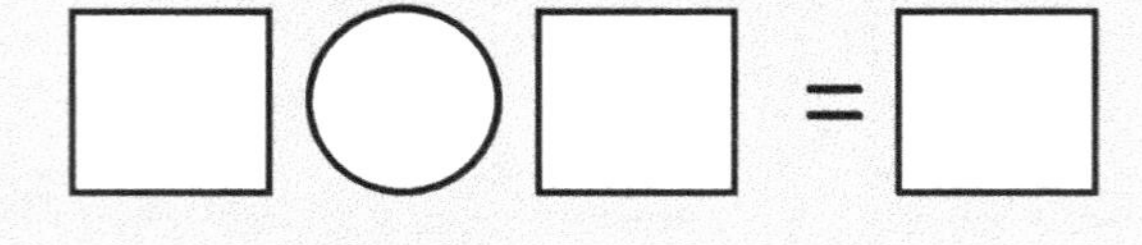

stickers

You have 16 stickers.

9 are green, and the rest are blue.

How many are blue?

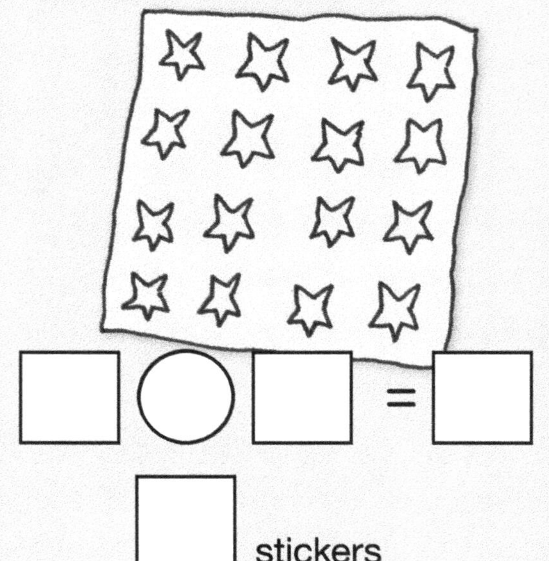

stickers

See the Instructor Guide for directions.

		+		=		
		+		=		
		+		=		

		+		=		
		+		=		
		+		=		

Match.

59 + 3	60	58 + 5
58 + 6	61	55 + 6
57 + 4	62	56 + 6
55 + 5	63	59 + 5
57 + 6	64	51 + 9

Jackson counted some of his toys. Use his chart to make a bar graph.

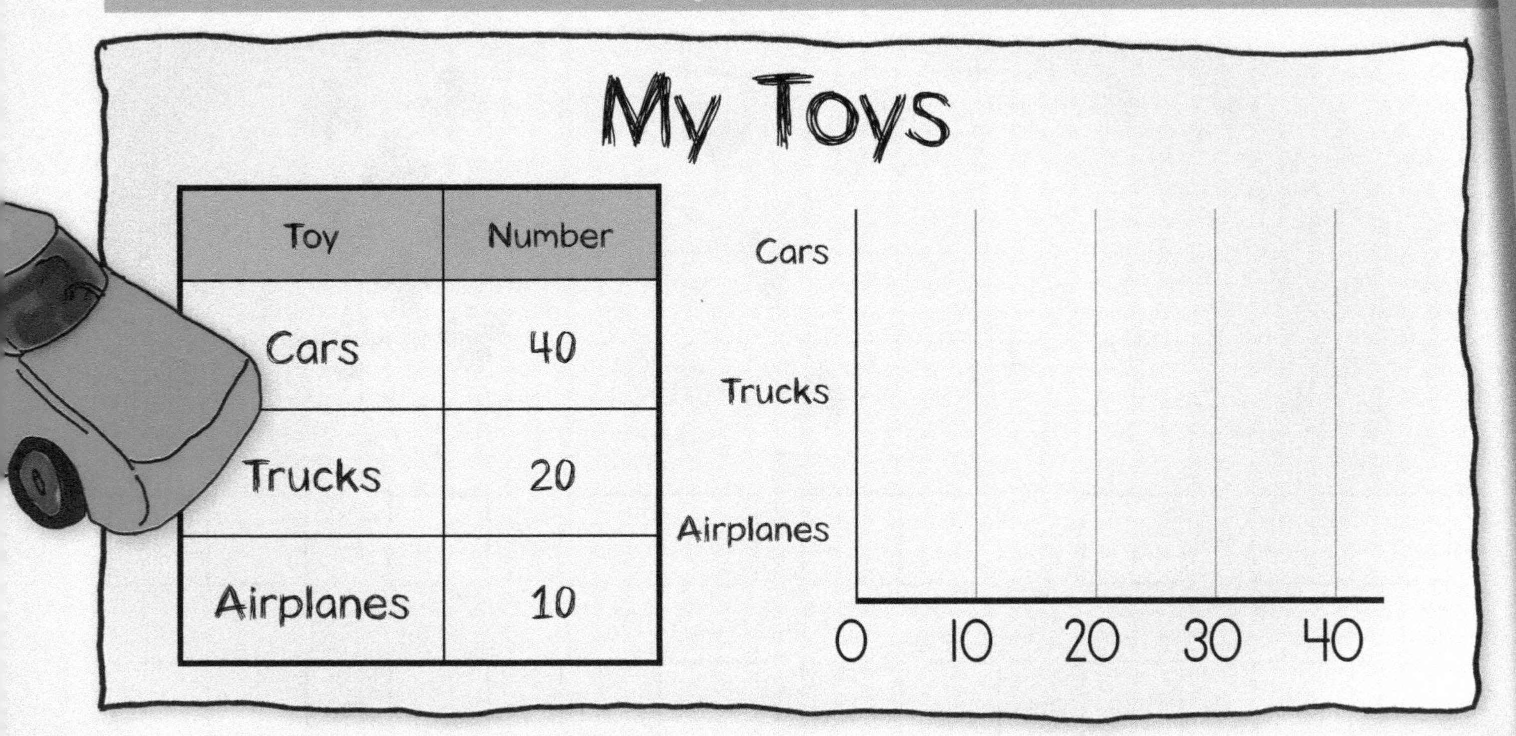

Toy	Number
Cars	40
Trucks	20
Airplanes	10

Match pairs that equal 100.

30 20 40 10 50

80 60 70 90 50

Complete.

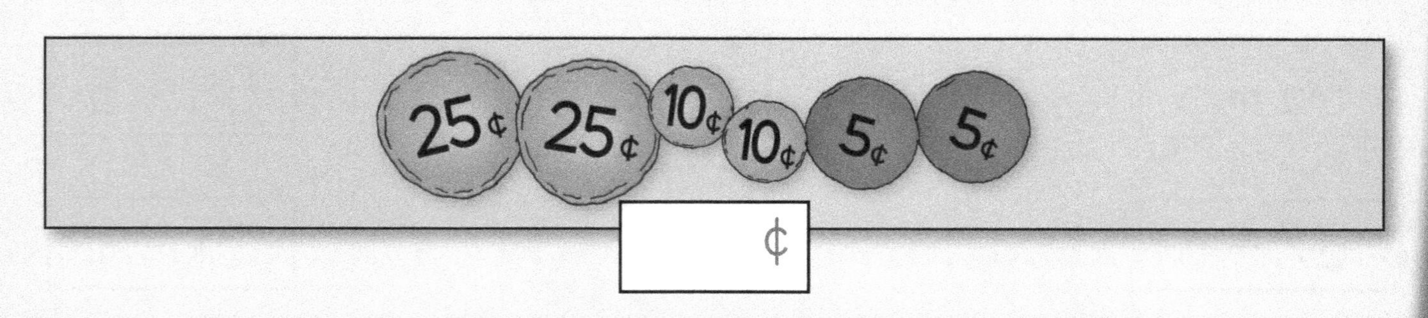

See the Instructor Guide for directions.

39 + 4 = ☐	65 + 7 = ☐
46 + 6 = ☐	78 + 9 = ☐

Color the addition problems that equal the number in the star.

39 + 5
40 + 4
38 + 6

31

25 + 6
28 + 3
27 + 5

50

47 + 2
45 + 5
49 + 1

62

56 + 8
59 + 3
57 + 6

68 + 5
69 + 2
65 + 8

78 + 6
77 + 5
75 + 9

Raj went on a nature walk. He made a pictograph about the animals he saw. Use the pictograph to complete the chart.

Animals I Saw

Birds

Lizards

Rabbits

= 2 animals

Animal	Number
Birds	
Lizards	
Rabbits	

How many more birds than lizards did he see?

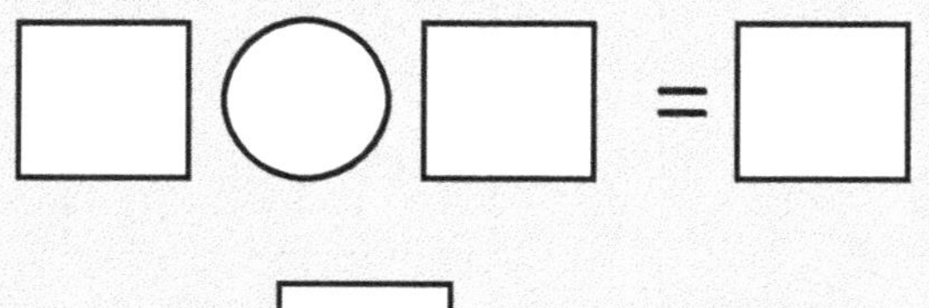

birds

How many animals did he see? Write your own equation.

animals

Label the numbers on the number line.

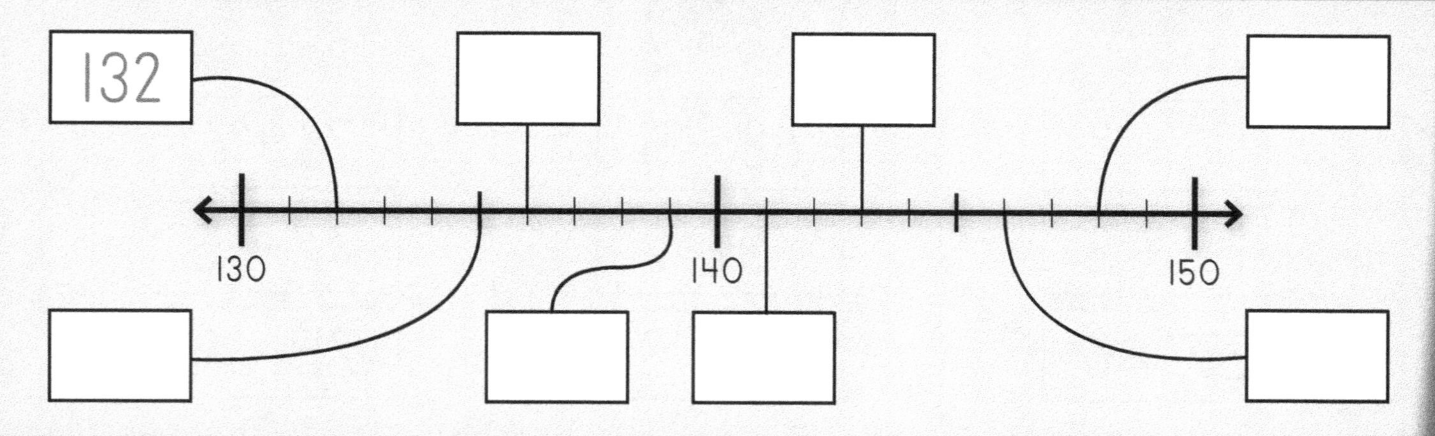

See the Instructor Guide for directions.

31 + 25 = ☐

43 + 32 = ☐

62 + 24 = ☐

25 + 34 = ☐

Complete. Then, use the key to color the stripes on the scarf.

53 + 24 = ☐

52 + 26 = ☐

67 + 32 = ☐

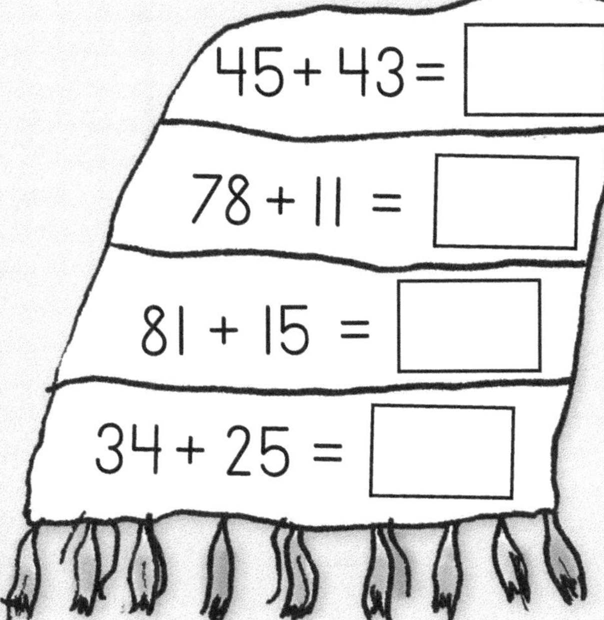

Match.

80¢	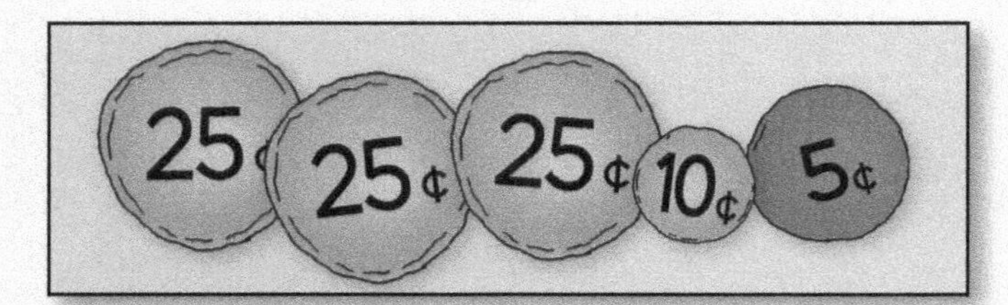	\$0.70
90¢	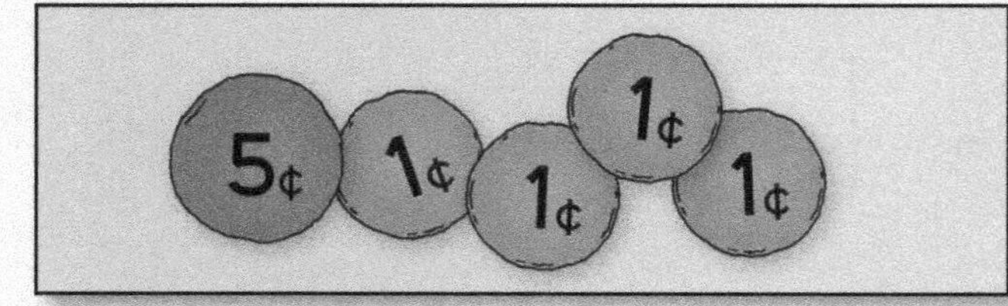	\$0.09
70¢		\$0.90
9¢		\$0.80

Solve.

You have \$30.

Then, you spend \$10.

How much money do you have left?

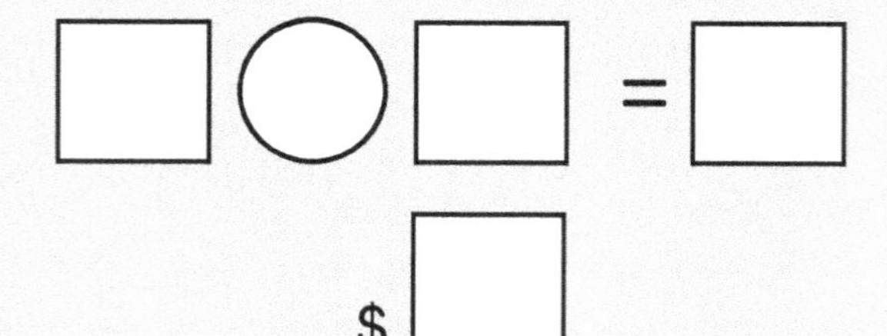

\$

You have \$20.

You spend \$9 on a shirt and the rest on a hat.

How much does the hat cost?

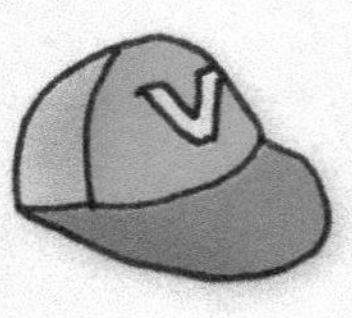

 = 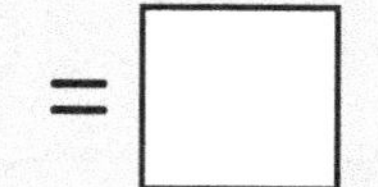

\$ 

See the Instructor Guide for directions.

35 + 15 = ☐	45 + 35 = ☐
55 + 25 = ☐	25 + 25 = ☐

Match.

55 + 15		25 + 55
	60	
25 + 45	70	35 + 55
45 + 25	80	35 + 35
	90	
45 + 45		15 + 45

Complete the circles with <, >, or =.

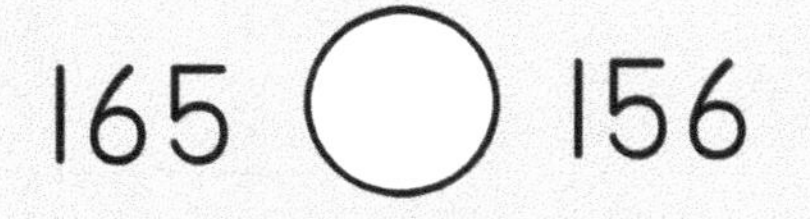

165 ◯ 156	101 ◯ 107	135 ◯ 135
38 ◯ 60	102 ◯ 120	150 ◯ 149

Complete the fact family to match the Part-Total Diagram.

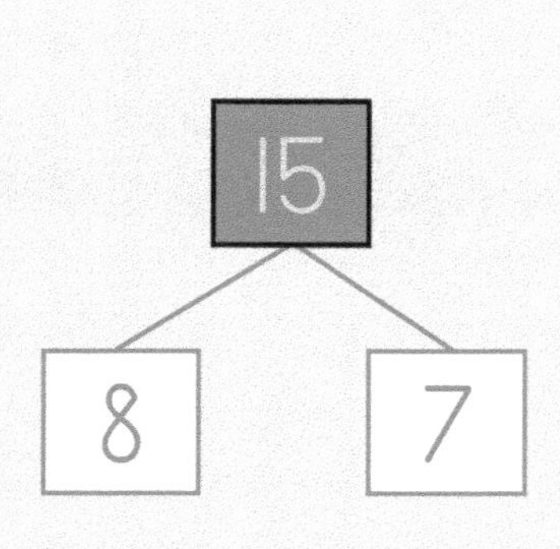

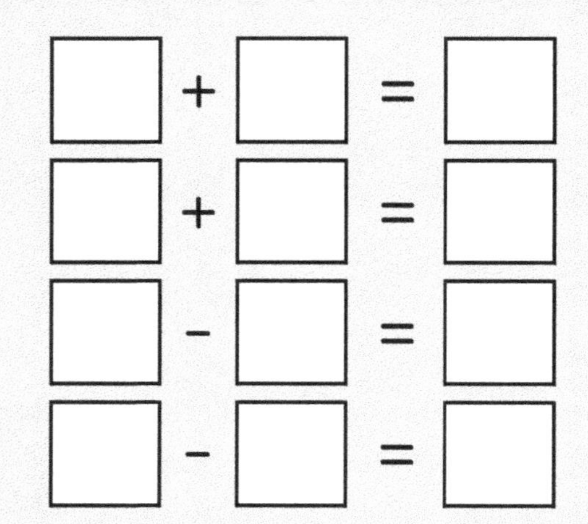

Count by 5s to connect the dots in order.

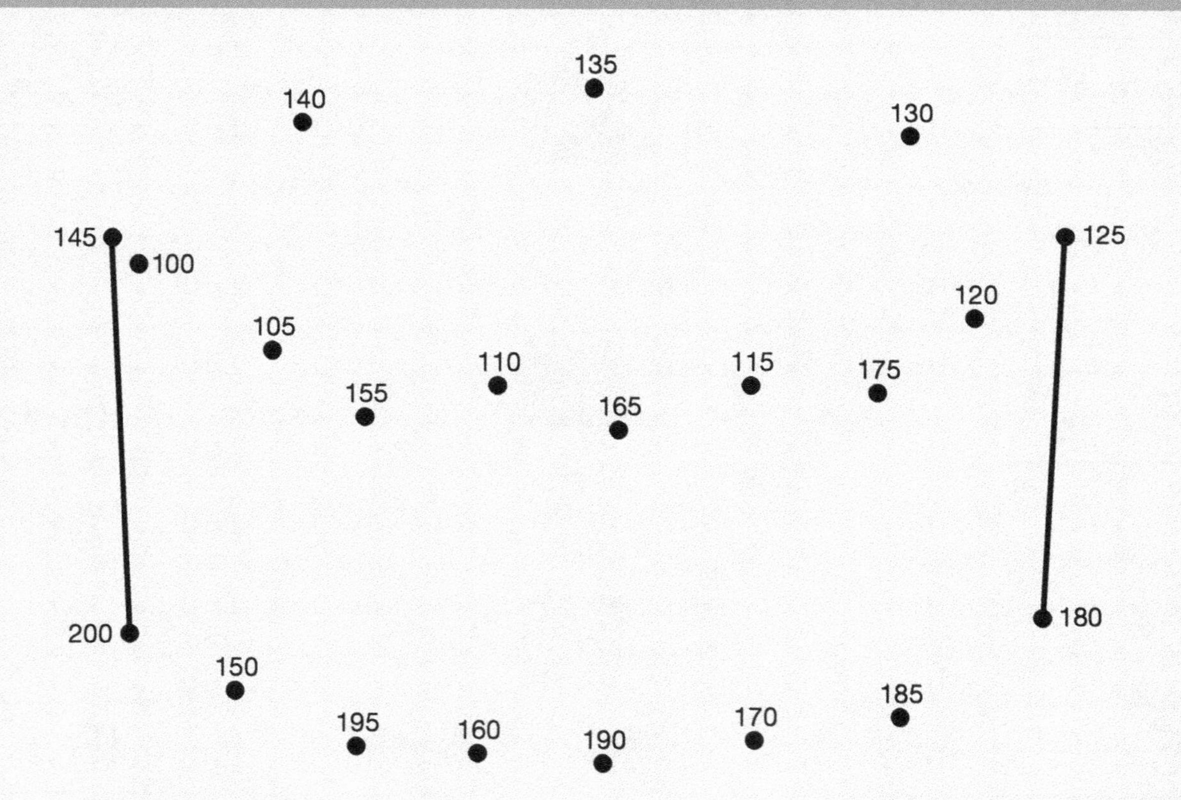

See the Instructor Guide for directions.

$39 + 23 =$ ☐

$68 + 14 =$ ☐

$25 + 37 =$ ☐

$56 + 24 =$ ☐

Snowball Fight

☐ + ☐ = ☐
☐ + ☐ = ☐

☐ + ☐ = ☐
☐ + ☐ = ☐

☐ + ☐ = ☐
☐ + ☐ = ☐

☐ + ☐ = ☐
☐ + ☐ = ☐

☐ + ☐ = ☐
☐ + ☐ = ☐

Samantha made a pictograph about how much time she spent practicing the piano. Use the pictograph to complete the chart and answer the questions.

Piano Practice

Day	Pictograph
Monday	♪ ♪ ♪
Tuesday	♪ ♪ ♪ ♪ ♪
Wednesday	♪ ♪ ♪ ♪
Thursday	♪ ♪

♪ = 5 minutes

Day	Minutes
Monday	
Tuesday	
Wednesday	
Thursday	

Which day did she practice the most?

Which day did she practice the least?

How much less did she practice on Monday than Tuesday? Write your own equation.

☐ minutes

How much did she practice in all? Write your own equation.

☐ minutes

Copy the shape.

See the Instructor Guide for directions.

$28 + 56 = \square$	$37 + 49 = \square$
$65 + 25 = \square$	$74 + 17 = \square$

Match.

79 + 5		58 + 15
	63	
38 + 35		53 + 41
	73	
47 + 33	80	45 + 18
	84	
39 + 24		64 + 16
	94	
56 + 38		36 + 48

Lucy made a bar graph about her art supplies.
Use the bar graph to complete the chart and answer the questions.

Art Supplies

Item	Number
Markers	
Colored Pencils	
Crayons	

How many more markers than colored pencils does she have?

☐ ○ ☐ = ☐

☐ markers

How many more crayons than colored pencils does she have?

☐ ○ ☐ = ☐

☐ crayons

Draw a line that splits each shape in half.

Draw lines that split each shape into fourths.

Label the hours on the clock.
Color the hour hand blue and the minute hand green.

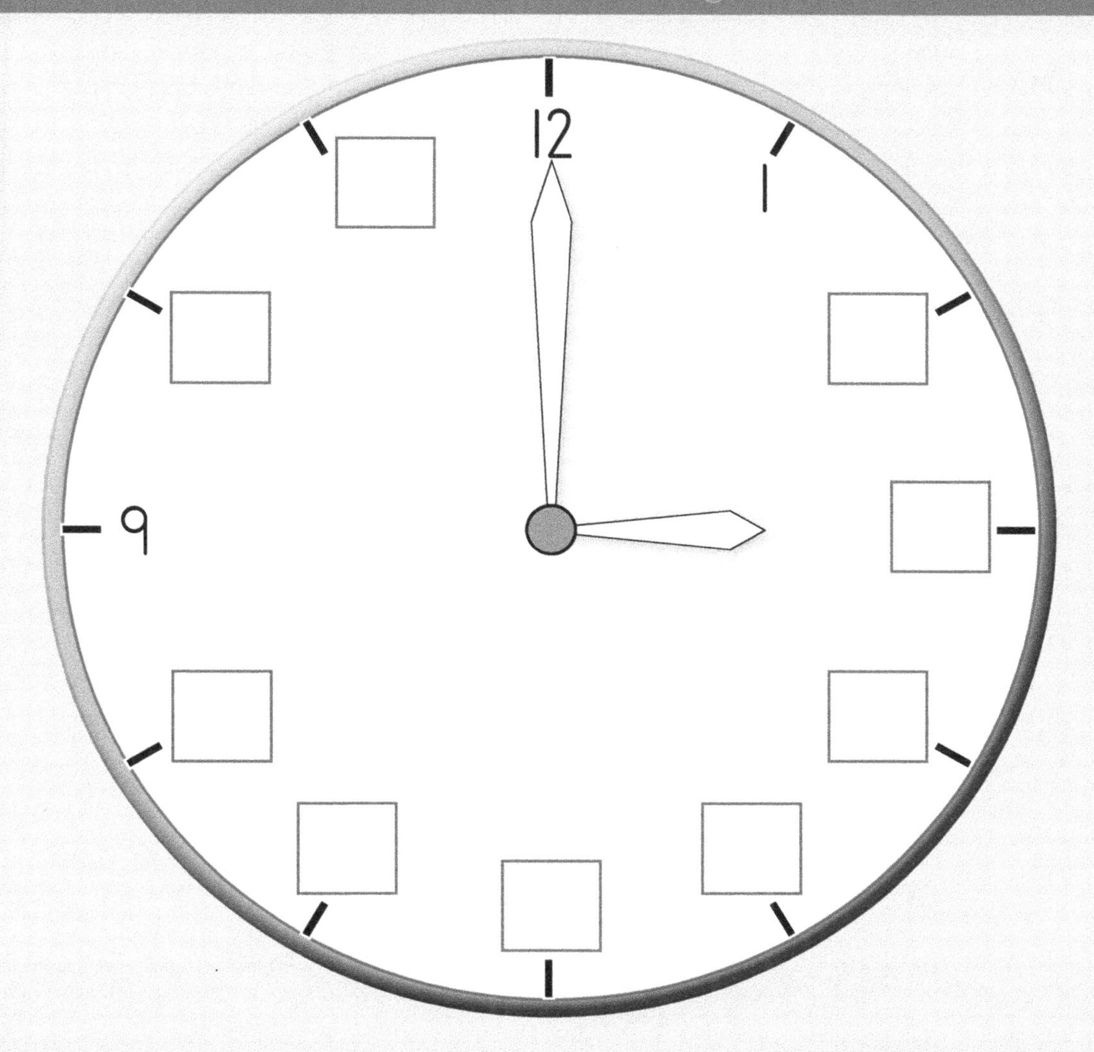

Write a.m. or p.m. for each time.

Complete.

48 + 27 = ☐

29 + 33 = ☐

52 + 38 = ☐

75 + 16 = ☐

61 + 24 = ☐

19 + 36 = ☐

Solve.

You have $38.
Then, you earn $5.
How much do you have now?

You have $29.
Then, you earn $7.
How much do you have now?

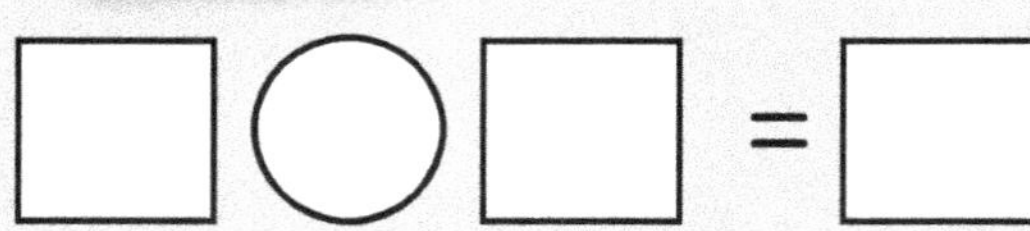

$ ☐

See the Instructor Guide for directions.

What hour does the hour hand show?

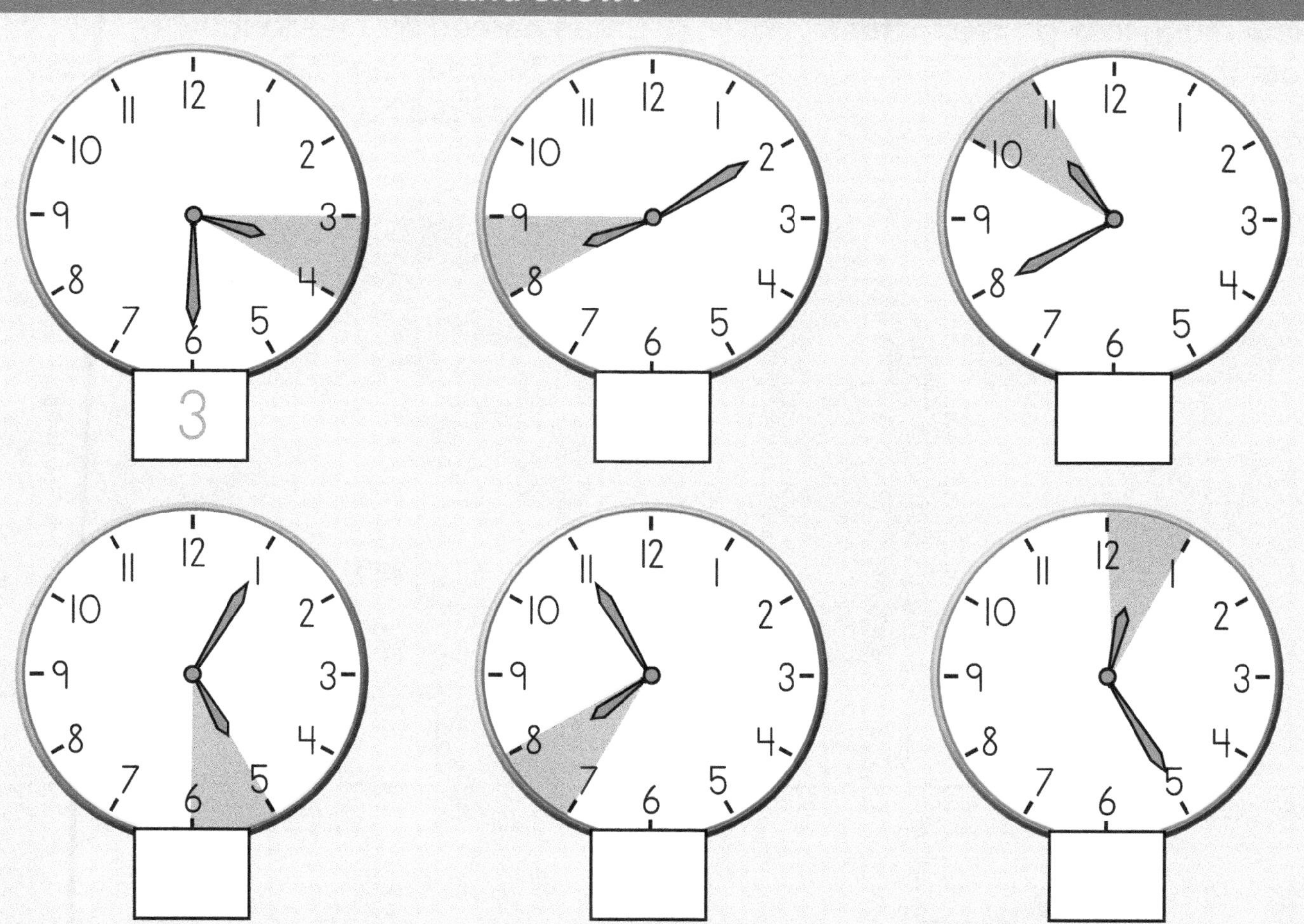

Match.

75 + 7	79	45 + 36
72 + 7	80	62 + 20
74 + 6	81	26 + 54
78 + 3	82	34 + 45

Solve.

How much less do the mittens cost than the scarf?

☐ ◯ ☐ = ☐

$ ☐

Ethan earned $9 on Monday, $7 on Tuesday, and $5 on Wednesday. How much did he earn in all?

☐ ◯ ☐ ◯ ☐ = ☐

$ ☐

Write the time.

Complete the sequence.

Complete.

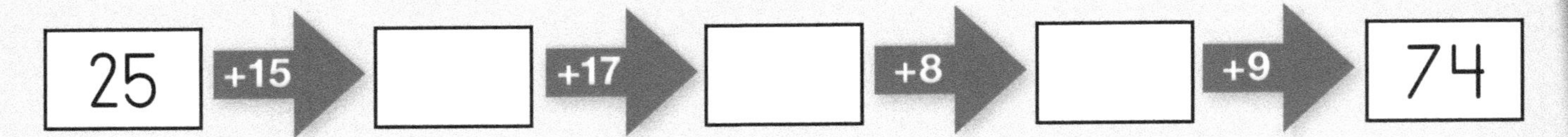

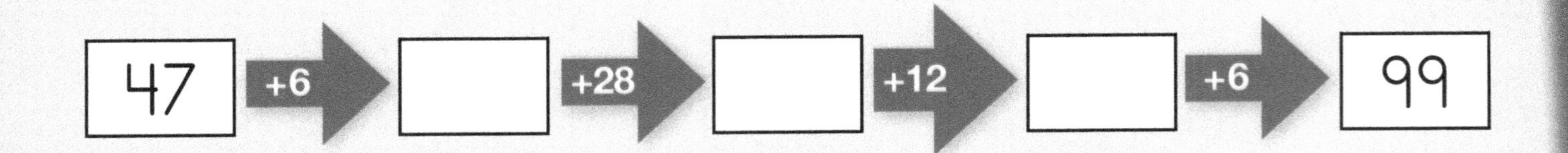

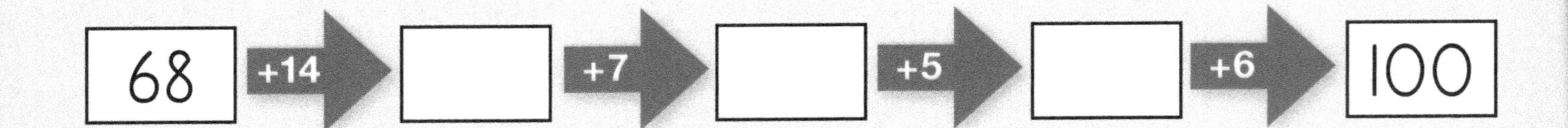

Write how many.

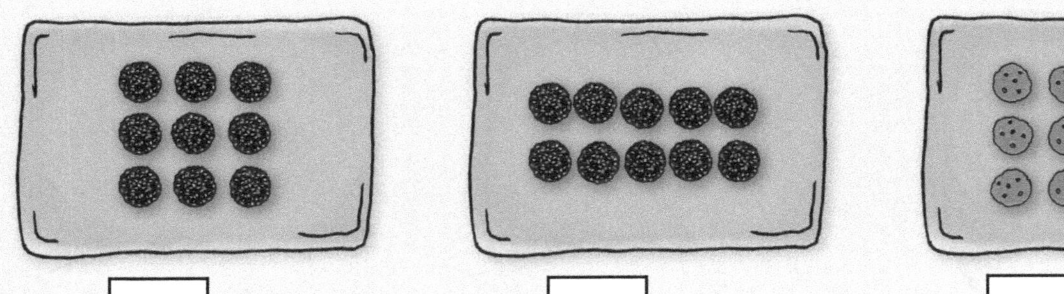

cookies

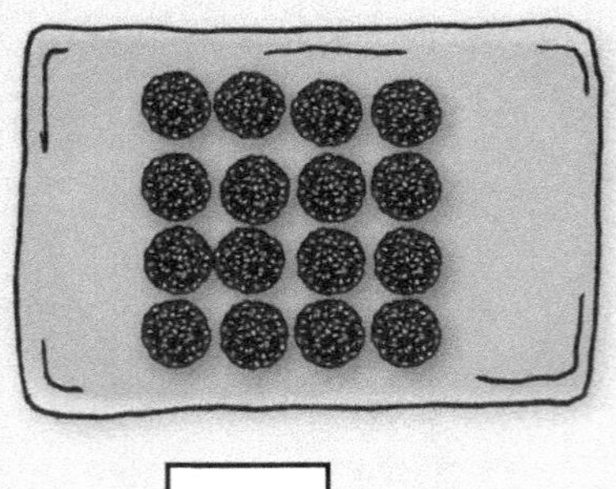

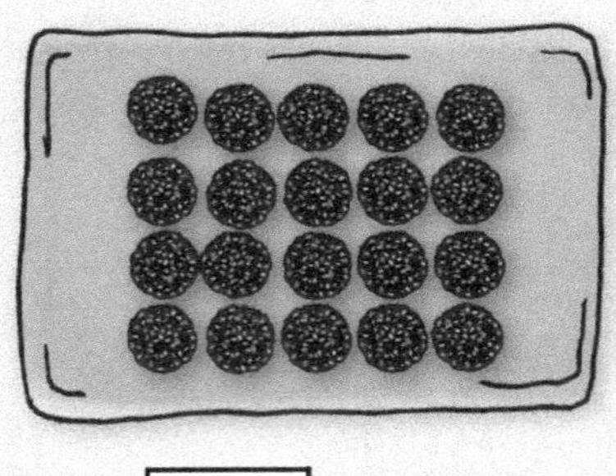

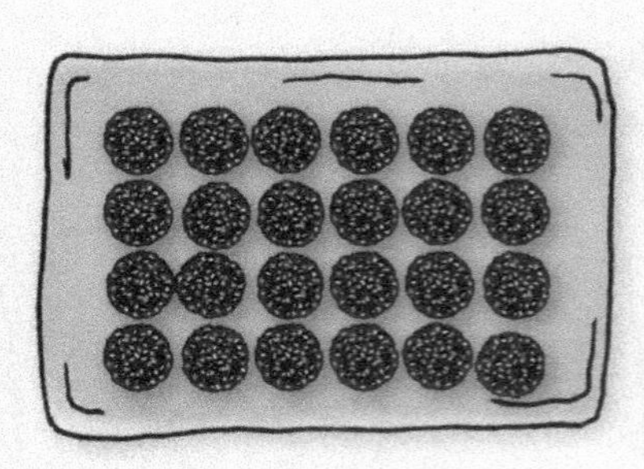

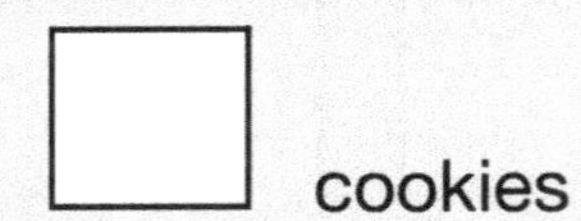

cookies

Label the minutes.

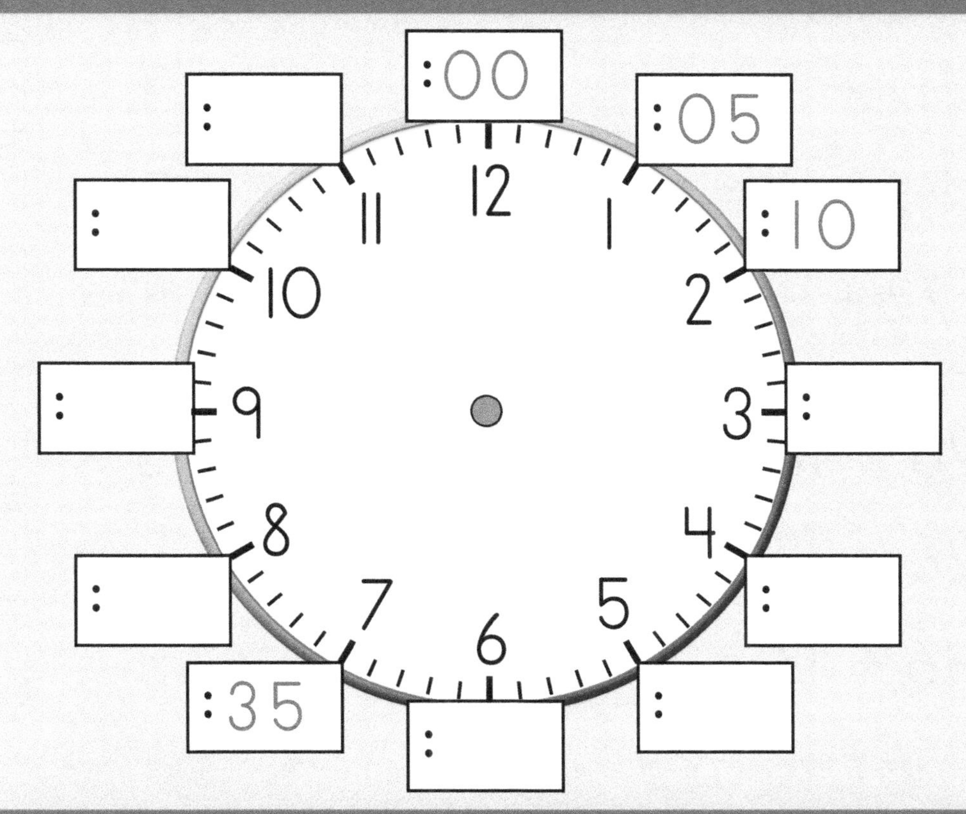

Write the time.

Complete.

$42 + 4 =$ ☐

$52 + 4 =$ ☐

$72 + 4 =$ ☐

$37 + 9 =$ ☐

$57 + 9 =$ ☐

$87 + 9 =$ ☐

$26 + 18 =$ ☐

$26 + 38 =$ ☐

$46 + 18 =$ ☐

$45 + 45 =$ ☐

$35 + 55 =$ ☐

$25 + 65 =$ ☐

Complete. Use a decimal point and dollar sign.

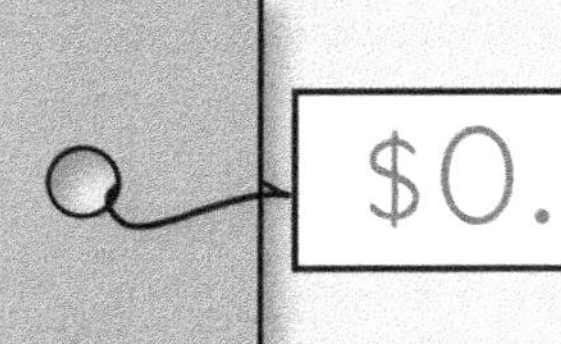

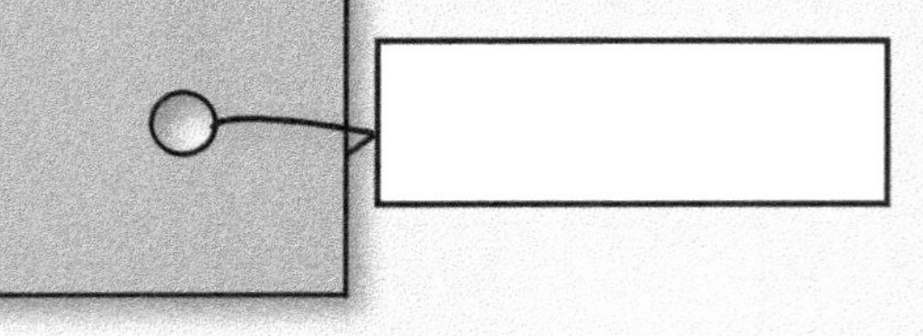

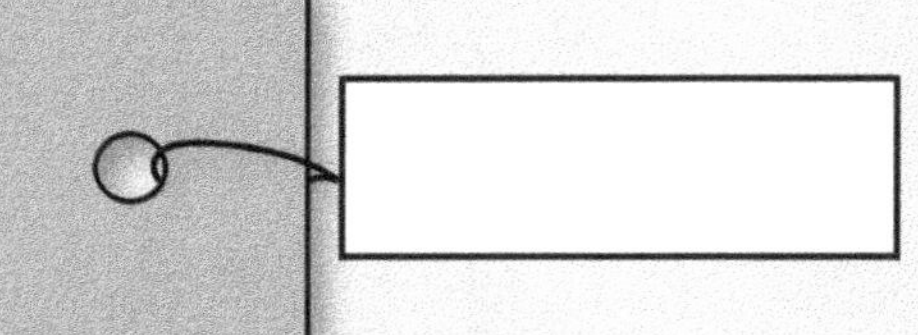

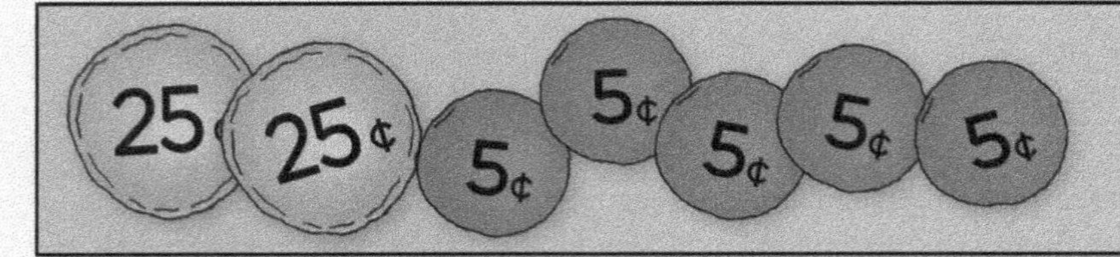

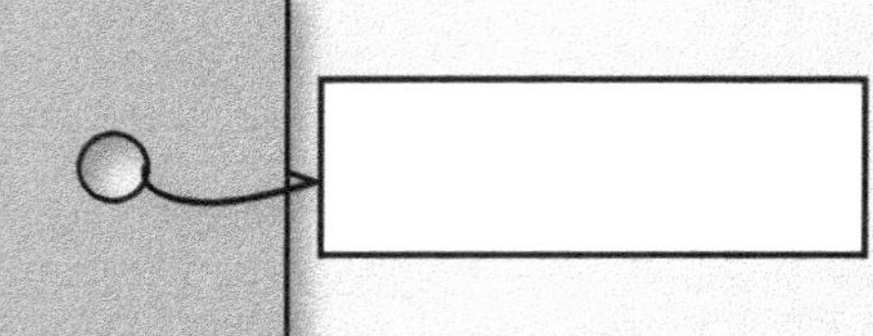

Match.

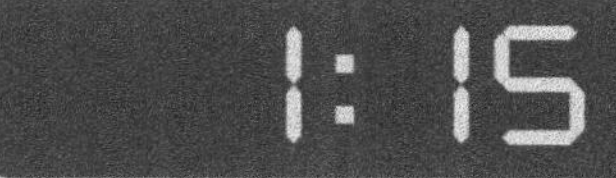

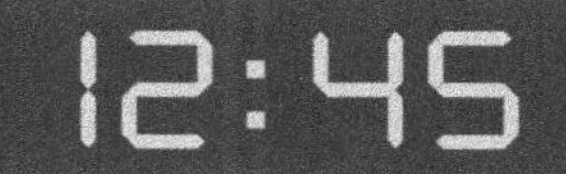

9:20

8:55

4:05

6:50

5:35

Write the time.

Complete.

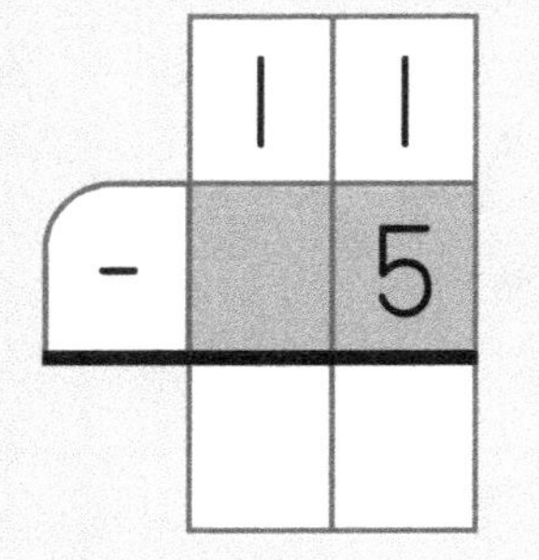

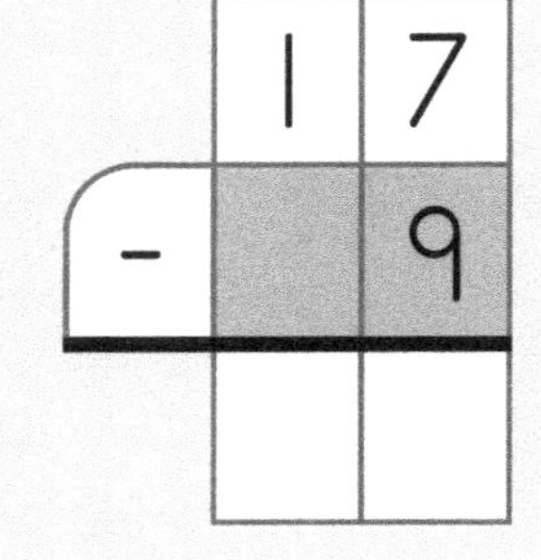

$$\begin{array}{r} 13 \\ -\ \ 8 \\ \hline \end{array}$$

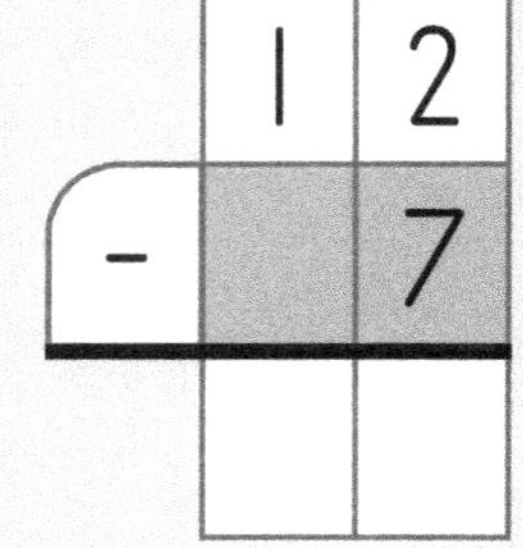

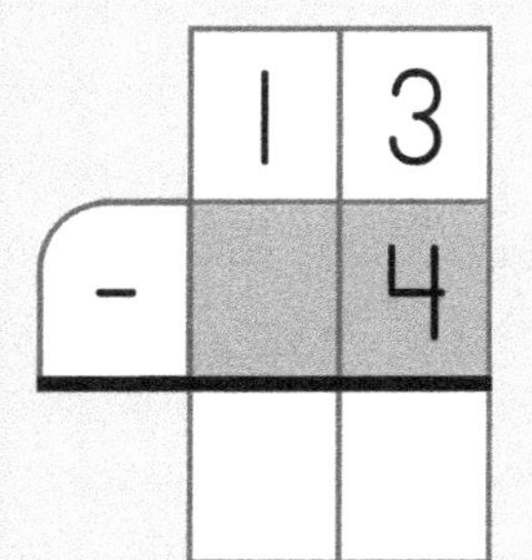

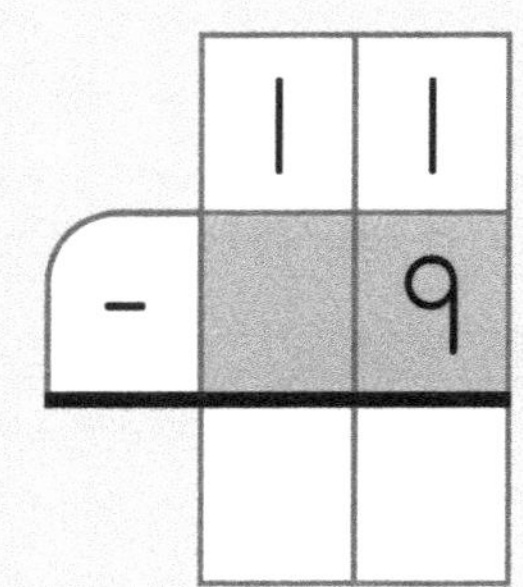

$$\begin{array}{r} 10 \\ -\ \ 8 \\ \hline \end{array}$$

$$\begin{array}{r} 13 \\ -\ \ 7 \\ \hline \end{array}$$

$$\begin{array}{r} 11 \\ -\ \ 3 \\ \hline \end{array}$$

$$\begin{array}{r} 13 \\ -\ \ 9 \\ \hline \end{array}$$

$$\begin{array}{r} 16 \\ -\ \ 8 \\ \hline \end{array}$$

$$\begin{array}{r} 15 \\ -\ \ 7 \\ \hline \end{array}$$

Write how much money is in each coin purse. Use a dollar sign and decimal point.

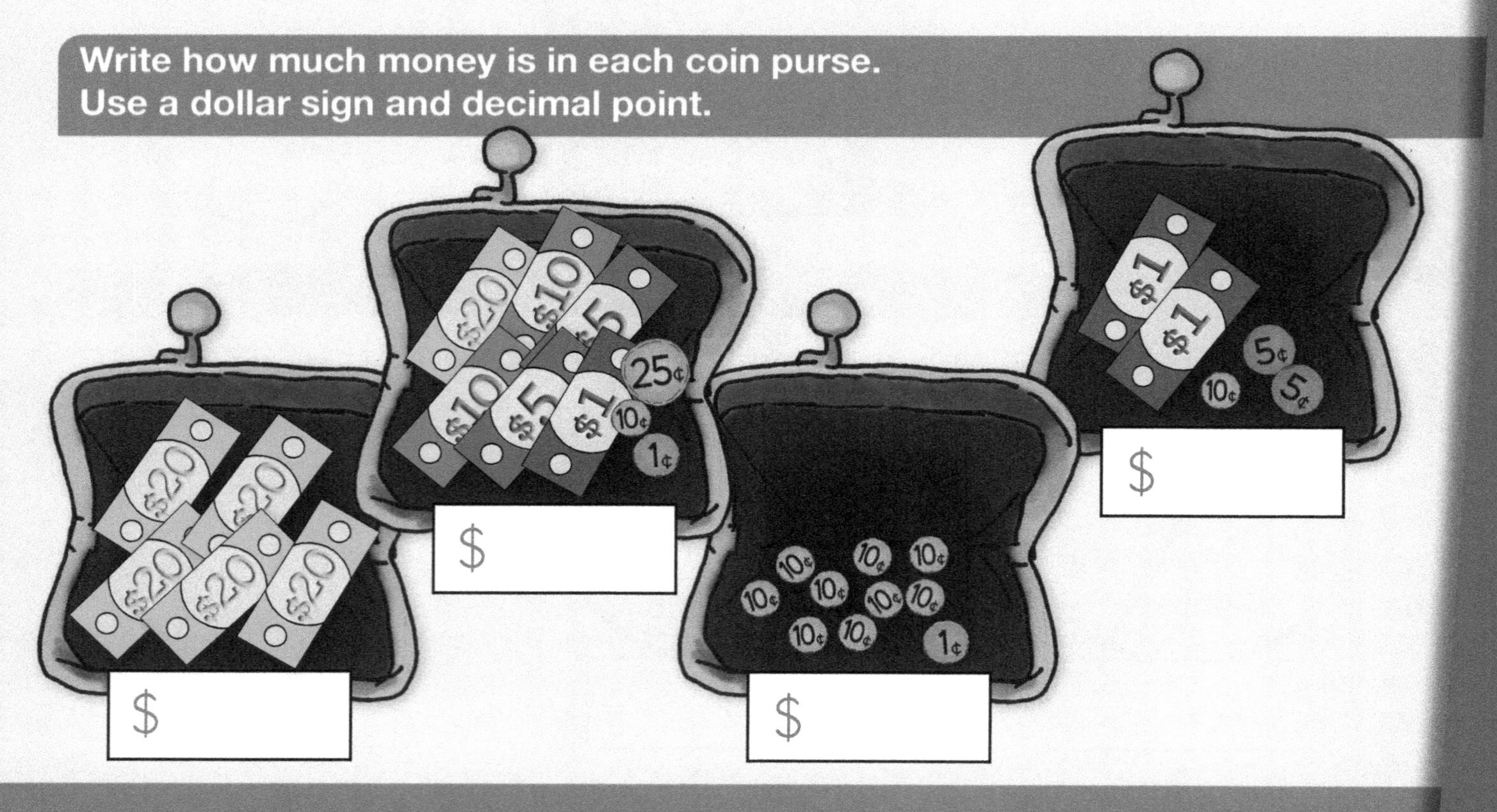

See the Instructor Guide for directions.

Write the time.

Complete.

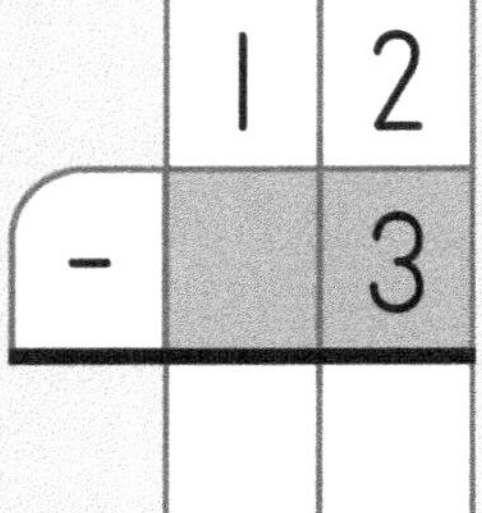

10 − 9 = ___

13 − 8 = ___

12 − 6 = ___

13 − 5 = ___

16 − 9 = ___

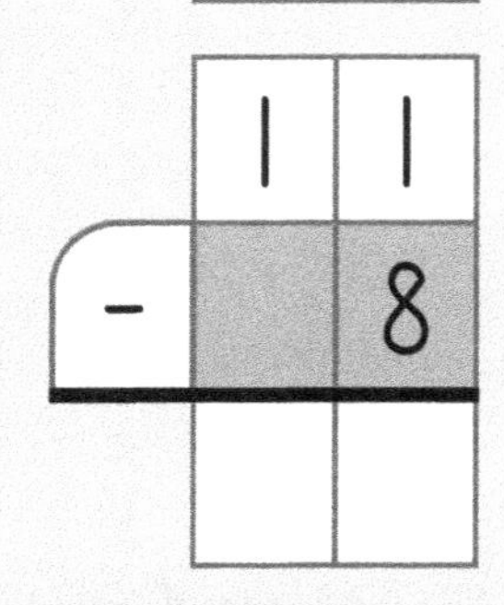

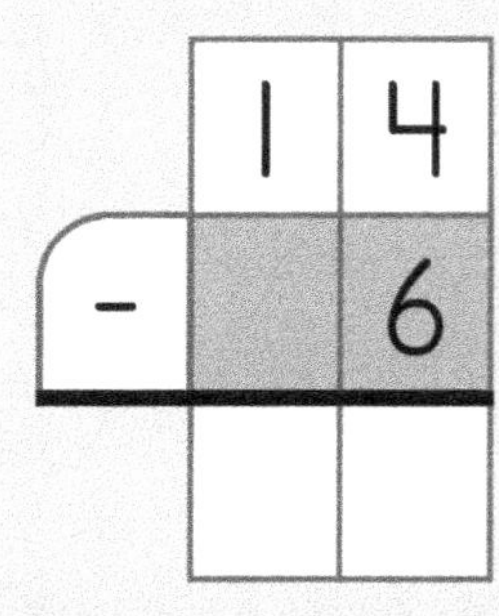

Complete.

7 double ___

Use the clues to complete the chart.

The wagon costs $15 more than the scooter.

The roller skates cost $20 less than the wagon.

The stilts cost $17 more than the roller skates.

Toy	Price
Scooter	$68
Wagon	
Roller Skates	
Stilts	

Match.

9:28

12:47

2:56

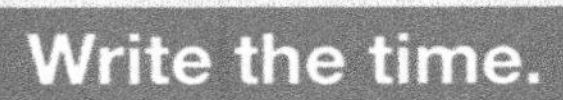

Write the time.

Complete.

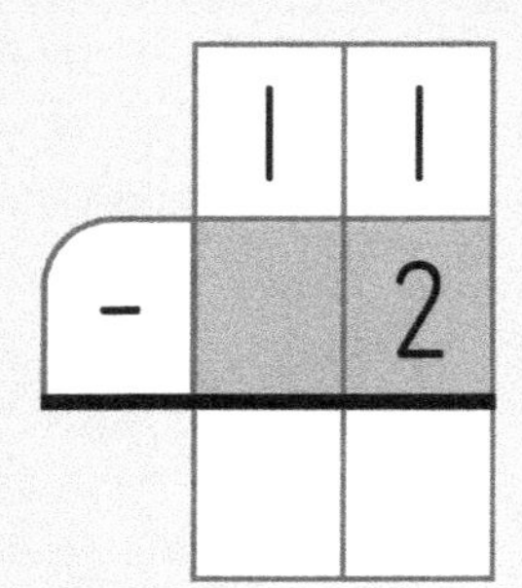

13
− 9

16
− 8

15
− 6

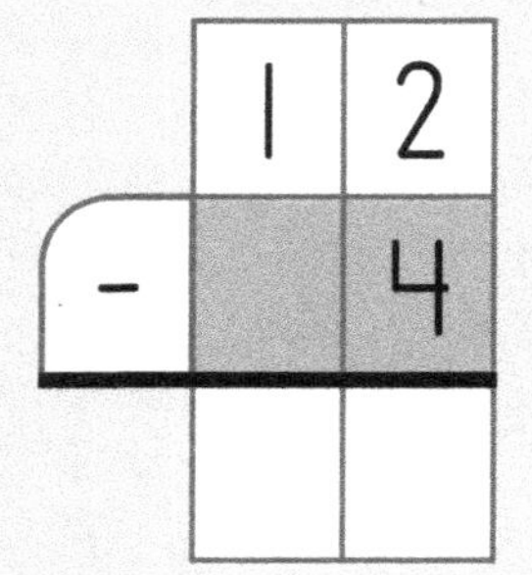

14
− 9

17
− 8

13
− 6

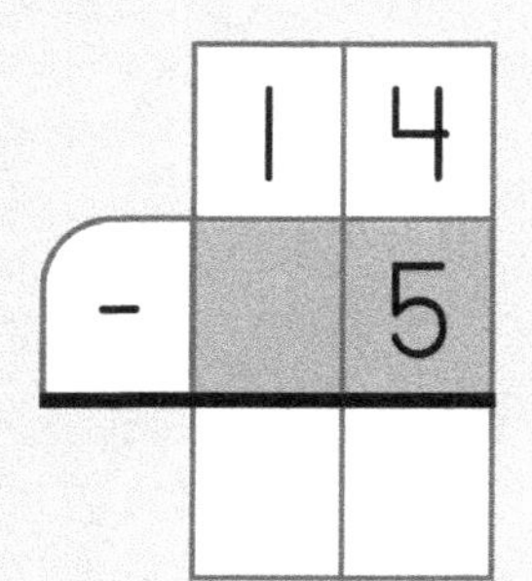

18
− 9

11
− 6

Complete the circles with <, >, or =.

40 ◯ 40	17 ◯ 71	76 ◯ 75
40 ◯ 4	104 ◯ 140	98 ◯ 89
148 ◯ 184	150 ◯ 160	200 ◯ 200

Write the time.

Complete the sequence.

Complete.

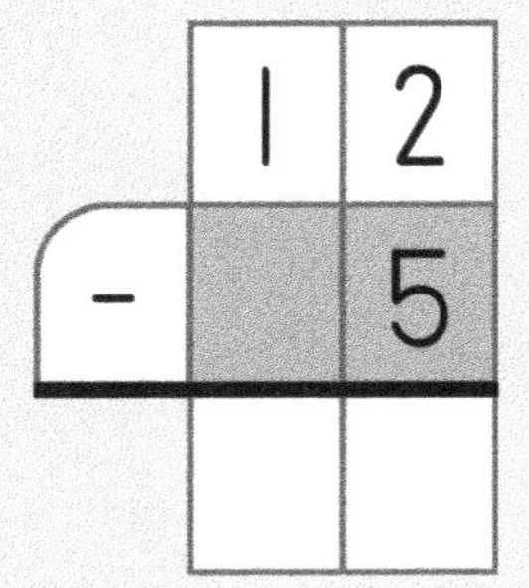

	1	5
-		9

	1	2
-		8

	1	4
-		7

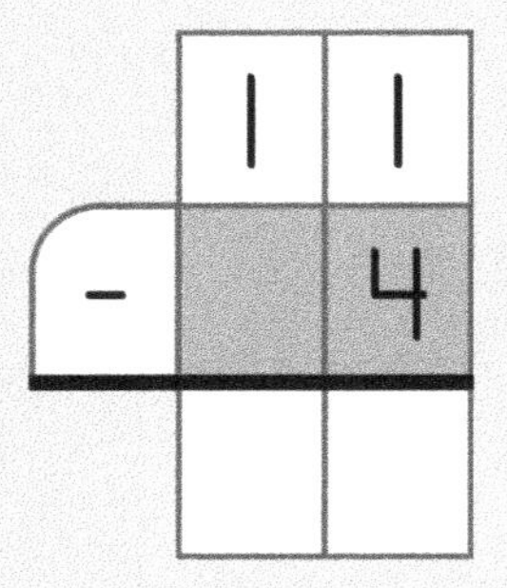

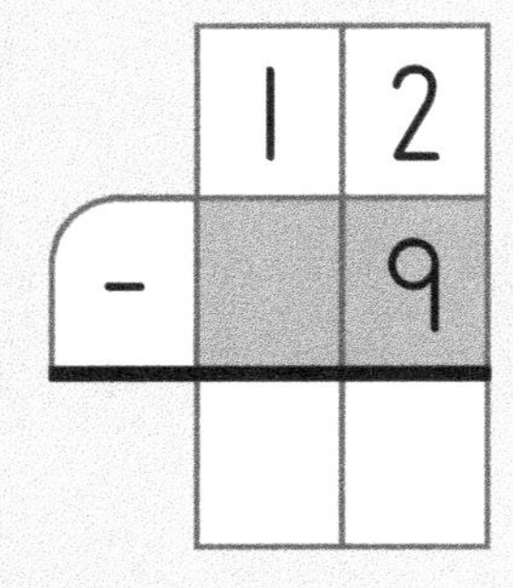

	1	7
-		8

	1	6
-		7

Solve.

You have $45.

The toy costs $50.

How much more money do you need?

You have $22.

The toy costs $30.

How much more money do you need?

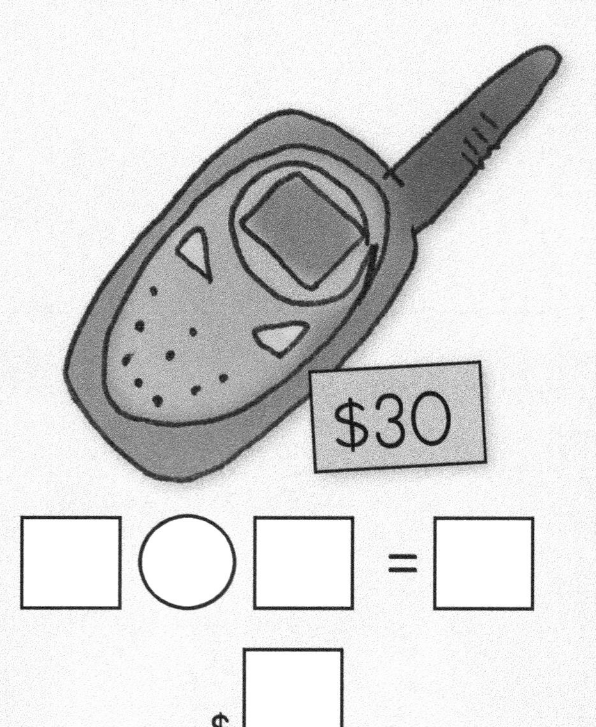

☐ ◯ ☐ = ☐

$ ☐

See the Instructor Guide for how to play.
Save this game board for future lessons.

Four in a Row

Subtract from Multiples of 10

80 - 2	30 - 8	40 - 7	70 - 7	60 - 9
70 - 4	90 - 6	80 - 3	50 - 5	30 - 6
60 - 1	40 - 3	50 - 4	70 - 8	90 - 2
40 - 9	30 - 2	60 - 1	80 - 4	40 - 5
80 - 5	90 - 1	70 - 6	30 - 7	50 - 3

Complete.

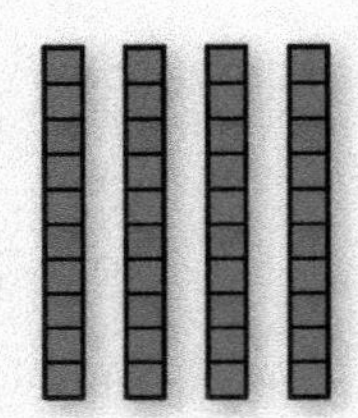

$40 - 2 =$ ☐

$50 - 2 =$ ☐

$70 - 2 =$ ☐

$30 - 2 =$ ☐

$30 - 5 =$ ☐

$40 - 5 =$ ☐

$90 - 5 =$ ☐

$60 - 5 =$ ☐

Label the numbers on the number line.

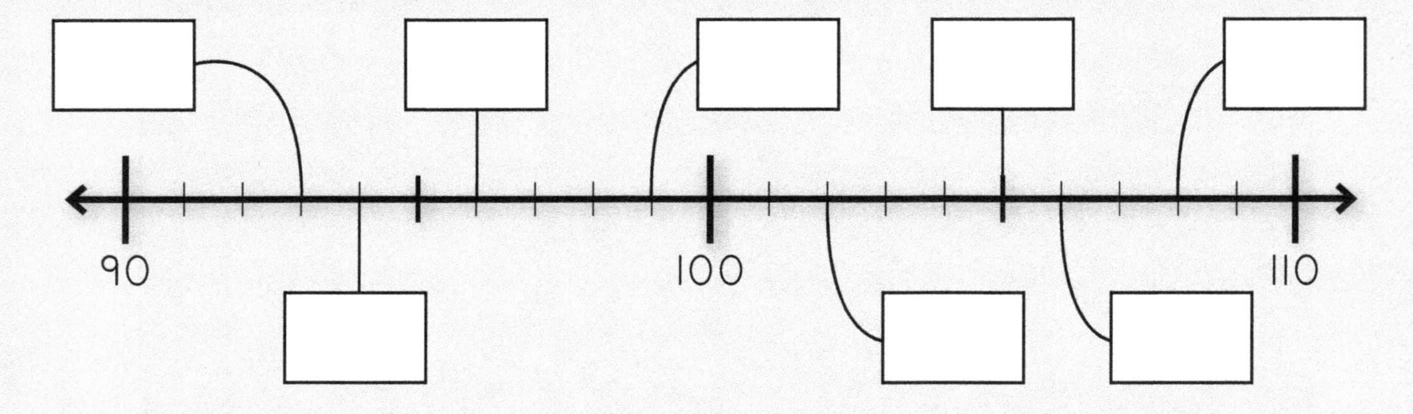

Write the time.

See the instructor Guide for directions.

53 - 4 = ☐	42 - 6 = ☐
61 - 3 = ☐	85 - 8 = ☐

Roll and Subtract

Player 1	Player 2
41 - ☐ = ☐	41 - ☐ = ☐
32 - ☐ = ☐	32 - ☐ = ☐
50 - ☐ = ☐	50 - ☐ = ☐
71 - ☐ = ☐	71 - ☐ = ☐
82 - ☐ = ☐	82 - ☐ = ☐

Write the time.

Josh made a bar graph about the books he read.
Use the bar graph to complete the chart and answer the questions.

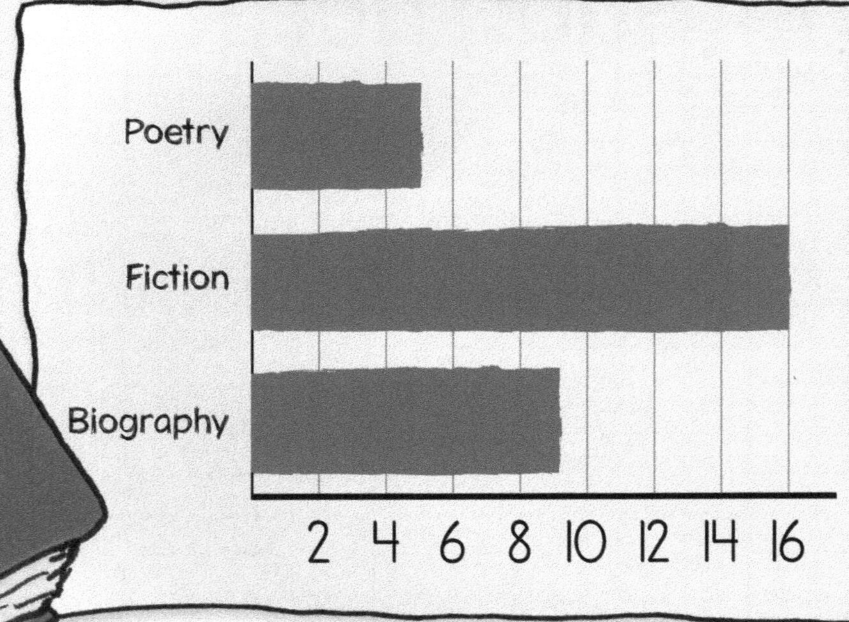

Poetry	
Fiction	
Biography	

How many poetry books and biographies did he read?

☐ books

How many more fiction books than biographies did he read?

☐ books

How many more fiction books than poetry books did he read?

☐ books

How many books did he read in all?

☐ books

See the Instructor Guide for directions.

62 - 5 = ☐	51 - 3 = ☐
45 - 6 = ☐	84 - 9 = ☐

Write the answer to each subtraction problem.
Use the key to color the quilt squares.

Odd answers - Yellow
Even answers - Red

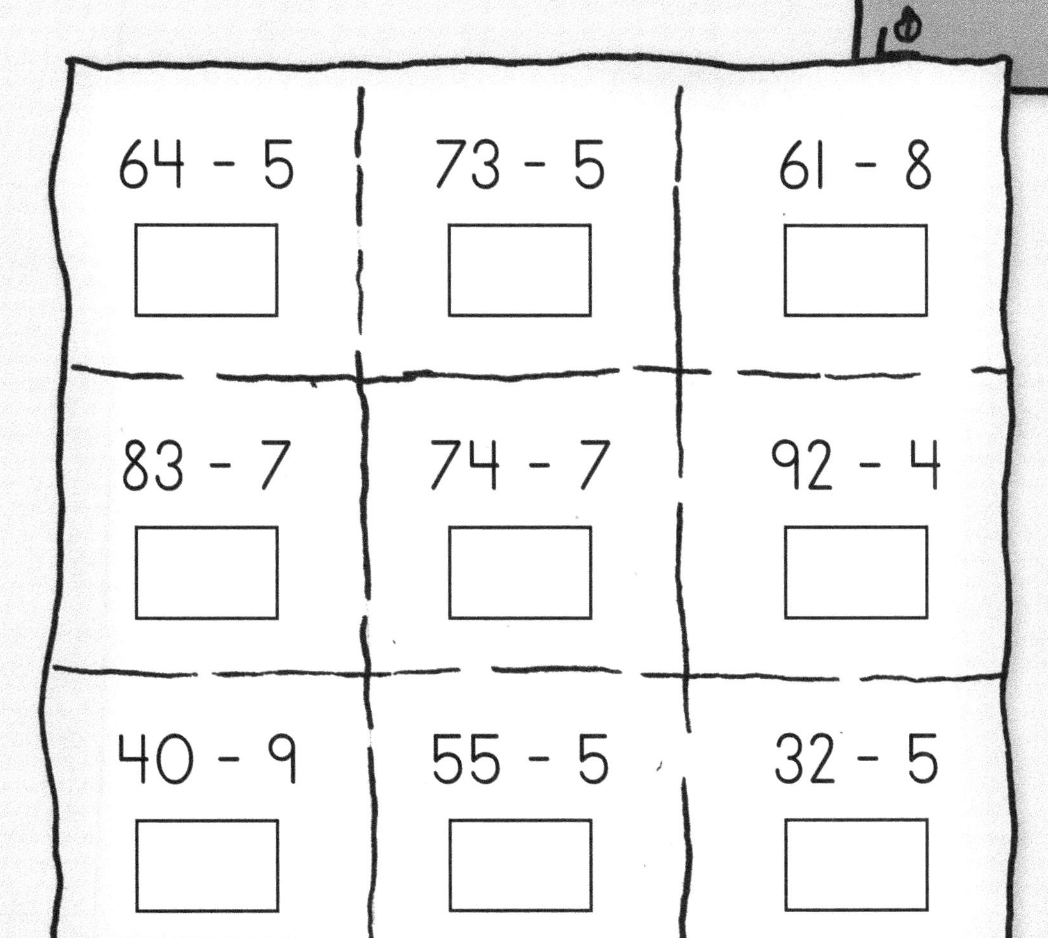

Complete the sequences.

Solve.

You have $40.
Then, you spend $6.
How much money do you have left?

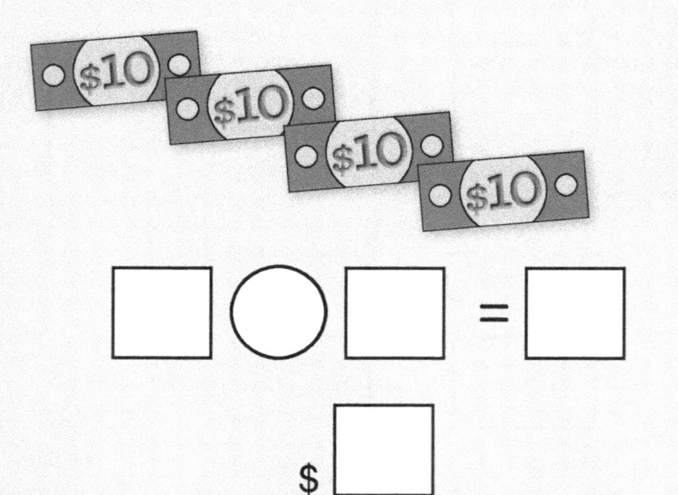

You have $40.
Then, you earn $6.
How much money do you have now?

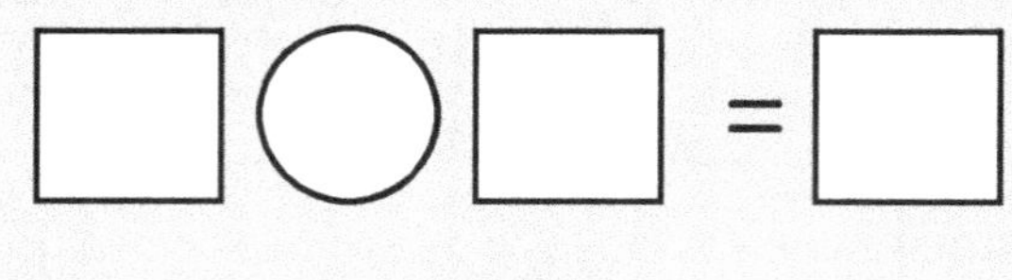

Solve.

You have $36.

Then, you spend $9.

How much money do you have left?

☐ ◯ ☐ = ☐

$ ☐

You have $53.

Then, you spend $5.

How much money do you have left?

☐ ◯ ☐ = ☐

$ ☐

Match.

73 - 4	69	73 - 7
	76	
	66	
71 - 6	75	80 - 5
	65	
84 - 7	77	85 - 9

Write the time.

Complete each box with a number that makes the statement true.

$20 > \square$	$98 < \square$	$146 > \square$
$\square = 80$	$\square < 146$	$\square > 150$
$0 < \square$	$\square = 32$	$156 < \square$

Copy the shape.

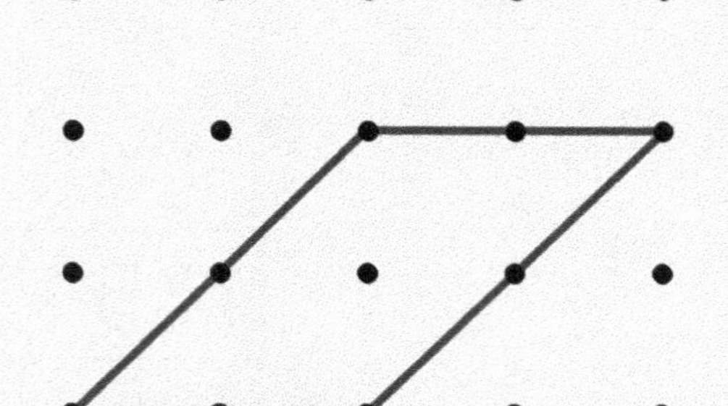

See the Instructor Guide for how to play.
Save this game board for future lessons.

Four in a Row

Two-Digit Subtraction

80 - 12	30 - 18	40 - 27	70 - 37	60 - 29
70 - 54	90 - 26	80 - 33	50 - 35	30 - 16
60 - 31	40 - 23	50 - 24	70 - 28	90 - 42
40 - 19	30 - 12	60 - 51	80 - 54	40 - 25
80 - 35	90 - 61	70 - 46	30 - 17	50 - 33

Complete the sequences.

Laura counted the children in each swim class. Use her chart to make a bar graph.

Class	Number of Children
Minnows	10
Fish	5
Dolphins	12

12
10
8
6
4
2

Minnows Fish Dolphins

See the Instructor Guide for directions.

$58 - 23 =$ ☐	$73 - 42 =$ ☐
$63 - 24 =$ ☐	$81 - 47 =$ ☐

Roll and Subtract

Player 1	Player 2
74 - ☐☐ = ☐	74 - ☐☐ = ☐
93 - ☐☐ = ☐	93 - ☐☐ = ☐
81 - ☐☐ = ☐	81 - ☐☐ = ☐
70 - ☐☐ = ☐	70 - ☐☐ = ☐
92 - ☐☐ = ☐	92 - ☐☐ = ☐

Solve. Write your own equation to match each word problem.

Eden does 35 jumping jacks and 20 sit-ups.
How many exercises does she do?

☐ ◯ ☐ = ☐

☐ exercises

Eden does 35 jumping jacks and 20 sit-ups.
How many more jumping jacks than sit-ups does she do?

☐ ◯ ☐ = ☐

☐ more

Complete.

25¢ 25¢ 10¢ 10¢ 1¢ 1¢

☐ ¢

Write the time.

See the Instructor Guide for directions.

85 - 16 = ☐	74 - 35 = ☐
95 - 47 = ☐	41 - 25 = ☐

Match.

53 - 25

85 - 46

81 - 33

93 - 64

28

29

38

39

48

87 - 58

91 - 53

80 - 32

66 - 27

Write the time.

Ian made a pictograph about how much time he spent playing outside. Use the pictograph to complete the chart and answer the questions.

Winter Activities

Skating	○○○○○○
Sledding	○○○○○○○
Building Snowmen	○○○

○ = 5 minutes

Activity	Minutes
Skating	
Sledding	
Building Snowmen	

Which activity did he do the longest?

Which activity did he do the shortest?

How much more time did he spend sledding than skating?

☐ minutes

How much less time did he spend making snowmen than sledding?

☐ minutes

Write the answer to each problem.
Then, use the key to color the pinwheel.

Key
16 - red
35 - orange
48 - yellow
66 - green
88 - blue

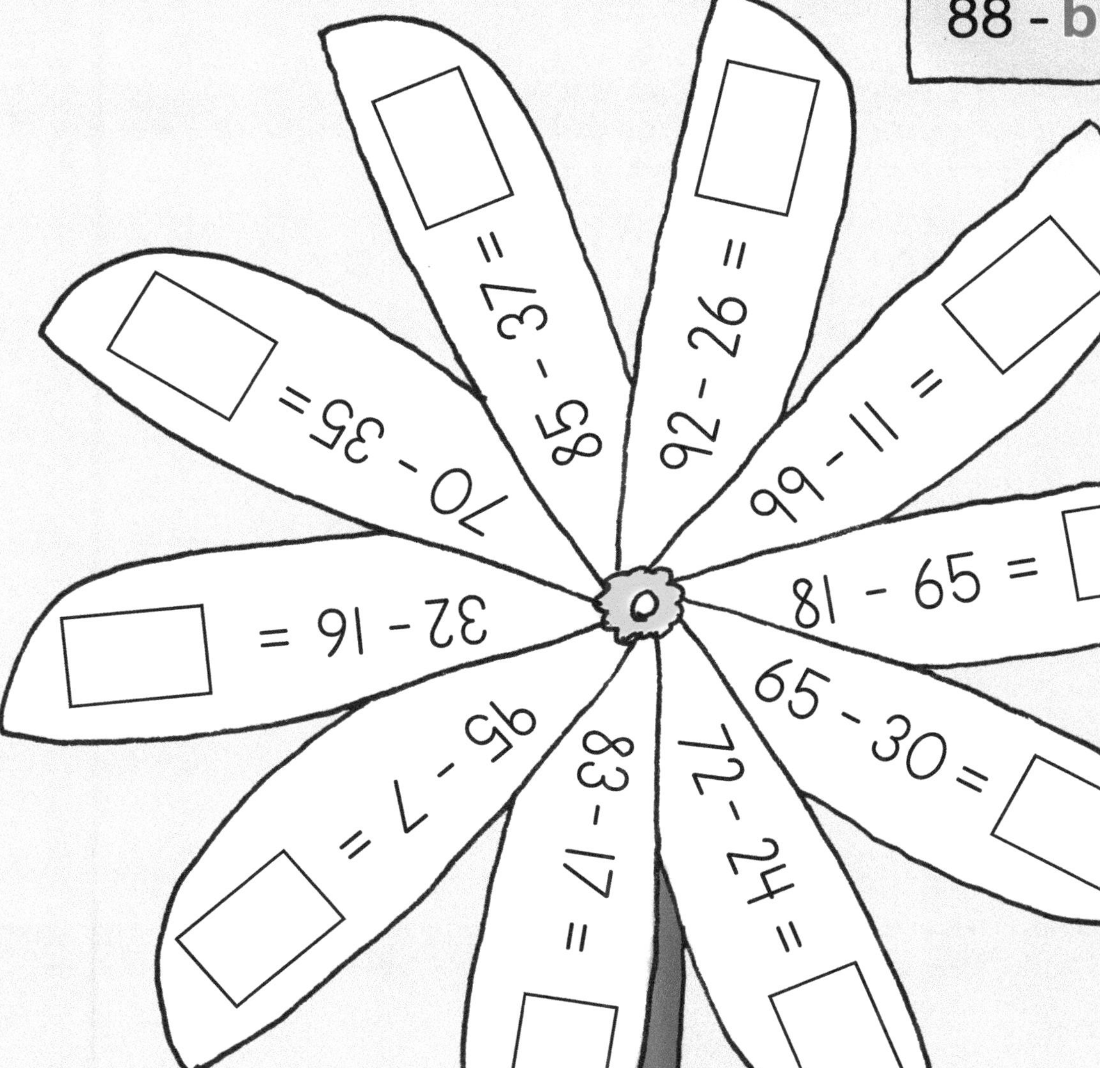

Complete.

1 year = ☐ months

1 week = ☐ days

1 day = ☐ hours

1 hour = ☐ minutes

1 minute = ☐ seconds

Color the even numbers yellow. Color the odd numbers red.

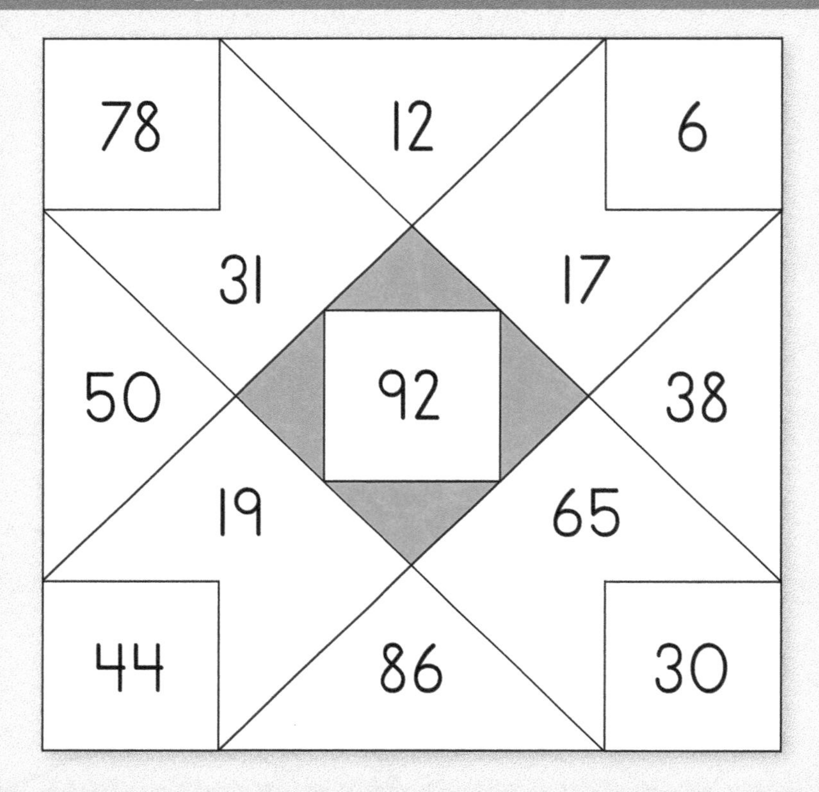

Write the time.

Use a ruler to measure the ribbons in inches.

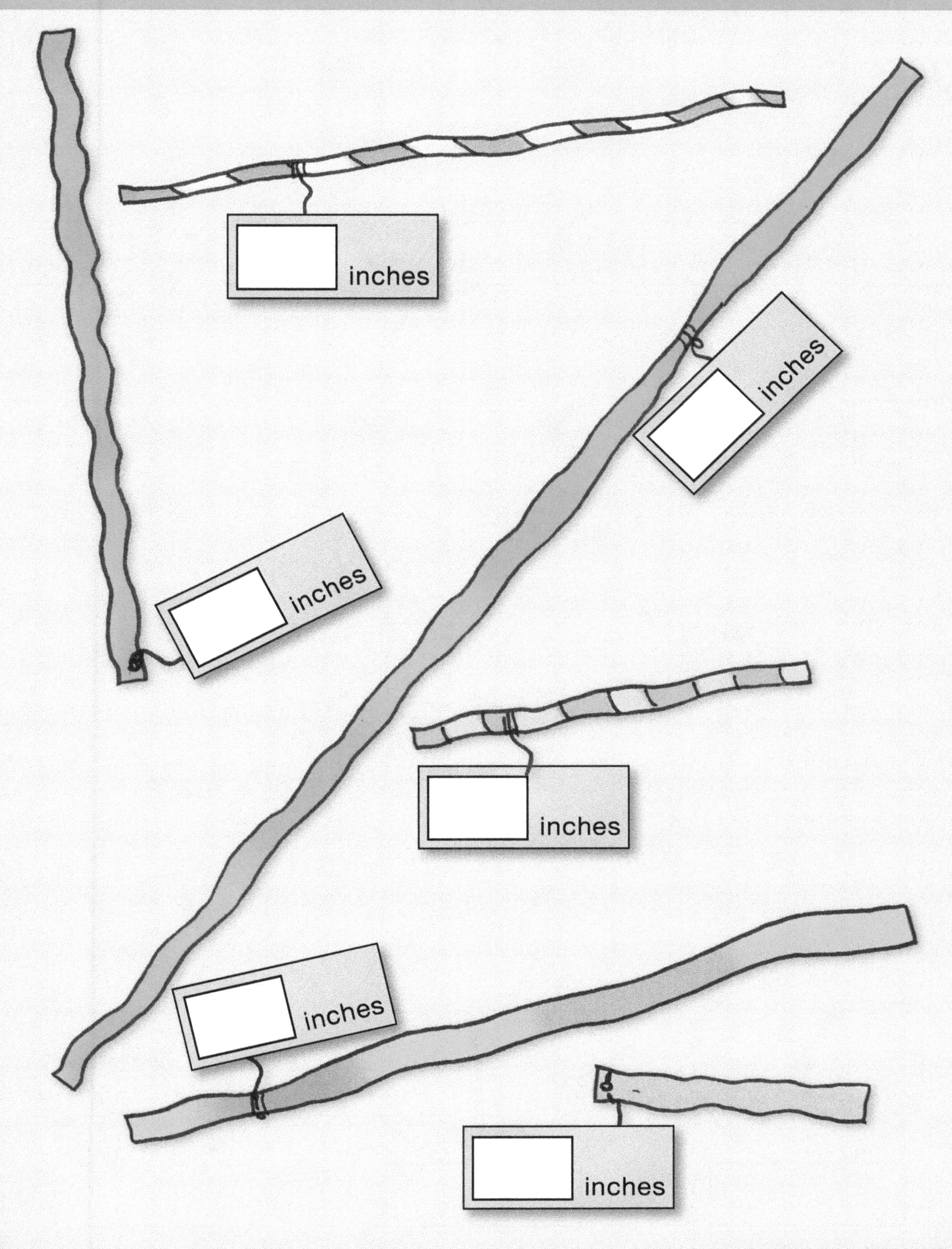

Complete.

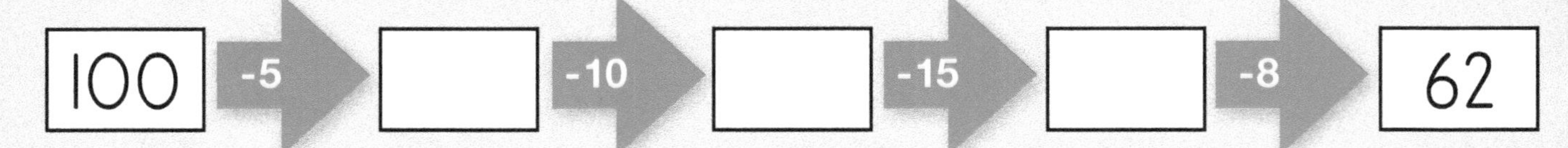

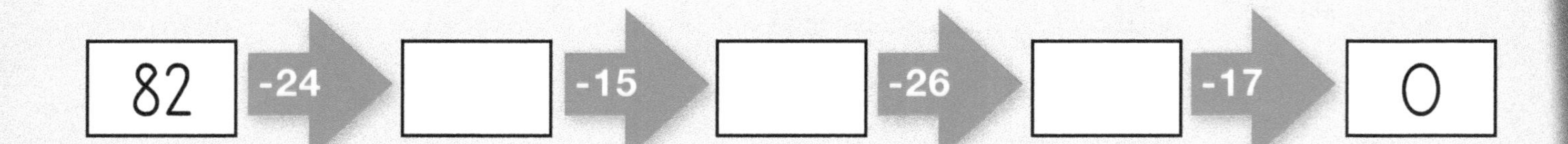

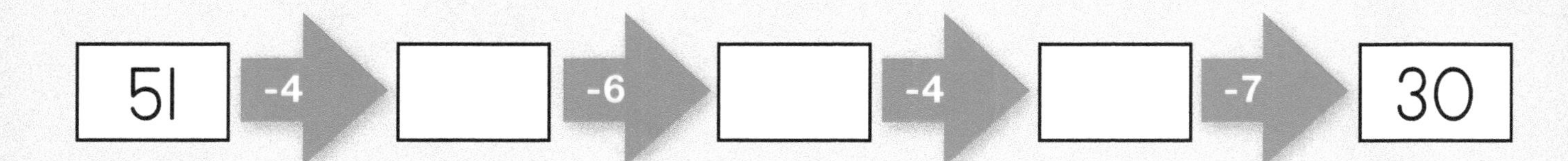

Complete the equations to match.

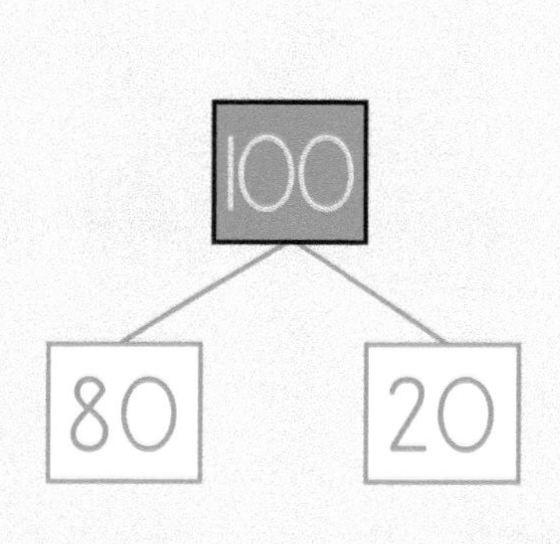

☐ + ☐ = ☐

☐ + ☐ = ☐

☐ − ☐ = ☐

☐ − ☐ = ☐

Write the time.

Use the "broken" rulers to measure the leaves.

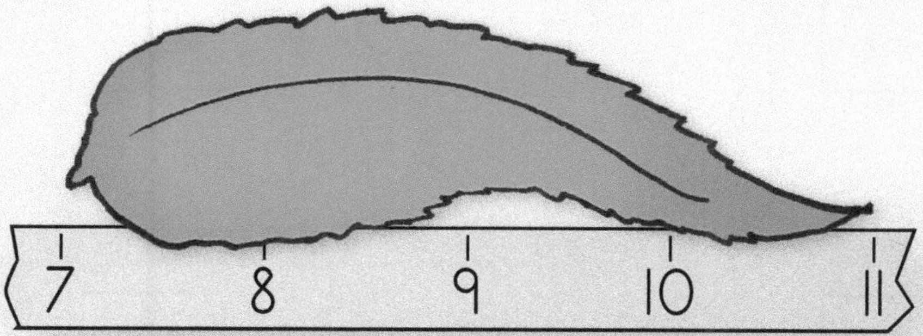

7 8 9 10 11

☐ inches

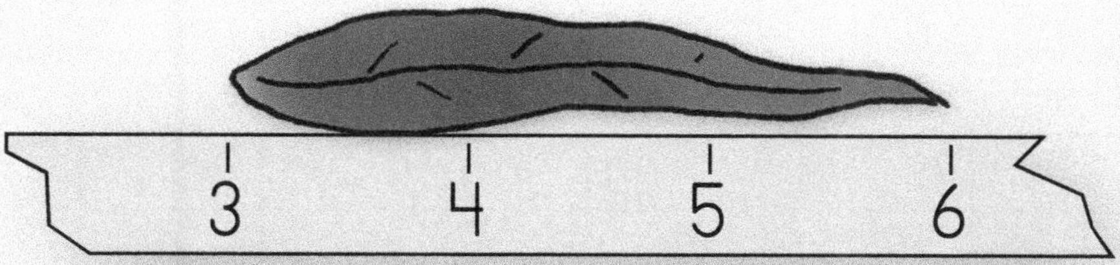

3 4 5 6

☐ inches

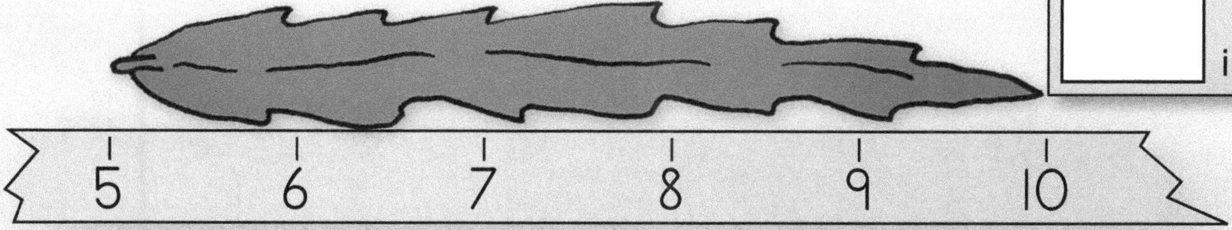

5 6 7 8 9 10

☐ inches

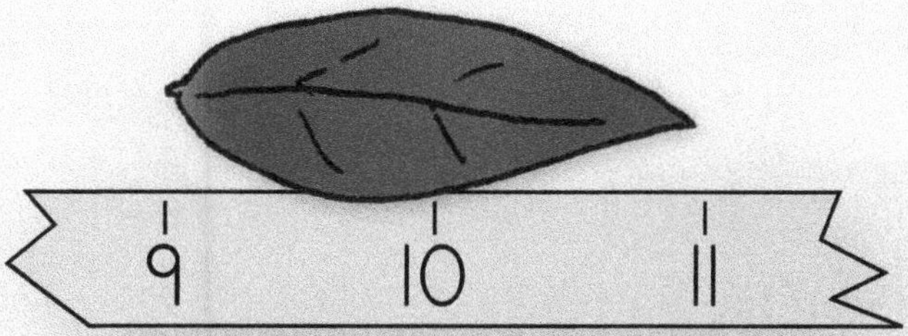

9 10 11

☐ inches

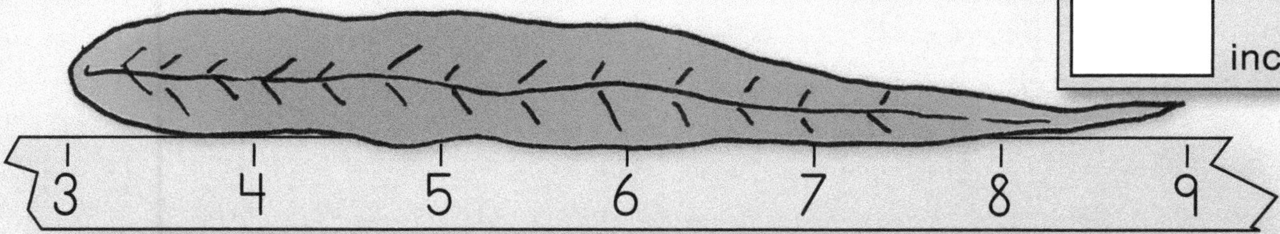

3 4 5 6 7 8 9

☐ inches

Complete.

45 - 32 = ☐	56 - 27 = ☐
80 - 76 = ☐	90 - 23 = ☐
62 - 16 = ☐	41 - 25 = ☐

Complete the missing numbers in the sequences.

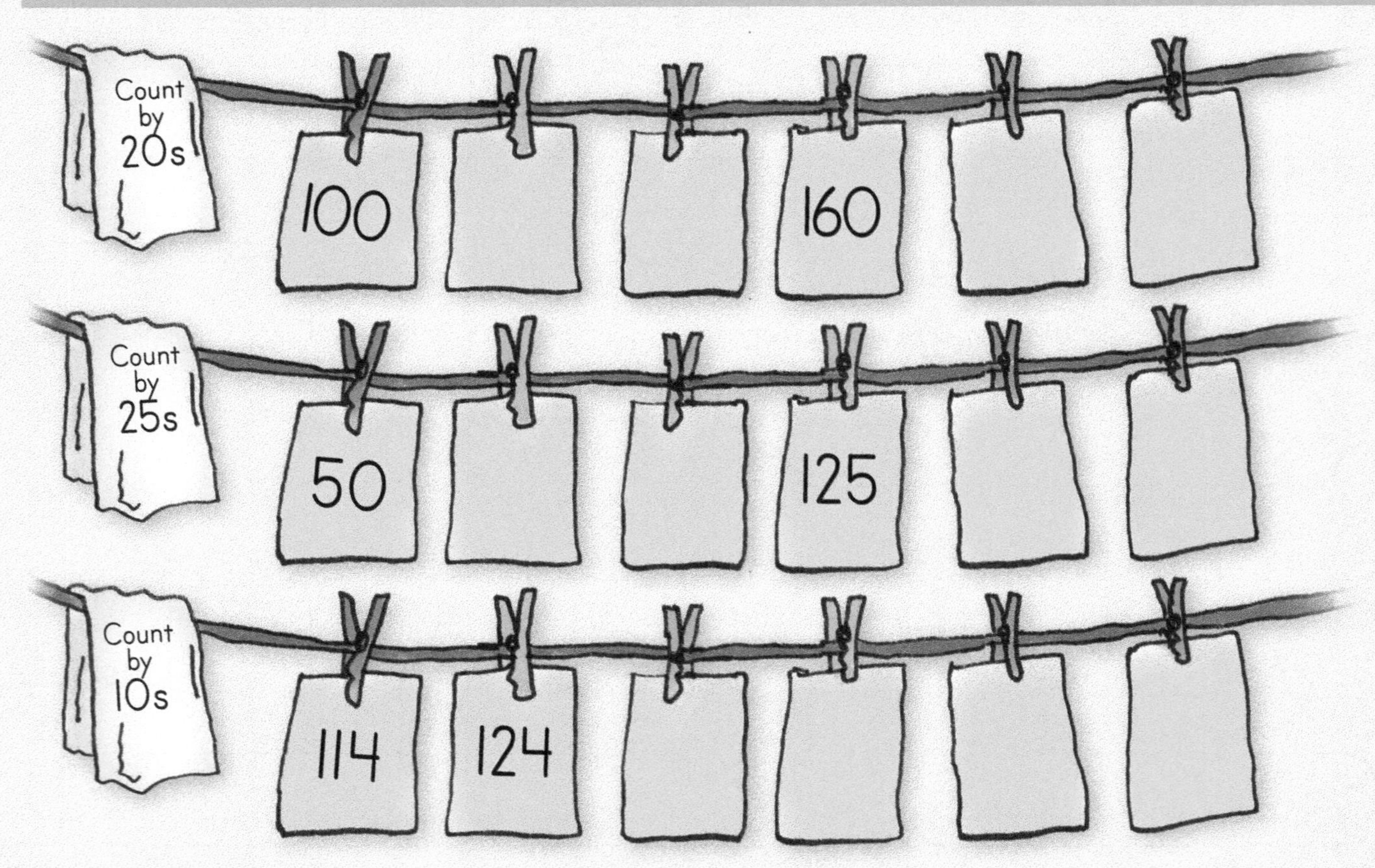

Match. Each ruler is 1 foot long.

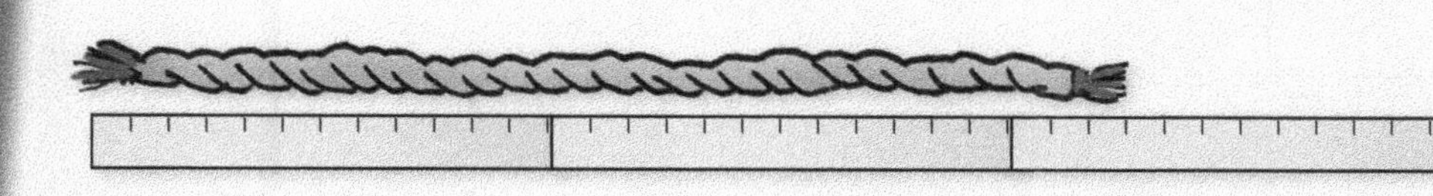

1 foot, 6 inches

2 feet, 3 inches

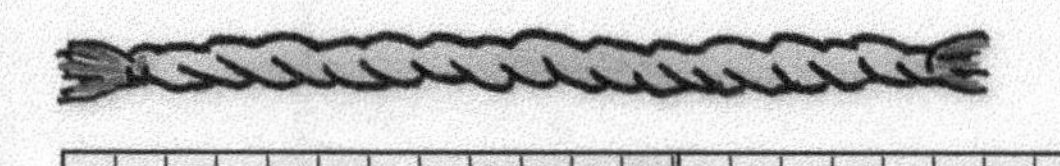

1 foot, 1 inch

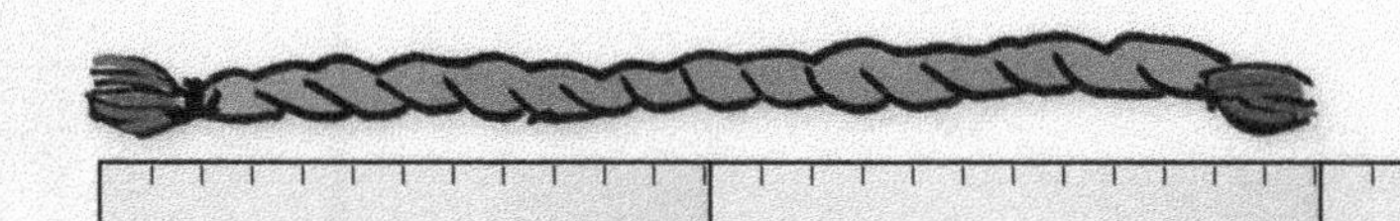

3 feet

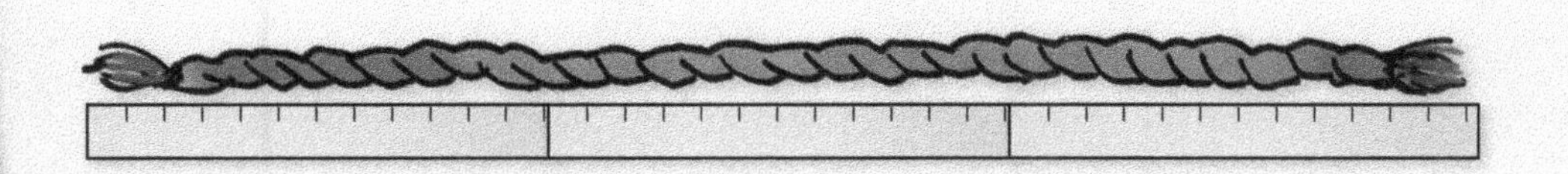

2 feet, 11 inches

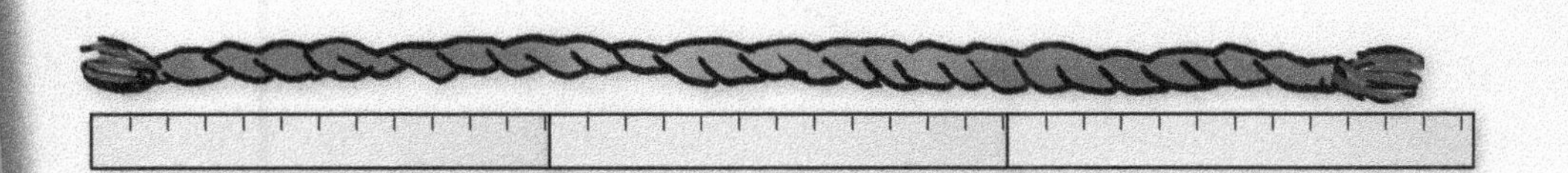

2 feet

Complete.

43 - 9 = ☐

62 - 8 = ☐

91 - 3 = ☐

76 - 7 = ☐

84 - 6 = ☐

55 - 9 = ☐

43 + 9 = ☐

62 + 8 = ☐

91 + 3 = ☐

76 + 7 = ☐

84 + 6 = ☐

55 + 9 = ☐

Use the key to color the hearts.

Complete.

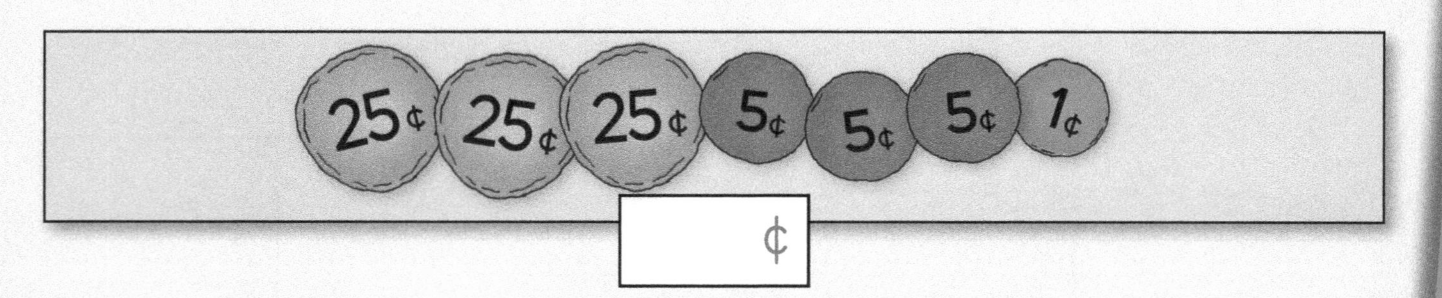

Circle the more sensible measurement for each item.

Height of a lamp

2 inches	2 feet

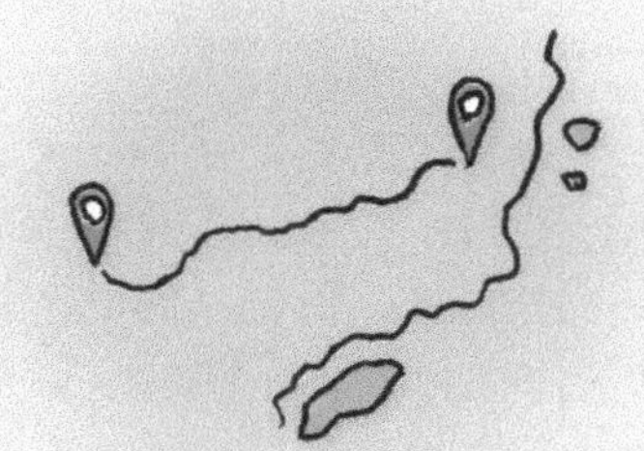

Distance between cities

50 yards	50 miles

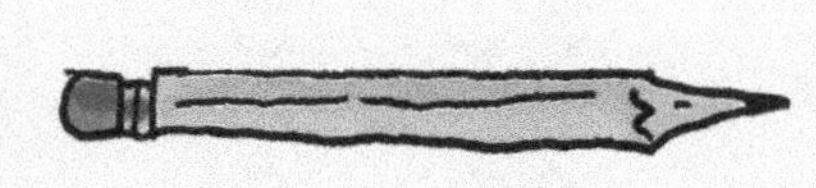

Length of a pencil

8 inches	8 feet

Height of a flagpole

30 inches	30 feet

Length of a bed

2 feet	2 yards

Length of a river

175 yards	175 miles

Length of a swimming pool

25 yards	25 miles

Height of a grown giraffe

5 feet	5 yards

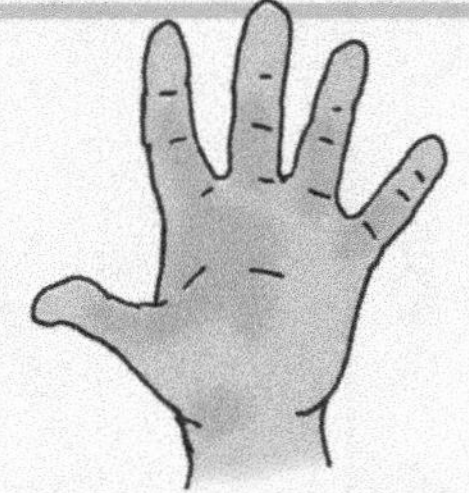

Width of your hand

5 inches	5 feet

Height of a tree

45 inches	45 feet

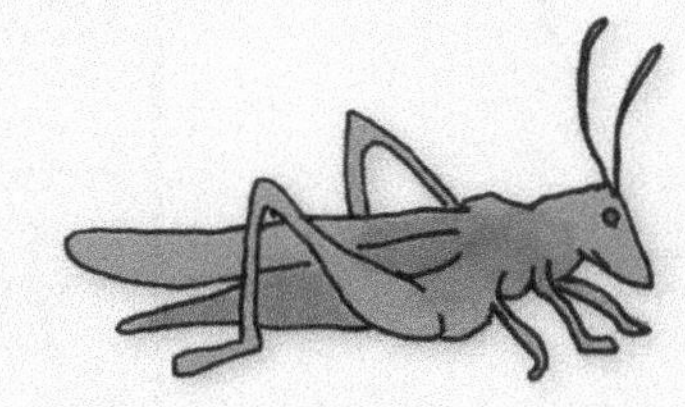

Length of a grasshopper

3 inches	3 feet

Length of a whale

82 inches	82 feet

Complete.

$70 - 5 =$ ☐

$80 - 3 =$ ☐

$30 - 8 =$ ☐

$50 - 4 =$ ☐

$60 - 9 =$ ☐

$40 - 7 =$ ☐

$71 - 5 =$ ☐

$81 - 3 =$ ☐

$31 - 8 =$ ☐

$51 - 4 =$ ☐

$61 - 9 =$ ☐

$41 - 7 =$ ☐

Cooper made a line graph of the high temperature each day. Use the graph to complete the chart.

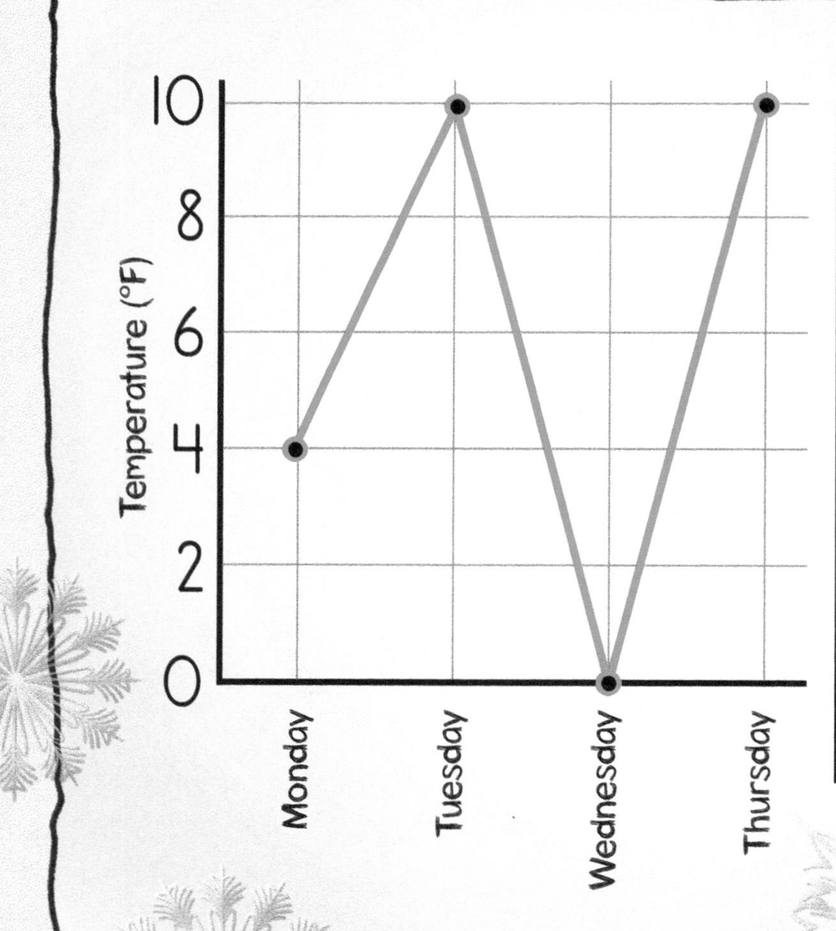

Day	High Temperature
Monday	
Tuesday	
Wednesday	
Thursday	

Use a ruler to measure the sticks in centimeters.

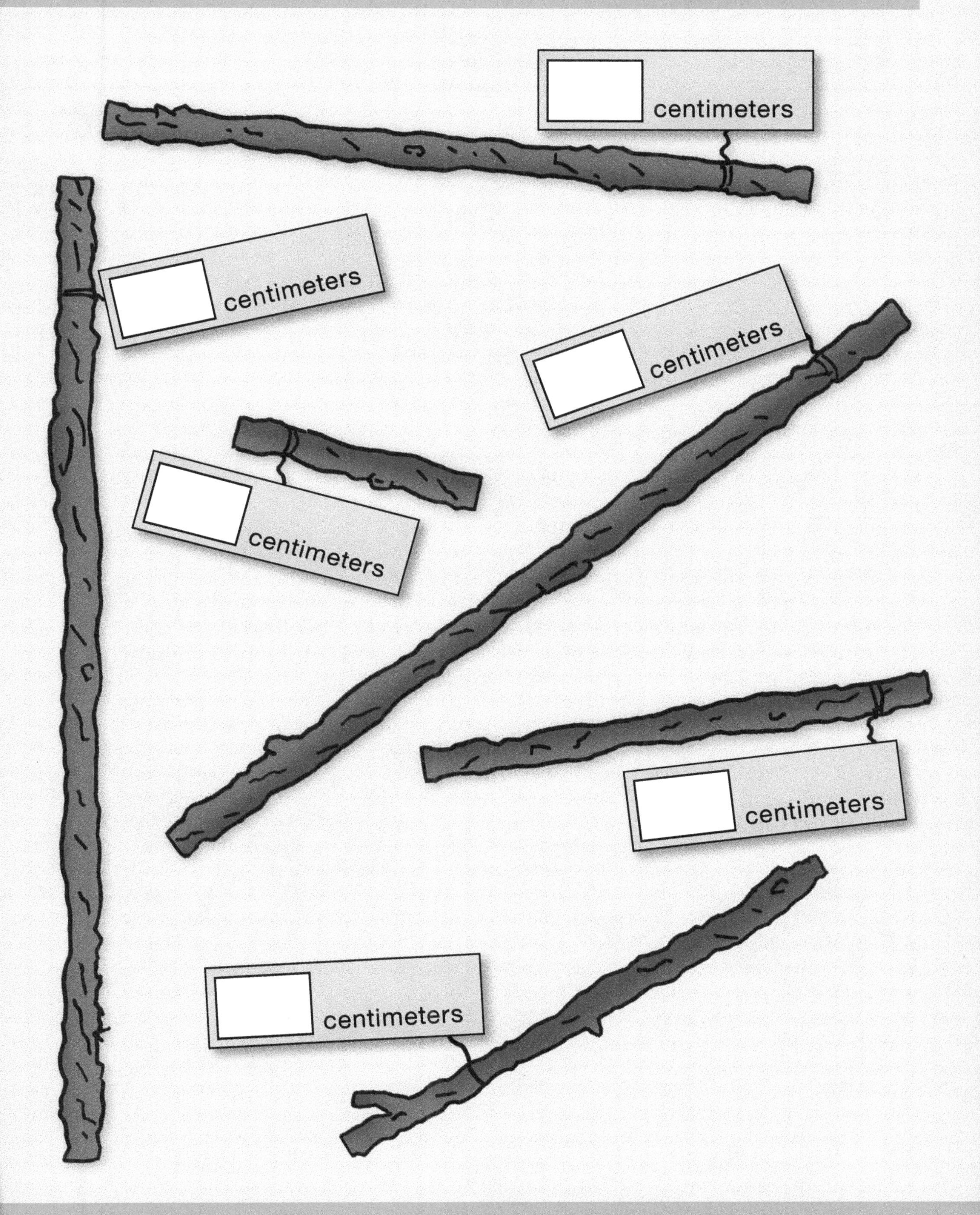

Match.

95 - 41	22	61 - 24
68 - 19	37	74 - 20
80 - 58	49	90 - 41
73 - 36	54	87 - 65

Solve.

Alice has $24. The skates cost $30. How much more money does she need to buy them?

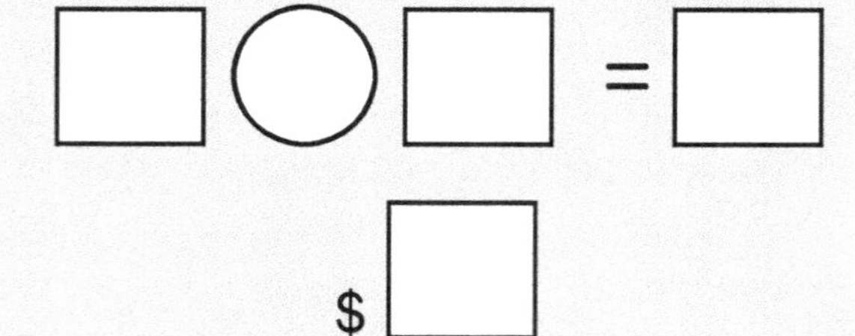

Simon has $9. The sled costs $23. How much more money does he need to buy it?

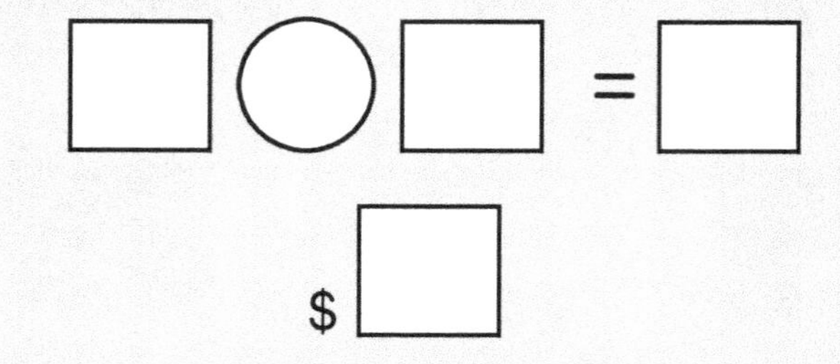

Use a ruler to measure the school supplies in centimeters.

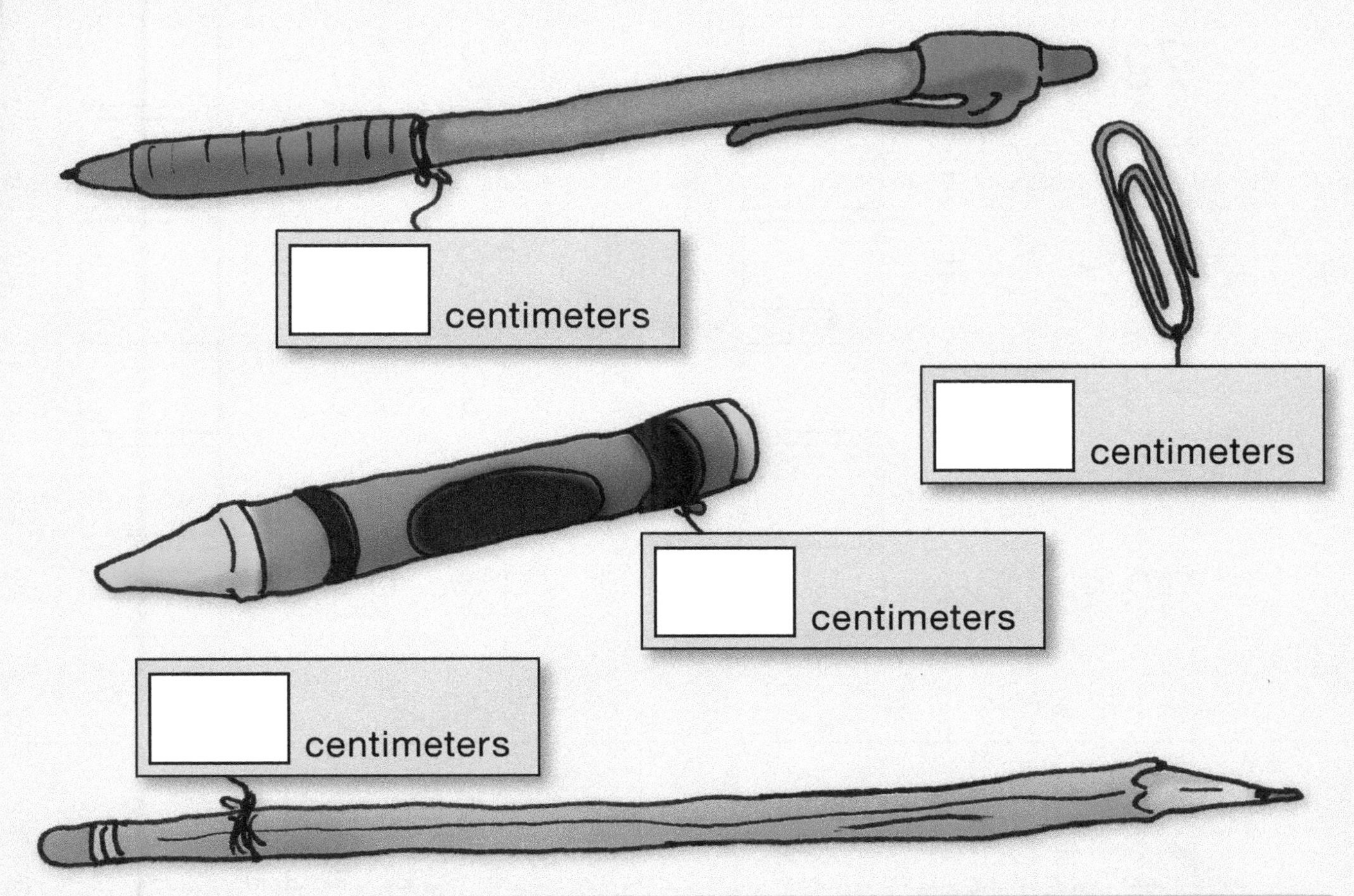

Use the measurements to complete the equations and answer the questions.

How much longer is the crayon than the paper clip?

☐ ◯ ☐ = ☐

☐ centimeters

How much longer is the pen than the paper clip?

☐ ◯ ☐ = ☐

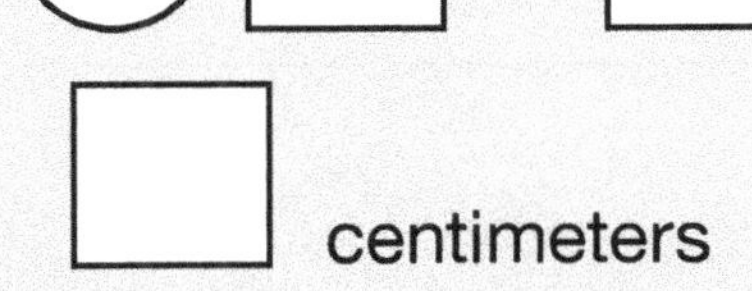

centimeters

How much shorter is the crayon than the pencil?

☐ ◯ ☐ = ☐

☐ centimeters

How much shorter is the pen than the pencil?

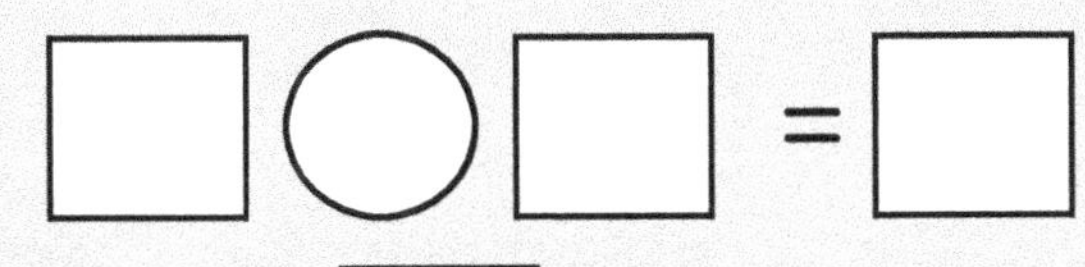

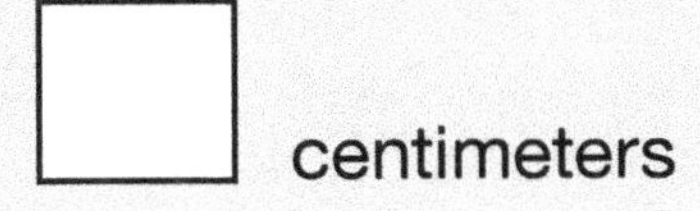

centimeters

Complete.

$73 - 23 =$ ☐

$72 - 23 =$ ☐

$71 - 23 =$ ☐

$83 - 23 =$ ☐

$83 - 22 =$ ☐

$83 - 21 =$ ☐

$63 - 23 =$ ☐

$53 - 23 =$ ☐

$43 - 23 =$ ☐

$93 - 23 =$ ☐

$93 - 33 =$ ☐

$93 - 43 =$ ☐

Write the value of the base-ten blocks.

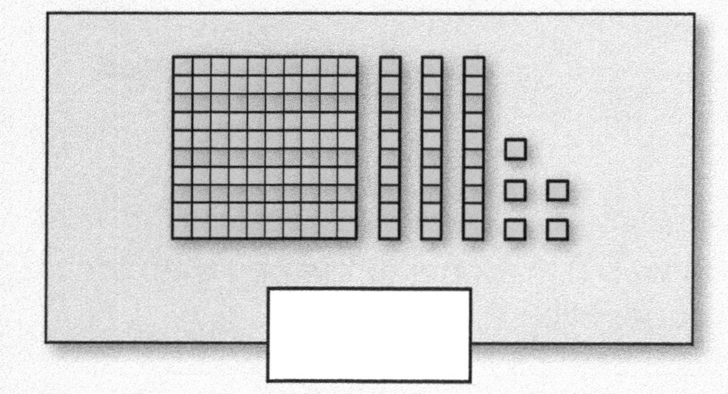

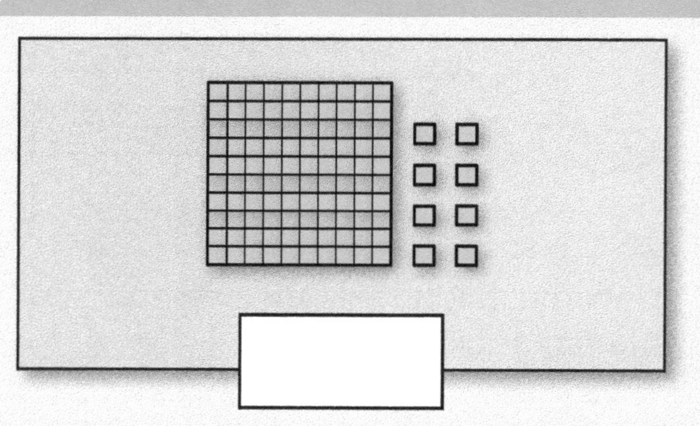

Complete. Use a decimal point and a dollar sign.

Circle the more sensible measurement for each item.

Height of a chair

1 centimeter | 1 meter

length of a hike

5 meters | 5 kilometers

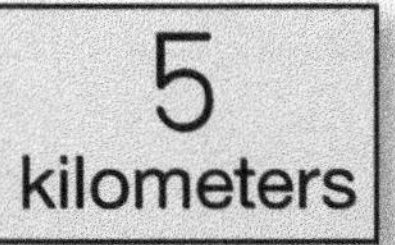

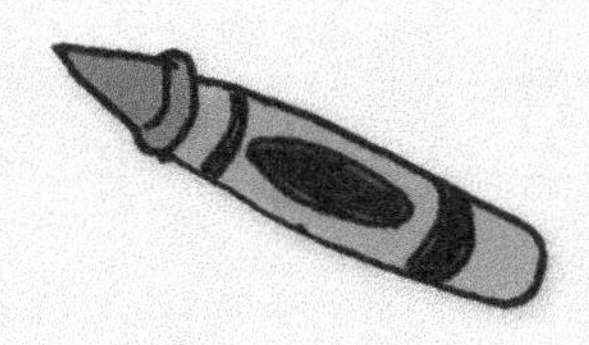

Length of a crayon

7 centimeters | 7 meters

Height of a house

6 meters | 6 kilometers

Length of a bathtub

150 centimeters | 150 meters

Height of a book

20 centimeters | 20 meters

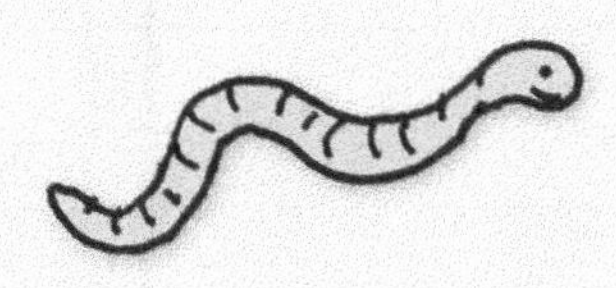

Length of a worm

12 centimeters | 12 meters

Length of a swimming pool

25 meters | 25 kilometers

Height of an elephant

2 centimeters | 2 meters

Length of a bus

12 centimeters | 12 meters

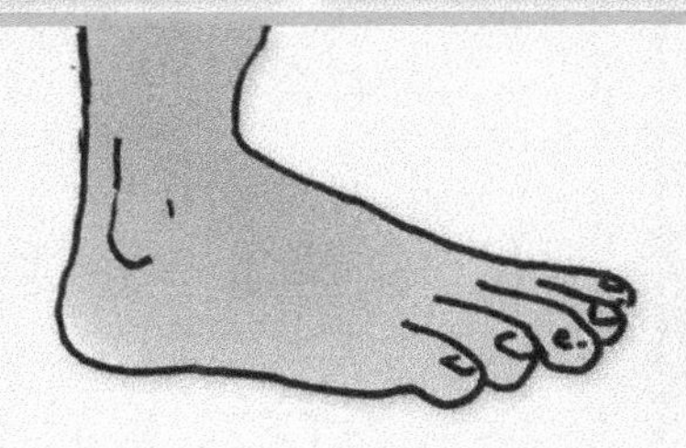

Length of your foot

18 centimeters | 18 meters

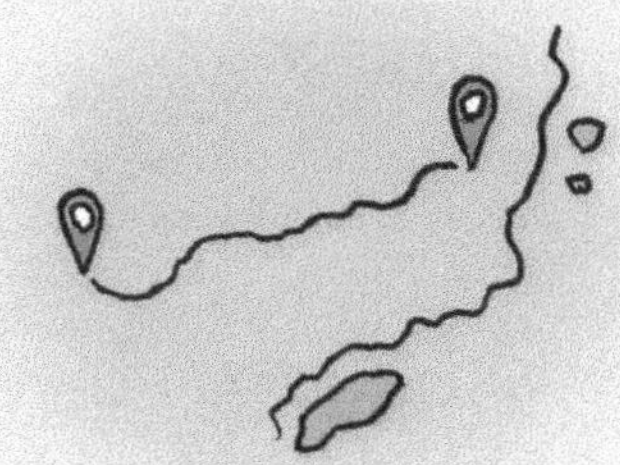

Distance between cities

40 meters | 40 kilometers

Complete.

29 → +6 → ☐ → +8 → ☐ → +8 → ☐ → +9 → 60

74 → -12 → ☐ → -12 → ☐ → -12 → ☐ → -12 → 26

85 → +4 → ☐ → +5 → ☐ → +5 → ☐ → +1 → 100

Connor, Santiago and Caroline played a game. Use their scorecard to answer the questions.

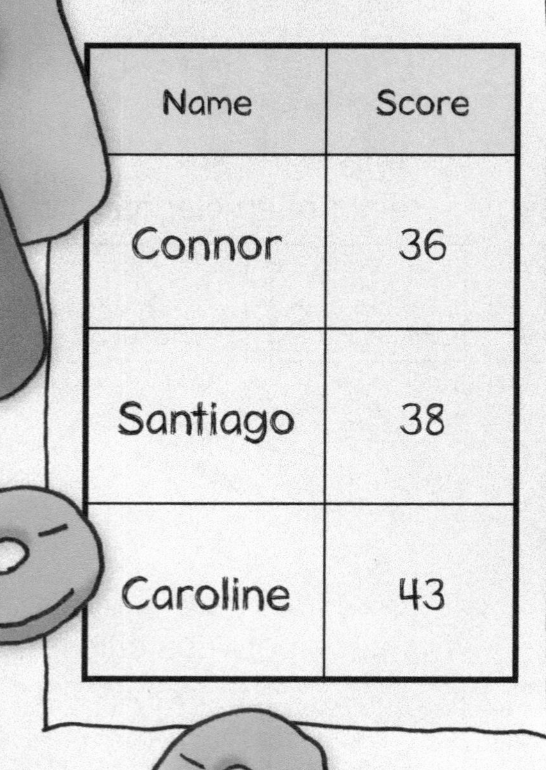

Scorecard

Name	Score
Connor	36
Santiago	38
Caroline	43

Who scored the most points? ☐

Who scored the fewest points? ☐

How many more points did Santiago score than Connor?

☐ ◯ ☐ = ☐

☐ points

How many more points did Caroline score than Santiago?

☐ ◯ ☐ = ☐

☐ points

Solve. Write your own equation to match each word problem.

Claire was 29 inches tall. Then, she grew 3 inches. How tall is she now?

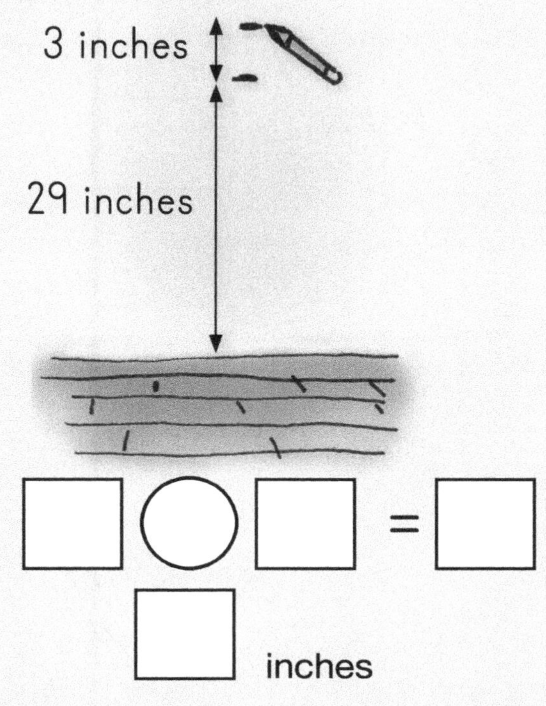

☐ ◯ ☐ = ☐

☐ inches

James has a ribbon 34 centimeters long. He uses 12 centimeters for a craft project. How many centimeters are left?

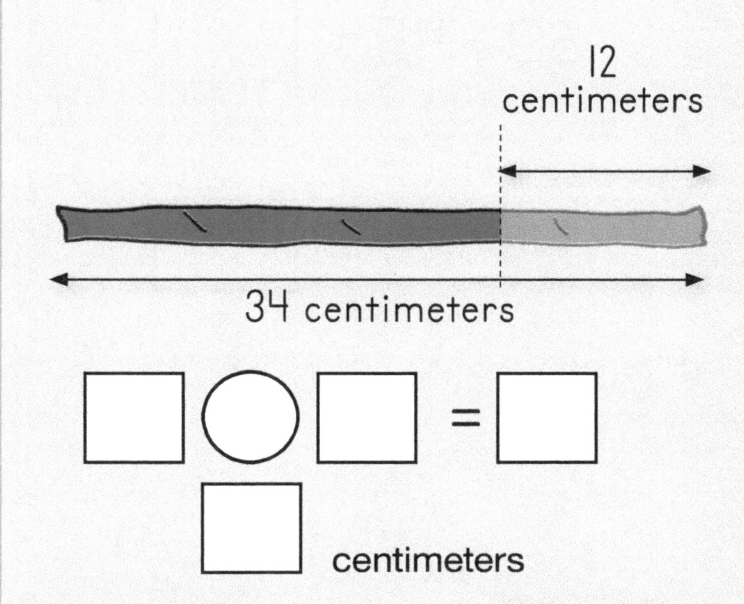

☐ ◯ ☐ = ☐

☐ centimeters

Caden's plant is 13 inches tall. Olivia's plant is 17 inches tall. How much taller is Olivia's plant than Caden's?

☐ ◯ ☐ = ☐

☐ inches

Amir's family hiked 2 kilometers on the red trail, 3 kilometers on the green trail, and 1 kilometer on the blue trail. How far did they hike in all?

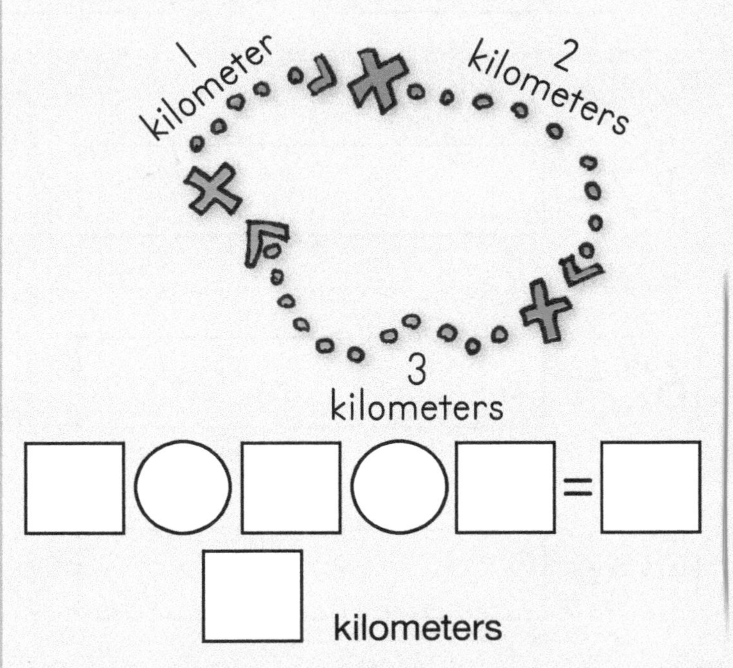

☐ ◯ ☐ ◯ ☐ = ☐

☐ kilometers

Complete.

42 - 26 = ☐	54 - 17 = ☐
60 - 45 = ☐	81 - 63 = ☐
93 - 34 = ☐	72 - 52 = ☐

Write the time.

Write the expanded form for each number.

87 = 80 + 7	134 = ☐
162 = ☐	151 = ☐
199 = ☐	109 = ☐

See the Instructor Guide for directions.

Chocolate Shop Packing Directions

1. Add the squares. 

2. If there are more than 9 squares, trade 10 squares for 1 bar.

3. Add the bars. 

	Bars	Squares
Order 1	4	8
Order 2	3	4
Total		

	Bars	Squares
Order 1	2	6
Order 2	6	7
Total		

	Bars	Squares
Order 1	5	9
Order 2	2	1
Total		

	Bars	Squares
Order 1	3	3
Order 2	6	6
Total		

	Bars	Squares
Order 1	8	2
Order 2		9
Total		

	Bars	Squares
Order 1	3	5
Order 2	5	9
Total		

Use a ruler to measure the straws in inches.

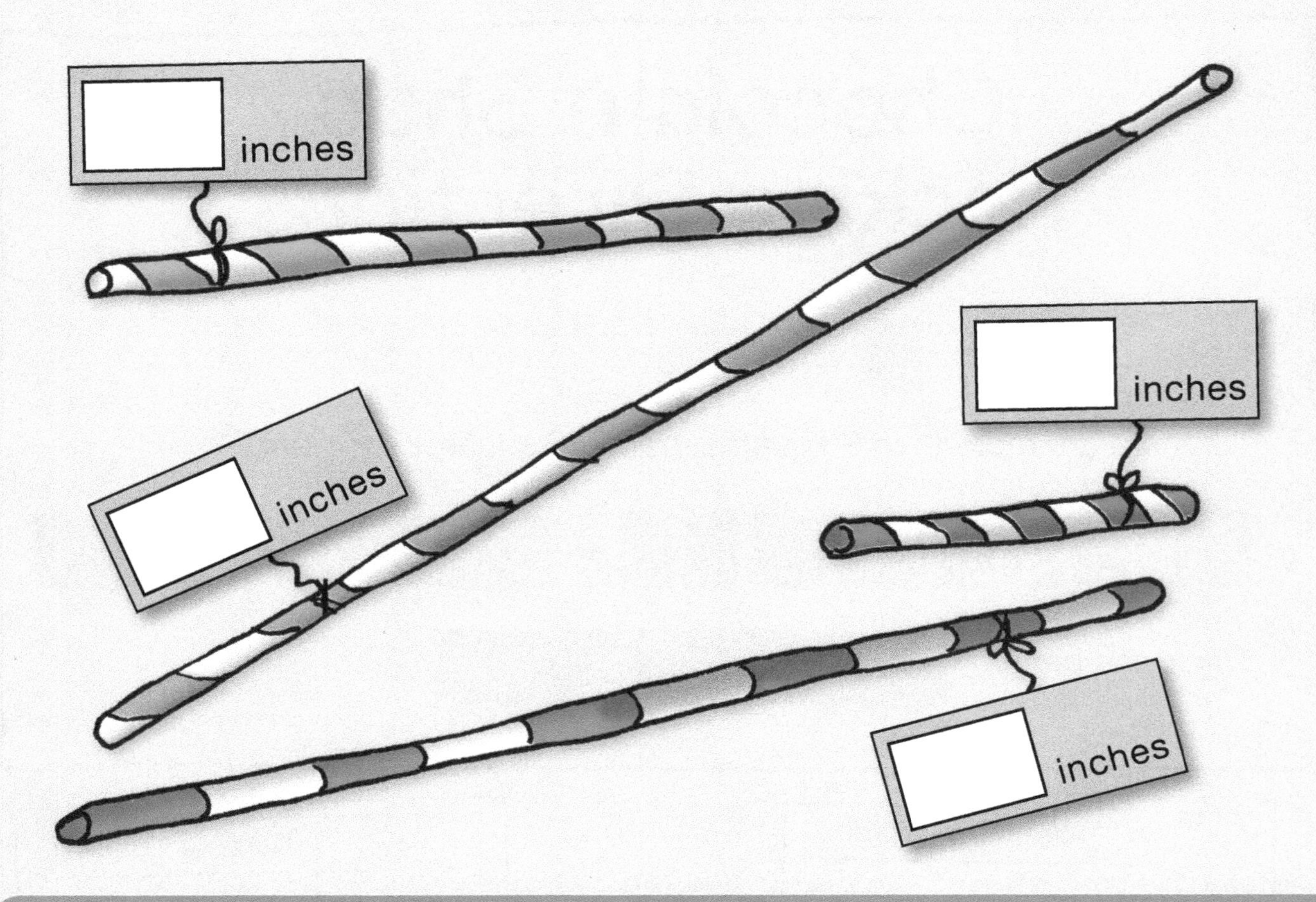

Solve.

The pink ribbon is 15 centimeters long. The red ribbon is 8 centimeters longer than the pink ribbon. How long is the red ribbon?

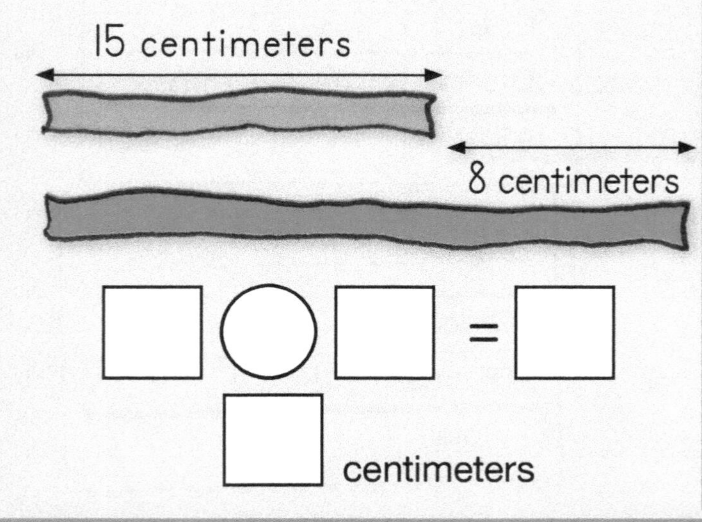

The purple ribbon is 34 centimeters long. The white ribbon is 10 centimeters shorter than the purple ribbon. How long is the white ribbon?

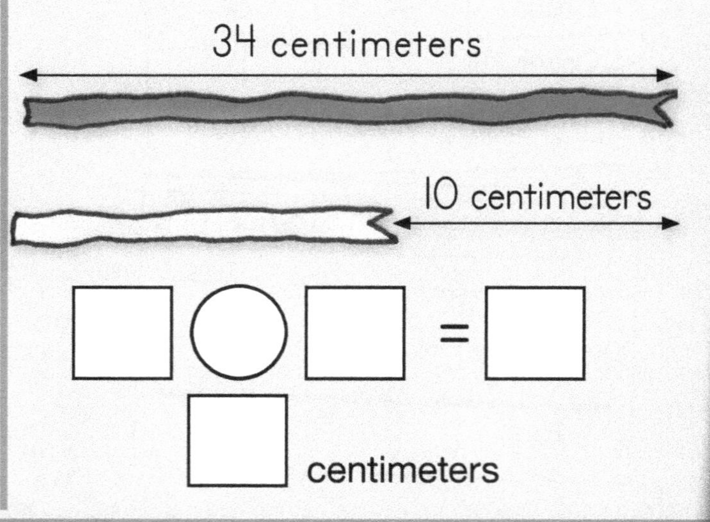

See the Instructor Guide for directions.

The Addition Algorithm

* * * Start with the ones-place.

* * * Follow the steps for all the places.

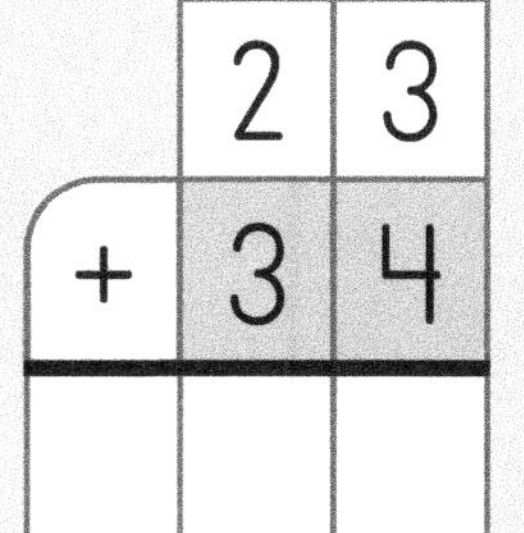

	2	3
+	3	4

	2	9
+	4	3

	3	5
+	2	5

	4	6
+		5

	2	8
+	4	5

	3	6
+	2	4

	5	2
+	4	6

	6	8
+		4

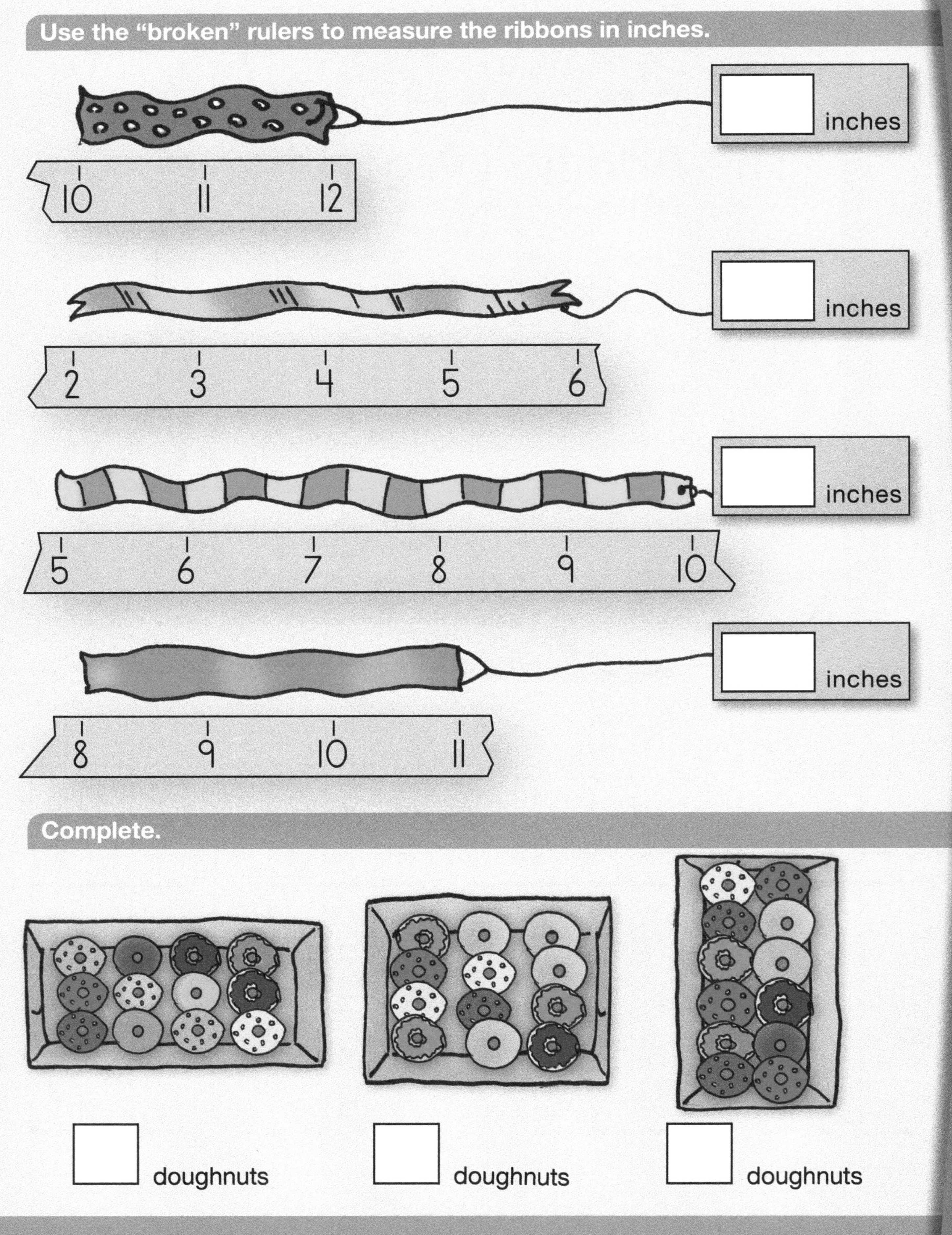
Use the "broken" rulers to measure the ribbons in inches.
inches
10
11
12
inches
2
3
4
5
6
inches
5
6
7
8
9
10
inches
8
9
10
11
Complete.
doughnuts
doughnuts
doughnuts

See the Instructor Guide for directions.

$\begin{array}{r} 71 \\ +\ 53 \\ \hline \end{array}$ $\begin{array}{r} 92 \\ +\ 35 \\ \hline \end{array}$ $\begin{array}{r} 37 \\ +\ 95 \\ \hline \end{array}$ $\begin{array}{r} 64 \\ +\ 43 \\ \hline \end{array}$

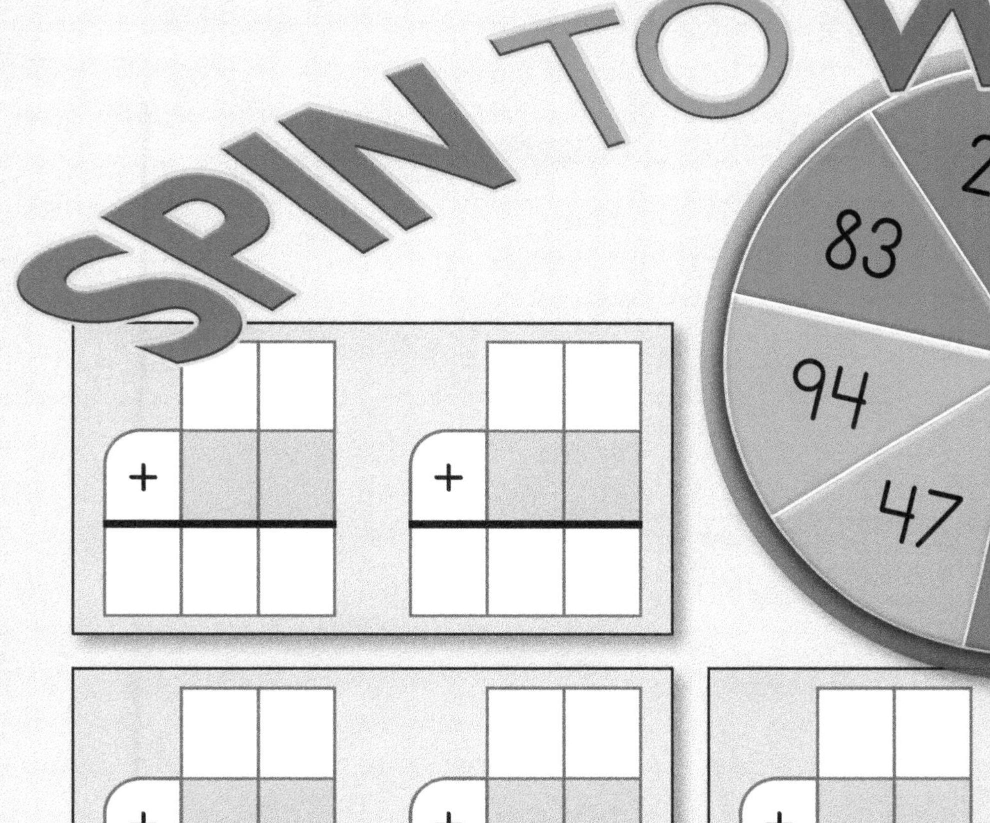

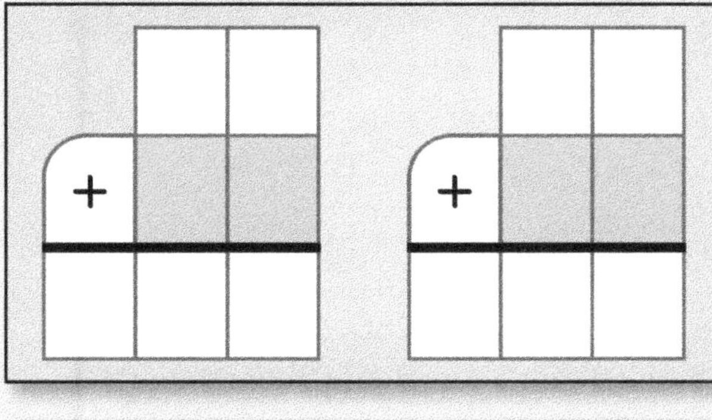

+ +

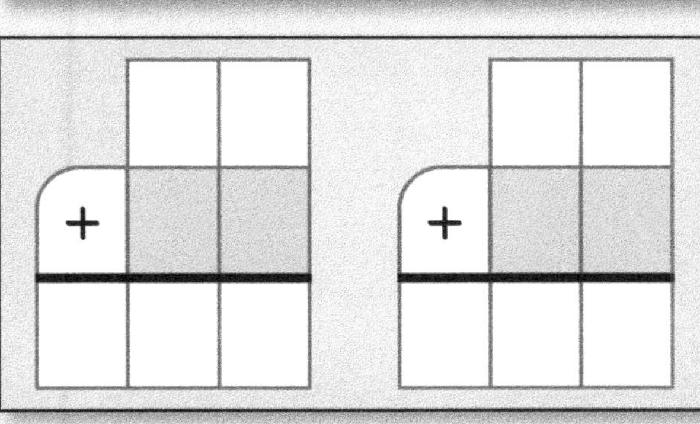

+ +

Complete.

1 foot = ☐ inches

1 yard = ☐ feet

1 yard = ☐ inches

1 day = ☐ hours

1 hour = ☐ minutes

1 minute = ☐ seconds

Match. Each ruler is 1 foot long.

2 feet, 4 inches

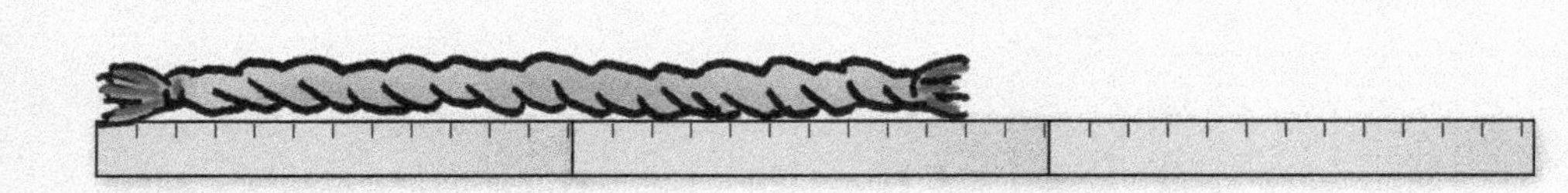

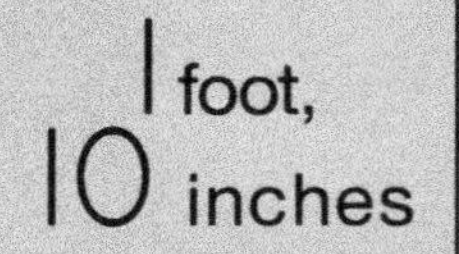

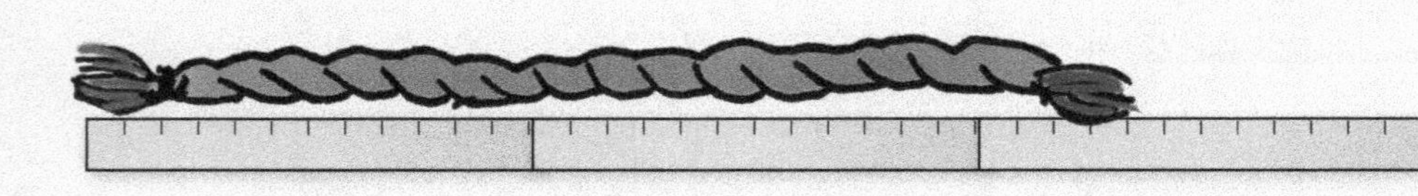

2 feet, 10 inches

Count by 25s to connect the dots in order.

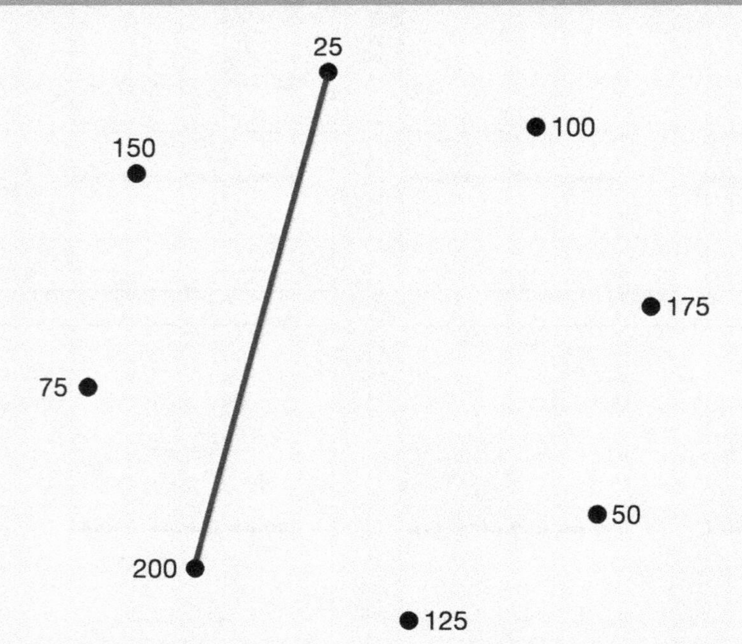

See the Instructor Guide for directions.

Two-Digit Plus Two-Digit War

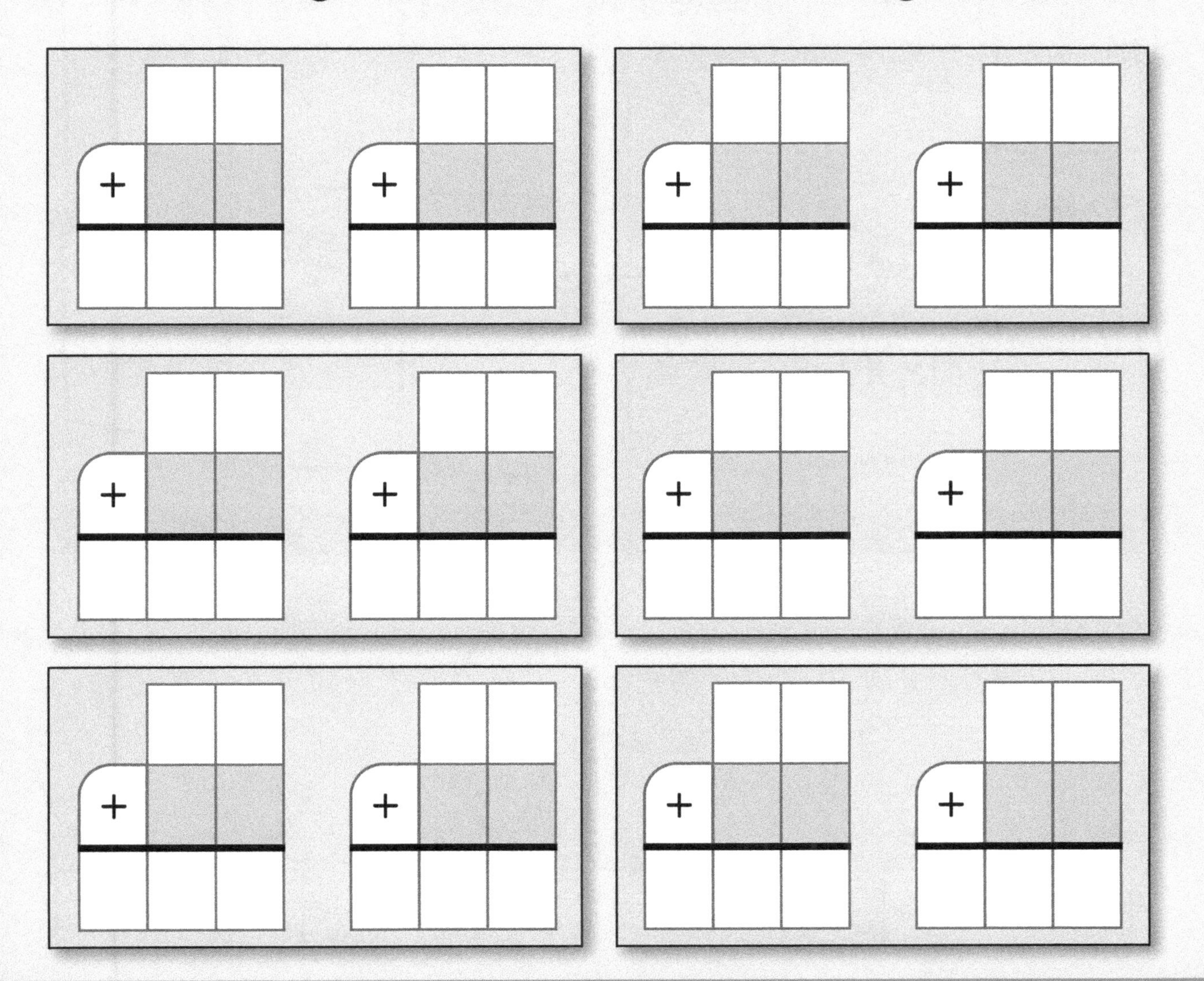

Choose the more sensible measurement for each item.

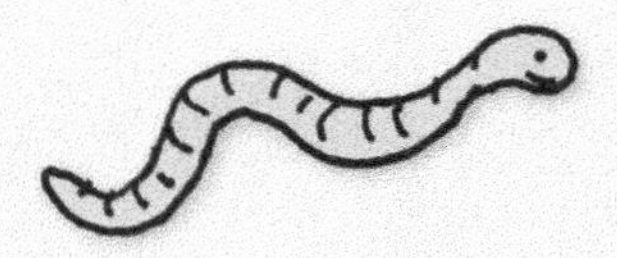

Length of a worm

6 inches	6 feet

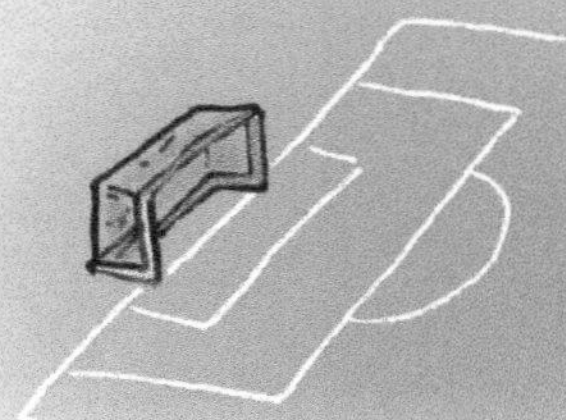

Length of a soccer field

100 yards	100 miles

Height of a house

30 feet	30 yards

Complete the sequences.

Write the time.

See the Instructor Guide for directions.

	7	6
+	1	9

	3	5
+	8	1

	6	2
+	5	3

	8	5
+		7

Snowball Fight

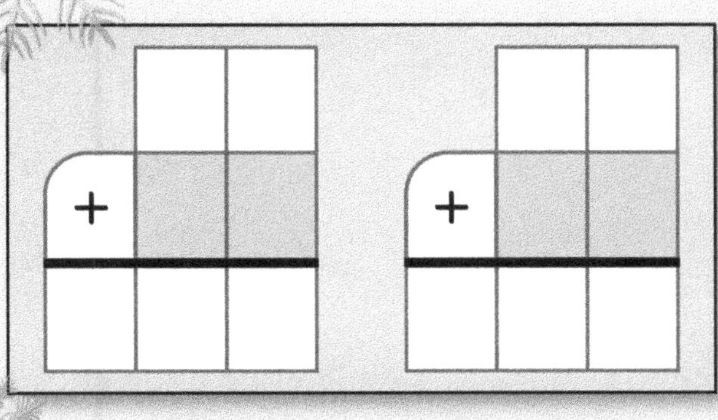

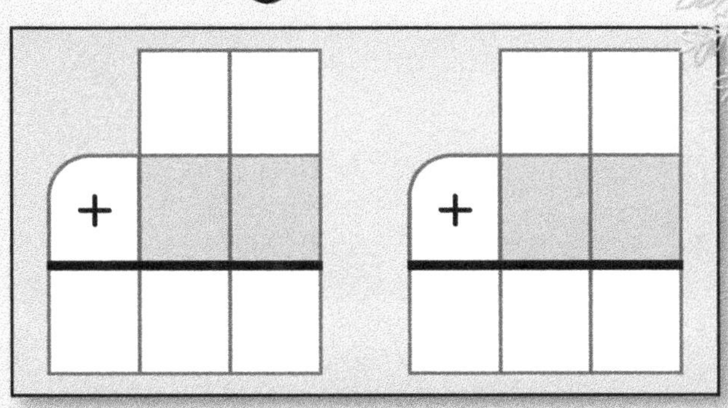

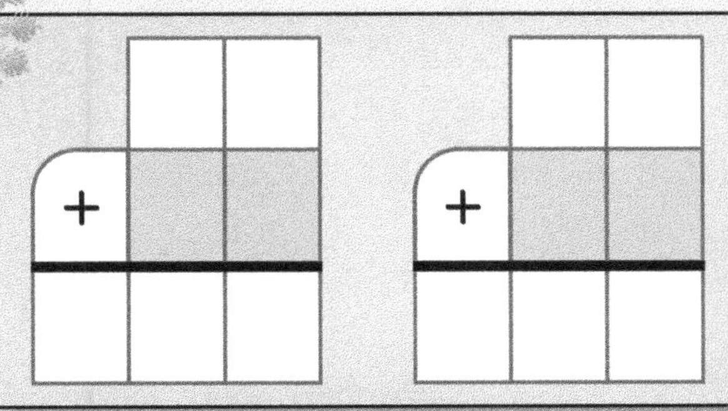

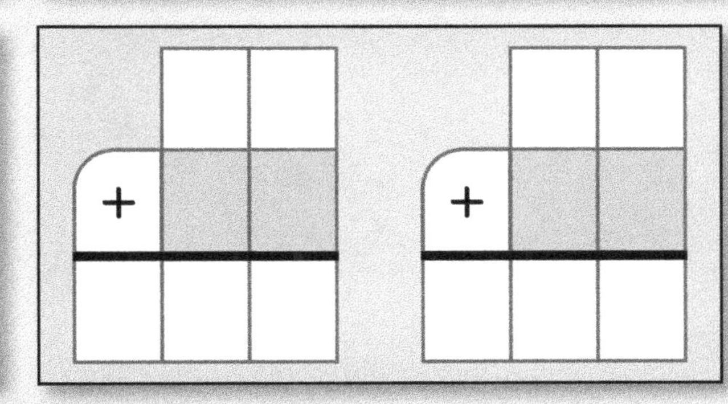

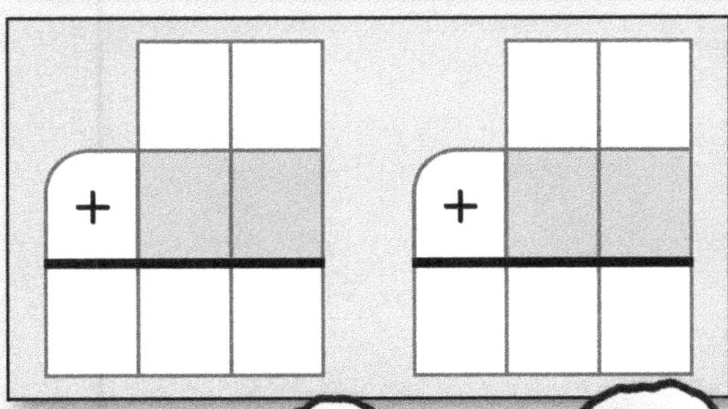

Use a ruler to measure the sticks in centimeters.

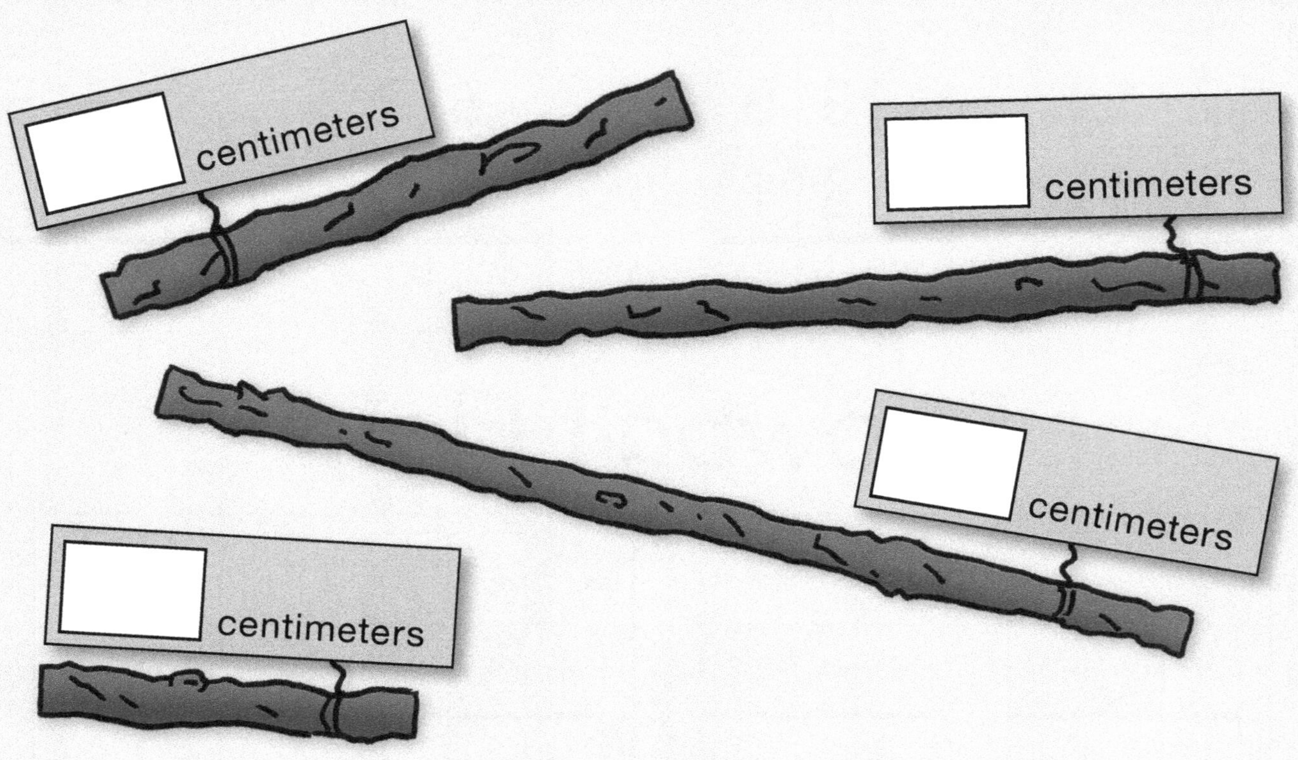

Write how much money is in each coin purse. Use a dollar sign and decimal point.

See the Instructor Guide for directions.

	5	6
+	6	8

	9	4
+	5	7

	4	9
+	5	1

	7	7
+	4	1

Connect the Boxes

	7	3
+	3	4

	9	8
+	4	0

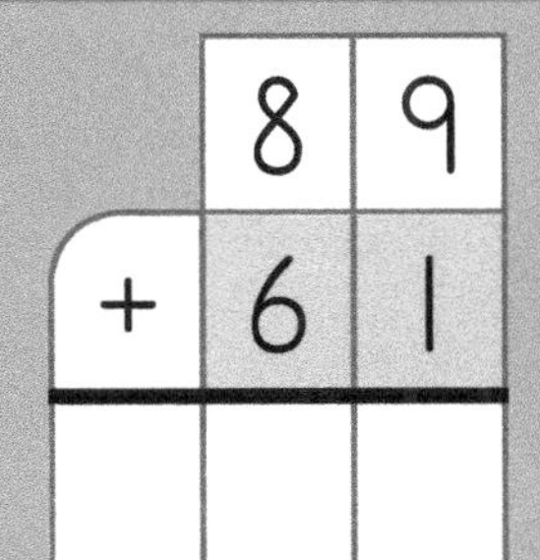

	8	9
+	6	1

	9	6
+	1	7

	6	6
+	7	8

	9	3
+	4	1

	8	1
+	6	3

	7	4
+	6	9

	8	0
+	5	6

	9	7
+	3	2

	9	9
+		8

	3	1
+	7	0

	2	2
+	5	8

	5	5
+	8	4

	8	8
+	6	2

	6	5
+	9	1

Choose the more sensible measurement for each item.

Height of a snowman

1 centimeter	1 meter

Length of a sledding hill

100 meters	100 kilometers

Height of a mug

9 meters	9 centimeters

Label the numbers on the number line.

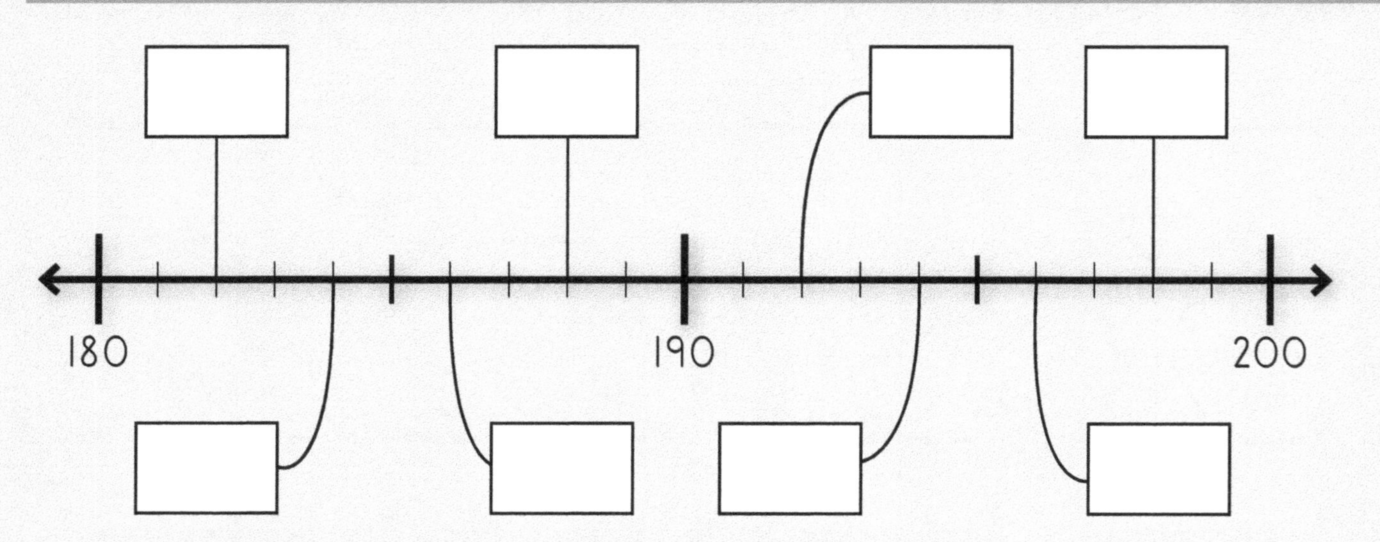

Complete.

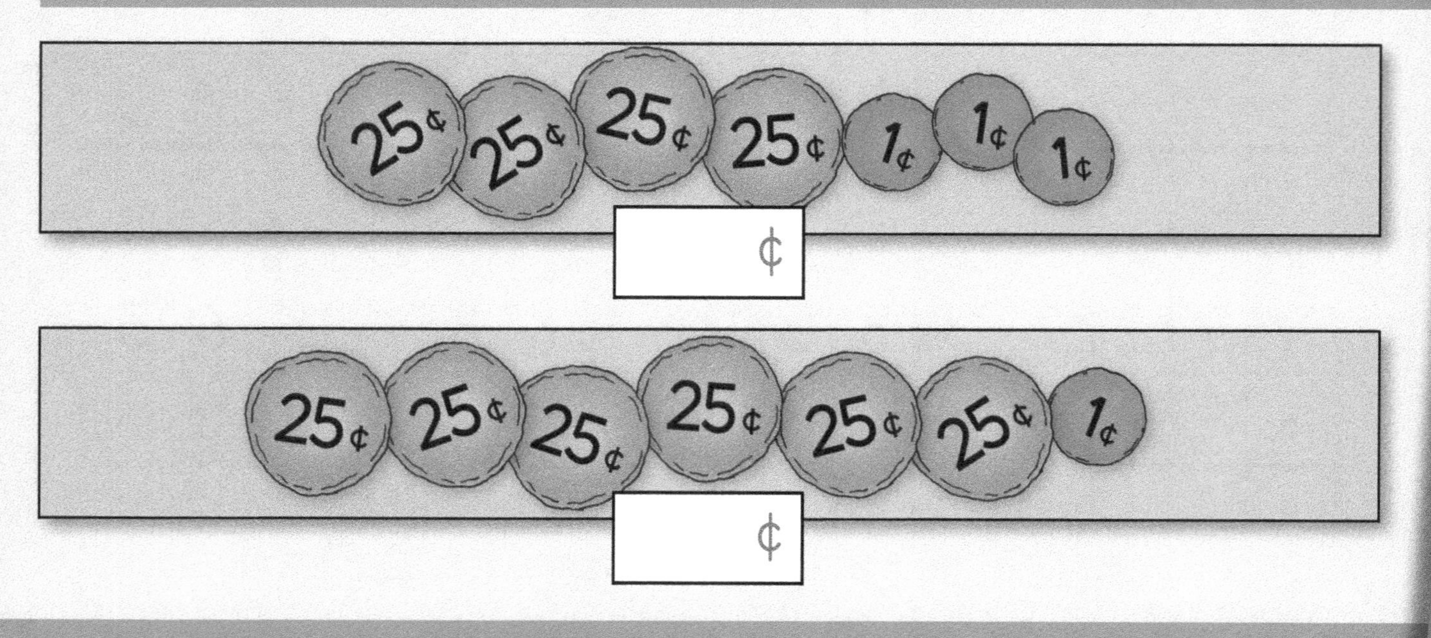

See the Instructor Guide for directions.

	3	7
+	4	4

	5	7
+	4	7

	3	8
+	9	5

	7	7
+	8	8

	5	5
+	2	5

	4	3
+	5	2

	6	5
+		7

	4	6
+	8	9

	1	6
+	8	6

	4	9
+	8	1

	7	9
+		8

	6	2
+	3	8

FINISH

Write an equation to match. Then, solve.

Roberto's foot is 8 inches long.
Mom's foot is 10 inches long.
How much longer is Mom's foot than Roberto's?

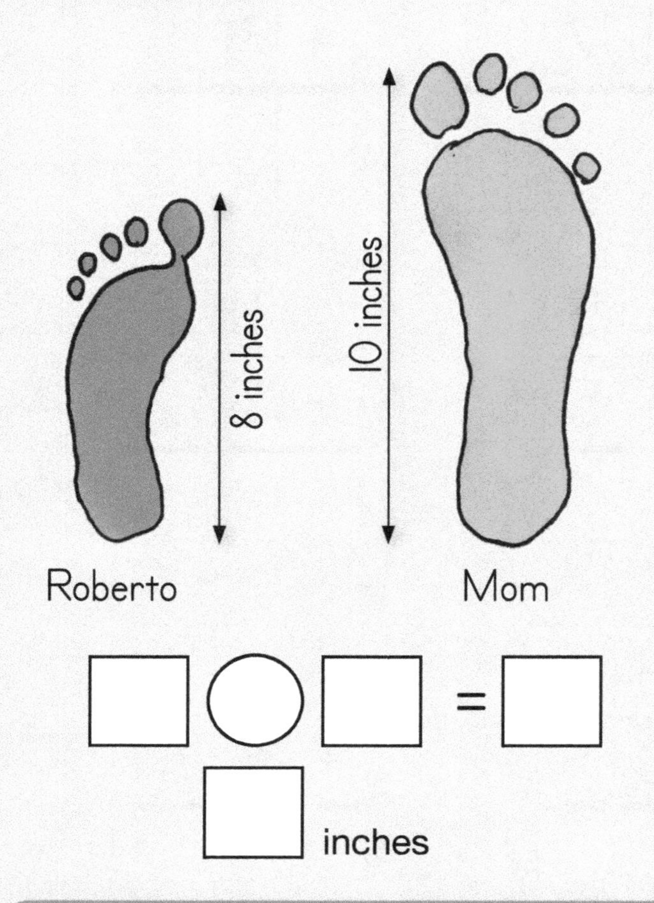

$\square \bigcirc \square = \square$

$\square$ inches

Charlotte's foot is 7 inches long.
Dad's foot is 12 inches long.
How much shorter is Charlotte's foot than Dad's?

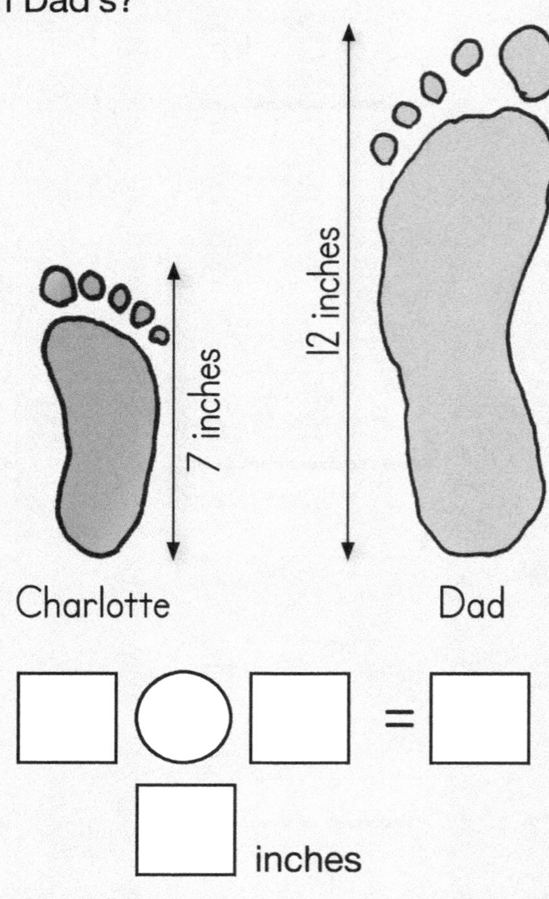

$\square \bigcirc \square = \square$

$\square$ inches

Complete each box with a number that makes the statement true.

$1 > \square$	$\square < 109$
$178 = \square$	$46 > \square$
$100 < \square$	$\square < 200$

Lincoln helped at the bake sale. He made a chart of how many cookies were sold. Use the chart to answer the questions.

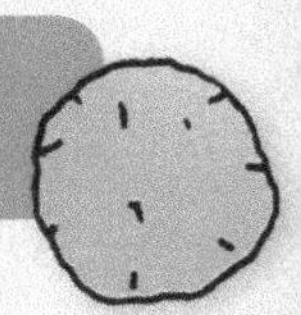

Type	Number Sold
Sugar	38
Peanut butter	43
Chocolate	59

How many sugar cookies and peanut butter cookies were sold?

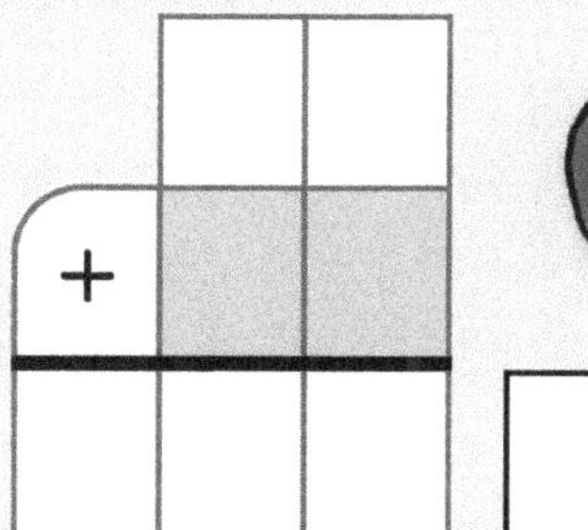

☐ cookies

How many sugar cookies and chocolate cookies were sold?

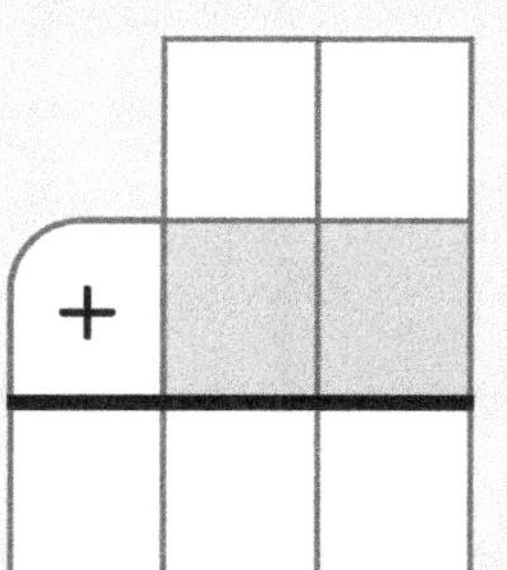

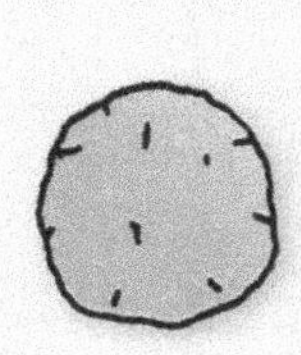

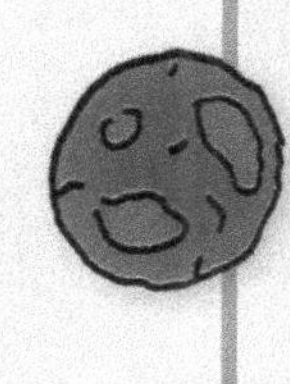

☐ cookies

How many peanut butter cookies and chocolate cookies were sold?

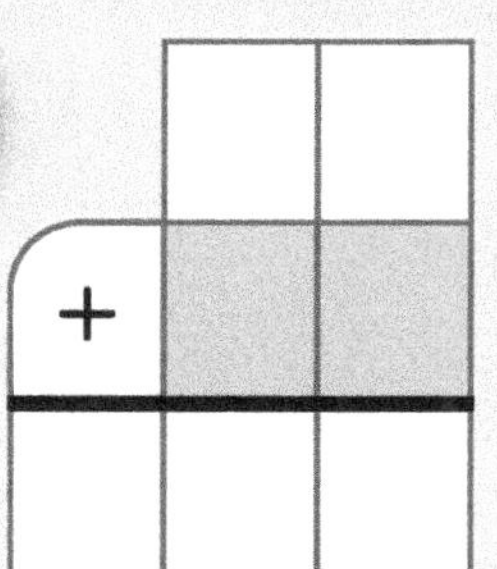

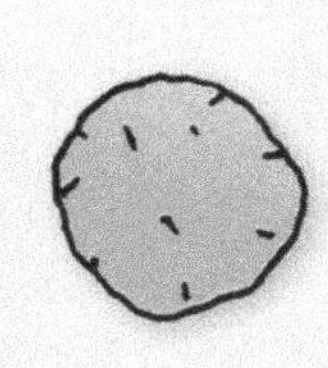

☐ cookies

Complete.

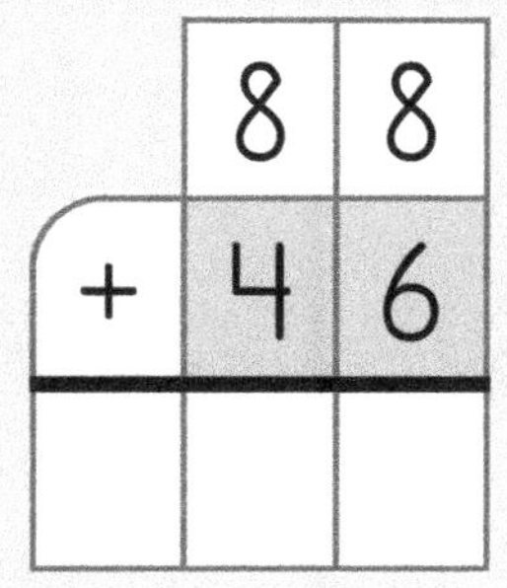

$$\begin{array}{r} 88 \\ +\ 46 \\ \hline \end{array}$$

$$\begin{array}{r} 49 \\ +\ 36 \\ \hline \end{array}$$

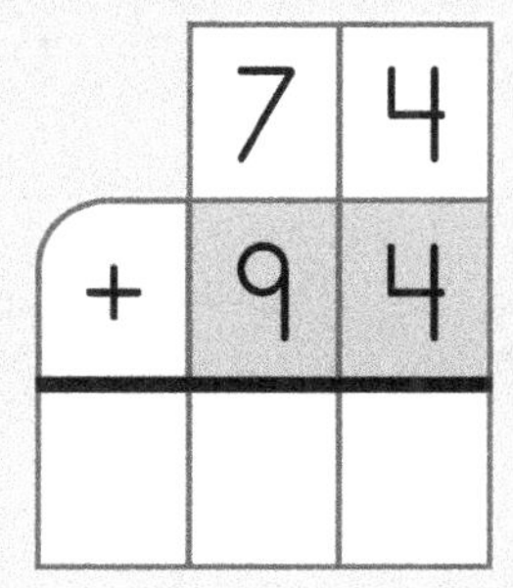

$$\begin{array}{r} 74 \\ +\ 94 \\ \hline \end{array}$$

$$\begin{array}{r} 56 \\ +\ 8 \\ \hline \end{array}$$

$$\begin{array}{r} 24 \\ +\ 67 \\ \hline \end{array}$$

$$\begin{array}{r} 74 \\ +\ 76 \\ \hline \end{array}$$

$$\begin{array}{r} 58 \\ +\ 80 \\ \hline \end{array}$$

$$\begin{array}{r} 42 \\ +\ 93 \\ \hline \end{array}$$

Write the time.

Complete the missing numbers in the sequences.

Copy the shape.

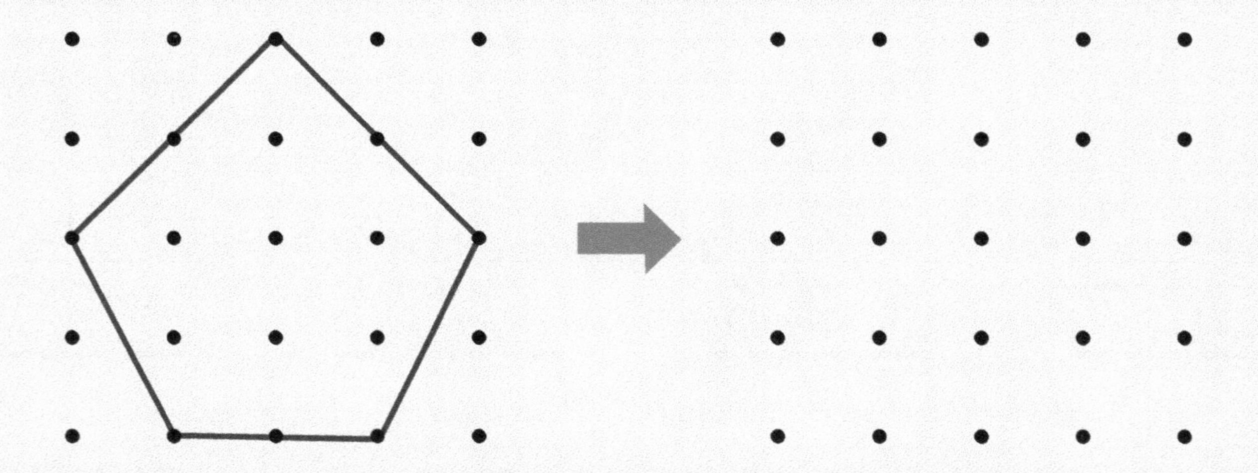

Circle the polygons. X the shapes that are not polygons.

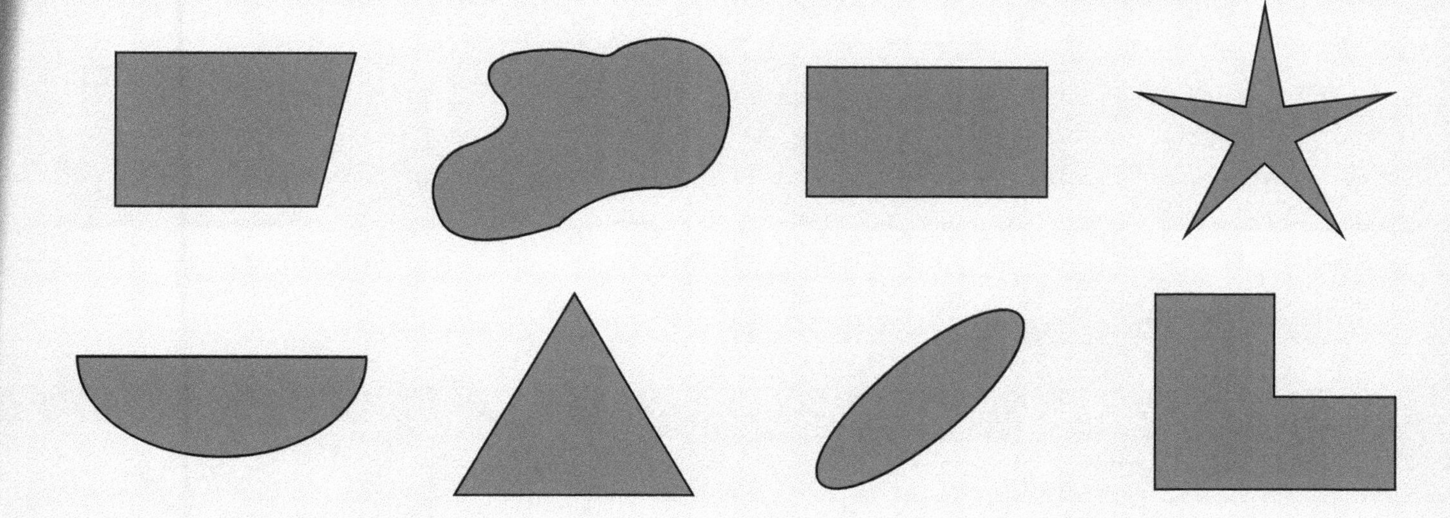

Match each polygon to its name.

Pentagon
(5 sides)

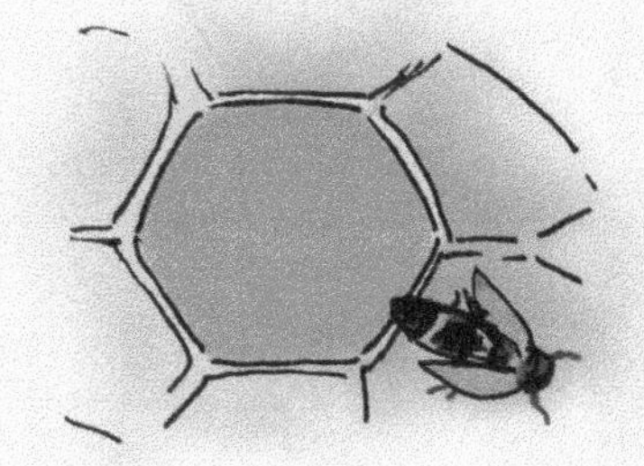

Triangle
(3 sides)

Hexagon
(6 sides)

Quadrilateral
(4 sides)

Octagon
(8 sides)

Complete.

	3	8
+	5	4

	7	6
+	4	1

	4	9
+		8

	9	9
+	3	2

Use the key to color the blocks.

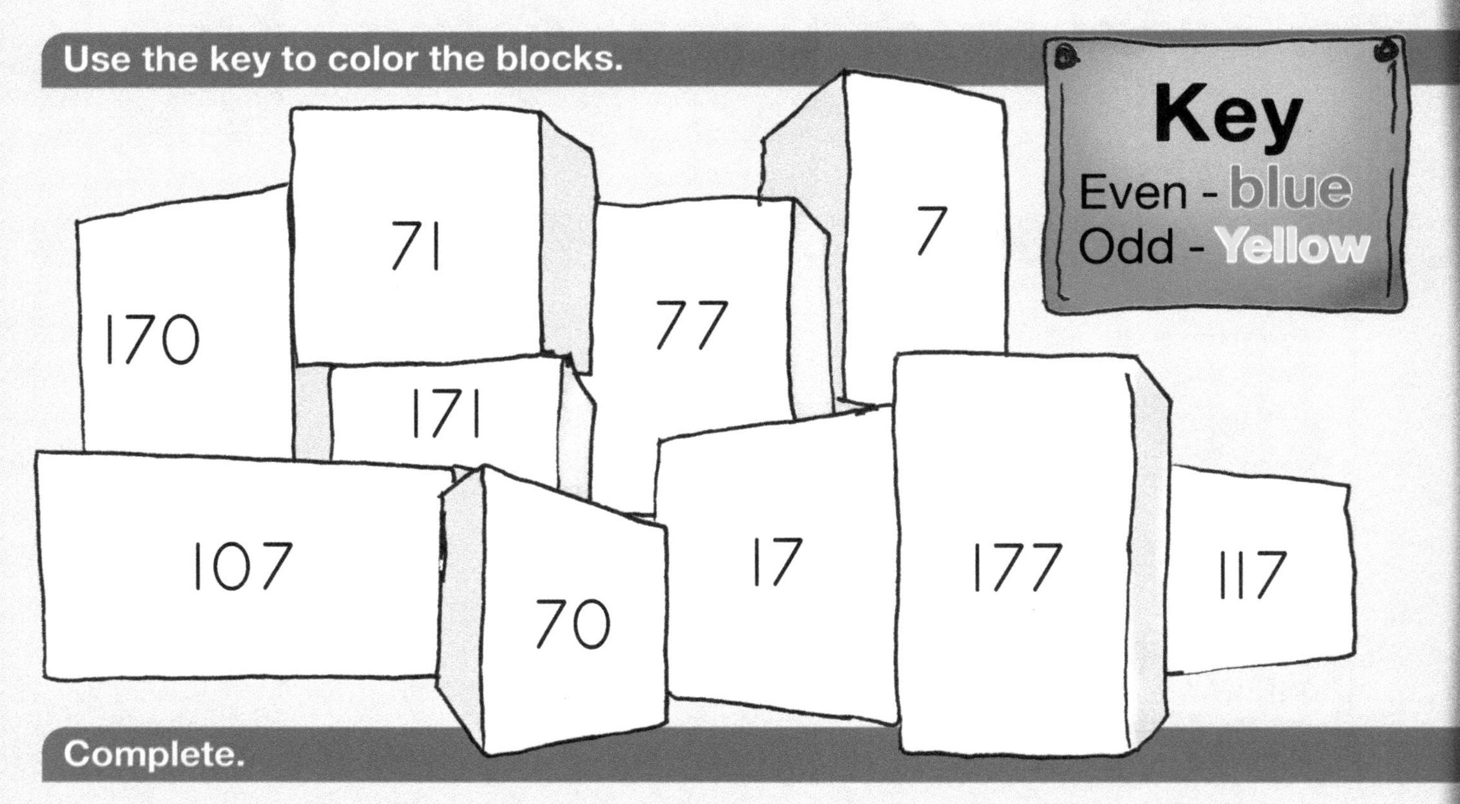

Complete.

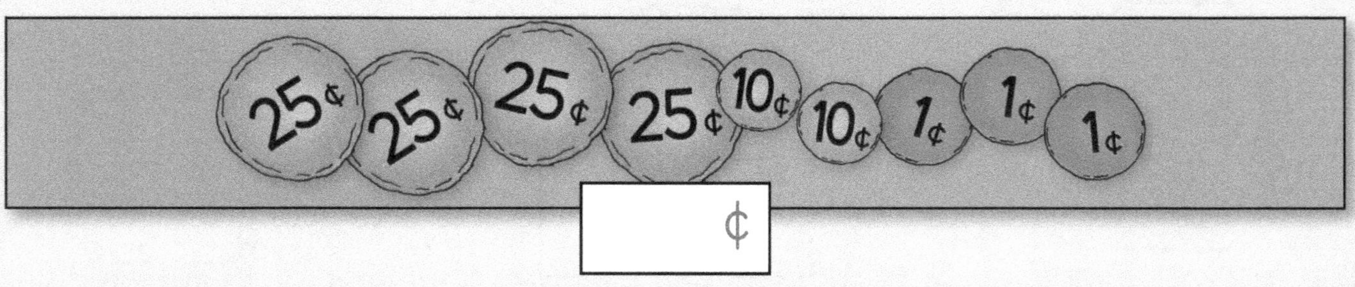

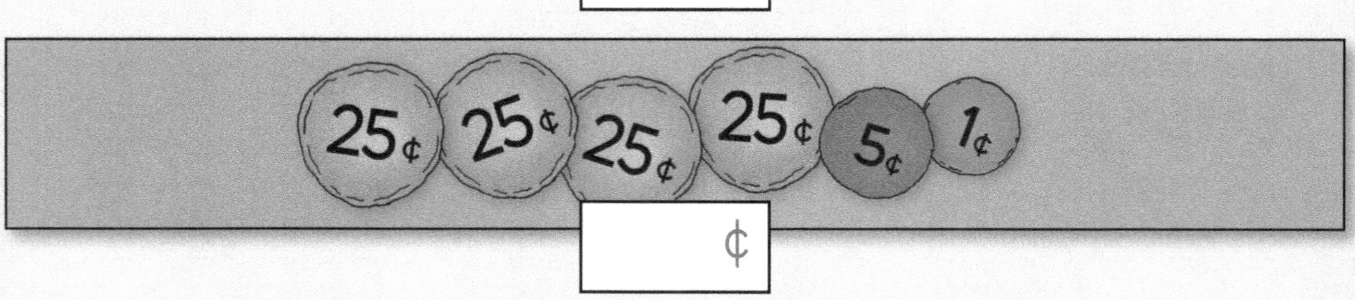

Use the puzzle pieces to cover the polygons.
Draw lines to show where you put each piece.

Use the chart to answer the questions.

Snowpants	$56
Coat	$65
Boots	$38
Gloves	$17
Hat	$12

How much does it cost to buy a coat and snowpants?

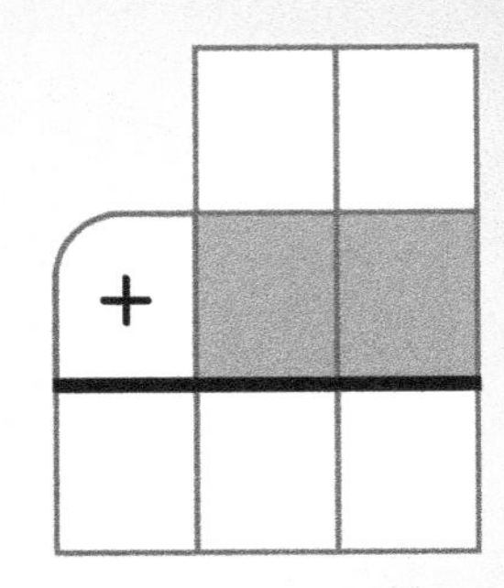

$ ______

How much does it cost to buy boots and gloves?

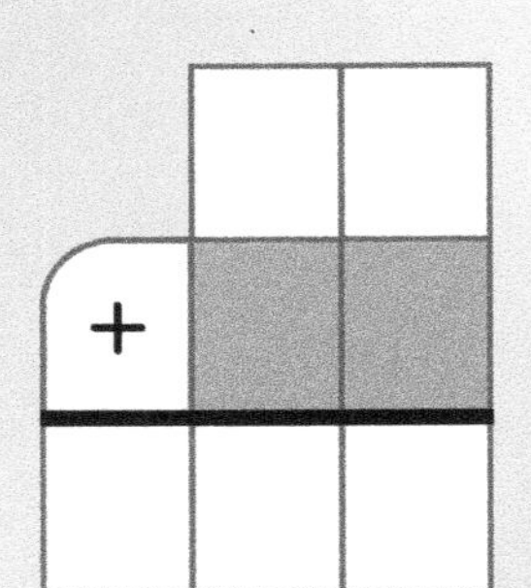

$ ______

How much does it cost to buy boots and a hat?

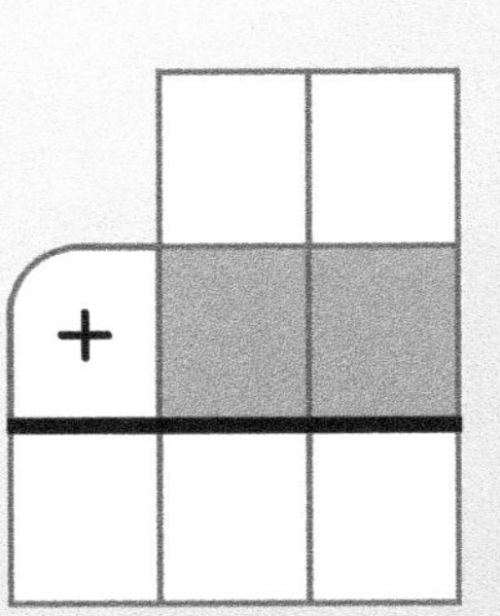

$ ______

Match the pairs that equal 100.

52 61 99 23 65

39 1 48 35 77

See Instructor Guide for directions.
Save this game board for future lessons.

Polygon Four in a Row

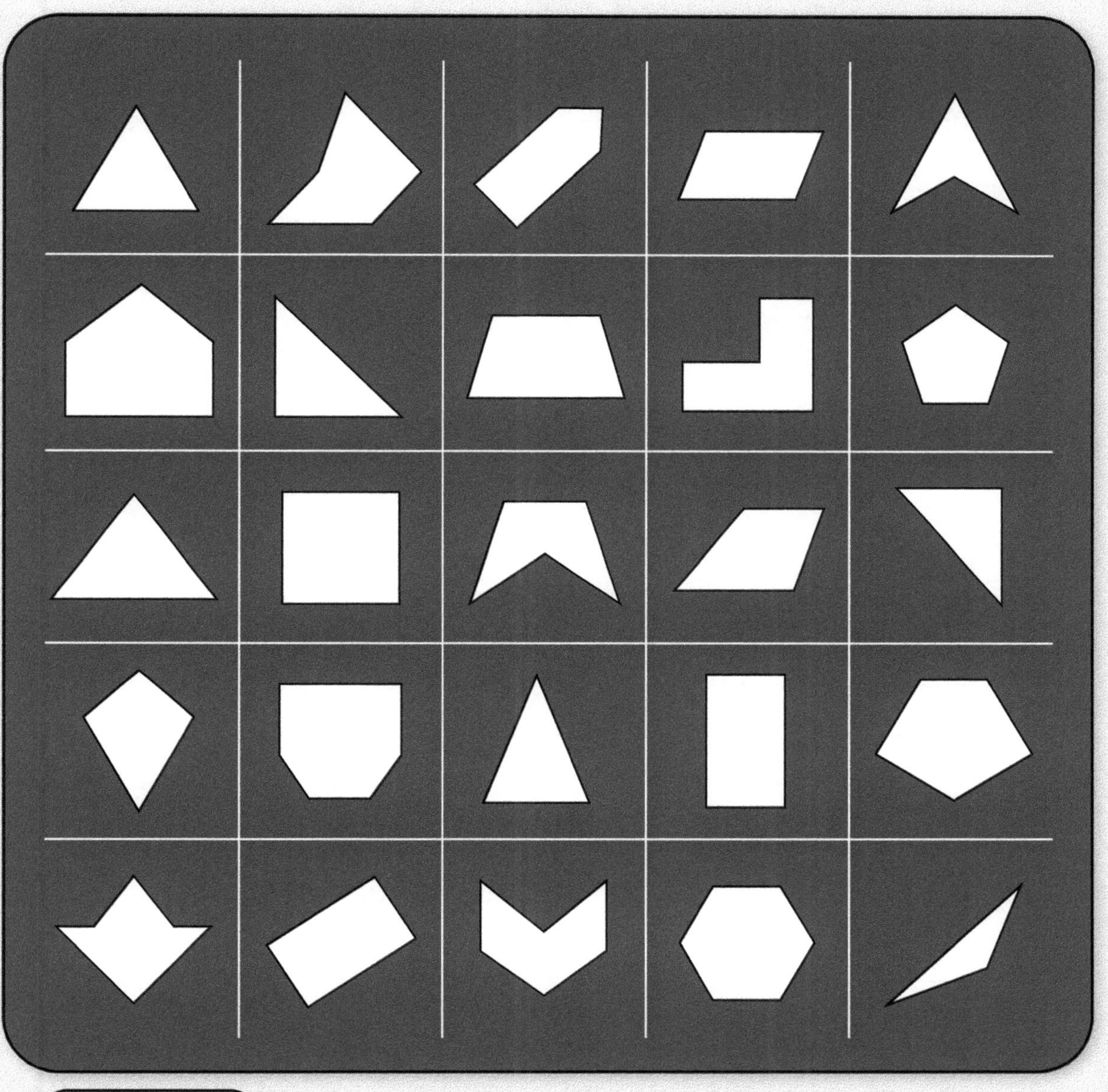

Key

 Wild

 Triangle

 Pentagon

 Any polygon with a right angle

 Quadrilateral

 Hexagon

Complete.

$$\begin{array}{r} 29 \\ +\ 35 \\ \hline \end{array}$$

$$\begin{array}{r} 85 \\ +\ 72 \\ \hline \end{array}$$

$$\begin{array}{r} 42 \\ +\ 58 \\ \hline \end{array}$$

$$\begin{array}{r} 79 \\ +\ 53 \\ \hline \end{array}$$

Harper made a graph about how much snow fell each month. Use the graph to complete the chart and answer the questions. Write your own equation for each question.

Total Snowfall

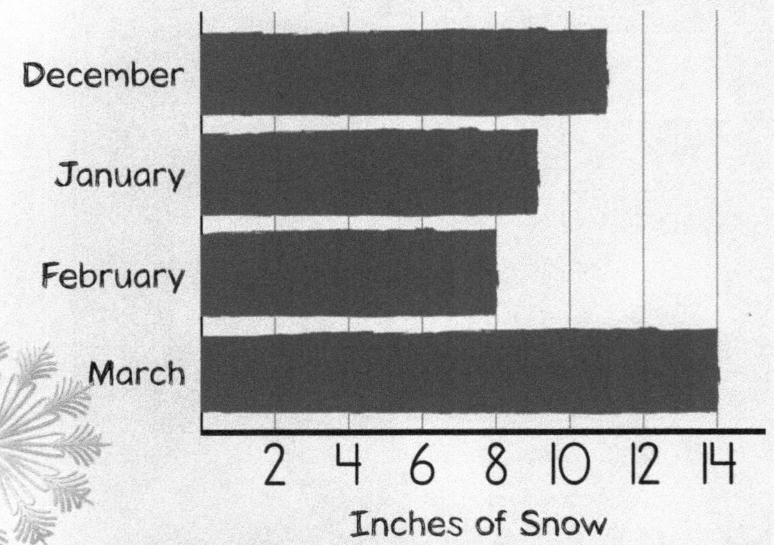

Month	Inches of Snow
December	
January	
February	
March	

How much snow fell in December and January?

inches

How much more snow fell in March than February?

inches

How much less snow fell in January than March?

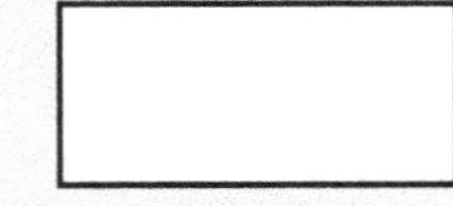
inches

How much snow fell in all 4 months?

inches

Match each shape to its name.

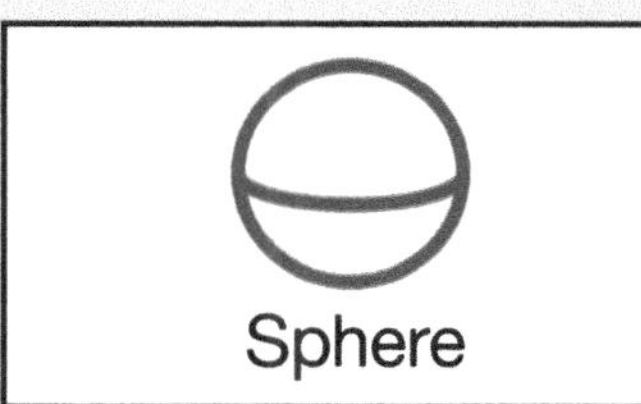

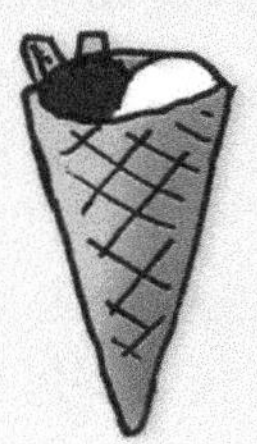

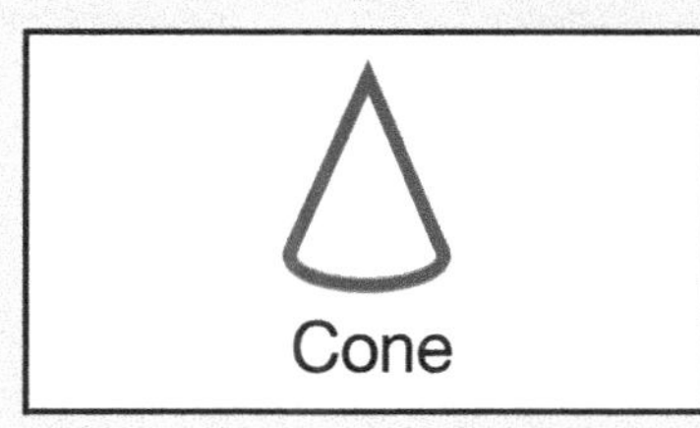

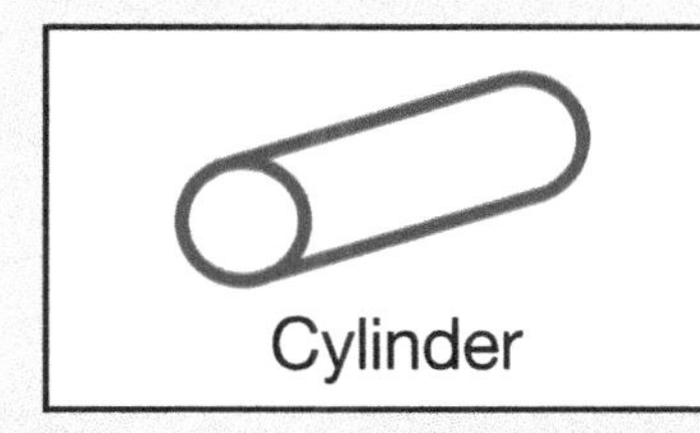

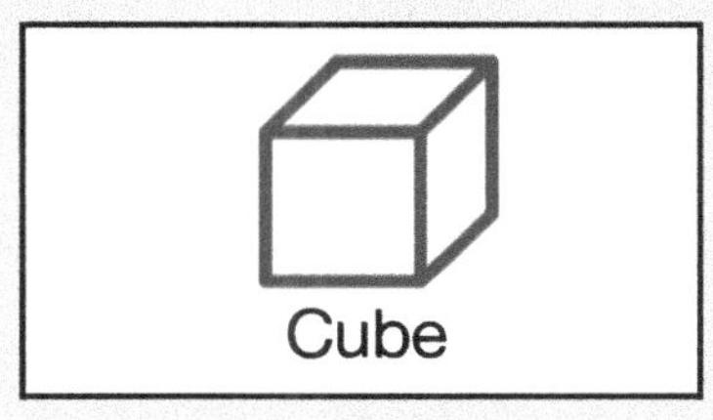

Draw a shape that matches each description.

A triangle

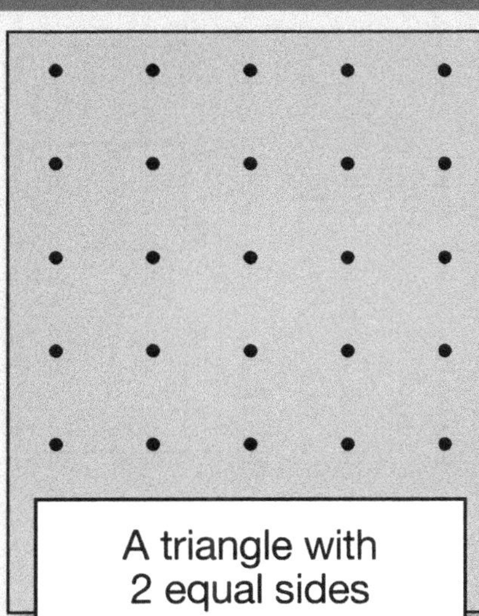

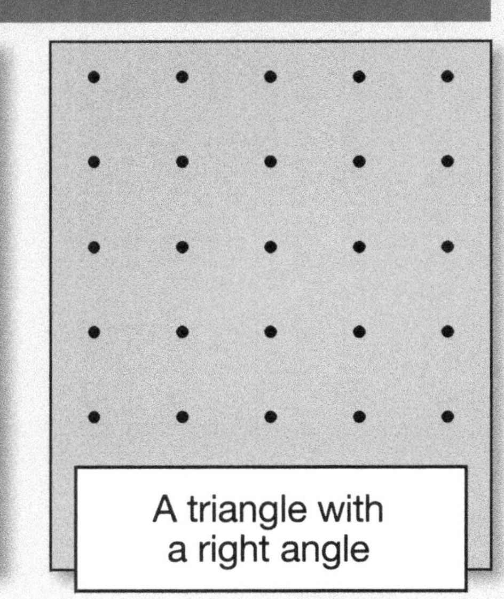

Complete.

	5	8
+	2	7

	7	0
+	8	2

	5	7
+	6	4

	7	5
+	6	3

Color the triangles blue. Color the quadrilaterals green.

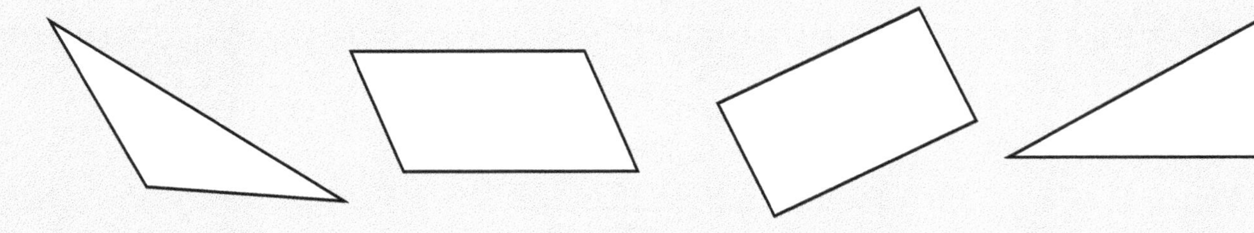

Complete.

11 - 5 = ☐　　17 - 9 = ☐　　13 - 8 = ☐

12 - 7 = ☐　　13 - 4 = ☐　　11 - 9 = ☐

10 - 8 = ☐　　13 - 7 = ☐　　11 - 3 = ☐

13 - 9 = ☐　　16 - 8 = ☐　　15 - 7 = ☐

Draw lines to cut each cake to match the label.

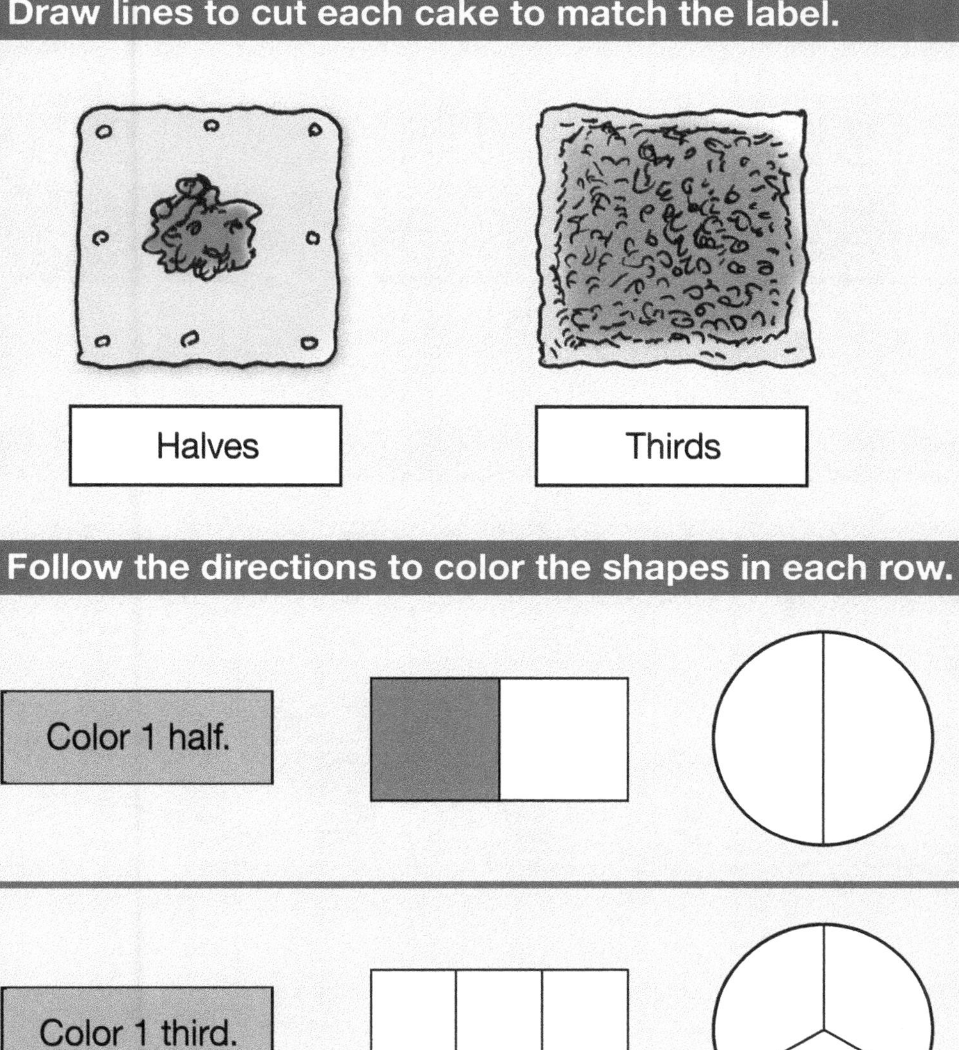

Halves

Thirds

Fourths

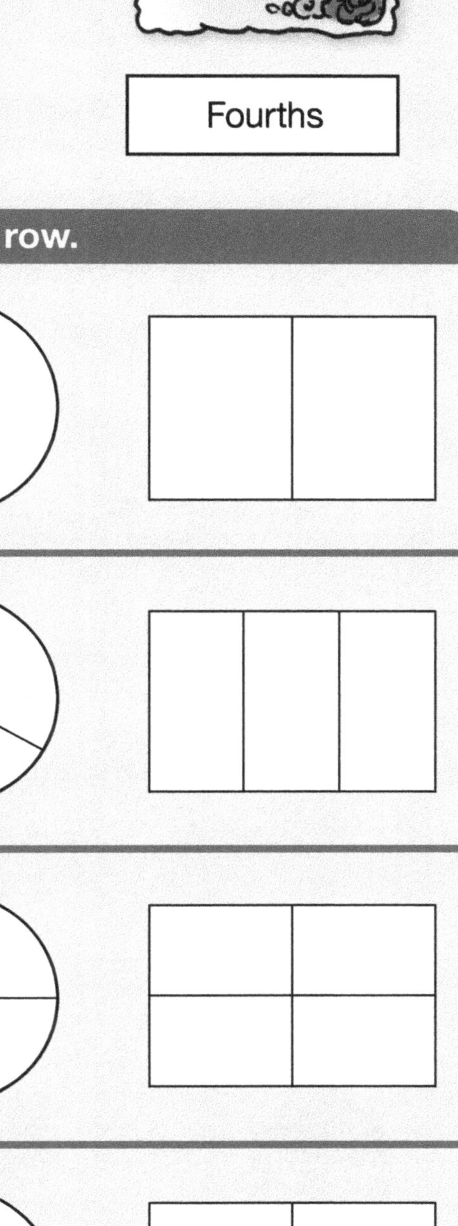

Follow the directions to color the shapes in each row.

Color 1 half.

Color 1 third.

Color 3 fourths.

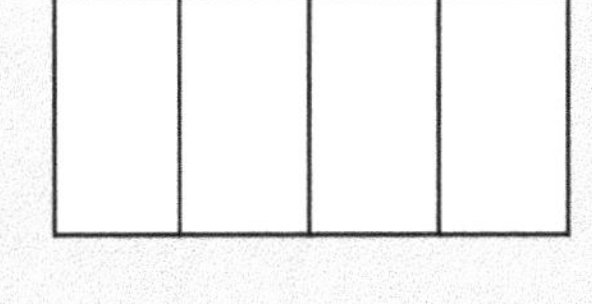

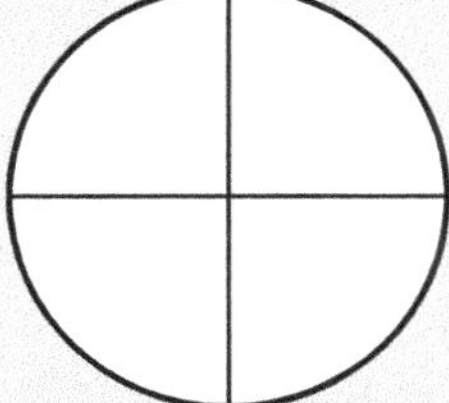

Color 4 fourths.

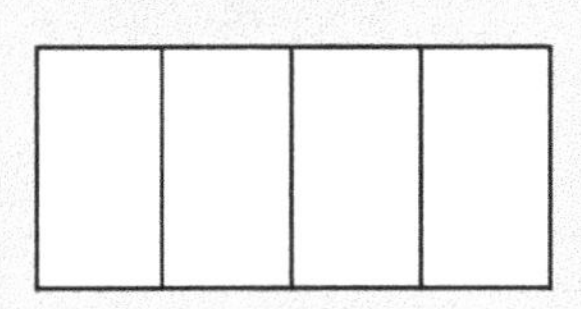

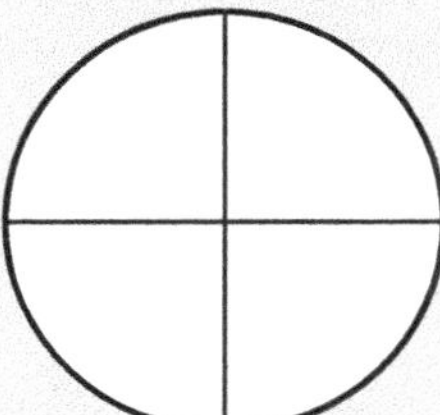

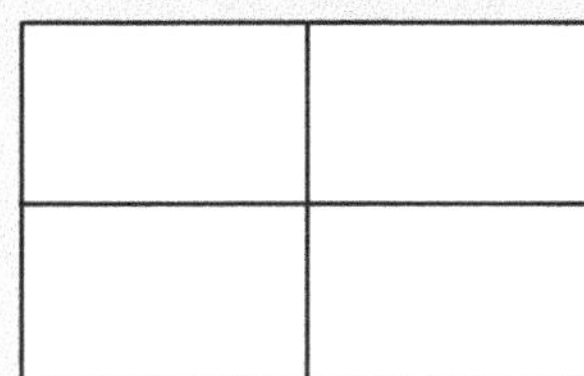

Complete.

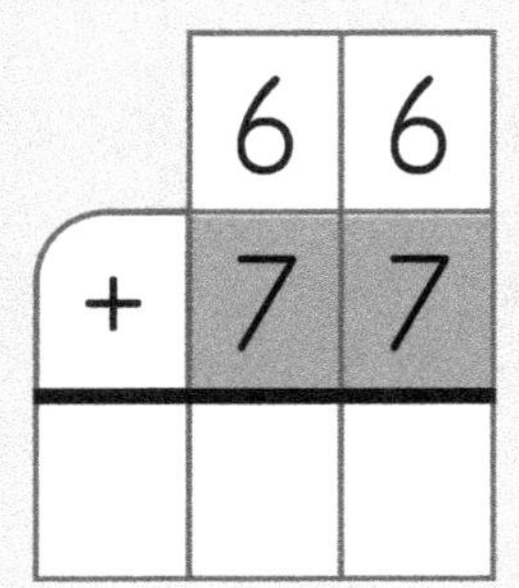

	2	4
+	5	2

	3	9
+	4	5

	2	6
+	8	3

Complete the missing numbers in the sequence.

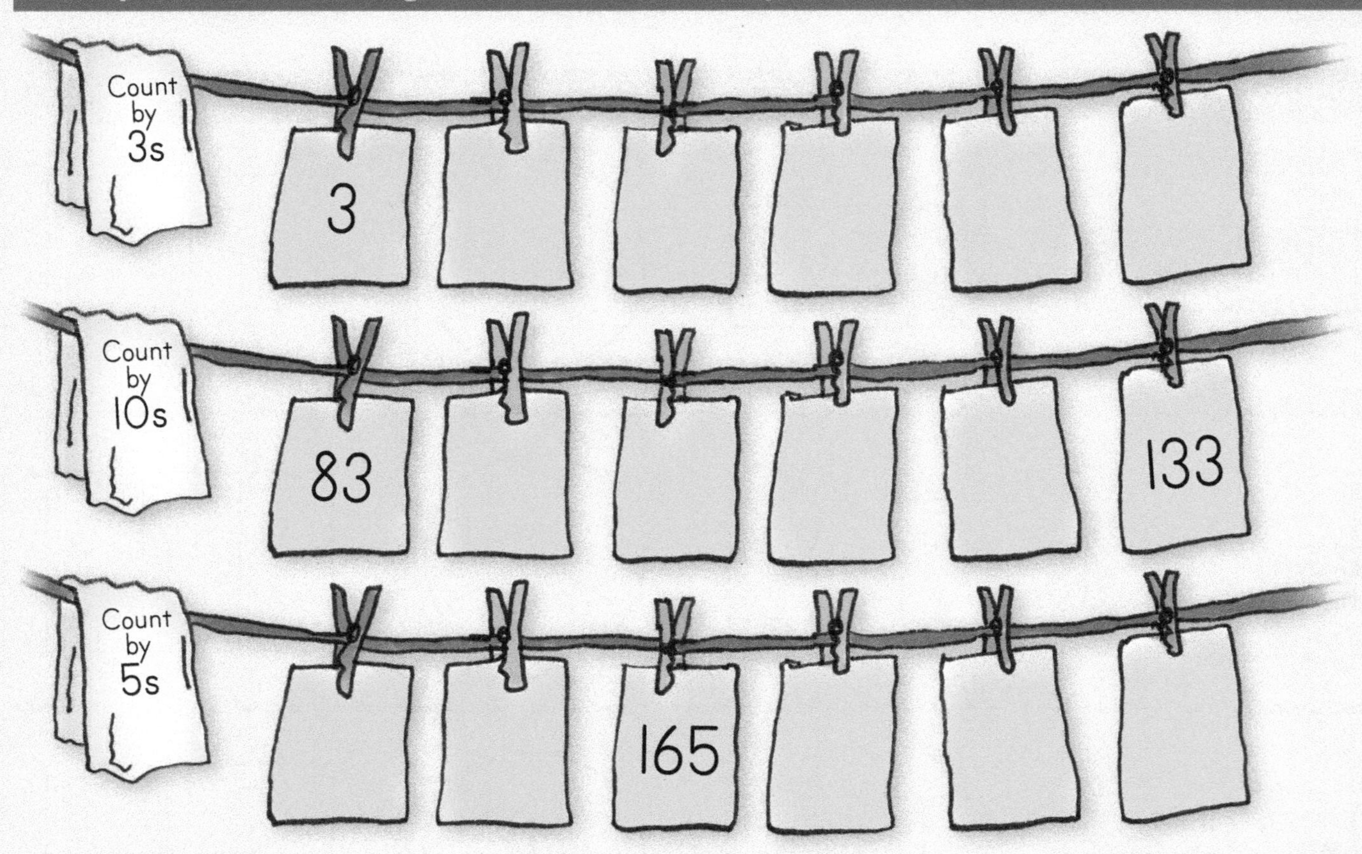

Match each shape to its name.

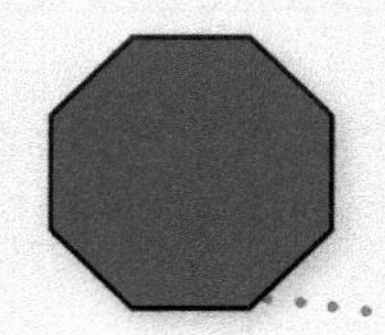

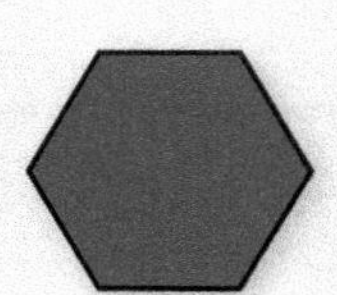

Quadrilateral	Hexagon	Octagon	Pentagon

See Instructor Guide for directions.
Save this game board for future lessons.

Fraction Bump

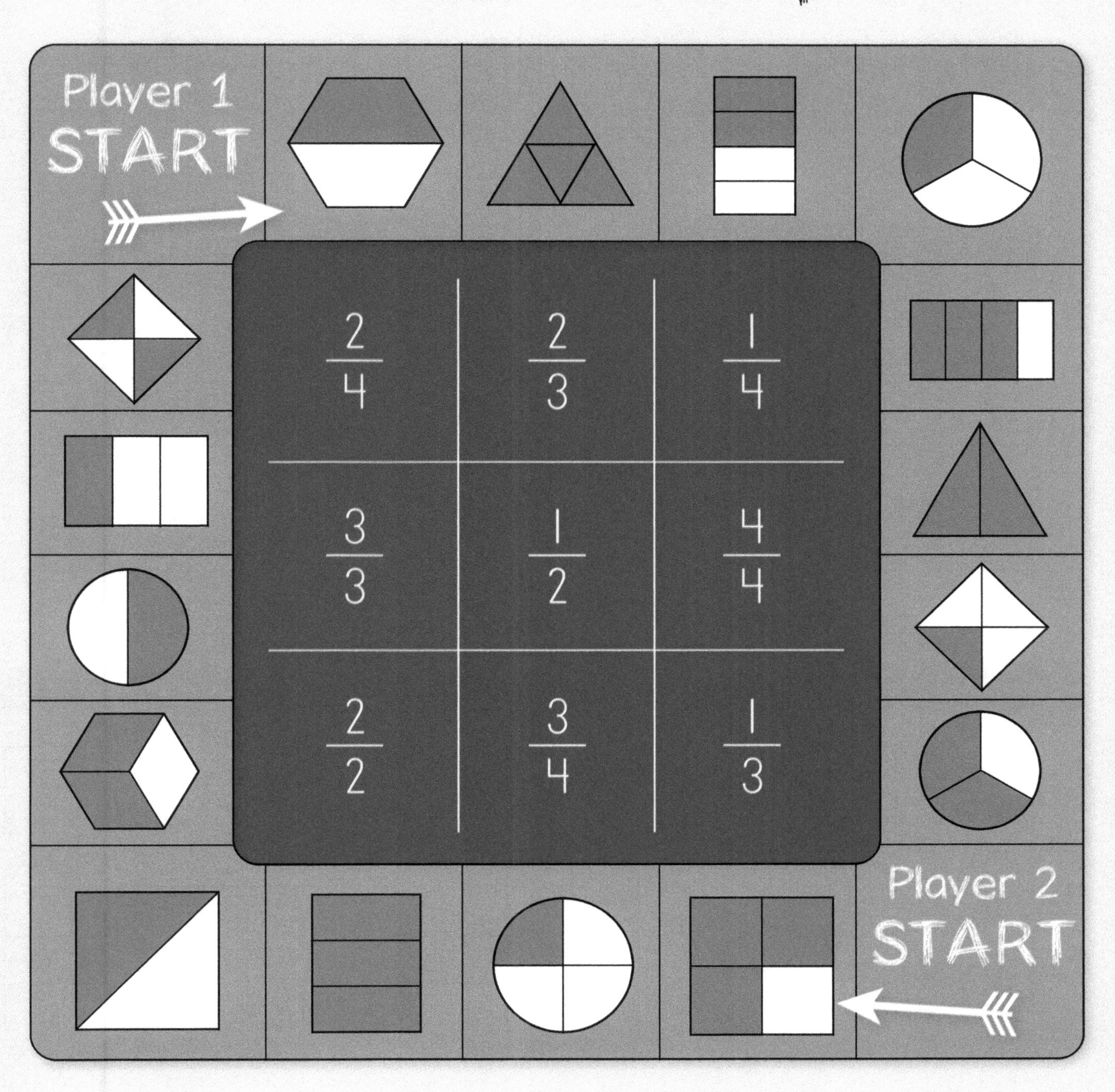

How much pizza is left? Match.

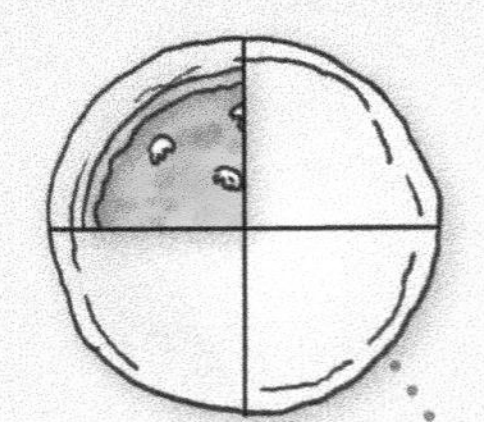
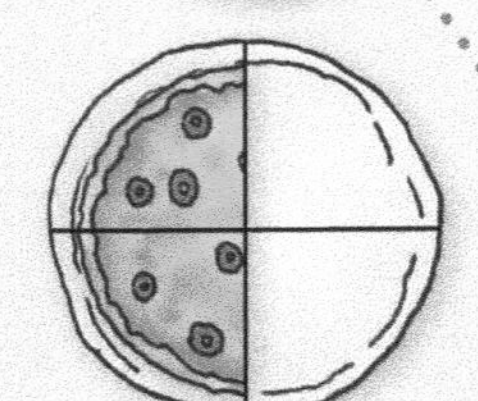
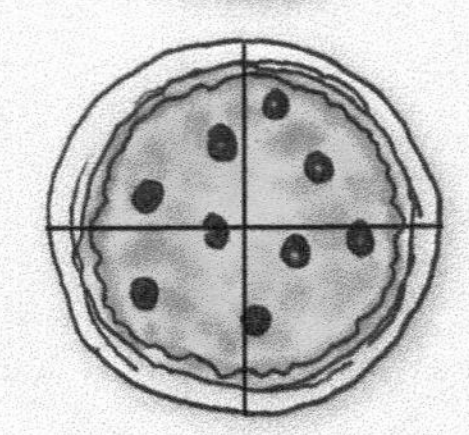
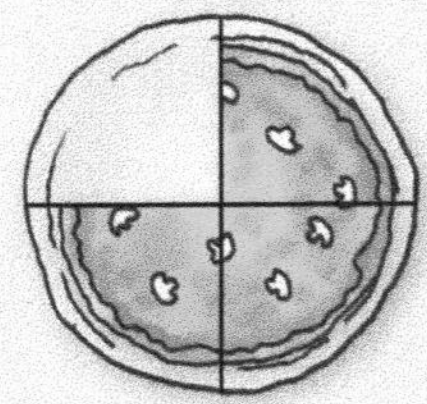
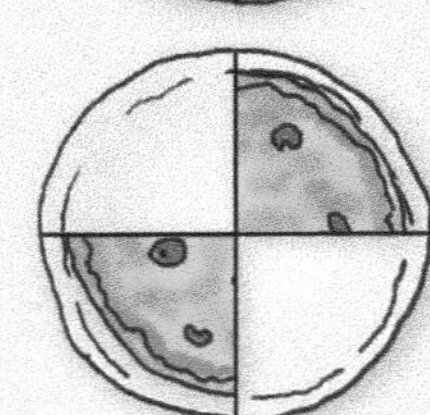

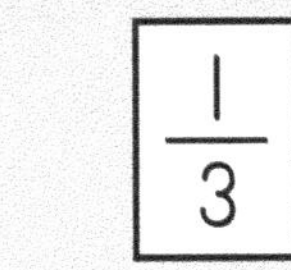

$\frac{4}{4}$

$\frac{2}{2}$

$\frac{2}{4}$

$\frac{2}{3}$

$\frac{1}{4}$

$\frac{1}{2}$

$\frac{3}{4}$

$\frac{3}{3}$

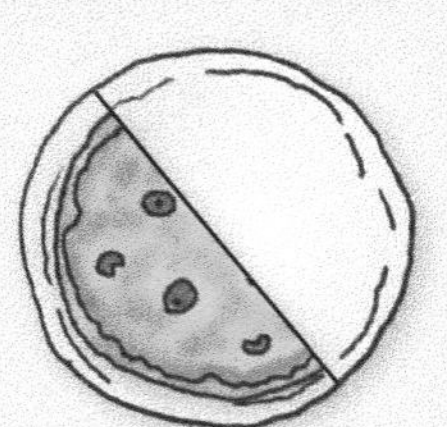

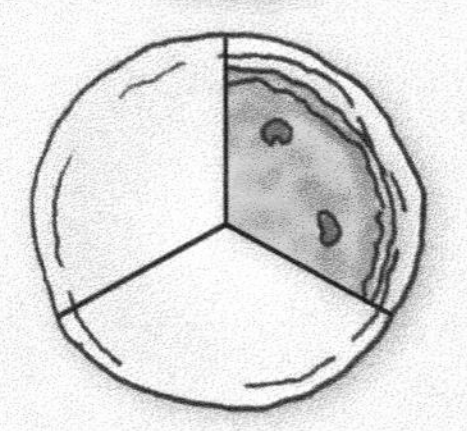
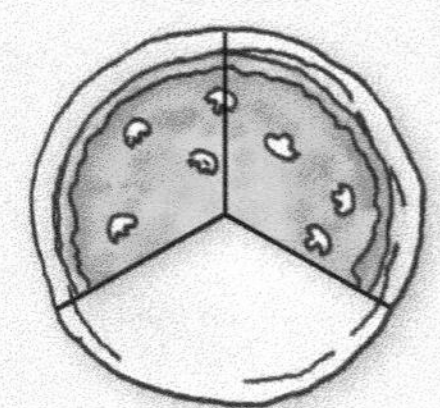
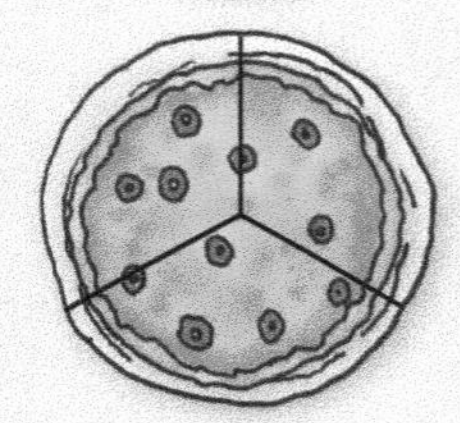

Complete.

11 - 2 = ☐	13 - 9 = ☐	15 - 6 = ☐
16 - 8 = ☐	12 - 4 = ☐	14 - 9 = ☐
17 - 8 = ☐	13 - 6 = ☐	18 - 9 = ☐
14 - 5 = ☐	15 - 8 = ☐	11 - 6 = ☐

Write a fraction for the purple part of each shape.

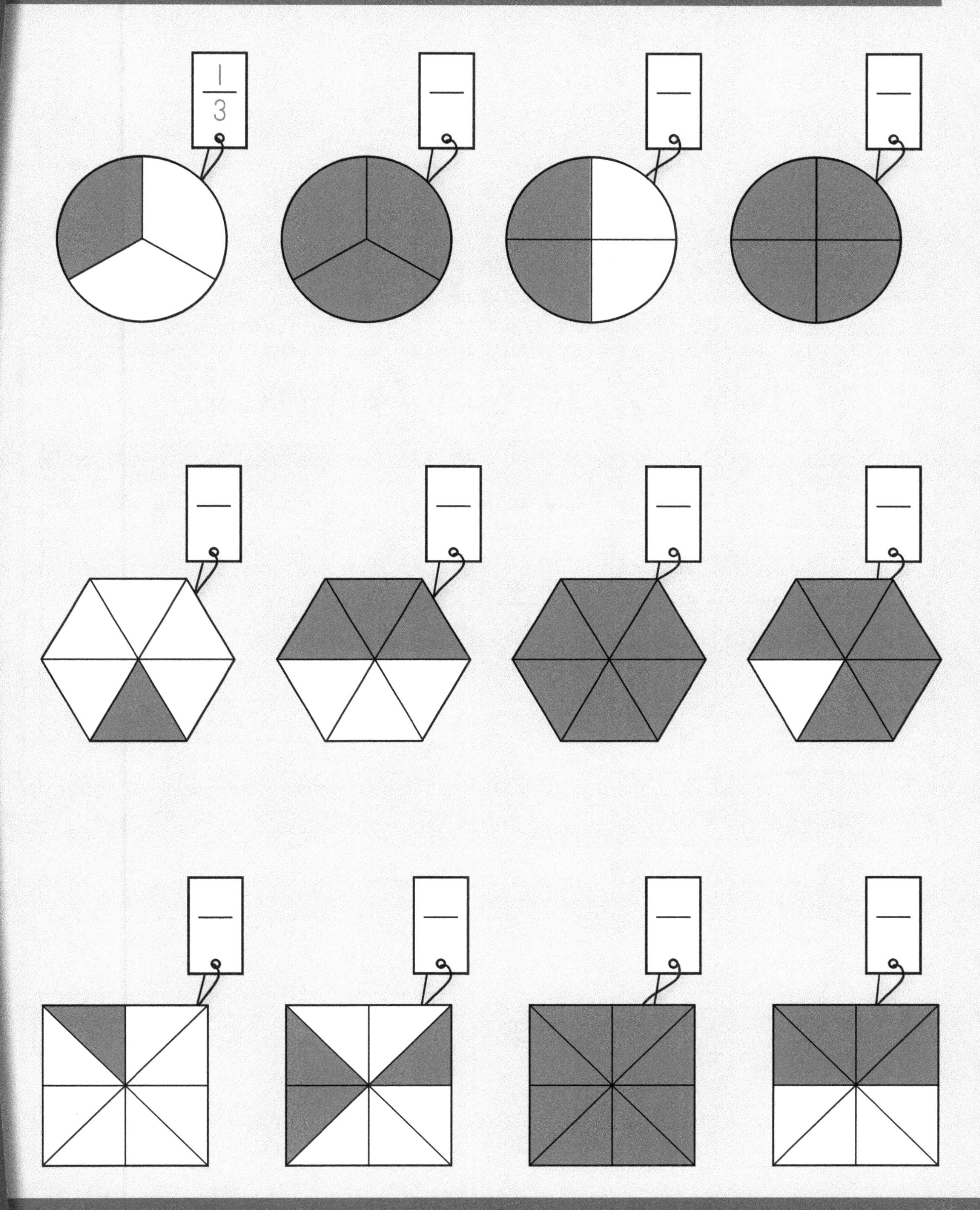

Complete.

	8	6
+		4

	6	8
+	3	4

	6	0
+	8	0

	9	5
+	6	5

Emma made a pictograph about her stuffed animals. Use the pictograph to complete the chart.

My Stuffed Animals

Pet animals 

Zoo animals 

Farm animals 

 = 3 stuffed animals

Type of Animal	Number
Pet	
Zoo	
Farm	

Complete.

12 - 3 = ☐ 10 - 9 = ☐ 13 - 8 = ☐

12 - 6 = ☐ 13 - 5 = ☐ 16 - 9 = ☐

11 - 8 = ☐ 14 - 6 = ☐ 10 - 5 = ☐

Color the shapes to match the fractions.
Then, complete each circle with <, >, or =.

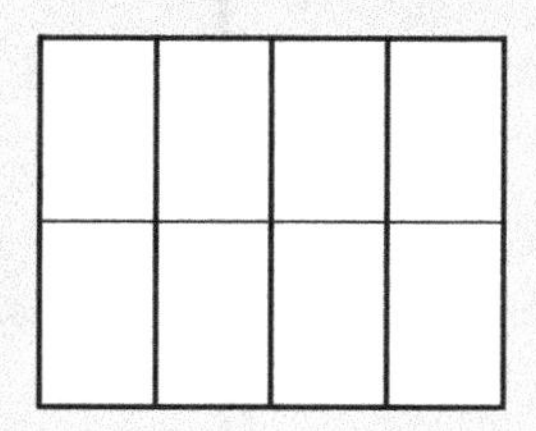 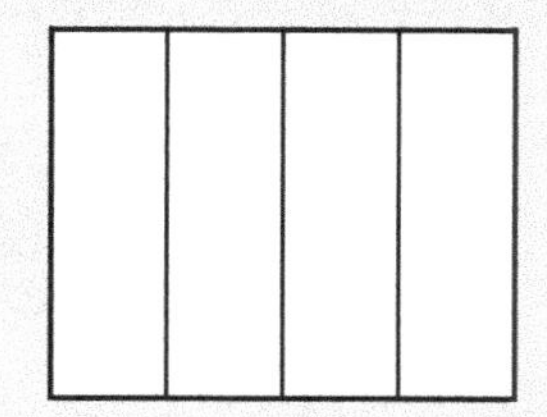

$\frac{1}{8} \bigcirc \frac{1}{4}$

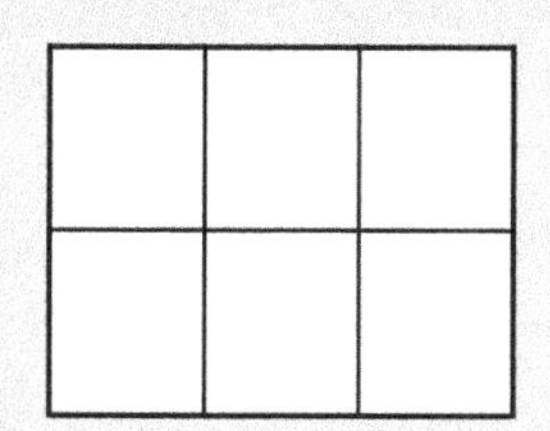 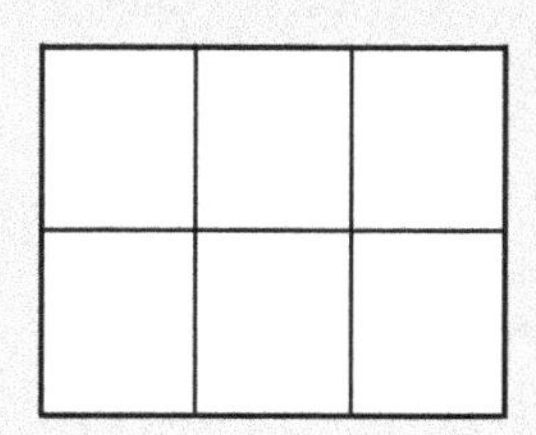

$\frac{5}{6} \bigcirc \frac{2}{6}$

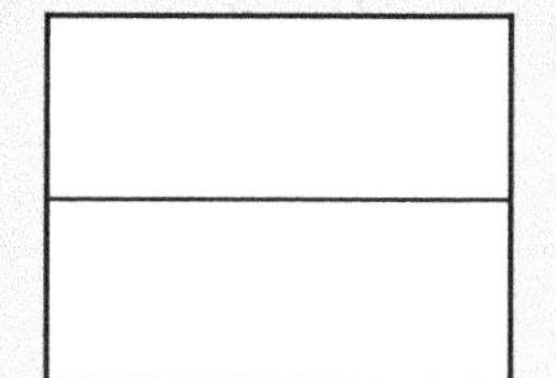 

$\frac{1}{2} \bigcirc \frac{3}{6}$

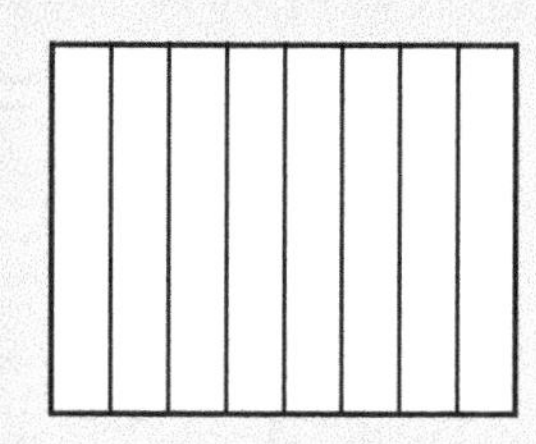 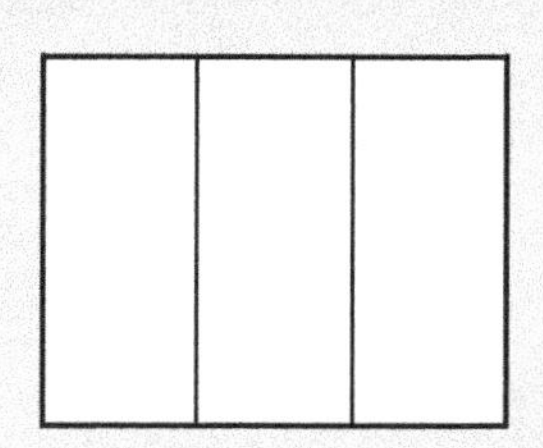

$\frac{5}{8} \bigcirc \frac{1}{3}$

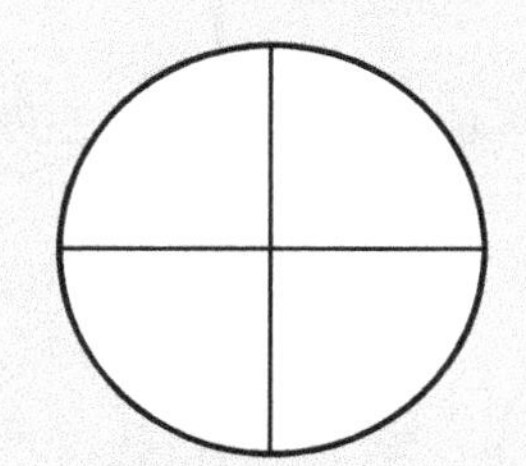 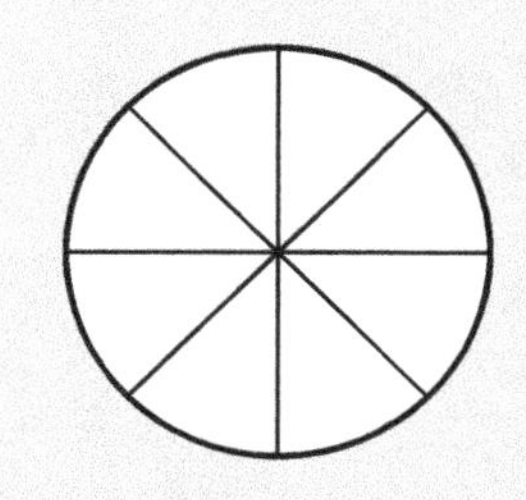

$\frac{3}{4} \bigcirc \frac{3}{8}$

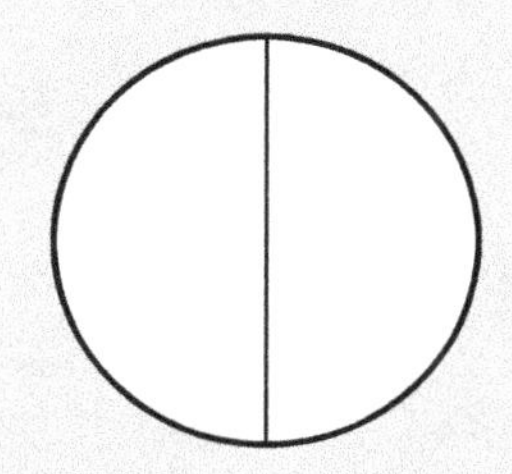 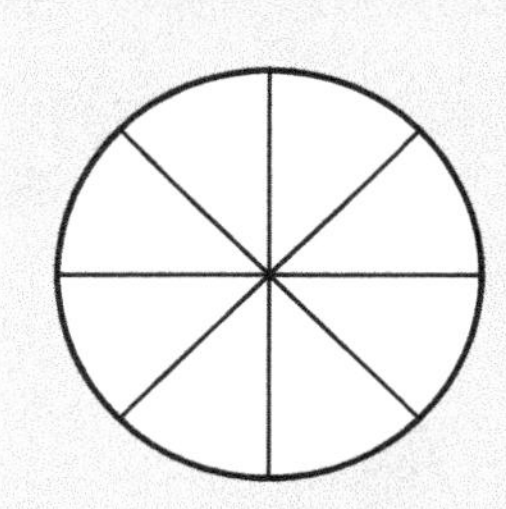

$\frac{2}{2} \bigcirc \frac{7}{8}$

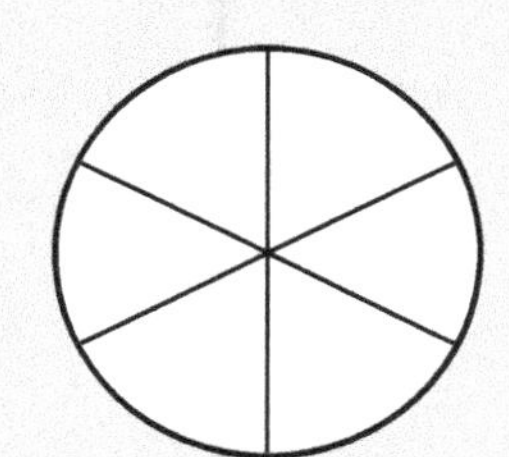 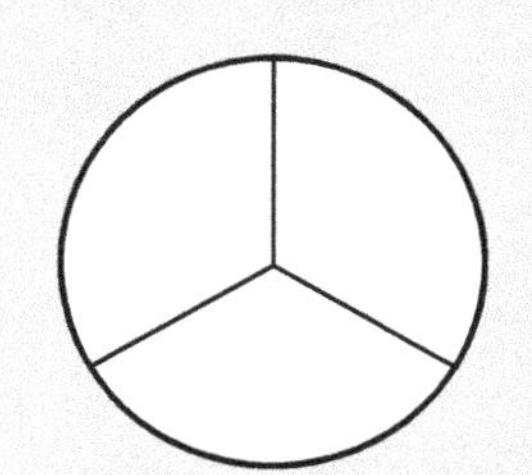

$\frac{4}{6} \bigcirc \frac{2}{3}$

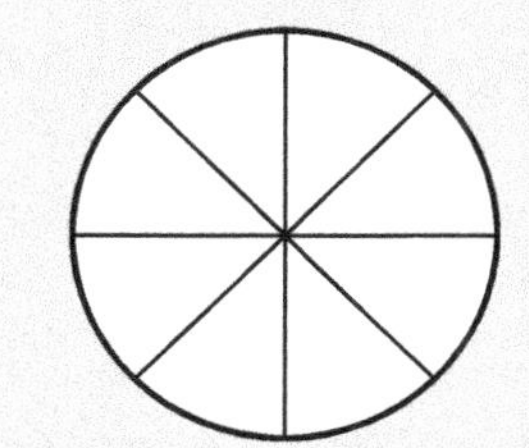 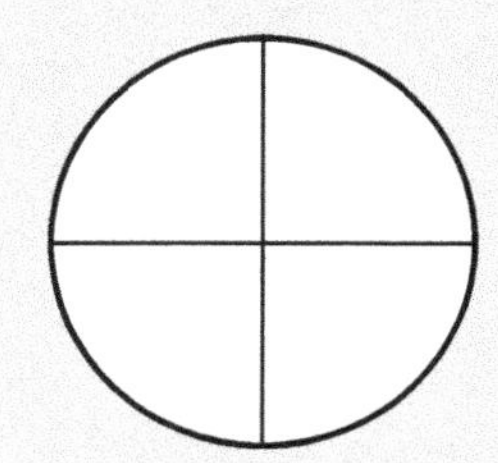

$\frac{7}{8} \bigcirc \frac{3}{4}$

Complete.

	5	5
+		9

	6	2
+	3	7

	5	9
+	7	4

	5	6
+	8	1

Complete.

12 - 5 = ☐ 15 - 9 = ☐ 12 - 8 = ☐

14 - 7 = ☐ 11 - 4 = ☐ 17 - 8 = ☐

12 - 9 = ☐ 16 - 7 = ☐ 13 - 5 = ☐

Match each shape to its name.

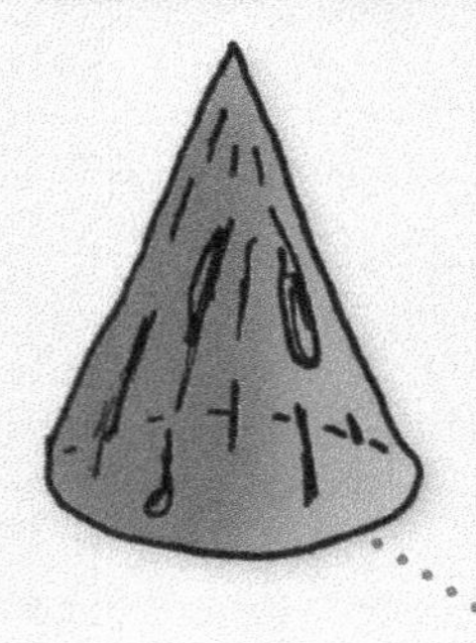

Cube	Rectangular prism	Cone	Cylinder	Sphere

See the Instructor Guide for directions.

Chocolate Shop Packing Directions

1. Check whether you have enough squares for the order. 
2. If you don't have enough squares, trade one bar for 10 squares.

3. Subtract the squares.
4. Subtract the bars.

	Bars	Squares
Total	9	5
Order 1	1	7
New Total		

	Bars	Squares
Total		
Order 2	2	3
New Total		

	Bars	Squares
Total		
Order 3		9
New Total		

	Bars	Squares
Total		
Order 4		6
New Total		

	Bars	Squares
Total		
Order 5	1	8
New Total		

	Bars	Squares
Total		
Order 6	1	4
New Total		

Solve.

Rodrigo's family drove 36 kilometers to his soccer game. Then, they drove 36 kilometers back. How far did they drive in all?

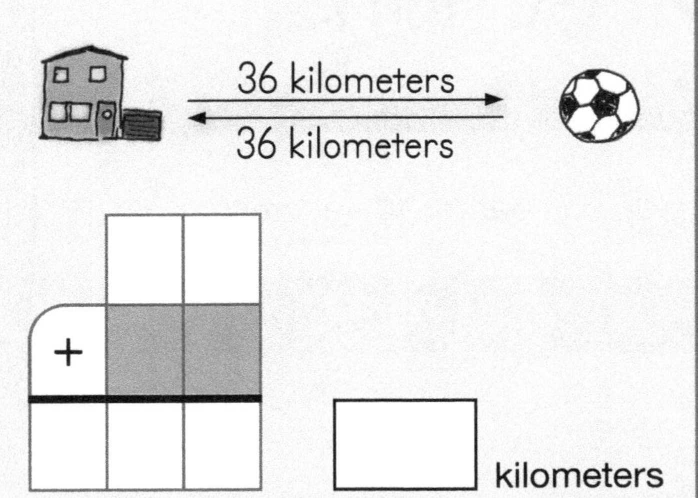

Kaylee's family drove 79 miles to her cousin's house. Then, they drove 79 miles back. How far did they drive in all?

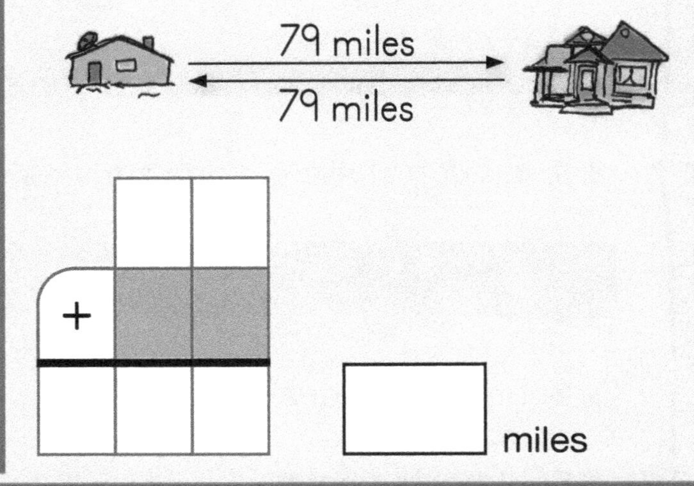

Complete the missing numbers in the sequences.

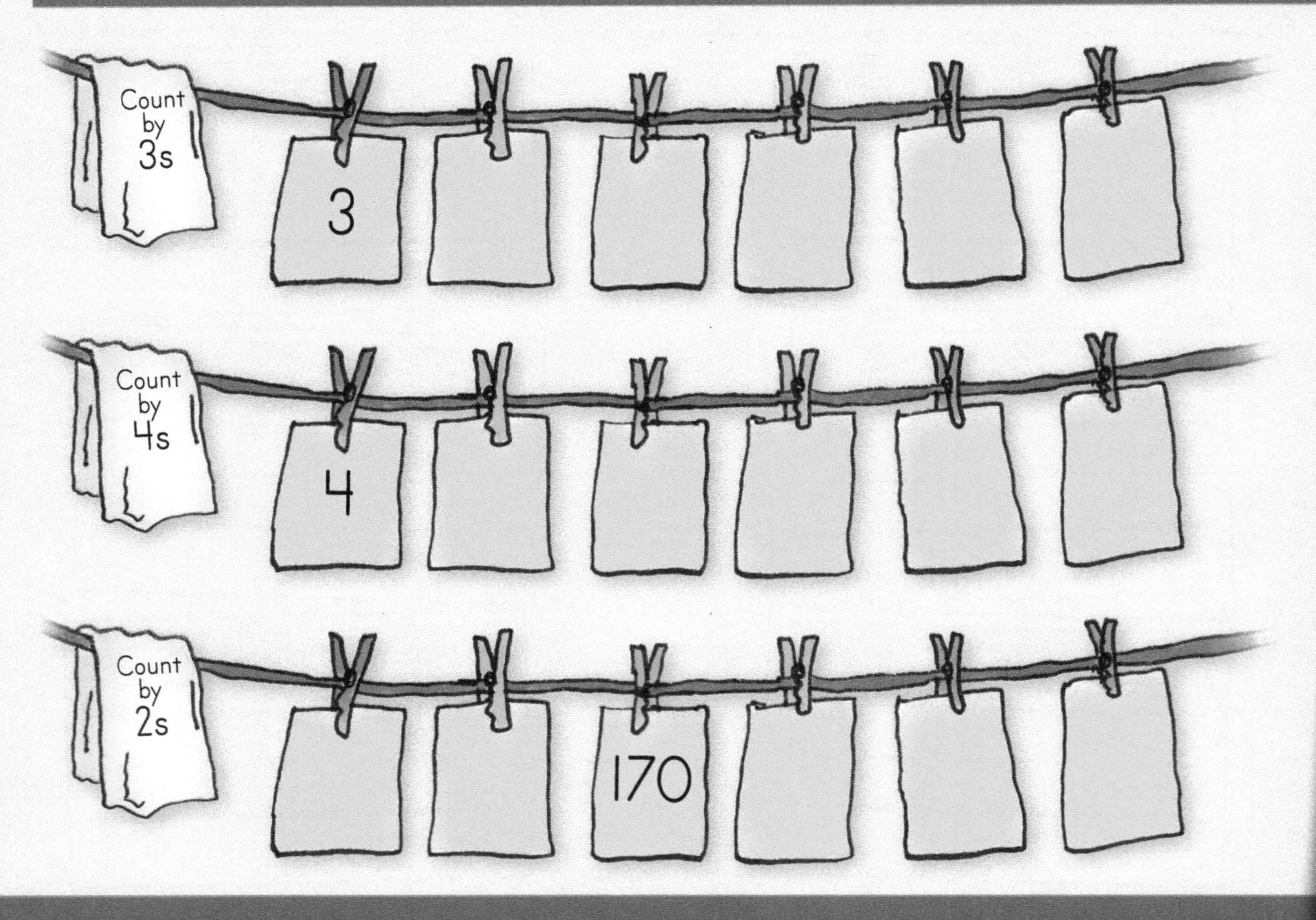

See the Instructor Guide for directions.

The Subtraction Algorithm

* * * Start with the ones-place.

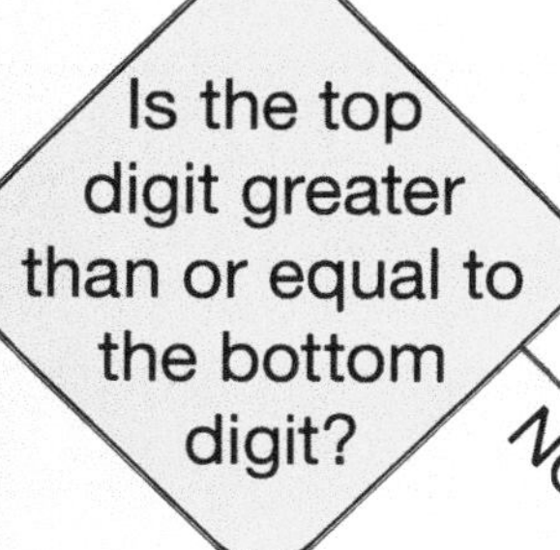

YES → Subtract.

NO → Trade. → Subtract.

* * * Follow the steps for all the places.

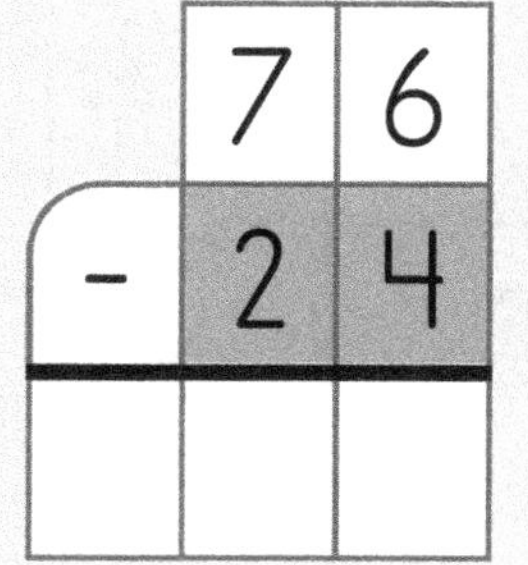

$$\begin{array}{r} 61 \\ -\ 19 \\ \hline \end{array} \qquad \begin{array}{r} 82 \\ -\ 57 \\ \hline \end{array} \qquad \begin{array}{r} 70 \\ -\ 47 \\ \hline \end{array}$$

$$\begin{array}{r} 94 \\ -\ 9 \\ \hline \end{array} \qquad \begin{array}{r} 89 \\ -\ 68 \\ \hline \end{array} \qquad \begin{array}{r} 43 \\ -\ 16 \\ \hline \end{array} \qquad \begin{array}{r} 52 \\ -\ 32 \\ \hline \end{array}$$

Choose the more sensible measurement for each item.

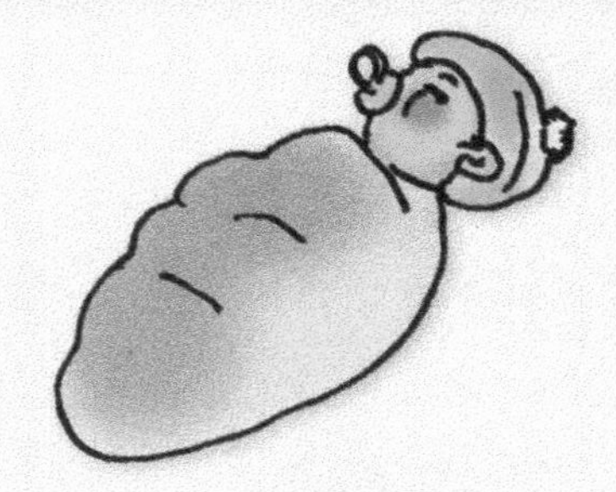

Length of a baby

2 feet | 2 yards

Length of a fork

8 feet

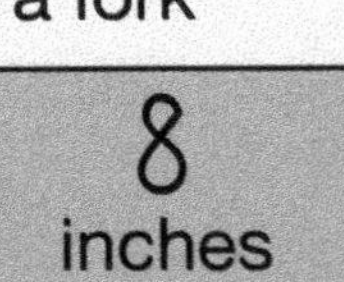

Length of a playground

50 miles | 50 yards

Label each spot on the number line.

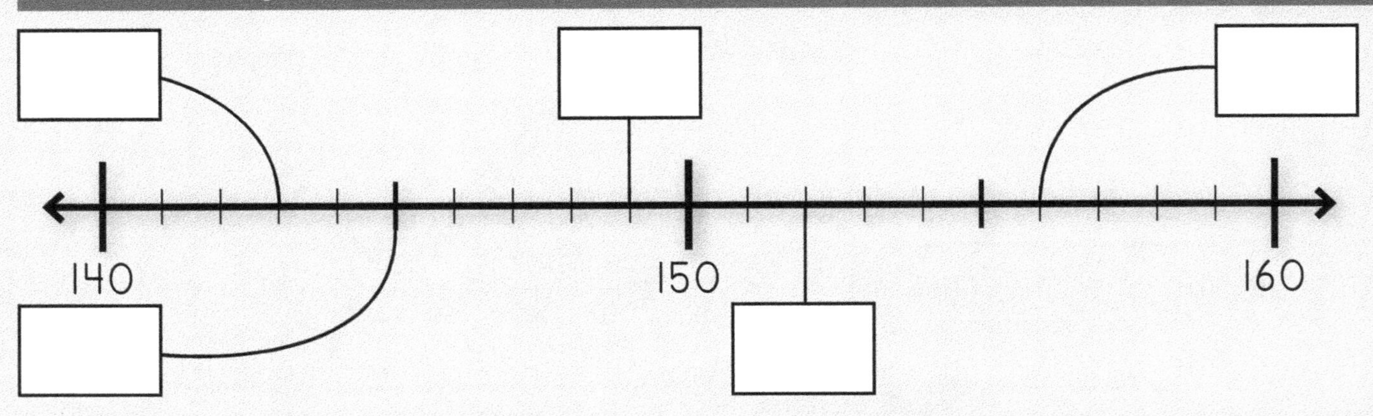

Color the shapes to match the fractions.

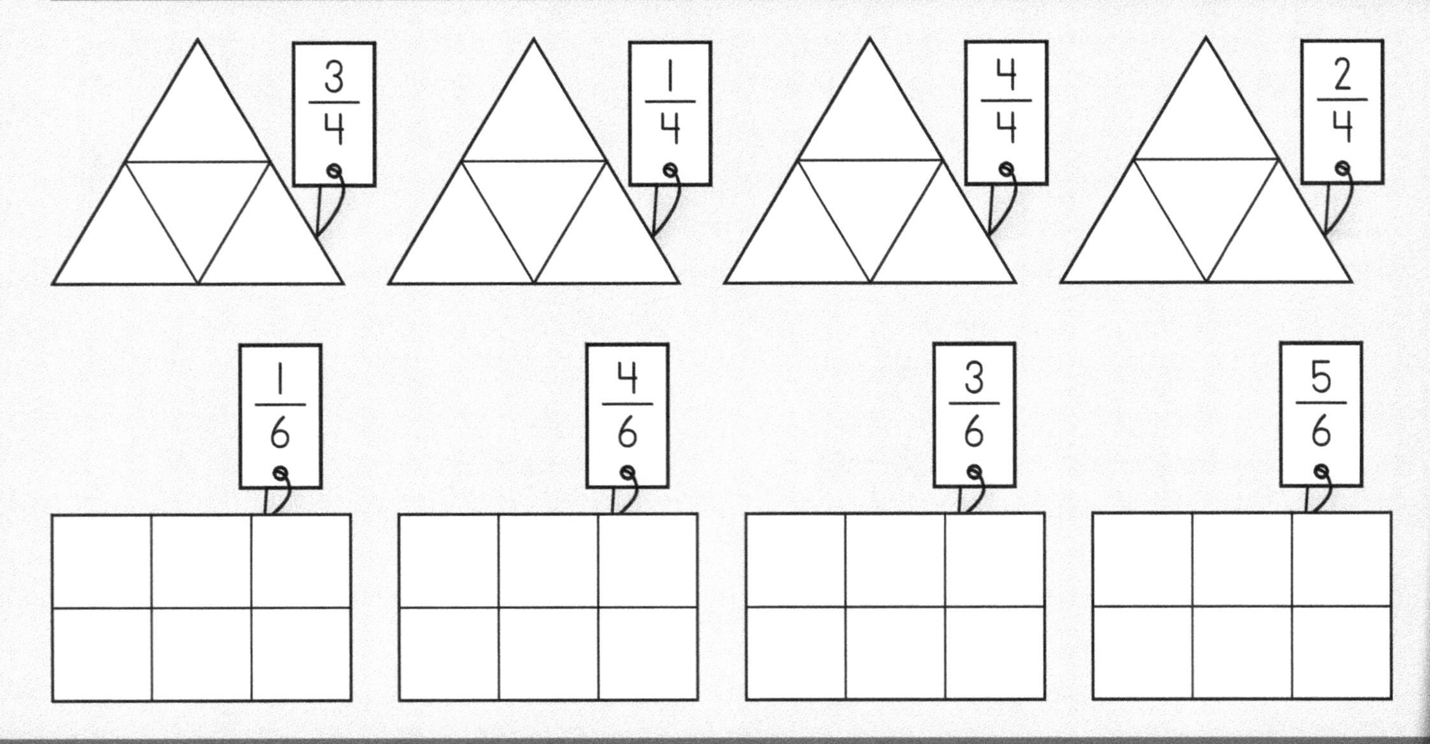

See the Instructor Guide for directions.

	1	6	5
−		3	8

	1	2	9
−		6	7

	1	3	7
−		5	4

SPIN TO WIN!

175 184 167 159 198 149

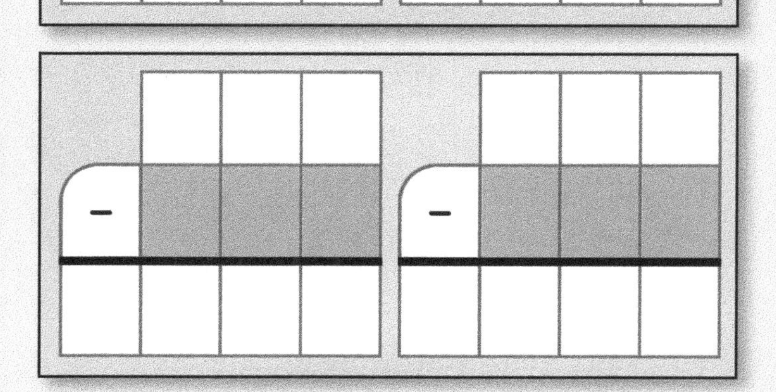

Complete.

1 week = ☐ days

1 day = ☐ hours

1 hour = ☐ minutes

1 minute = ☐ seconds

1 yard = ☐ feet

1 yard = ☐ inches

1 foot = ☐ inches

1 meter = ☐ centimeters

Complete the missing numbers in the 200 chart.

	152	153	154	155	156	157	158	159	160
161	162	163	164	165	166	167		169	
	172	173	174		176	177	178	179	180
181	182	183				187	188	189	
191		193	194	195	196	197			

Write how many.

☐ doughnuts

☐ doughnuts

☐ doughnuts

☐ doughnuts

☐ doughnuts

☐ doughnuts

See the Instructor Guide for directions.

	1	3	4
-		5	6

	1	5	2
-		7	9

	1	4	0
-		8	5

SPIN TO WIN!

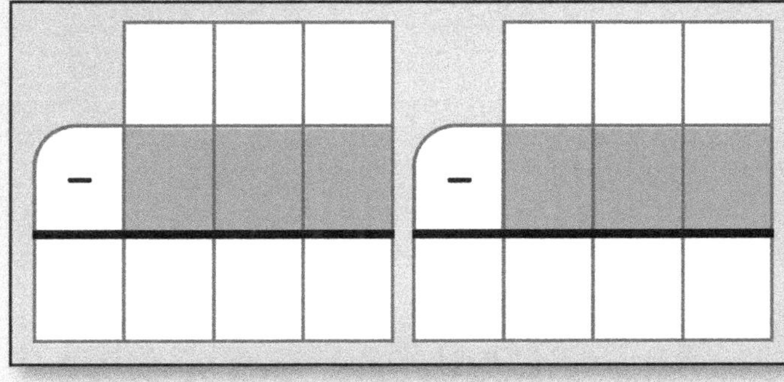

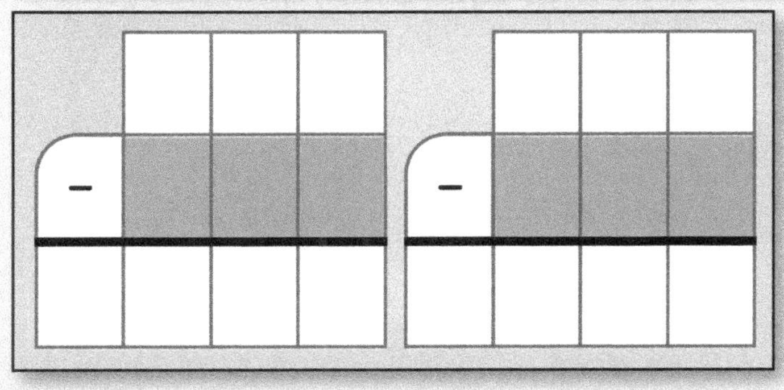

Complete.

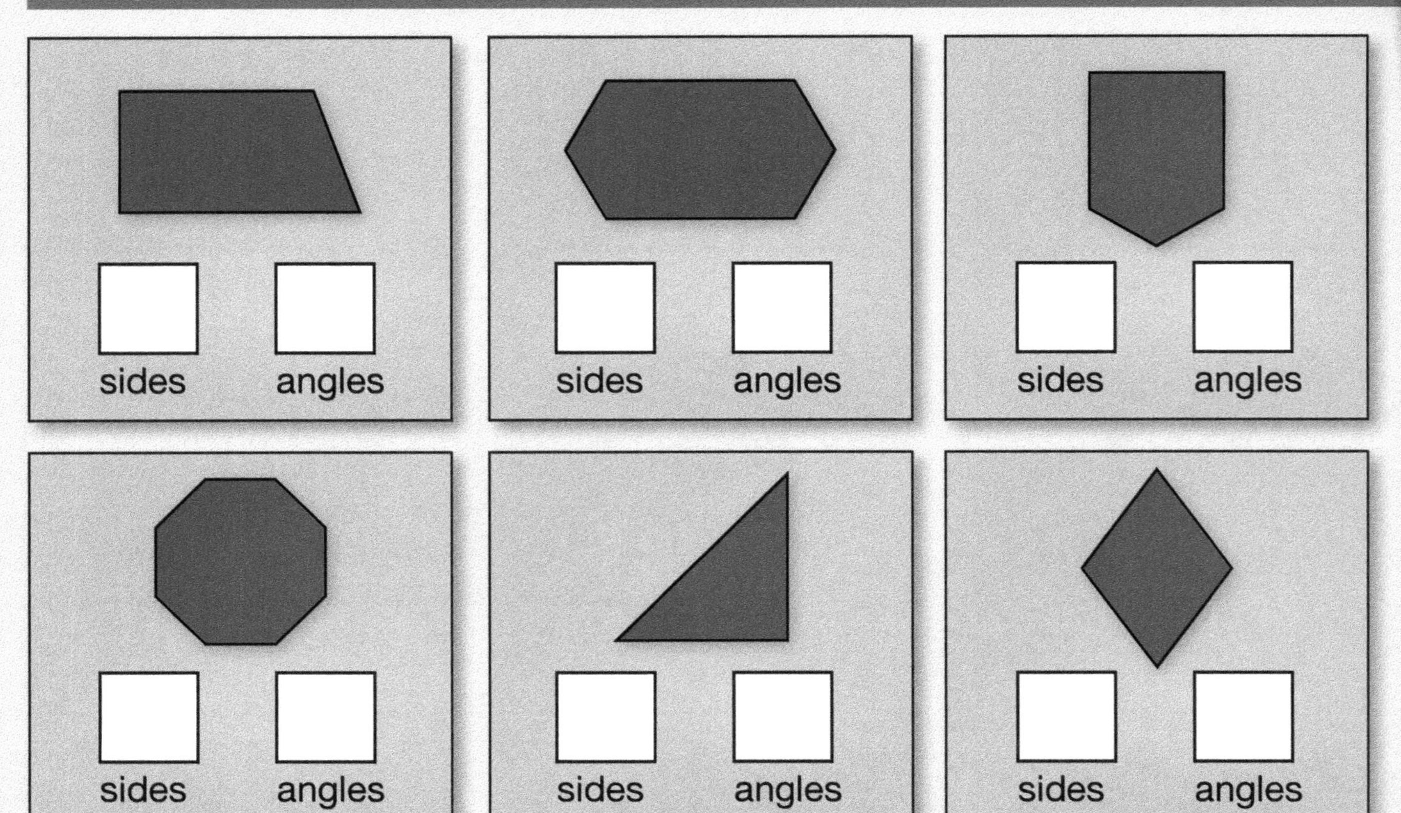

Write a fraction for the pink part of each shape.

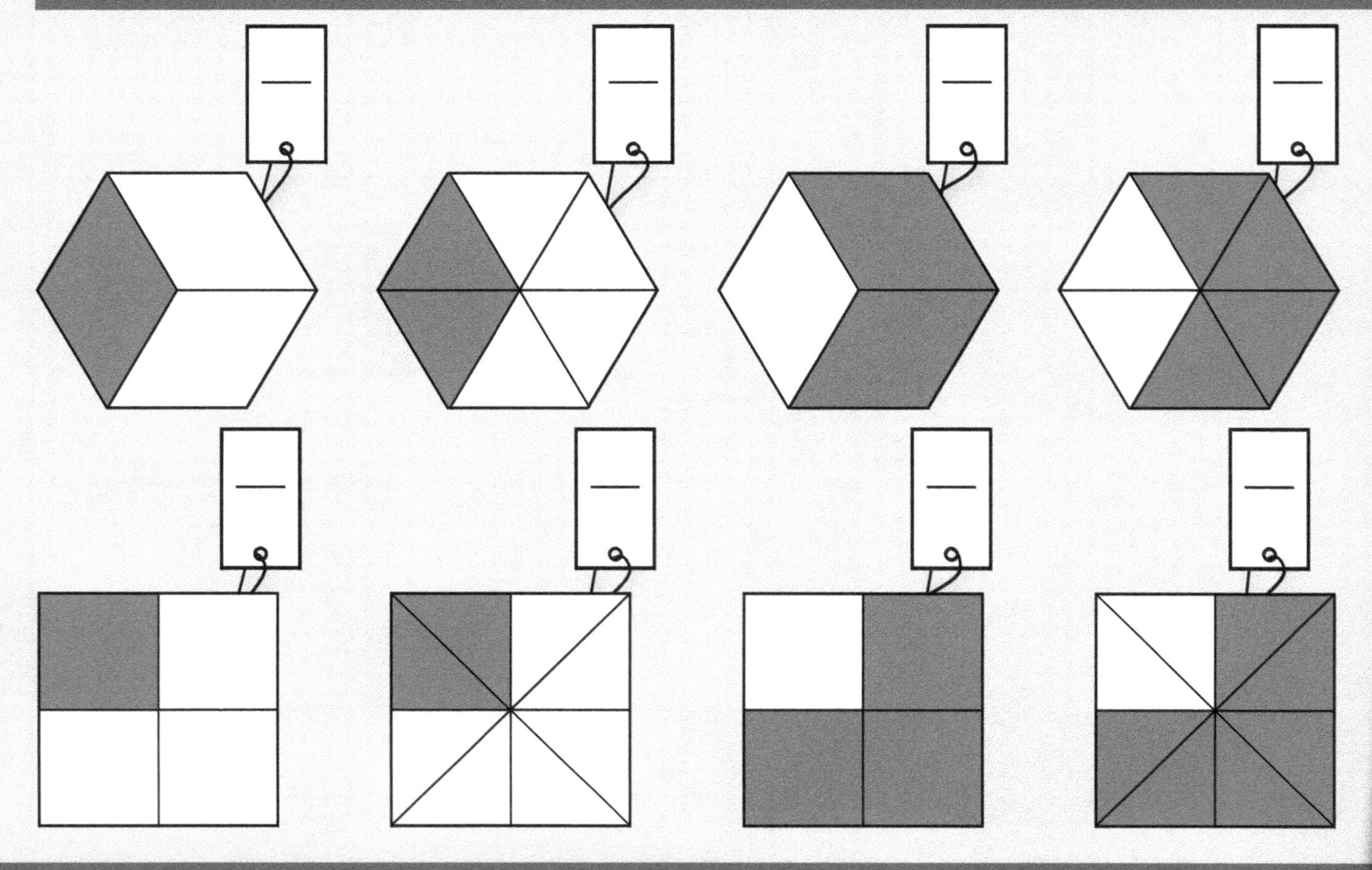

See the Instructor Guide for directions.

	1	1	8
-		6	2

	1	7	2
-		5	9

	1	4	3
-		6	5

What's the Difference?

147 155 87 58

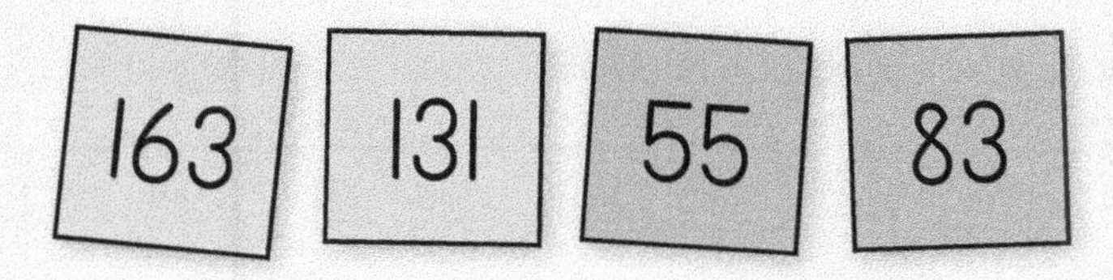

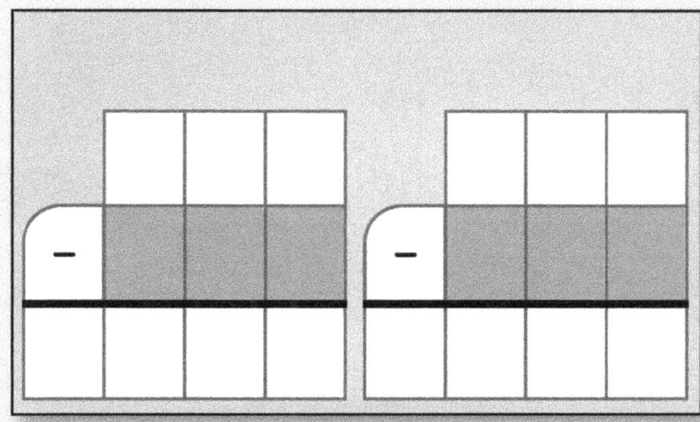

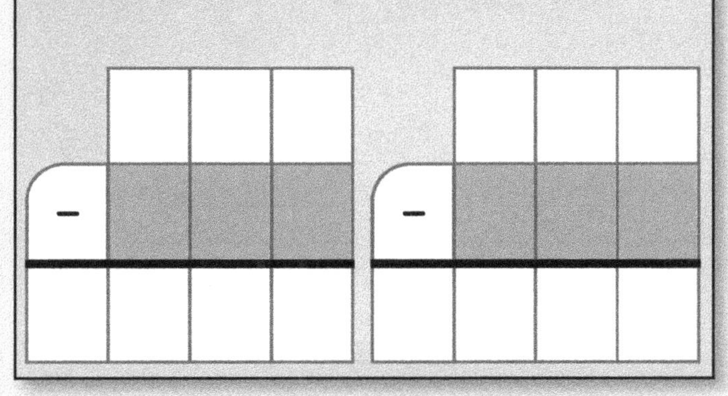

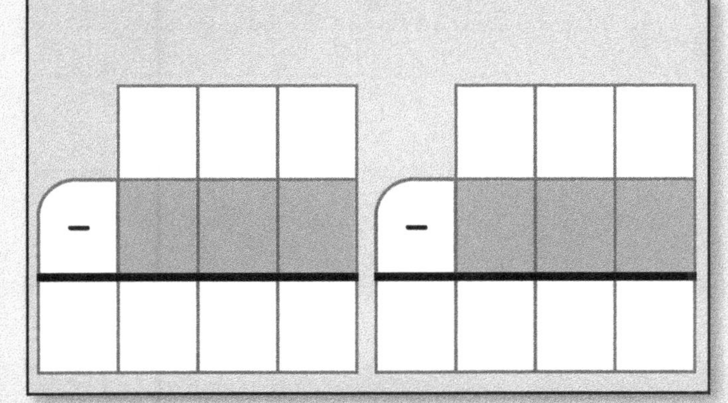

Match.

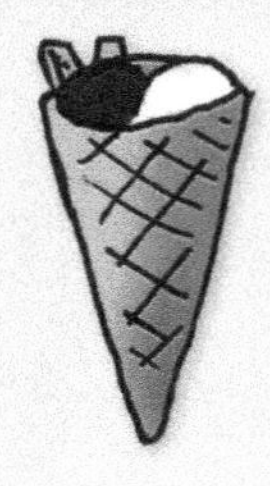

Cone	Rectangular prism	Cube	Sphere	Cylinder

Use a ruler to measure the ribbons in inches.

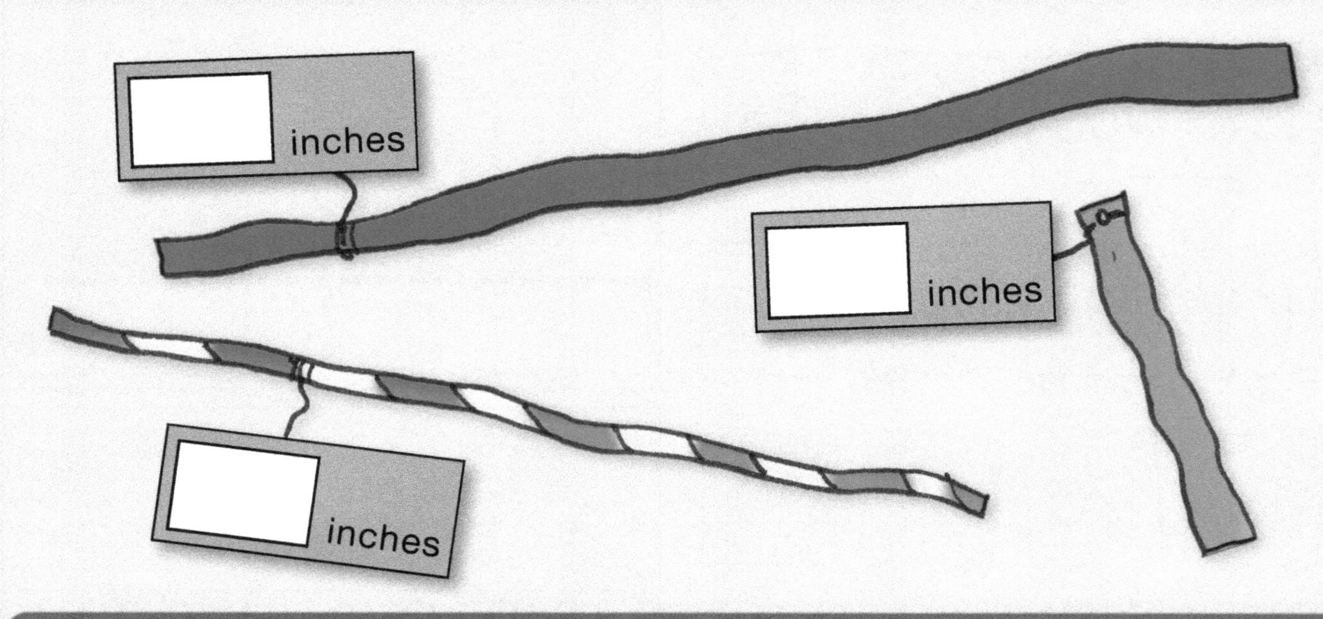

Write the expanded form for each number.

41 = 40 + 1	140 =
141 =	104 =
144 =	114 =

See the Instructor Guide for directions.

	1	2	6
-		7	8

	1	5	1
-		7	3

	1	9	5
-		6	9

Connect the Boxes

	1	7	1
-		5	4

		7	1
-		3	6

		8	4
-		6	9

		9	1
-		3	5

	1	4	6
-		6	8

		9	2
-		5	6

		6	3
-		2	8

		5	1
-		3	7

	1	8	2
-		5	7

		9	7
-		5	4

		8	0
-		4	7

		6	5
-			9

	1	2	5
-		9	2

		9	8
-		5	2

		5	5
-		3	6

		9	3
-		6	4

Choose the more sensible measurement for each item.

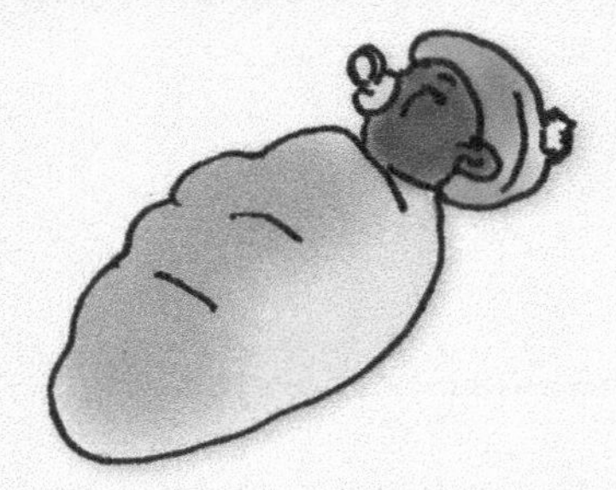

Length of a baby

50 centimeters	50 meters

Length of a fork

20 meters	20 centimeters

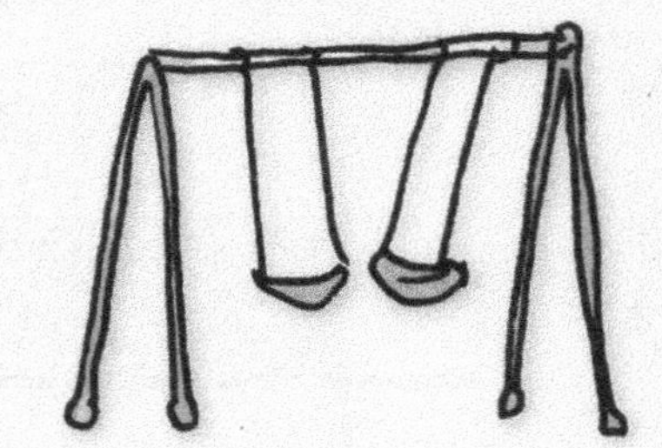

Length of a playground

45 kilometers	45 meters

Write the time.

Color the shapes to match the fractions. Then, complete each circle with <, >, or =.

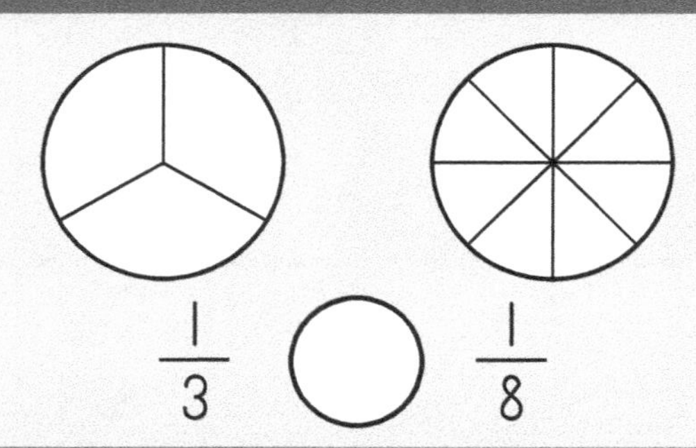

$\frac{1}{3}$ ◯ $\frac{1}{8}$

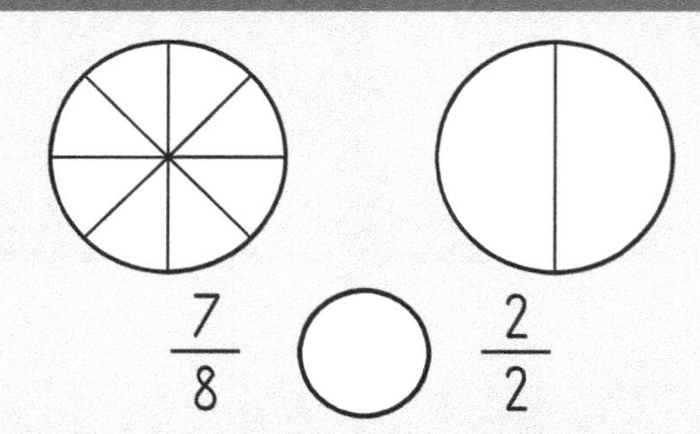

$\frac{7}{8}$ ◯ $\frac{2}{2}$

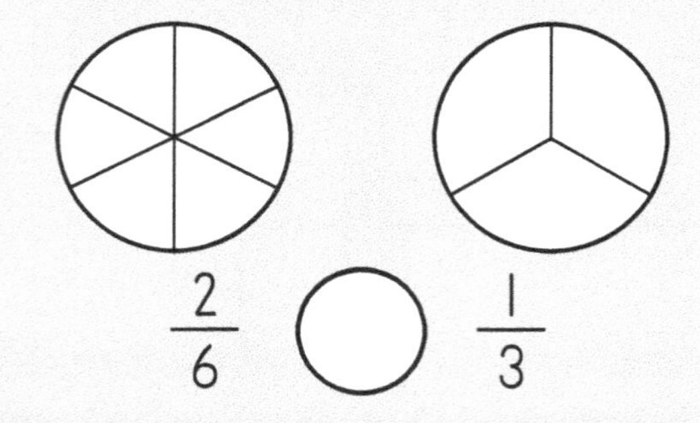

$\frac{2}{6}$ ◯ $\frac{1}{3}$

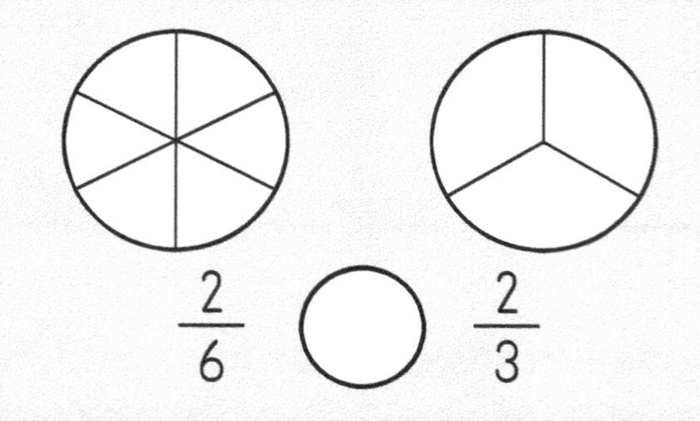

$\frac{2}{6}$ ◯ $\frac{2}{3}$

See the Instructor Guide for directions.

15

7 8

☐ + ☐ = ☐

☐ + ☐ = ☐

☐ - ☐ = ☐

☐ - ☐ = ☐

20 30

☐ + ☐ = ☐

☐ + ☐ = ☐

☐ - ☐ = ☐

☐ - ☐ = ☐

		9	5
-		2	8

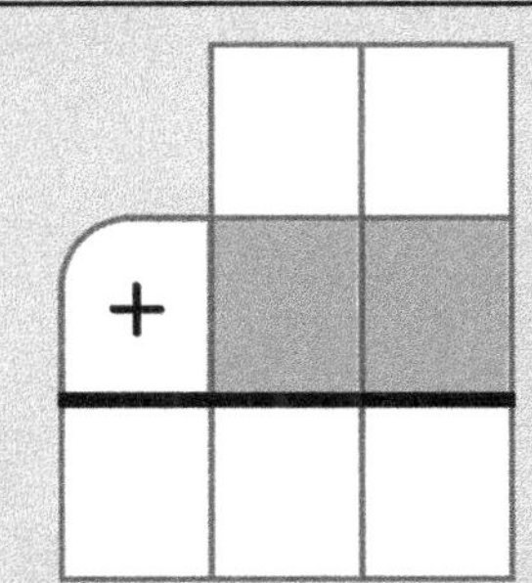

	1	5	9
-		7	4

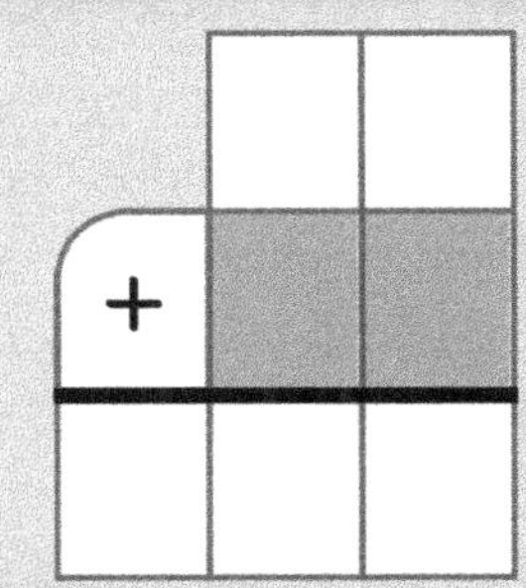

	1	3	6
-		8	8

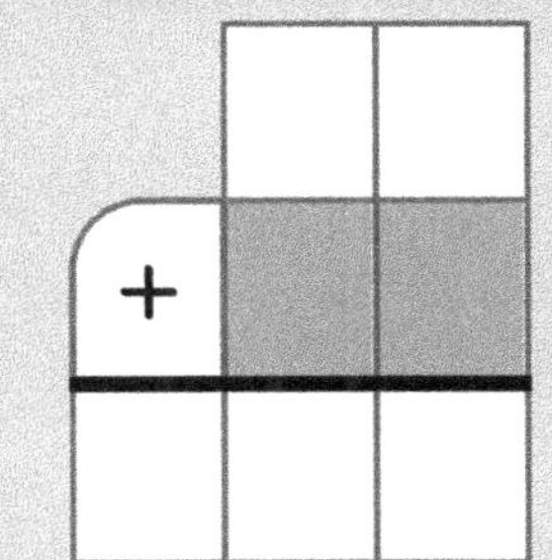

Write a fraction for the pink part of each shape.

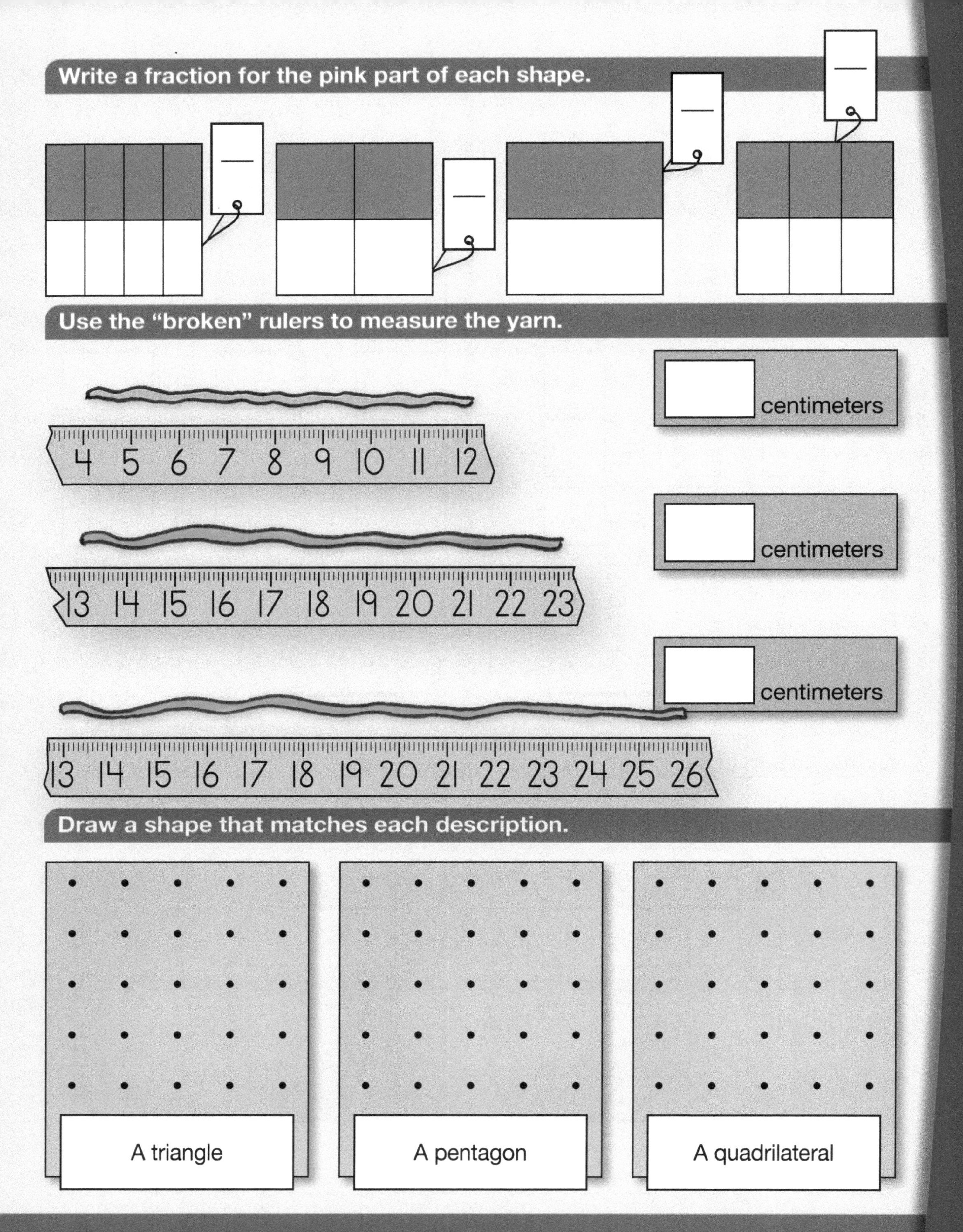

Use the "broken" rulers to measure the yarn.

Draw a shape that matches each description.

Neveah helped at the bake sale. She made a chart of how many cookies were sold. Use the chart to answer the questions.

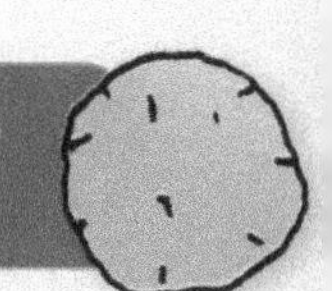

Type	Number Sold
Oatmeal Raisin	123
Chocolate Chip	87
Lemon	49

How many more oatmeal raisin cookies than lemon cookies were sold?

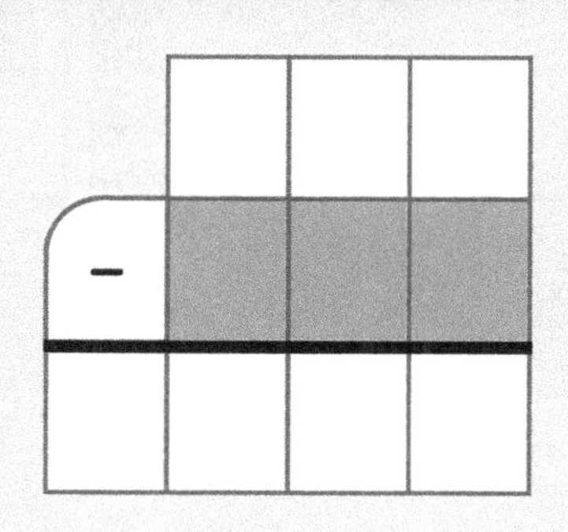

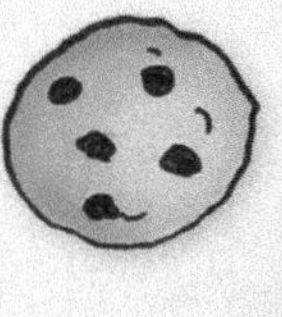

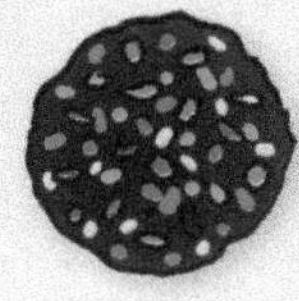

☐ cookies

How many more oatmeal raisin cookies than chocolate chip cookies were sold?

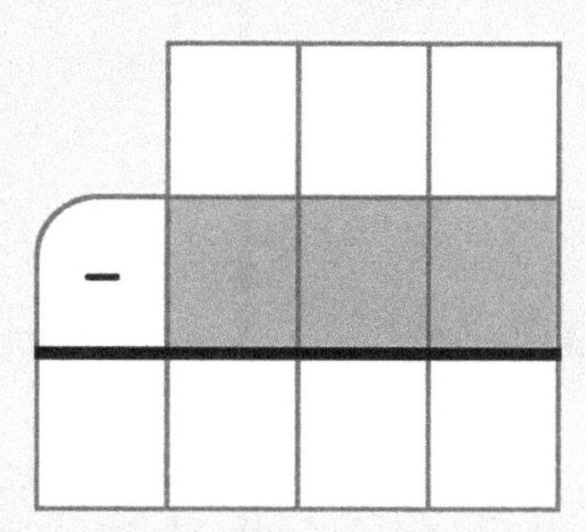

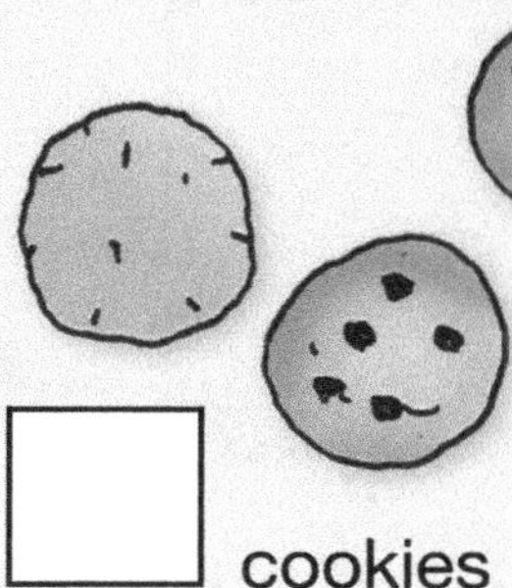

☐ cookies

How many fewer lemon cookies than chocolate chip cookies were sold?

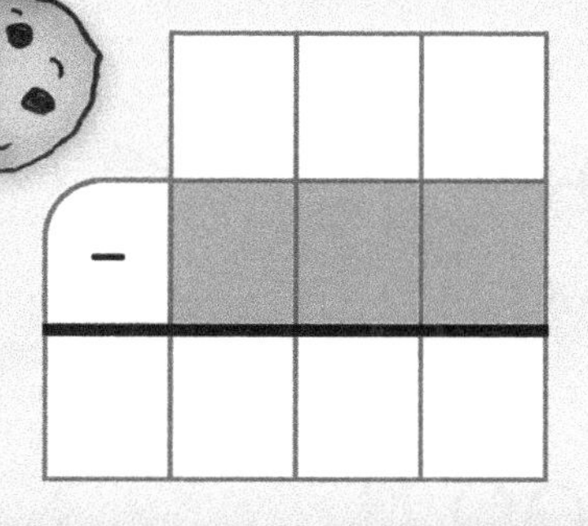

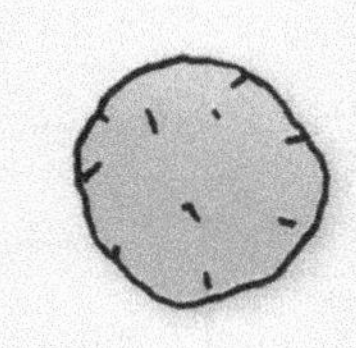

☐ cookies

Complete.

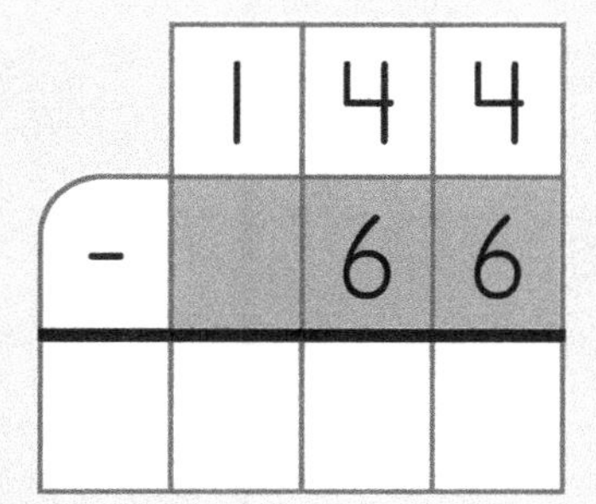

$$
\begin{array}{r} 196 \\ -\ 79 \\ \hline \end{array}
\qquad
\begin{array}{r} 116 \\ -\ 27 \\ \hline \end{array}
$$

$$
\begin{array}{r} 180 \\ -\ 56 \\ \hline \end{array}
\qquad
\begin{array}{r} 135 \\ -\ 87 \\ \hline \end{array}
\qquad
\begin{array}{r} 174 \\ -\ 36 \\ \hline \end{array}
$$

Write a fraction for the pink part of each shape.

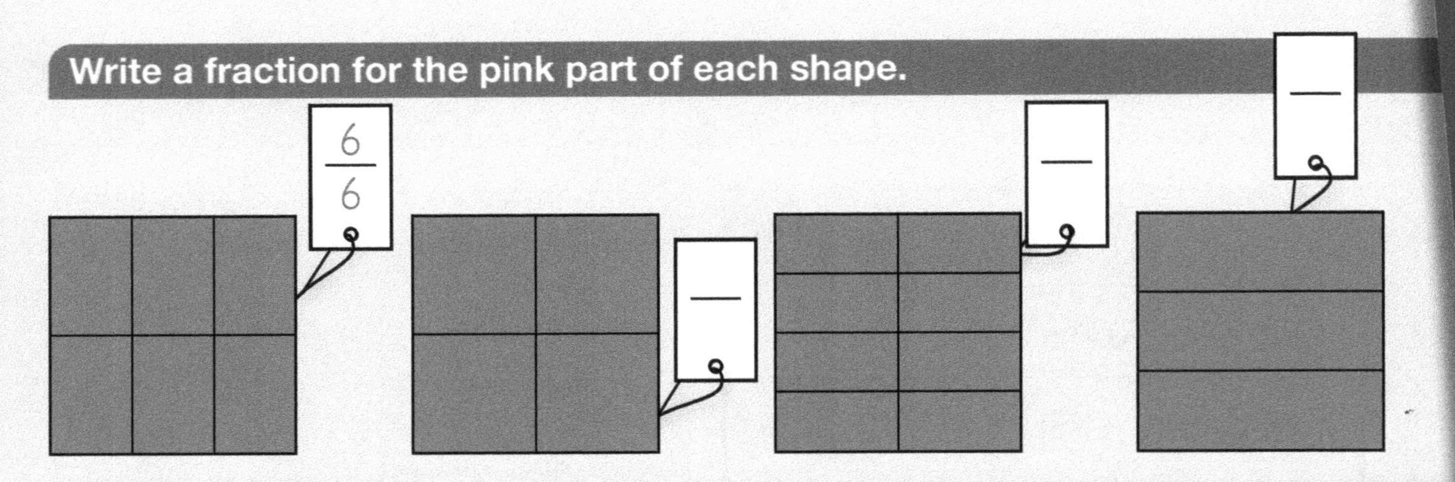

Complete the sequences.

Draw a shape that matches each description.

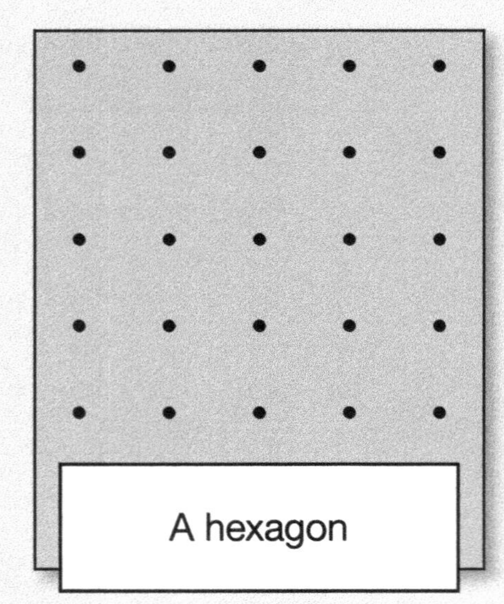

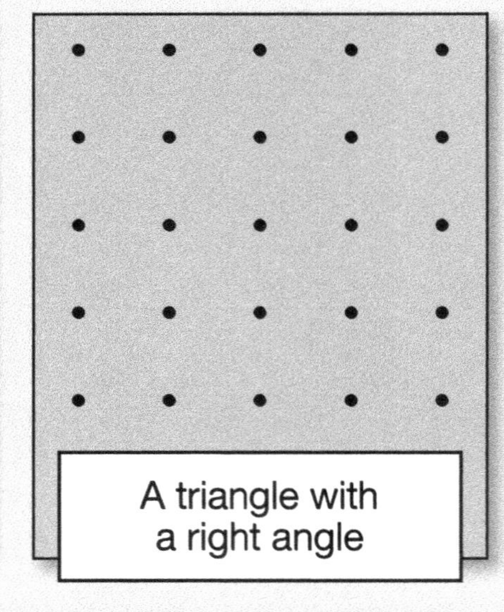

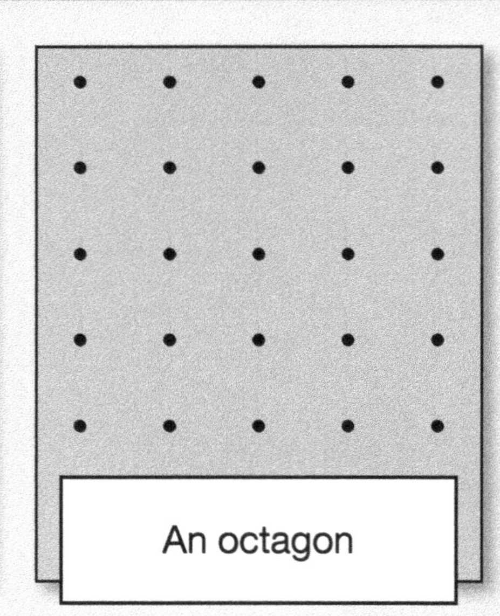

Write the value of each set of base-ten blocks.

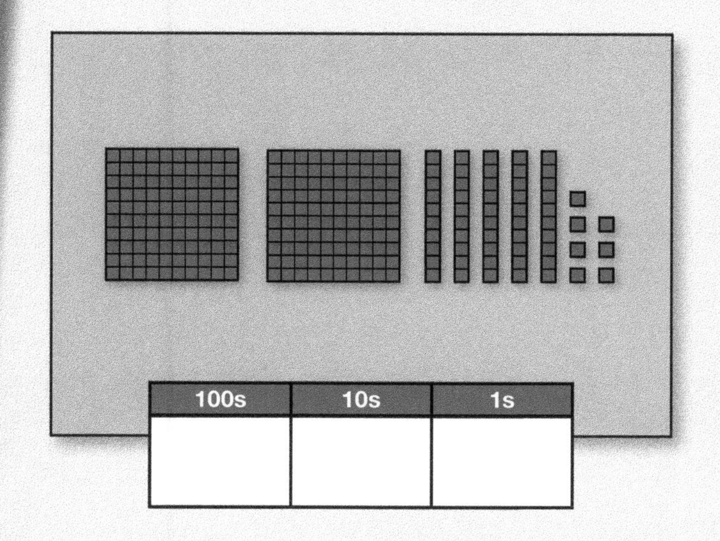

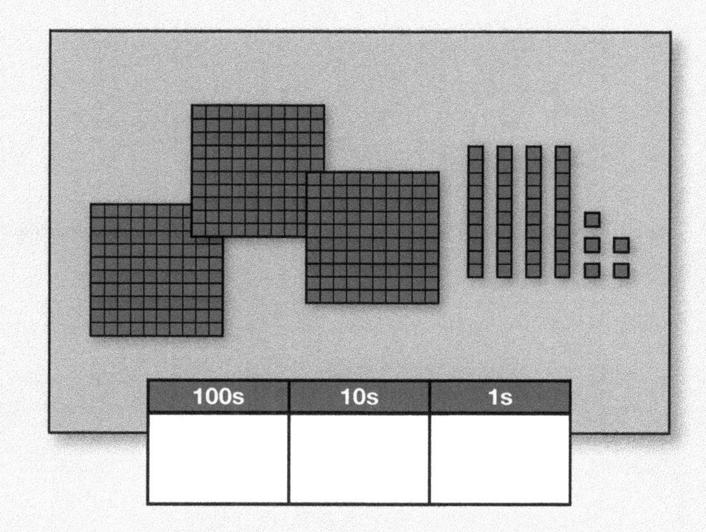

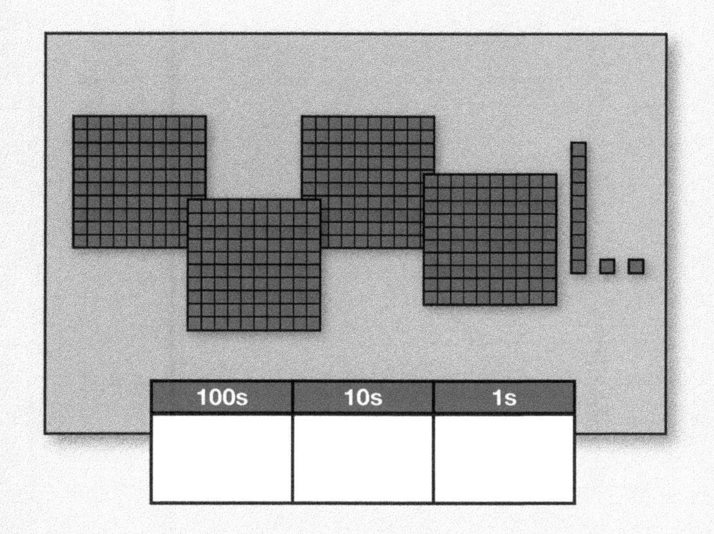

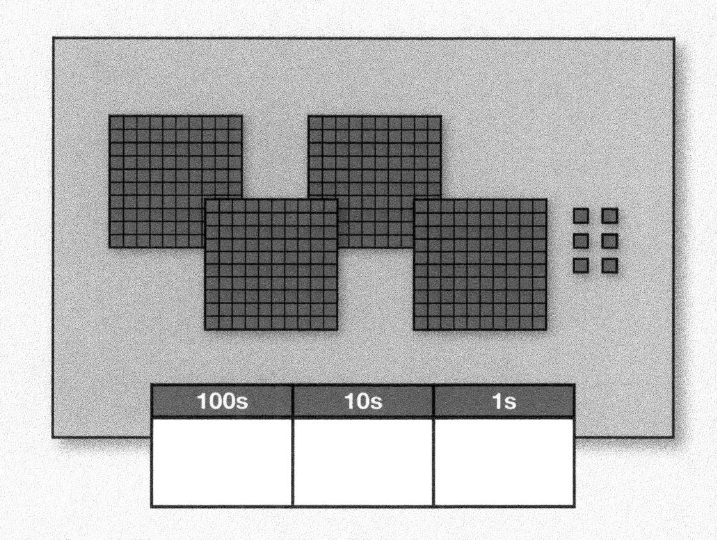

Complete the circles with <, >, or =.

425 ◯ 525	628 ◯ 618	923 ◯ 924
847 ◯ 609	352 ◯ 352	714 ◯ 900
700 ◯ 450	809 ◯ 890	600 ◯ 599

Complete.

$$\begin{array}{r} 154 \\ -\ 81 \\ \hline \end{array}$$

$$\begin{array}{r} 136 \\ -\ 99 \\ \hline \end{array}$$

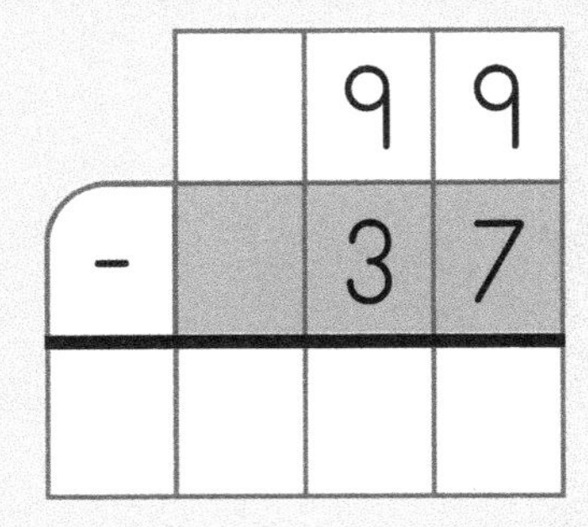

Elena made a graph about the spring flowers at the park.
Use the graph to complete the chart and answer the questions.

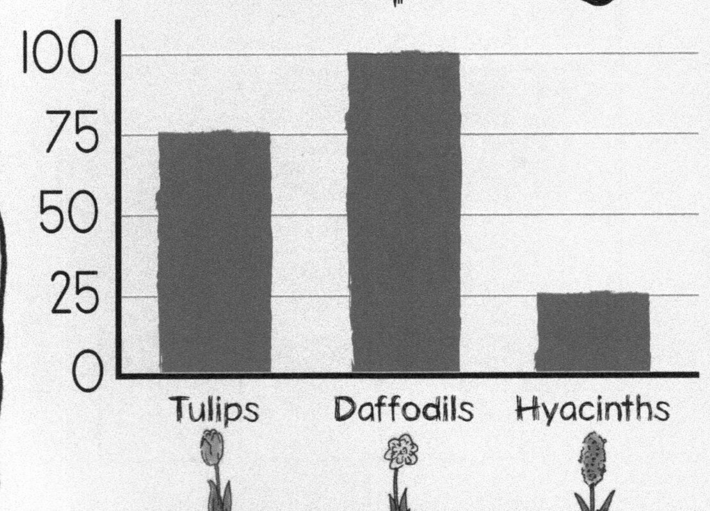

Flower	Number
Tulips	
Daffodils	
Hyacinths	

How many more daffodils than tulips are there?

☐ more

How many fewer hyacinths than tulips are there?

☐ fewer

How many more daffodils then hyacinths are there?

☐ more

How many flowers are there in all?

☐ flowers

Match.

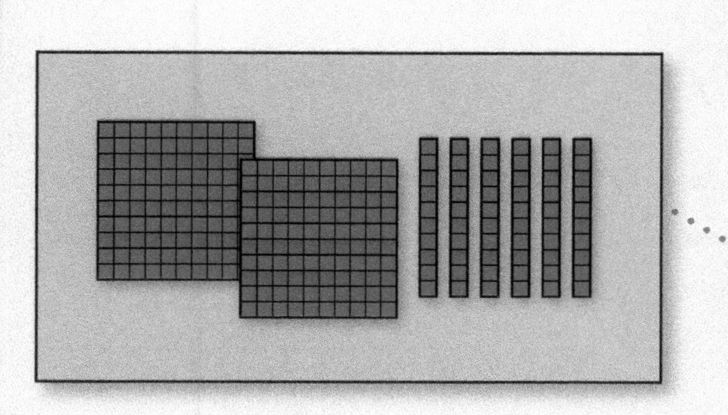

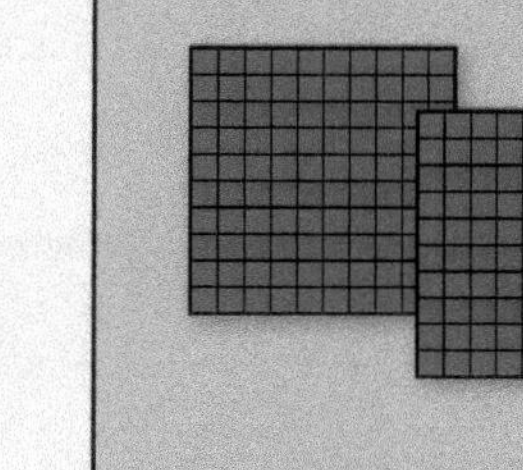

261

260

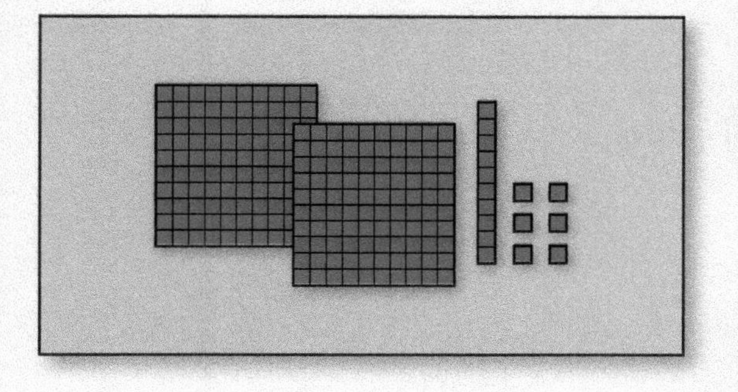

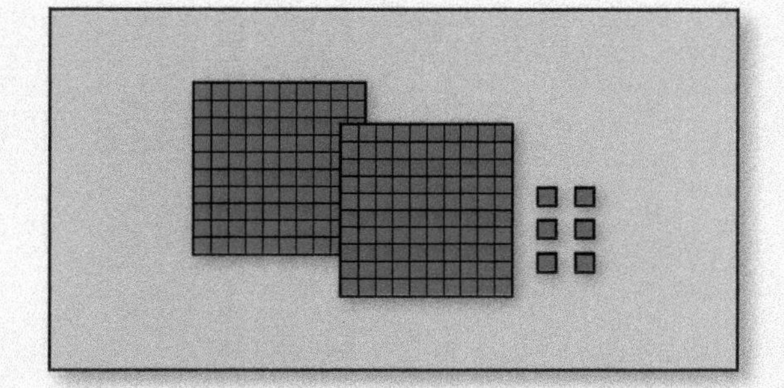

206

216

Write the expanded form for each number.

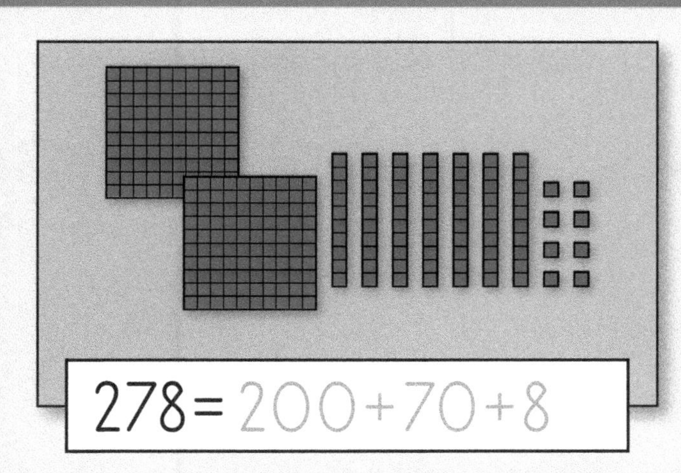

278= 200+70+8

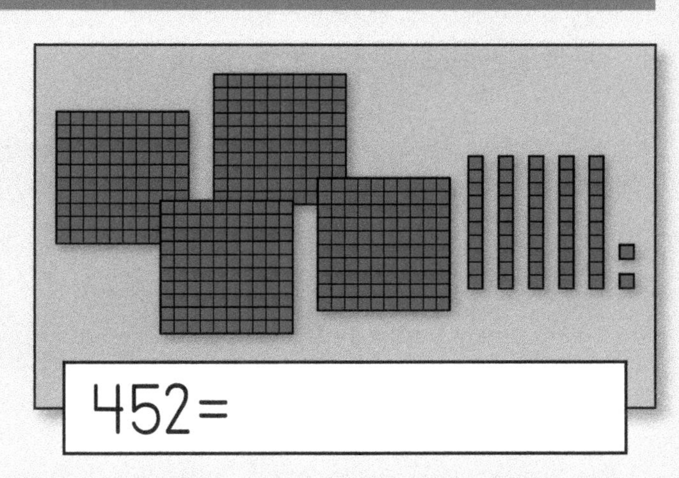

452=

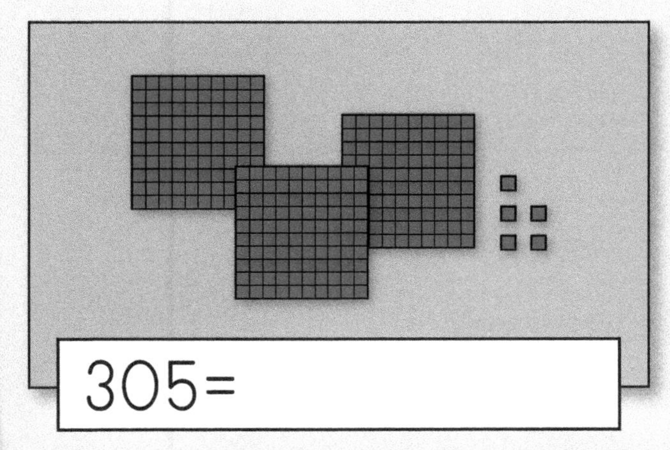

305=

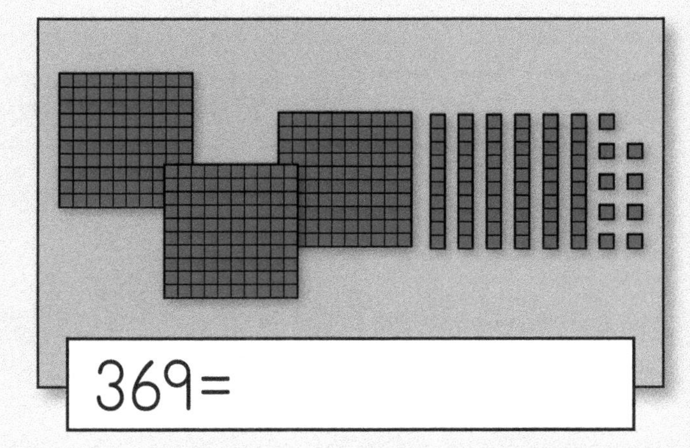

369=

Complete.

		8	2
-		5	6

	1	5	7
-		7	4

	1	3	2
-		8	5

Complete.

1 week = ☐ days

1 day = ☐ hours

1 hour = ☐ minutes

1 minute = ☐ seconds

1 yard = ☐ feet

1 yard = ☐ inches

1 foot = ☐ inches

1 meter = ☐ centimeters

Match. Each ruler is 1 foot long.

1 foot, 2 inches

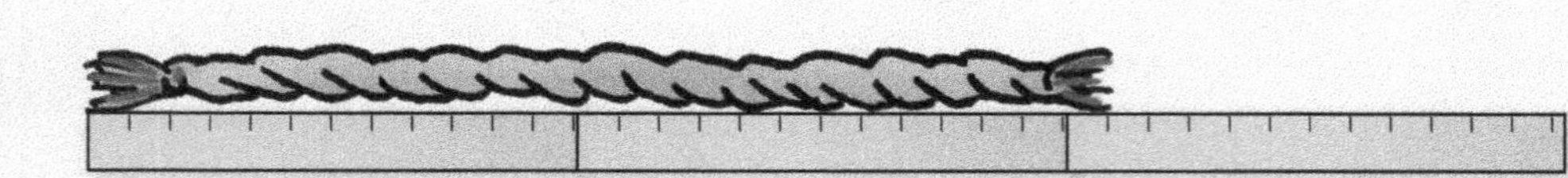

3 feet

2 feet, 1 inches

Complete the missing numbers in the sequences.

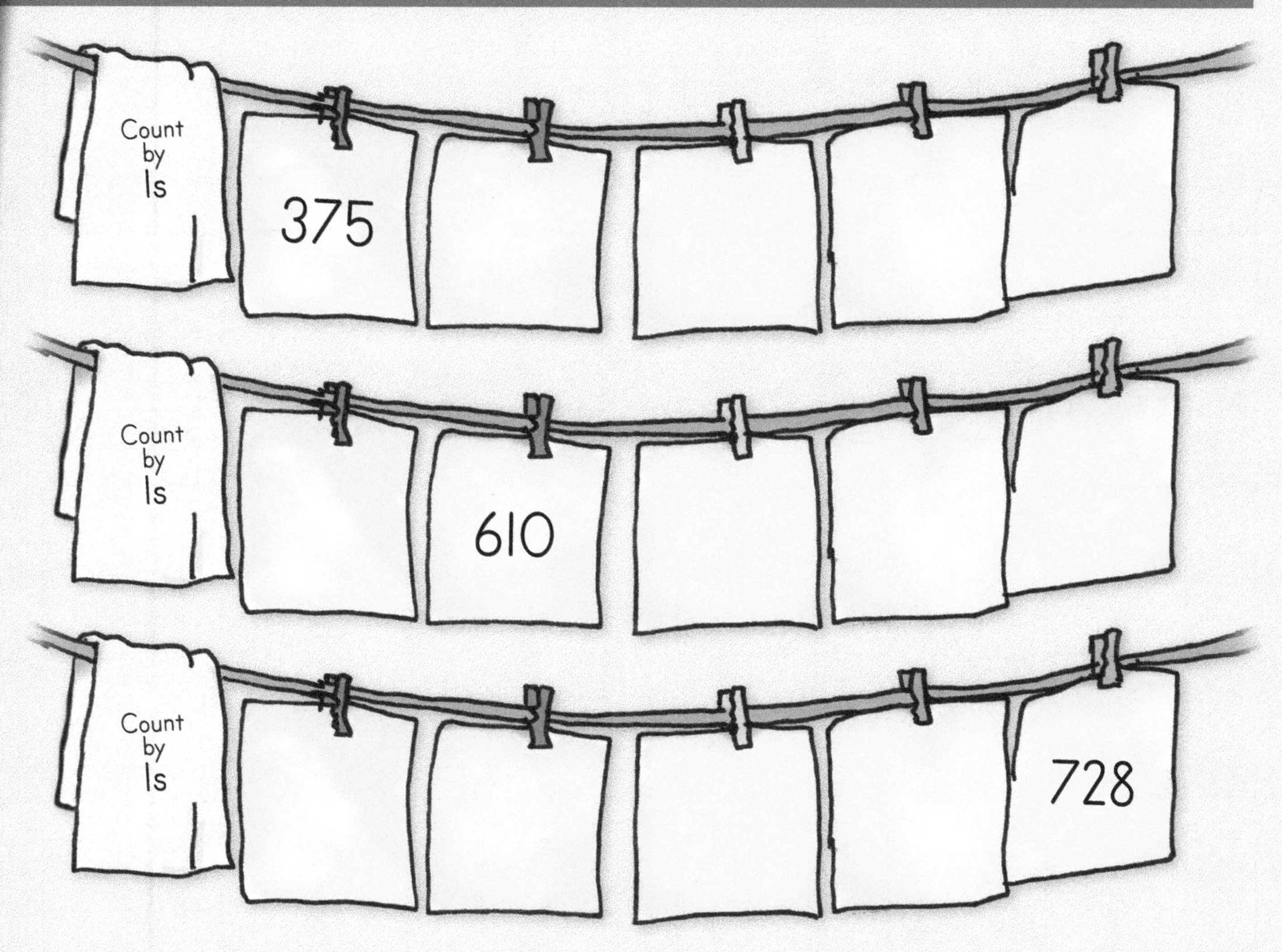

Write the numbers that come before and after.

	374	
	247	
	932	
	486	

	565	
	799	
	608	
	853	

Complete.

		9	0
-		3	9

	1	2	5
-		6	8

	1	9	9
-		7	6

Shade the shapes to match the fractions. Then, complete each circle with <, >, or =.

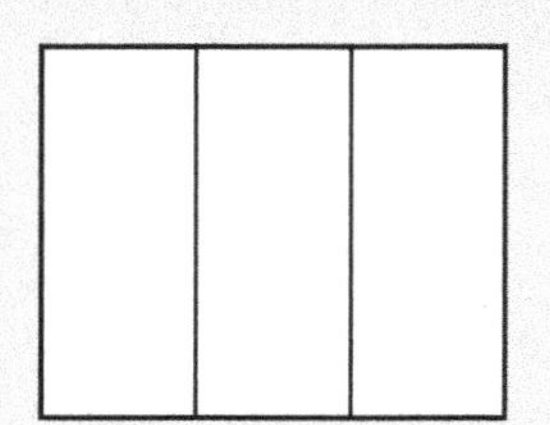 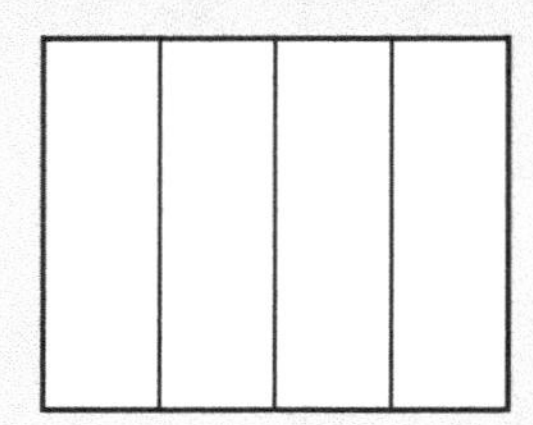

$\frac{2}{3}$ ◯ $\frac{2}{4}$

 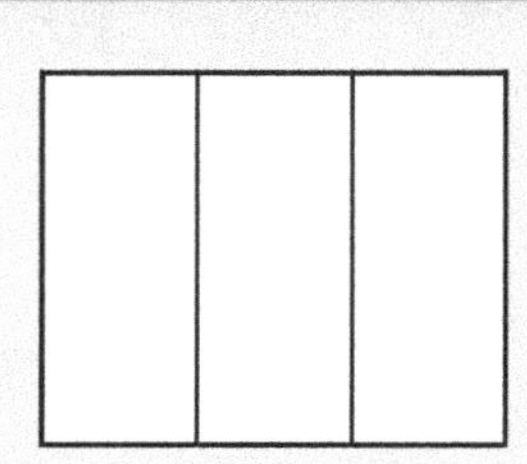

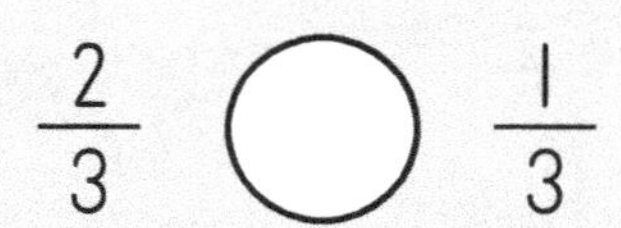

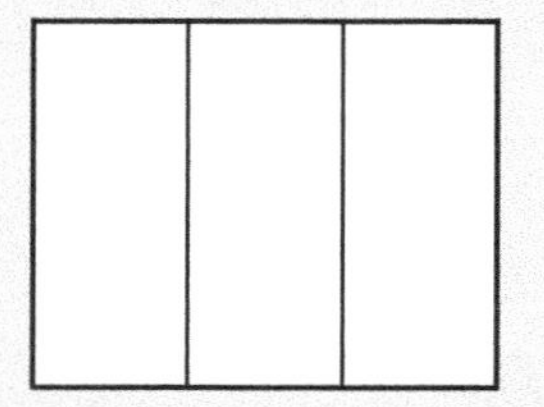 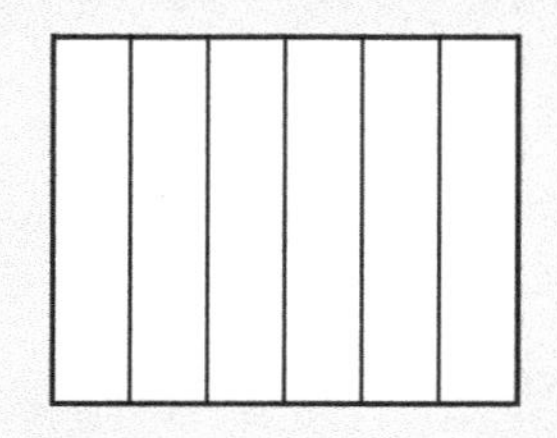

$\frac{2}{3}$ ◯ $\frac{2}{6}$

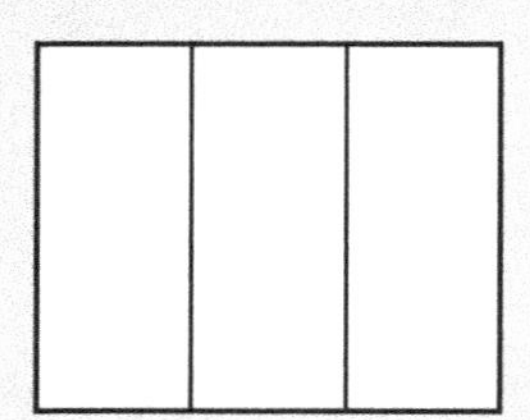 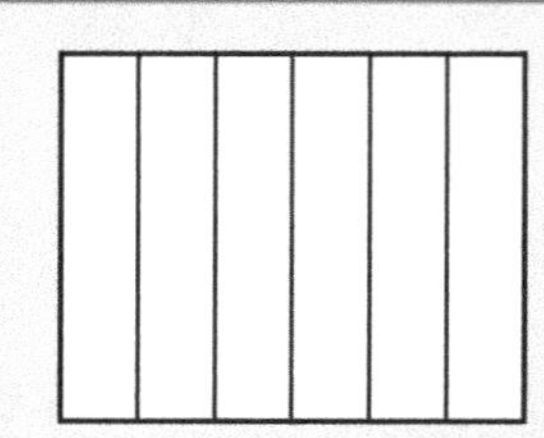

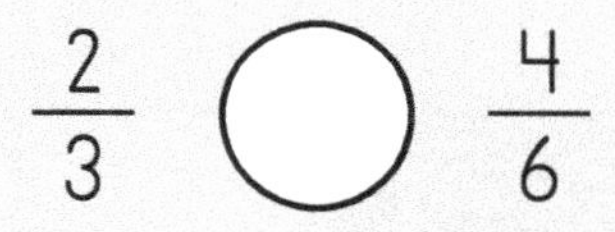

Complete. Use a decimal point.

Connect each number to its spot on the number lines.

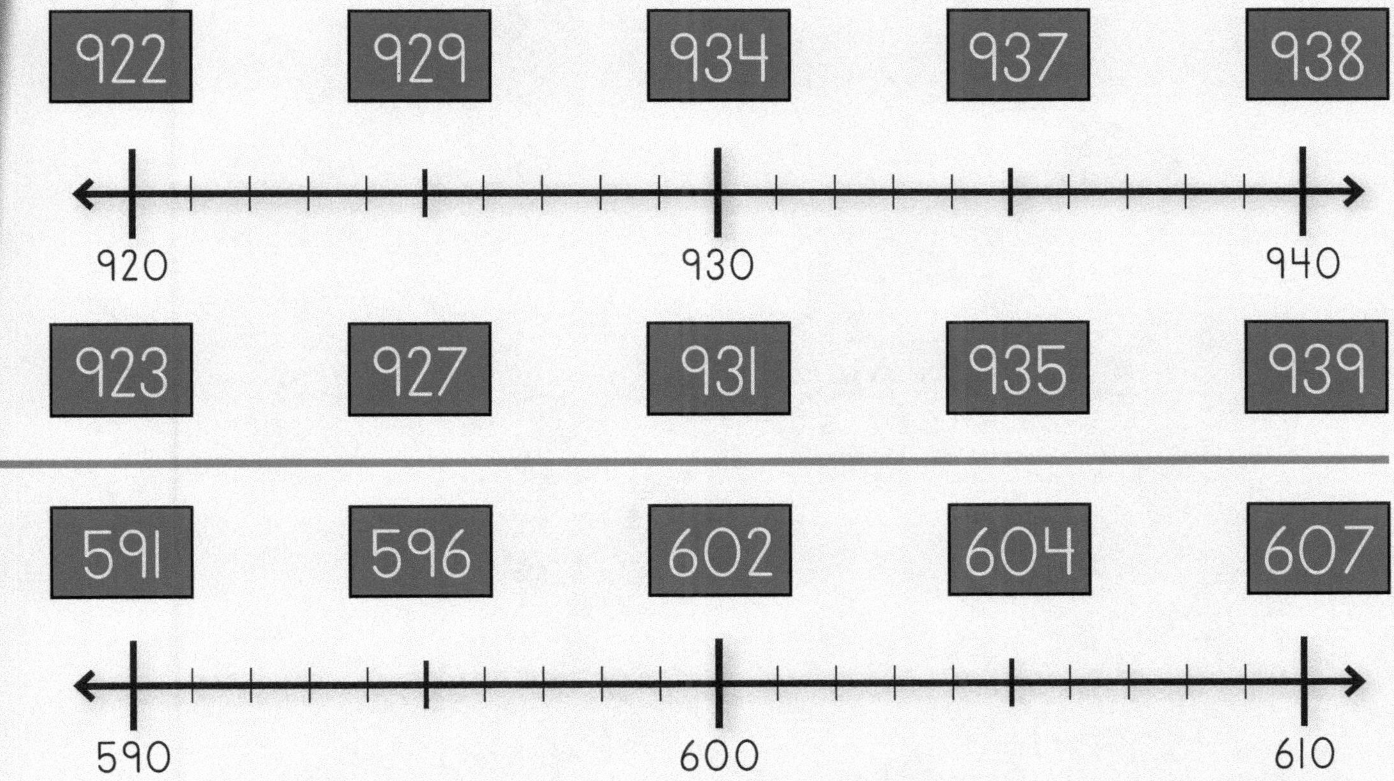

Color the even numbers blue. Color the odd numbers yellow.

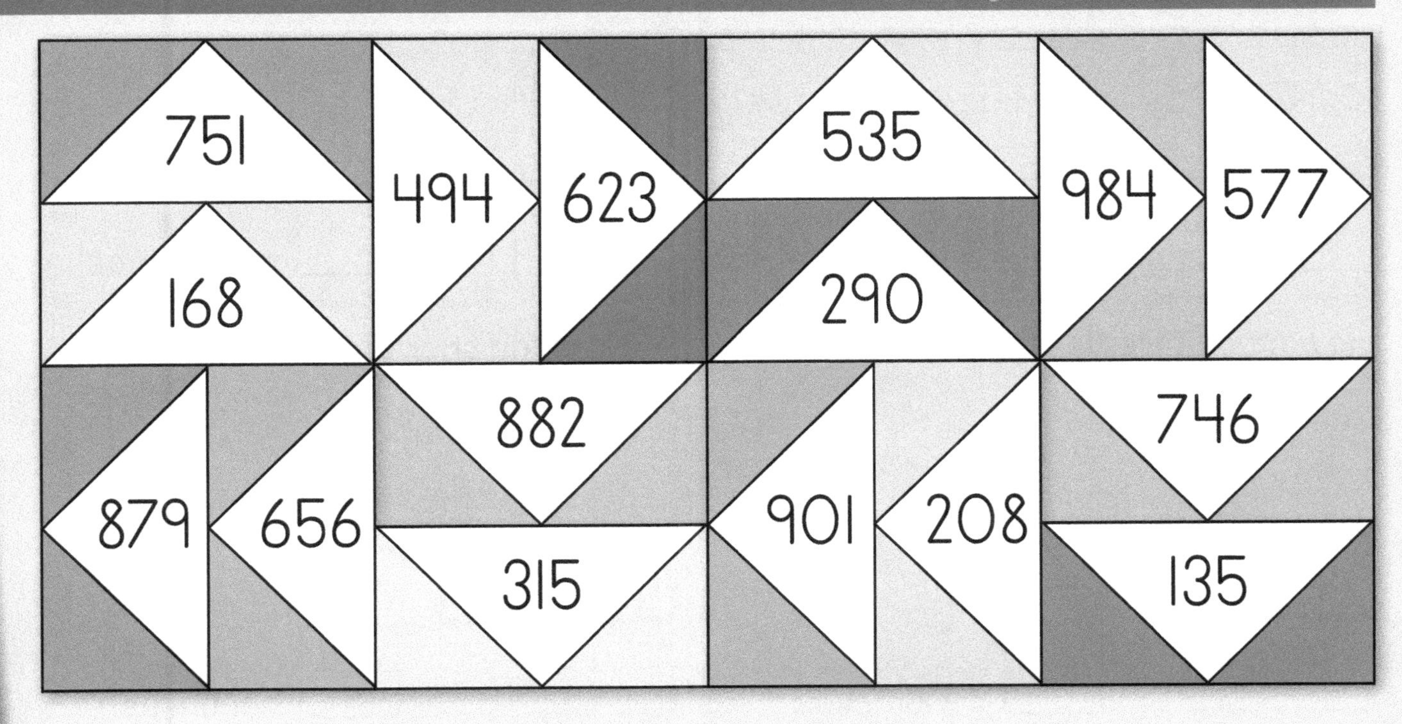

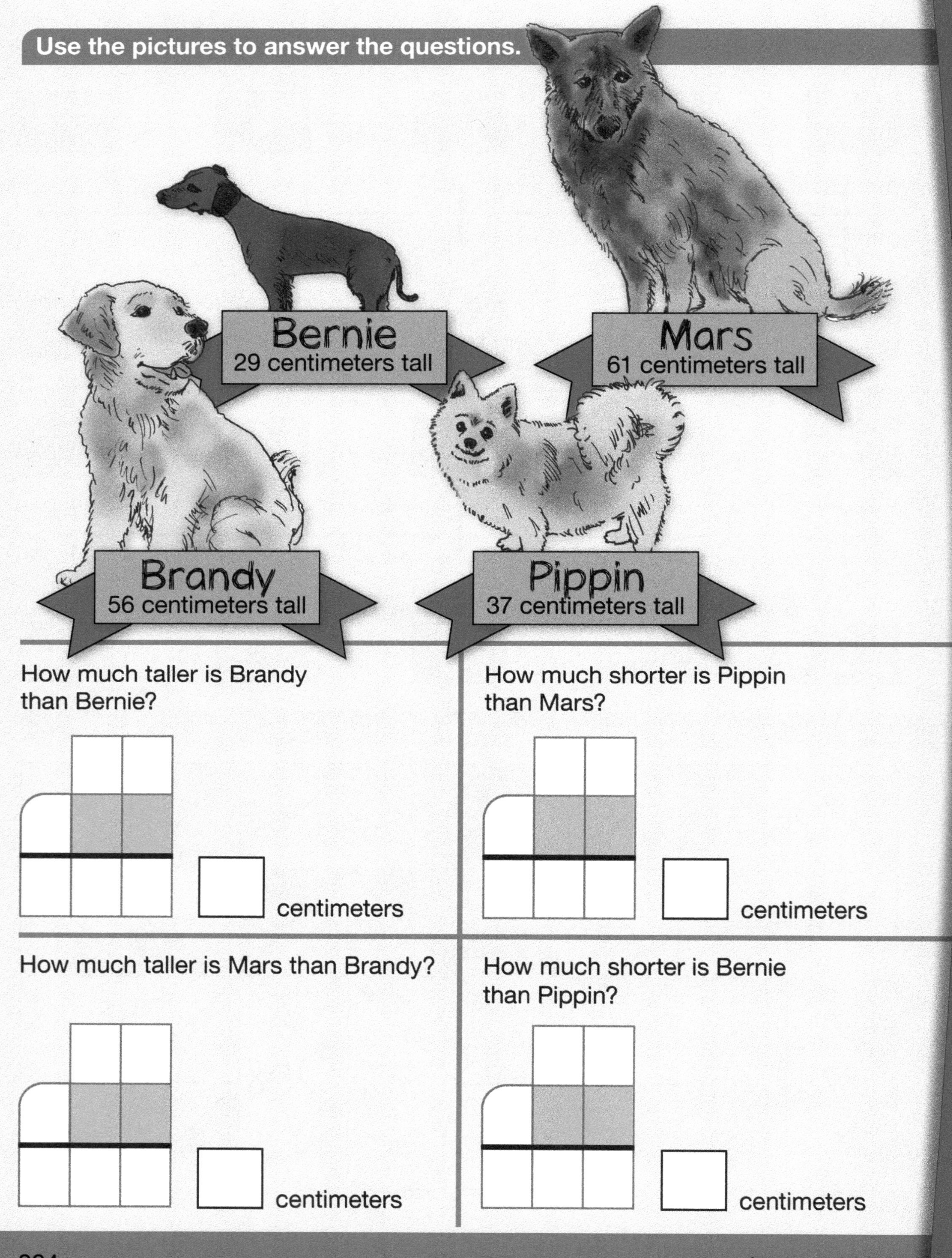
Use the pictures to answer the questions.
Bernie
29 centimeters tall
Mars
61 centimeters tall
Brandy
56 centimeters tall
Pippin
37 centimeters tall
How much taller is Brandy than Bernie?
centimeters
How much shorter is Pippin than Mars?
centimeters
How much taller is Mars than Brandy?
centimeters
How much shorter is Bernie than Pippin?
centimeters

Complete.

328 + 1 = ☐	739 + 1 = ☐
328 + 10 = ☐	739 + 10 = ☐
328 + 100 = ☐	739 + 100 = ☐
645 + 2 = ☐	562 + 3 = ☐
645 + 20 = ☐	562 + 30 = ☐
645 + 200 = ☐	562 + 300 = ☐

Match.

499 + 2	500	498 + 2
497 + 6	501	496 + 6
498 + 4	502	495 + 6
494 + 6	503	499 + 3

Complete.

	1	4	8
-		9	2

	1	8	1
-		2	7

		6	7
+		2	5

Complete.

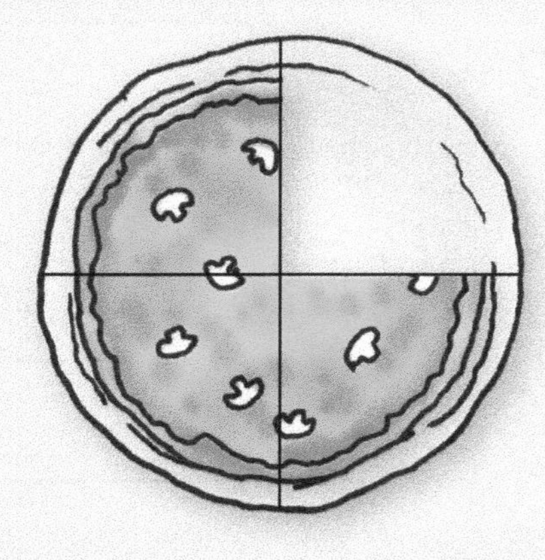

$\frac{\square}{\square}$ of the pizza is left.

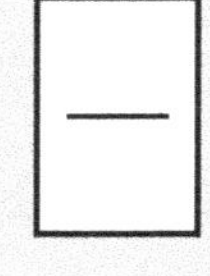

$\frac{\square}{\square}$ of the pizza has been eaten.

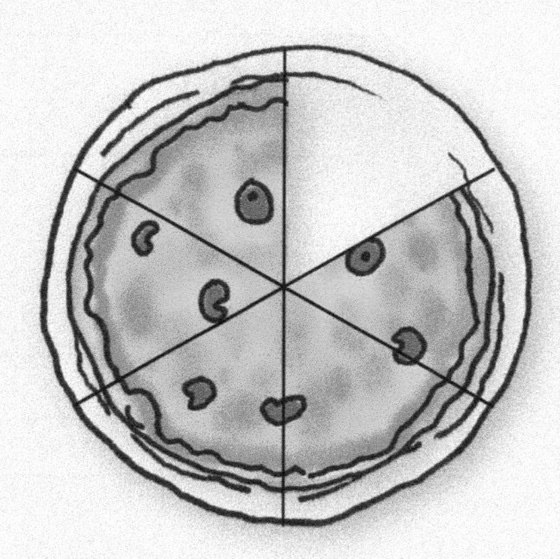

$\frac{\square}{\square}$ of the pizza is left.

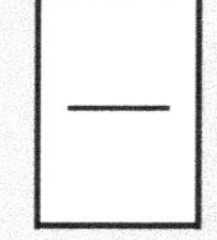

$\frac{\square}{\square}$ of the pizza has been eaten.

Write a.m. or p.m. for each time.

Complete.

$328 - 1 =$ ☐

$328 - 10 =$ ☐

$328 - 100 =$ ☐

$739 - 1 =$ ☐

$739 - 10 =$ ☐

$739 - 100 =$ ☐

$645 - 2 =$ ☐

$645 - 20 =$ ☐

$645 - 200 =$ ☐

$562 - 3 =$ ☐

$562 - 30 =$ ☐

$562 - 300 =$ ☐

Complete.

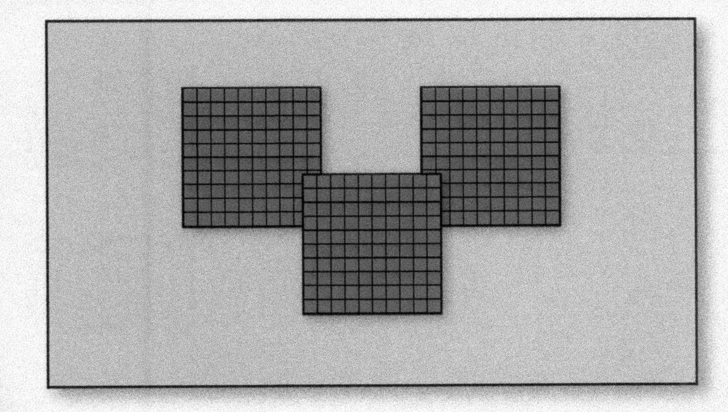

$300 - 1 =$ ☐

$300 - 5 =$ ☐

$300 - 6 =$ ☐

$300 - 9 =$ ☐

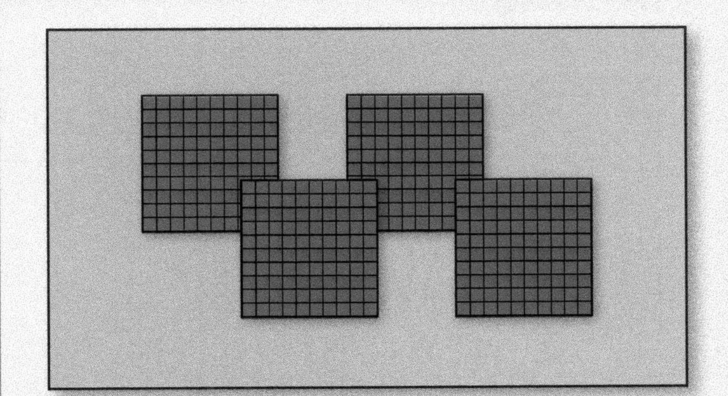

$400 - 2 =$ ☐

$400 - 4 =$ ☐

$400 - 8 =$ ☐

$400 - 3 =$ ☐

Complete.

	1	2	9
-		7	5

		7	3
+		8	2

	1	3	0
-		5	4

Match.

385 750 363 412 907

odd

even

441 536 198 629 724

Write the time.

Complete.

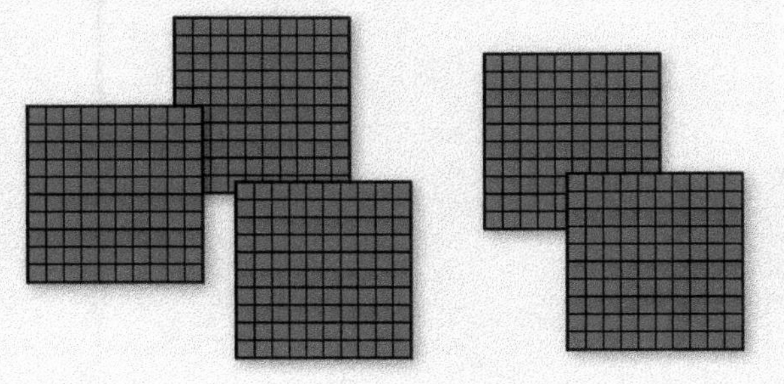

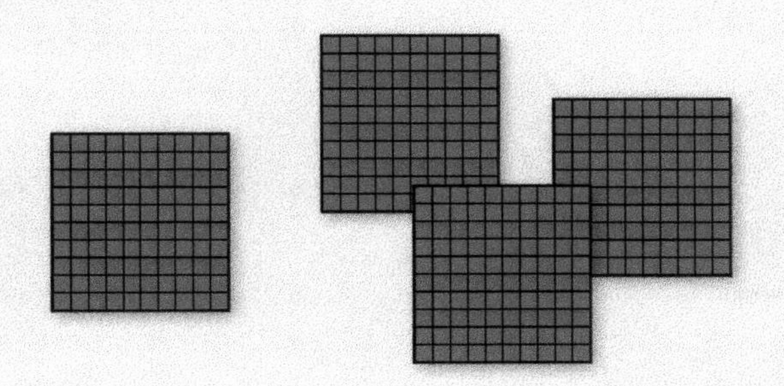

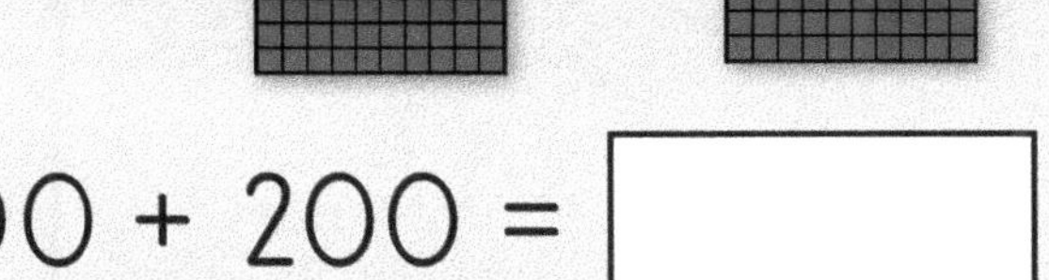

300 + 200 = ☐	100 + 300 = ☐
500 + 200 = ☐	400 + 400 = ☐
100 + 800 = ☐	600 + 200 = ☐
300 + 400 = ☐	200 + 700 = ☐

Match the pairs that make 1000.

500	300
600	500
700	100
800	400
900	200

Complete.

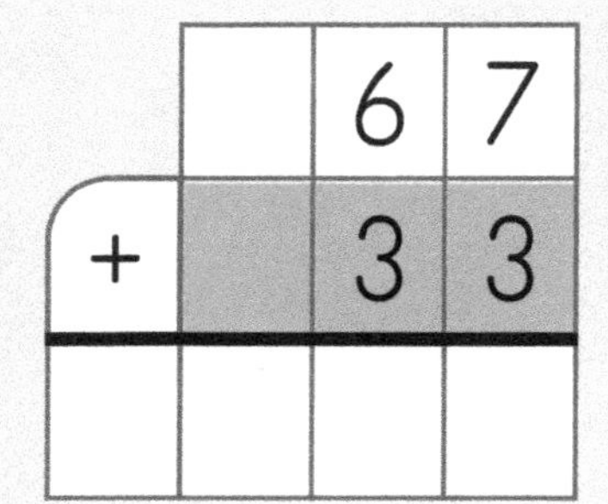

	6	8
+	4	9

	9	2
-	5	3

Complete the sequences.

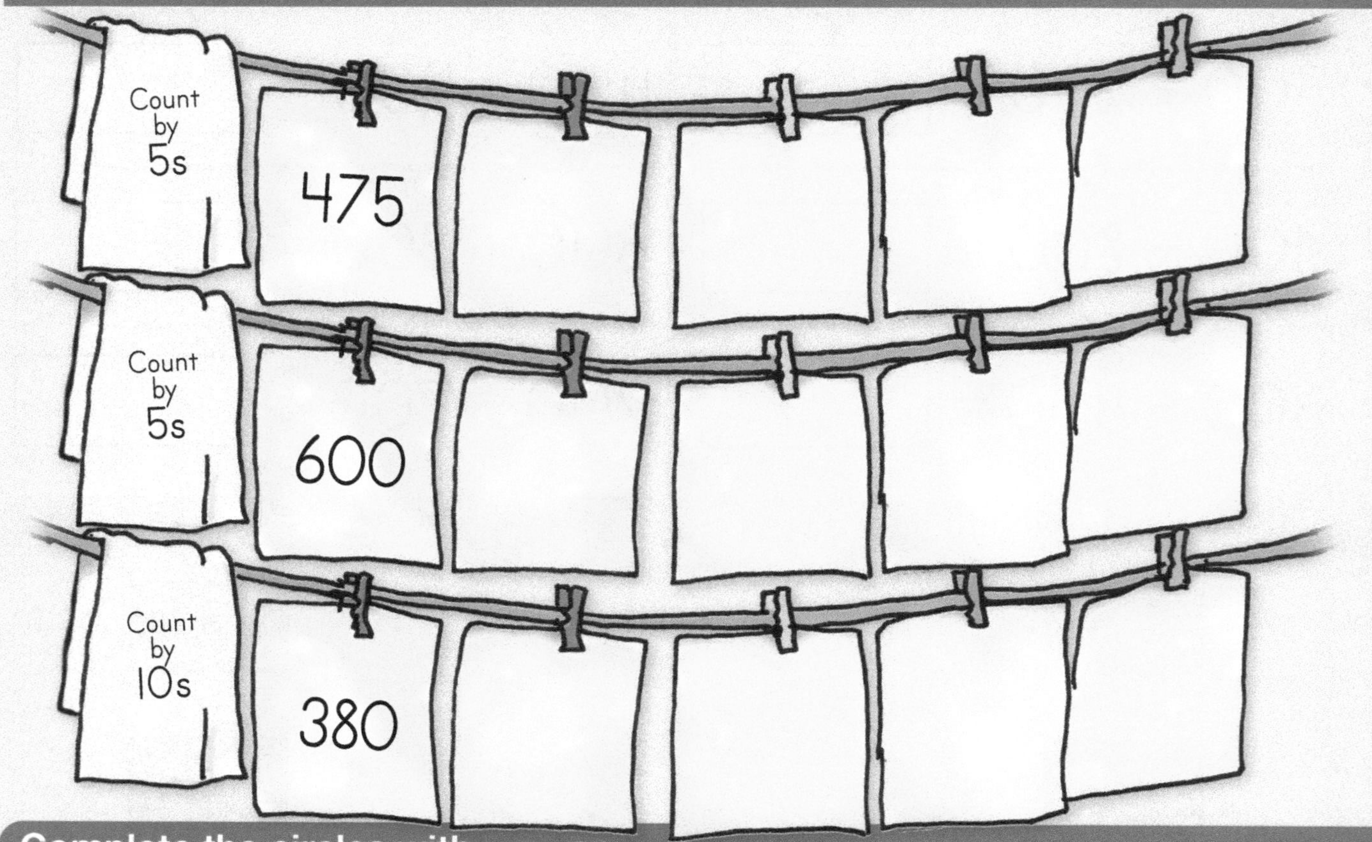

Complete the circles with <, >, or =.

516 ◯ 517	500 ◯ 499	345 ◯ 254
500 ◯ 500	890 ◯ 809	708 ◯ 808
275 ◯ 396	600 ◯ 900	999 ◯ 1000

Complete.

Use the clues to complete the chart.

- The table costs $200 less than the bed.
- The bookcase costs $1 more than the table.
- The desk costs $5 less than the bookcase.
- The lamp costs $300 less than the desk.

Furniture Sale

Item	Price
Bed	$699
Table	
Bookcase	
Desk	
Lamp	

Complete.

$$\begin{array}{r} 186 \\ -\ \ 75 \\ \hline \end{array}$$

$$\begin{array}{r} 94 \\ -\ 49 \\ \hline \end{array}$$

$$\begin{array}{r} 47 \\ +\ 63 \\ \hline \end{array}$$

Write how many.

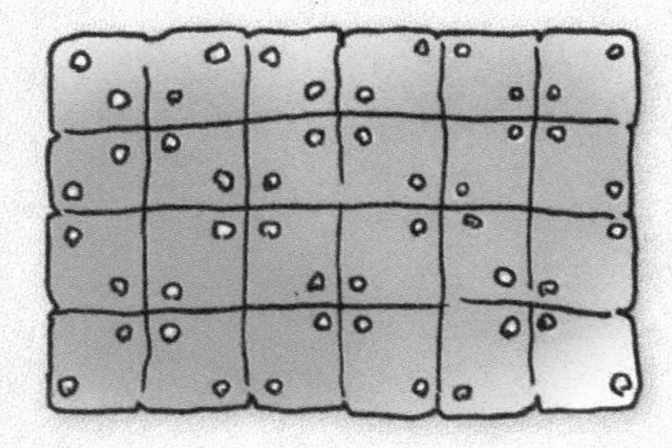

 tiles

 tiles

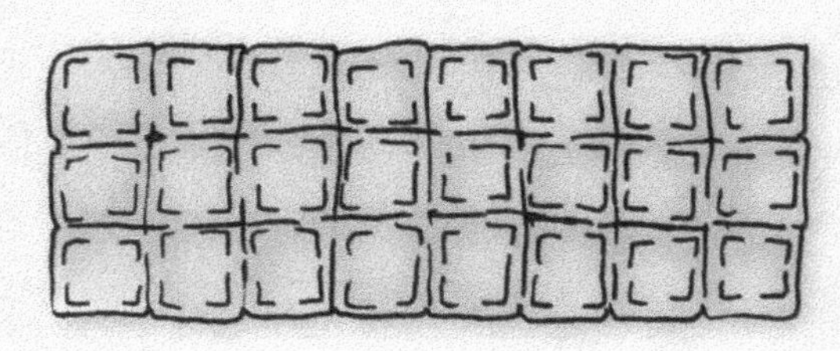

 tiles

Solve.

Mateo has $46. He spends $24 on a toy. How much money does he have left?

$ [ ]

Emerson has $41. She spends $17 on a toy. How much money does she have left?

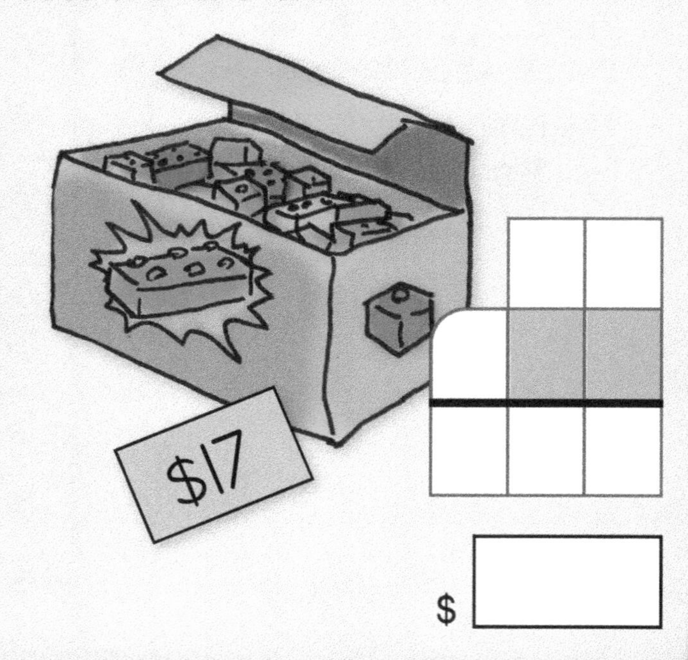

$ [ ]

See the Instructor Guide for directions.

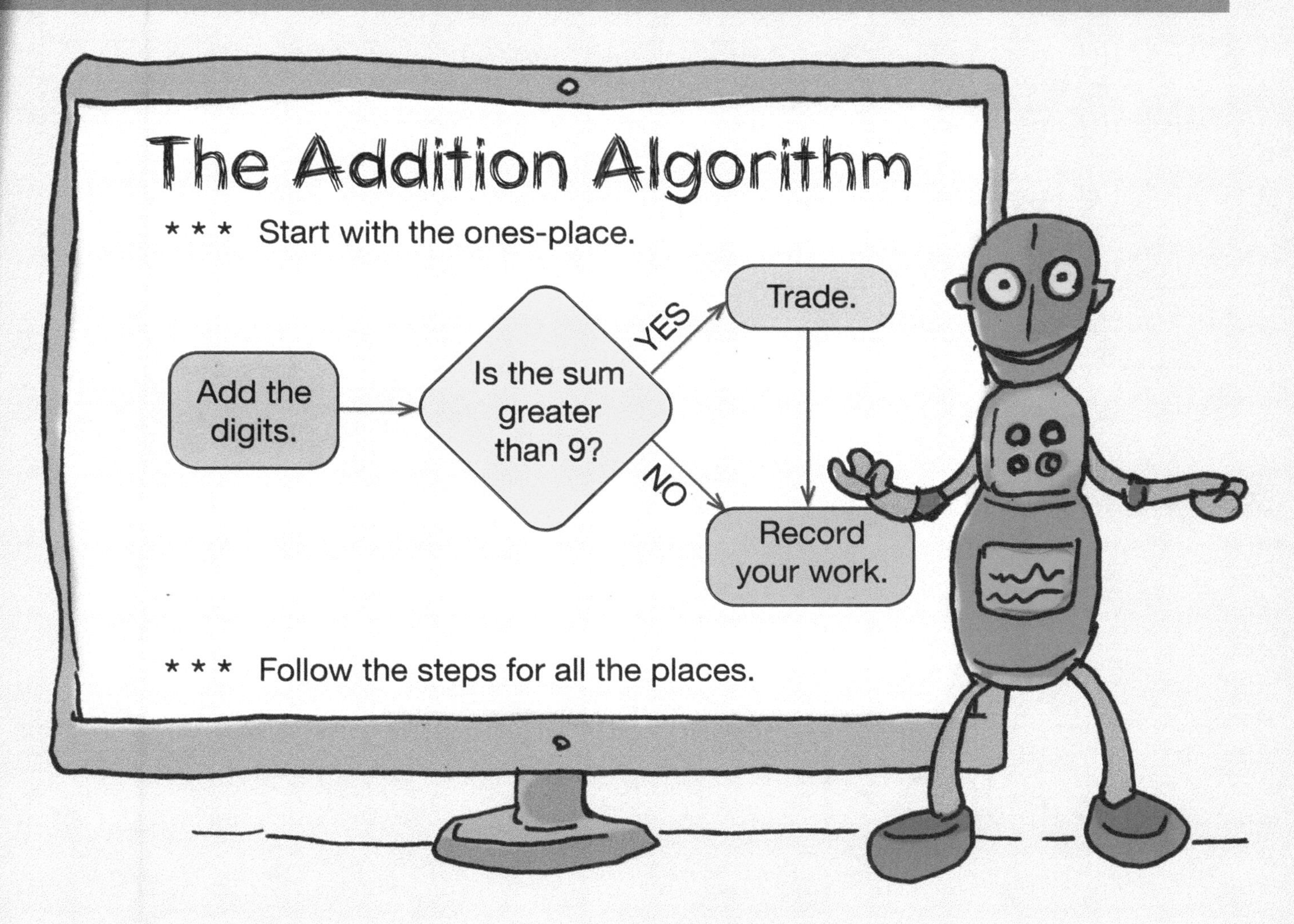

	2	1	3
+	3	4	5

	1	9	4
+	4	2	0

	6	1	6
+	1	7	5

	6	8	1
+		7	2

	4	5	7
+	2	5	1

	3	7	4
+	5	4	8

Label the numbers on the number line.

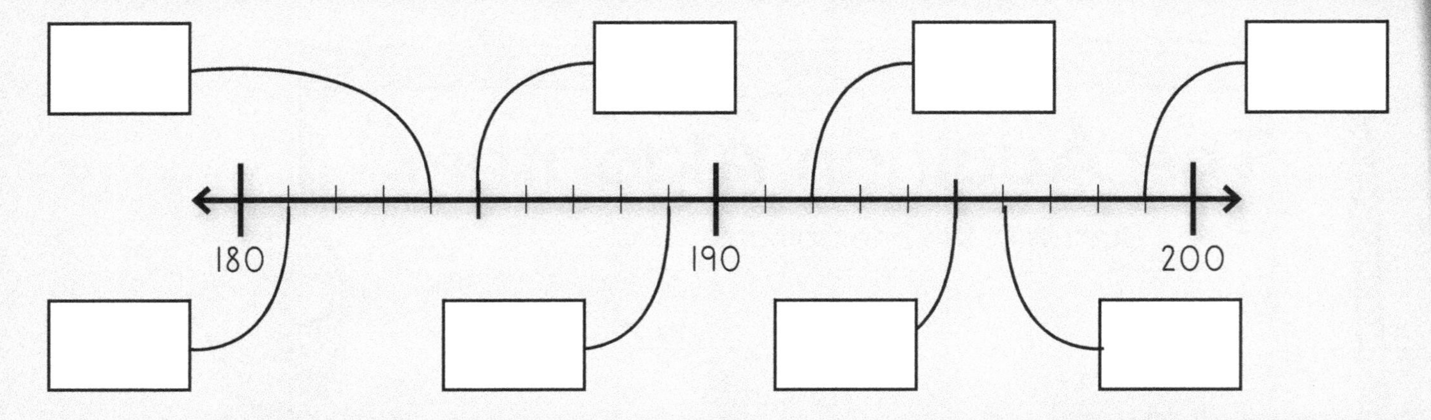

Complete.

425 + 3 = ☐	708 - 7 = ☐
619 + 20 = ☐	840 - 30 = ☐
332 + 400 = ☐	523 - 200 = ☐

Zoe counted some of her toys. Use her chart to make a bar graph.

Toy	Number
Dolls	8
Stuffed Animals	12
Puppets	4

My Toys

Dolls

Stuffed Animals

Puppets

2 4 6 8 10 12

See the Instructor Guide for directions.

Snowball Fight

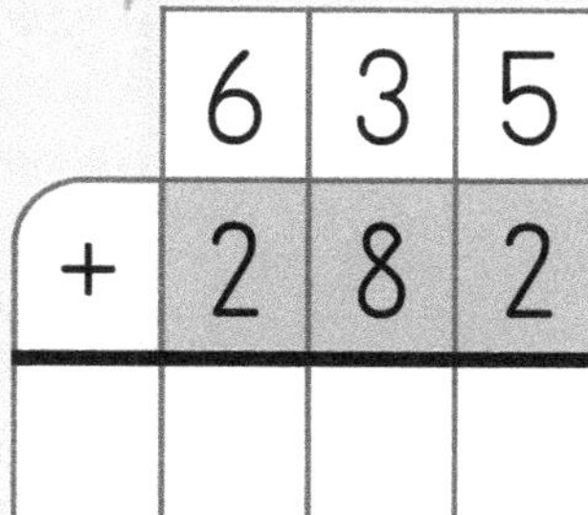

	4	7	5
+	3	6	9

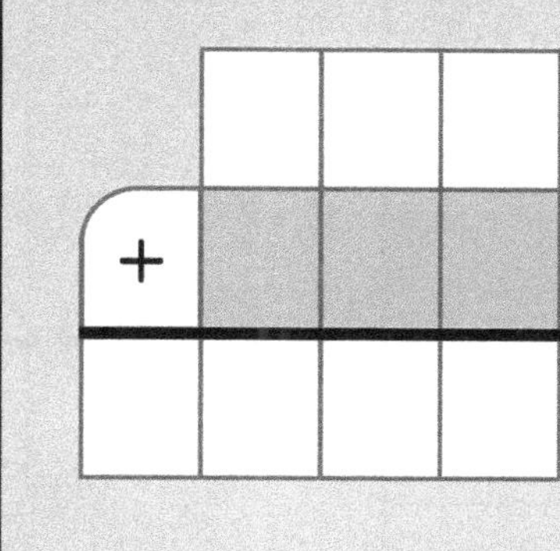

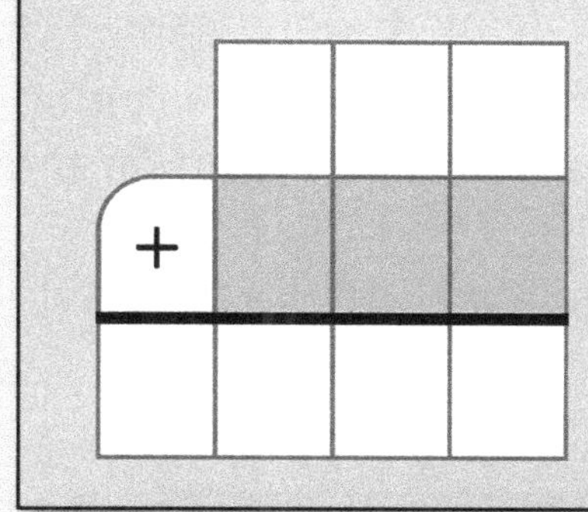

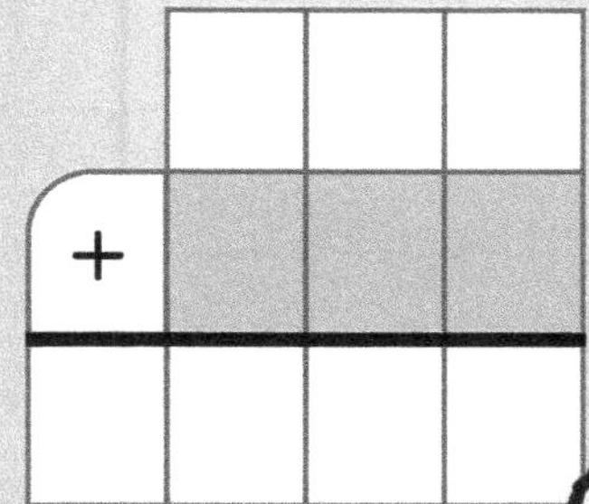

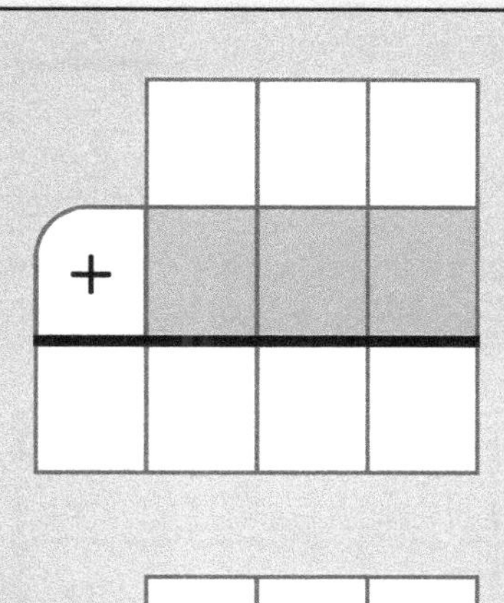

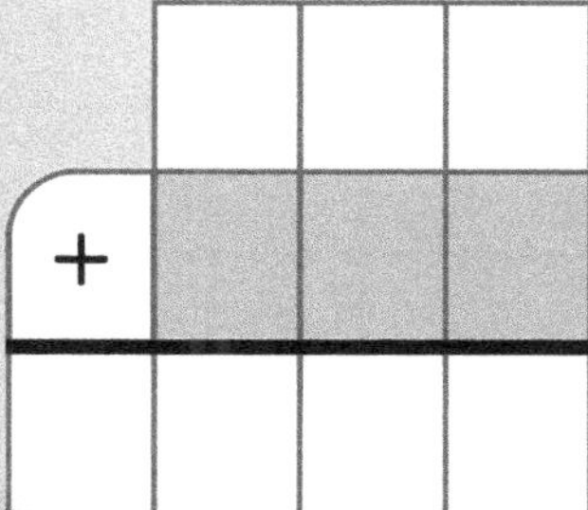

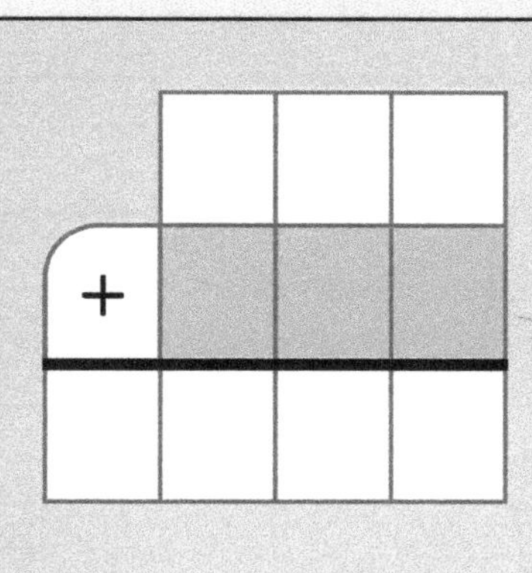

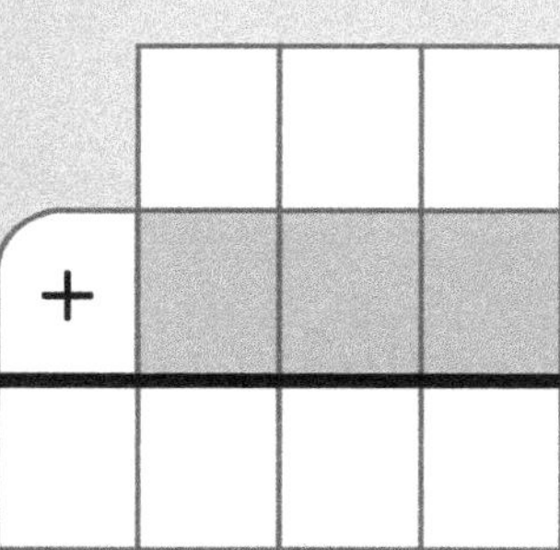

175 162 247 254 451 106 379 493 360 387 286 498

Use the chart to answer the questions.

Name	Age
Grandma	61
Grandpa	60
Mom	33
Dad	34
Caleb	7

How much older is Grandma than Mom?

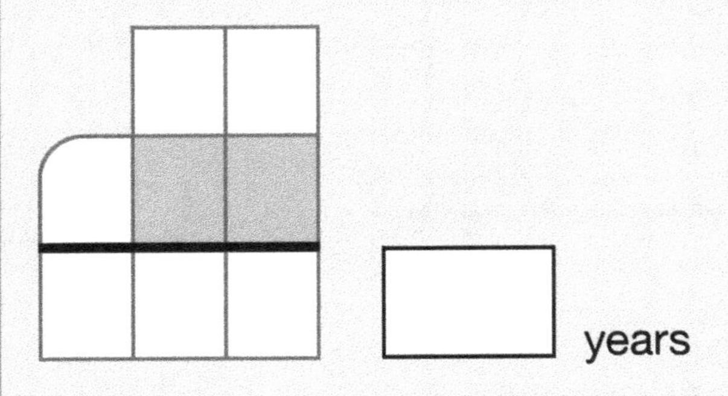

years

How much older is Grandpa than Dad?

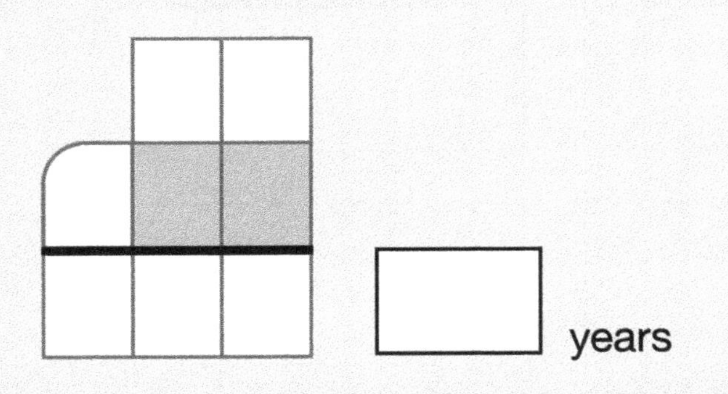

years

How much younger is Caleb than Grandma?

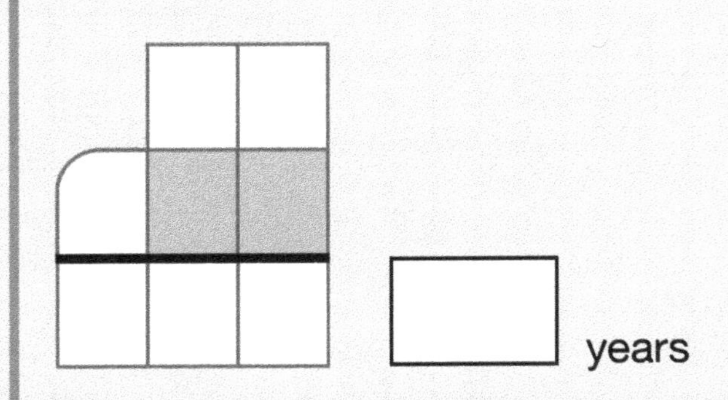

years

Color the shapes to match the fractions.

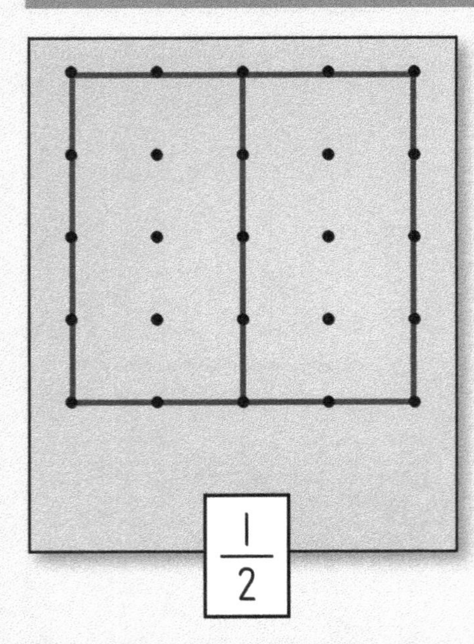

$\frac{1}{2}$

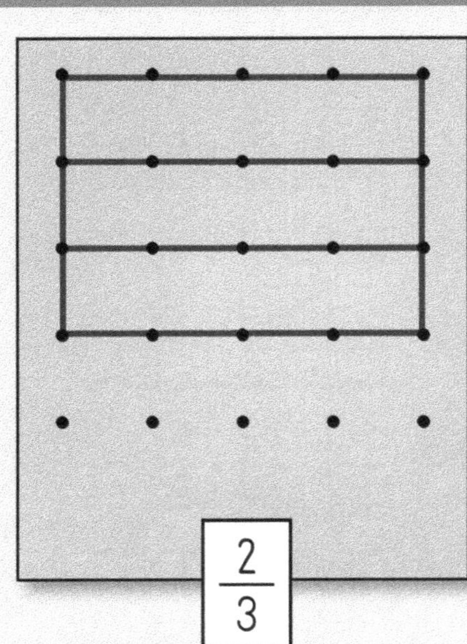

$\frac{2}{3}$

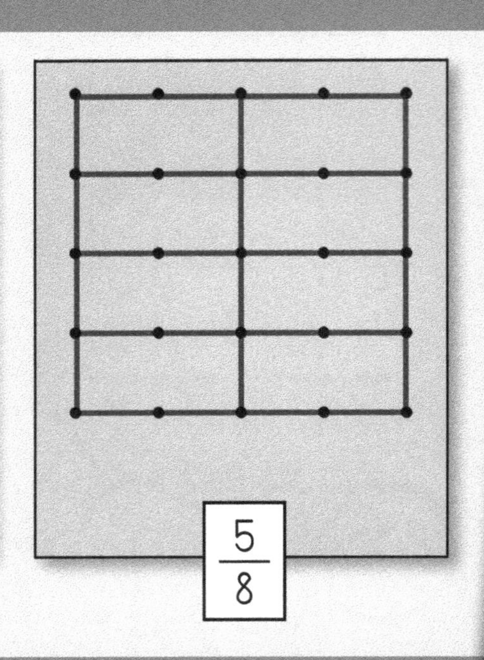

$\frac{5}{8}$

See the Instructor Guide for directions.

	3	5	4
	1	3	3
+	2	4	5

	4	0	6
	1	9	8
+	3	6	3

	2	4	1
	2	1	8
	2	2	5
+	2	0	7

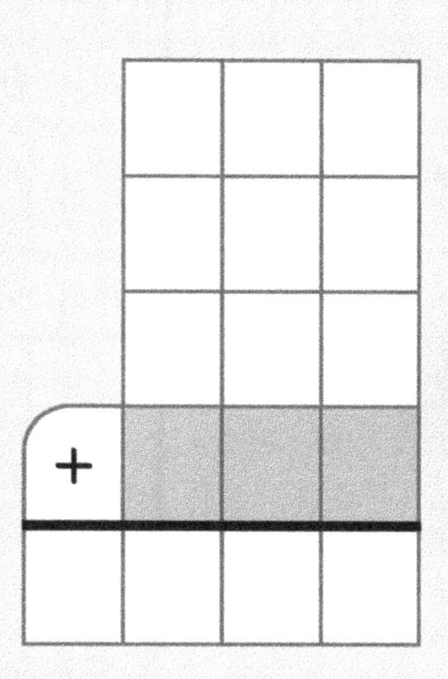

Complete.

	5	5	0
	1	3	2
+	2	6	4

	2	2	3
	2	7	1
	2	4	0
+	2	6	1

	1	5	1
	2	0	9
	1	4	5
	3	2	0
+	1	3	6

Match.

Cylinder	Sphere	Cube	Rectangular prism	Cone

Write the numbers that come before and after.

	438	
	600	
	399	

	559	
	830	
	709	

Use a ruler to draw lines that match the lengths.

4 inches

12 centimeters

Use the chart to answer the questions.

Bike Shop Prices

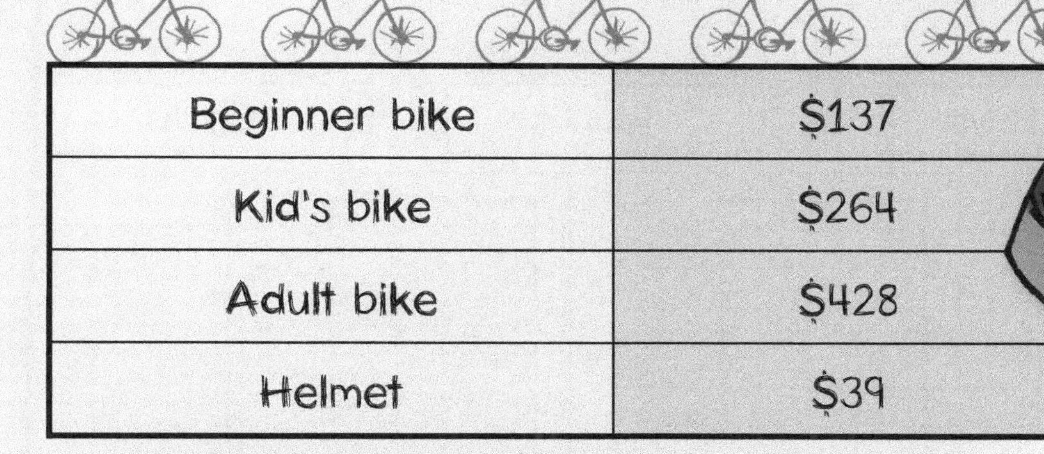

Beginner bike	$137
Kid's bike	$264
Adult bike	$428
Helmet	$39

How much does it cost to buy a kid's bike and adult bike?

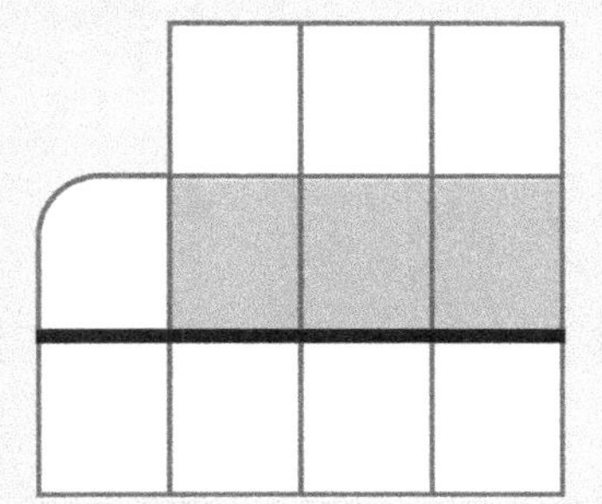

$ ______

How much does it cost to buy a beginner bike and helmet?

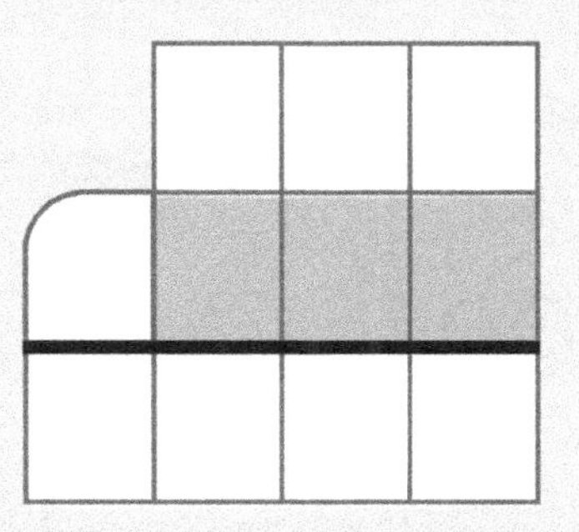

$ ______

How much does it cost to buy 2 beginner bikes?

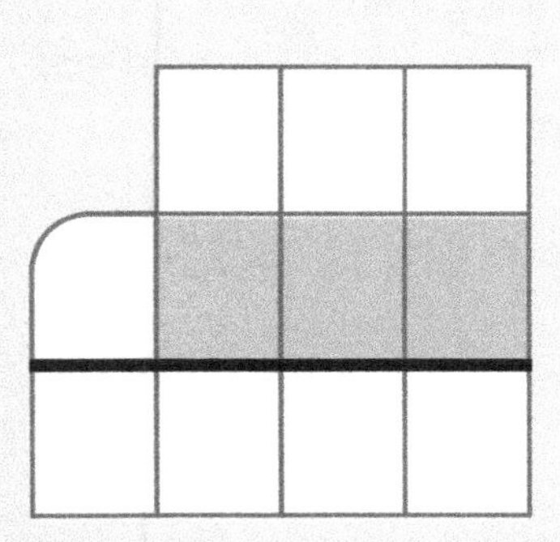

$ ______

How much does it cost to buy a beginner bike, kid's bike, and adult bike?

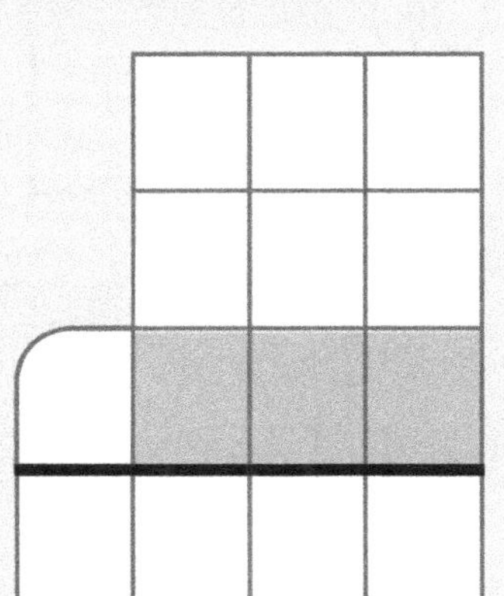

$ ______

Draw lines to split the shapes into the matching parts.

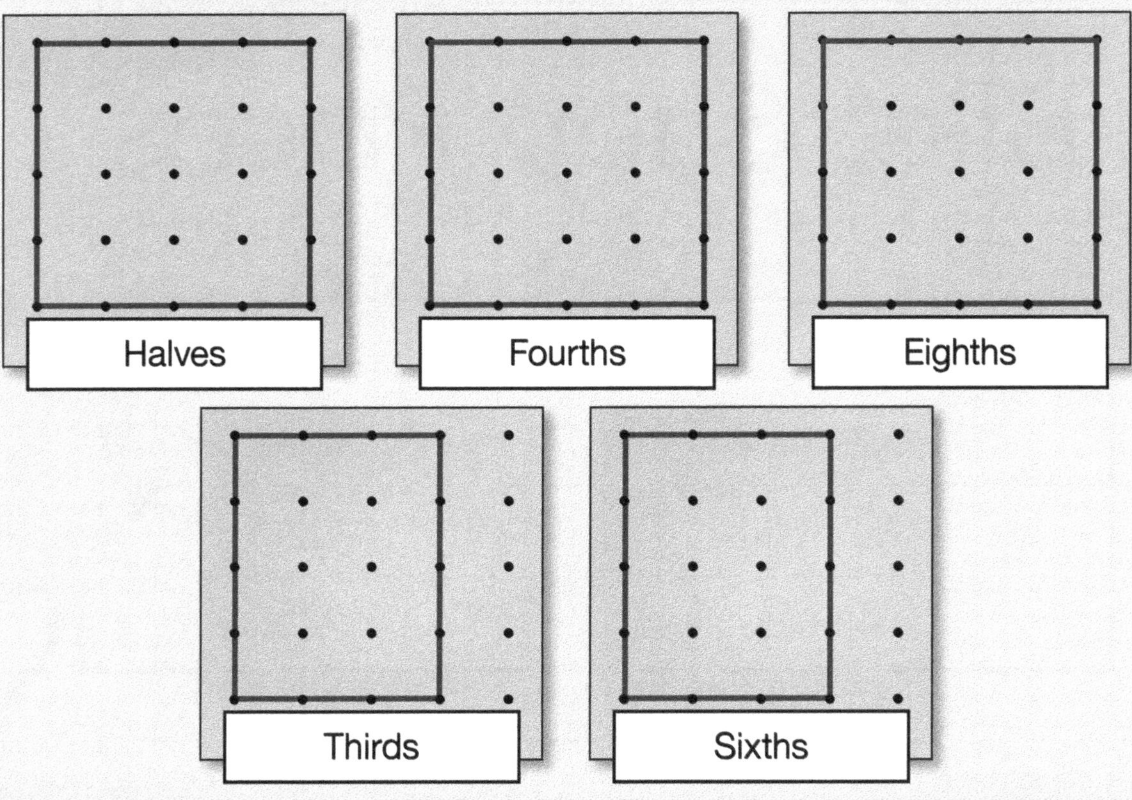

Complete the sequences.

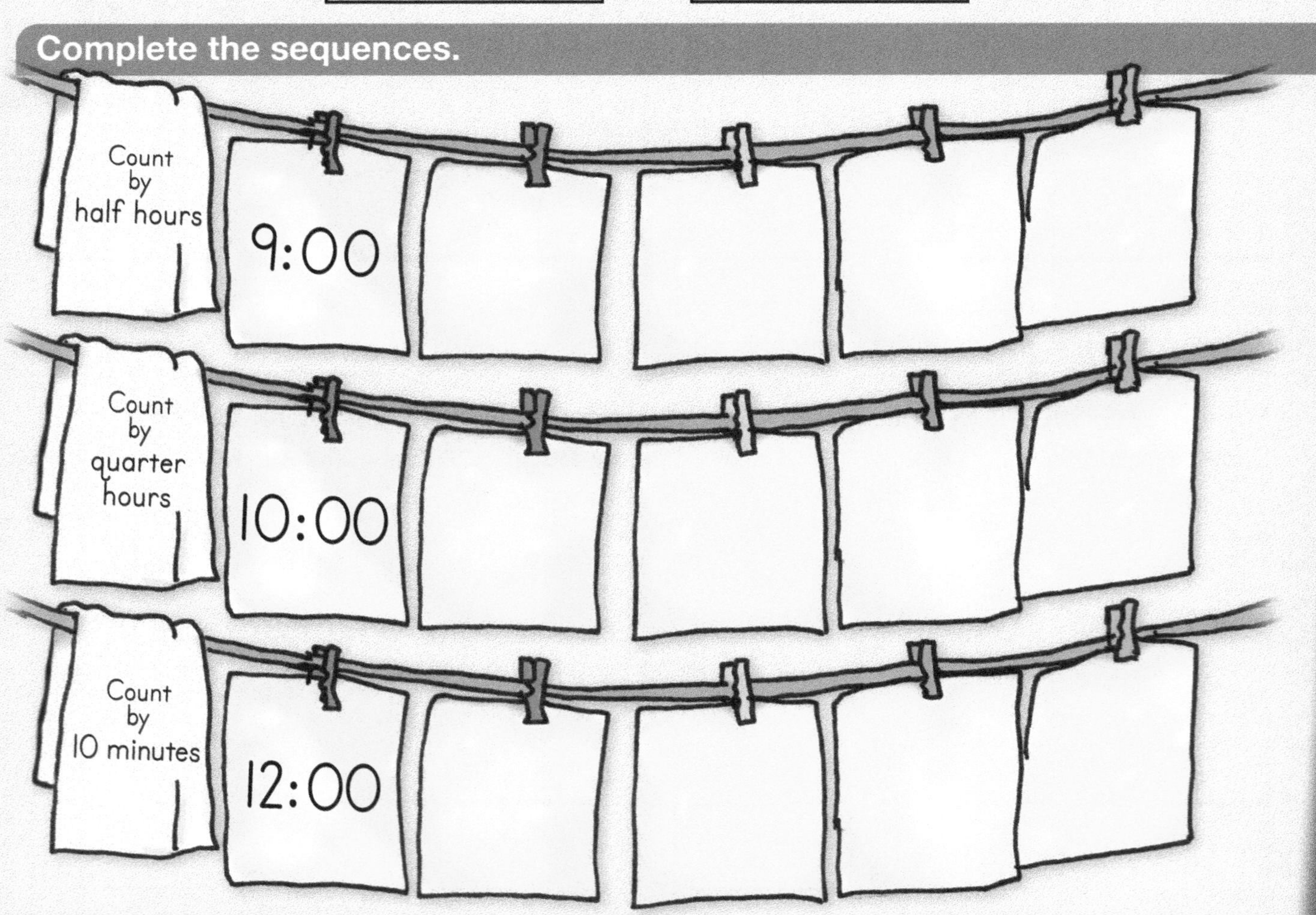

See the Instructor Guide for directions.

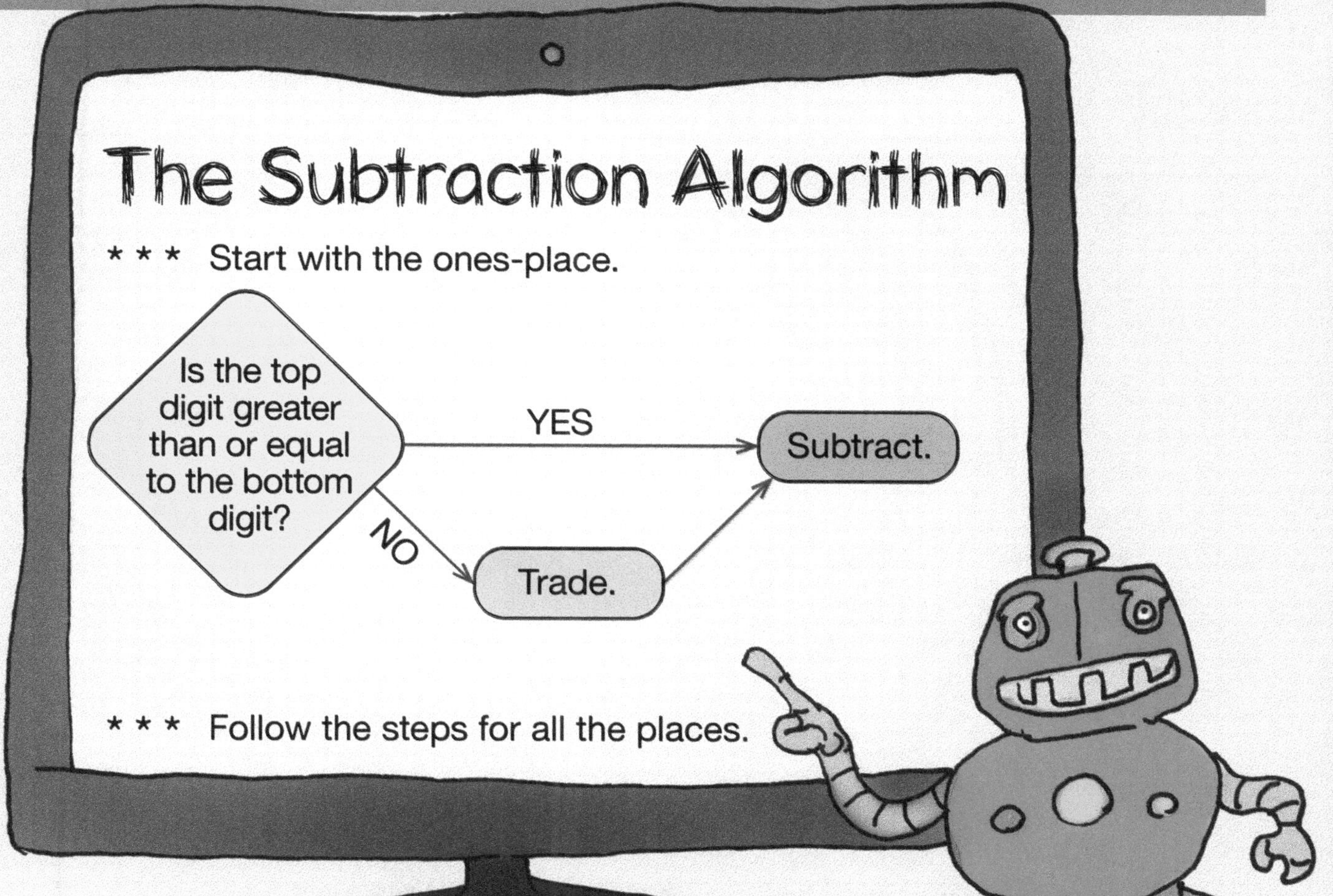

	7	8	6
-	3	1	4

	6	2	9
-	2	4	8

	5	9	1
-	3	3	8

	5	7	0
-	2	3	6

	8	1	7
-		8	4

	4	3	5
-	2	6	8

Complete each box with a number that makes the statement true.

500	>		236	<		499	=	
	=	8		<	301		>	301
1000	>		0	<			<	5

Count by 2s to connect the dots in order.

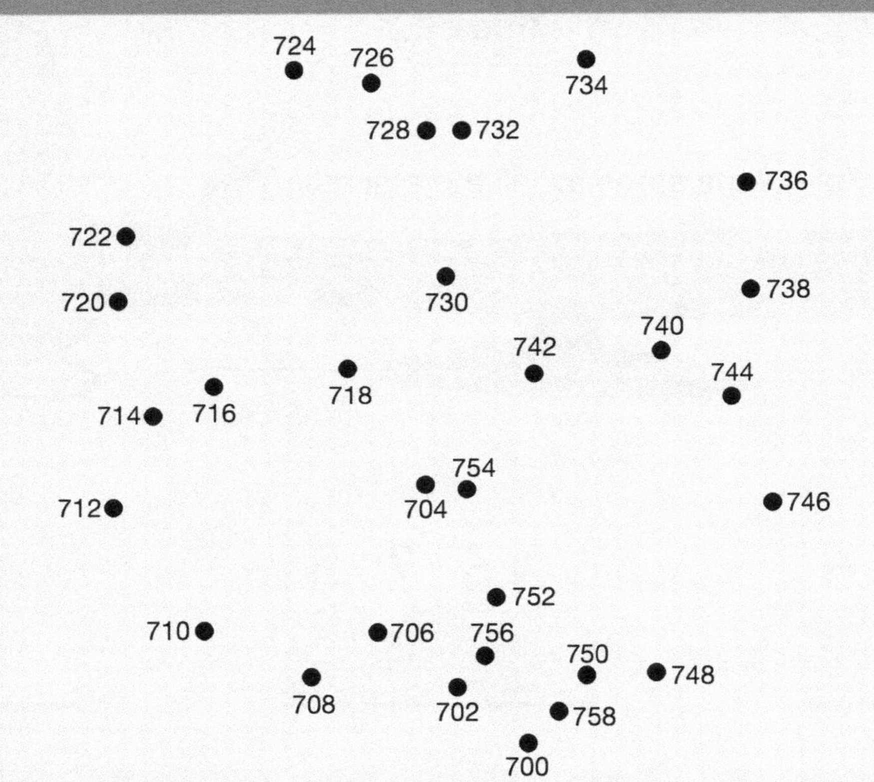

Complete.

$

$$\begin{array}{r} 504 \\ -\ 351 \\ \hline \end{array} \qquad \begin{array}{r} 602 \\ -\ 476 \\ \hline \end{array} \qquad \begin{array}{r} 800 \\ -\ 439 \\ \hline \end{array}$$

What's the Difference?

902 605 359 268

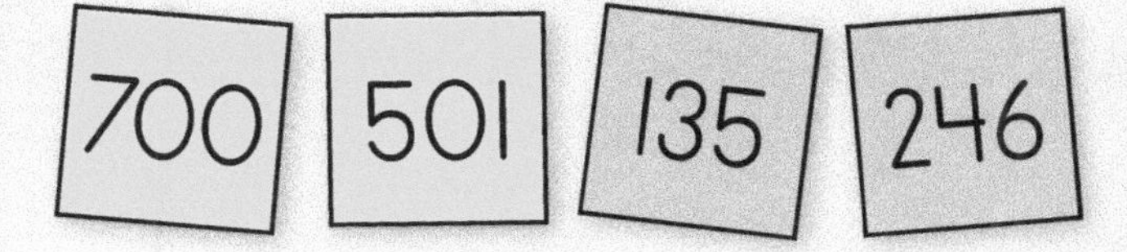

906 900 279 317

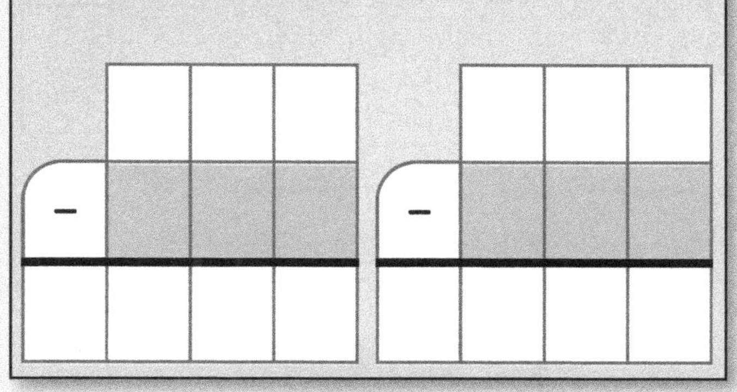

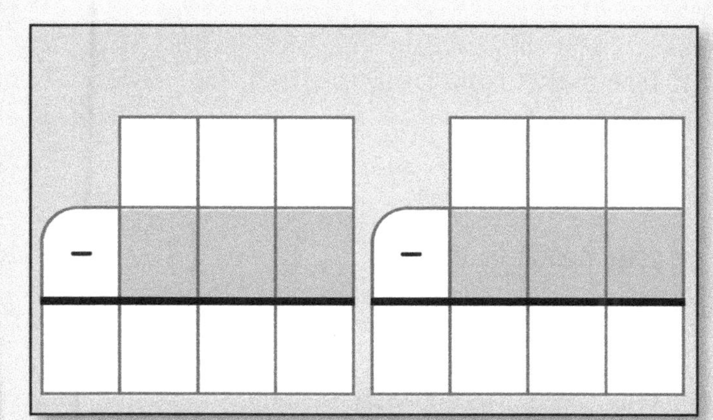

Solve.

Eliana's stick is 83 centimeters long. Leah's stick is 67 centimeters long. How much longer is Eliana's stick than Leah's stick?

83 centimeters

67 centimeters

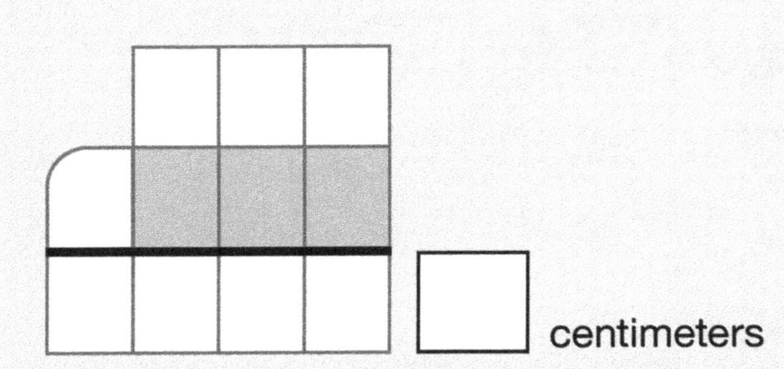

centimeters

Nolan's stick is 76 centimeters long. Adrian's stick is 124 centimeters long. How much shorter is Nolan's stick than Adrian's stick?

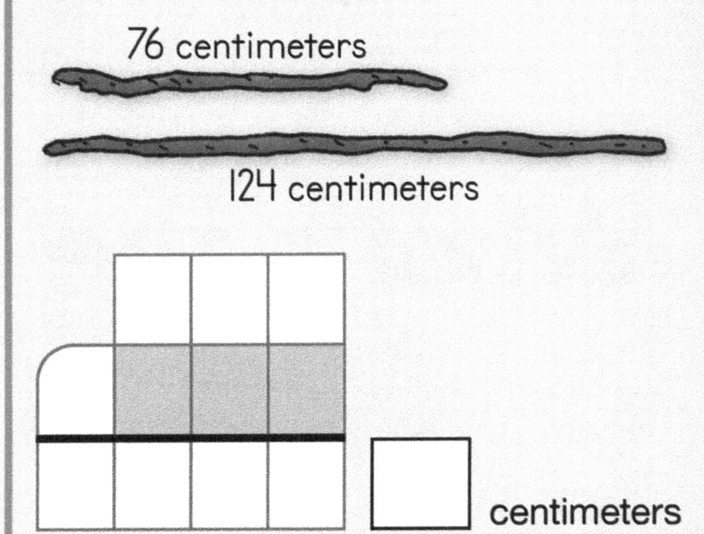

centimeters

Complete.

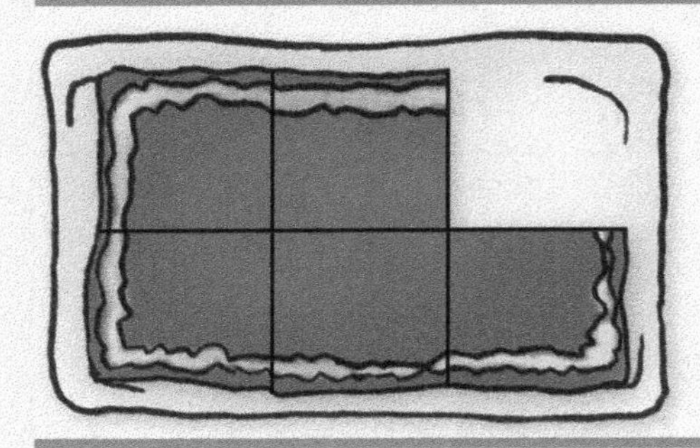

$\frac{5}{6}$ of the cake is left.

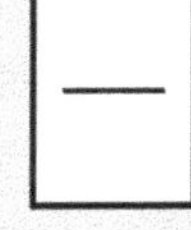

of the cake has been eaten.

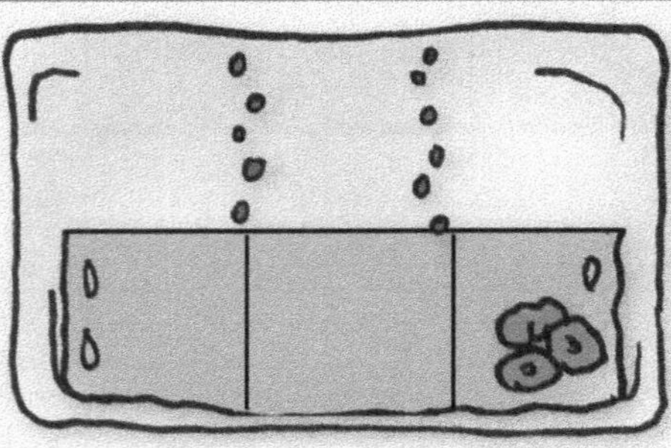

of the cake is left.

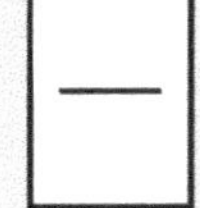

of the cake has been eaten.

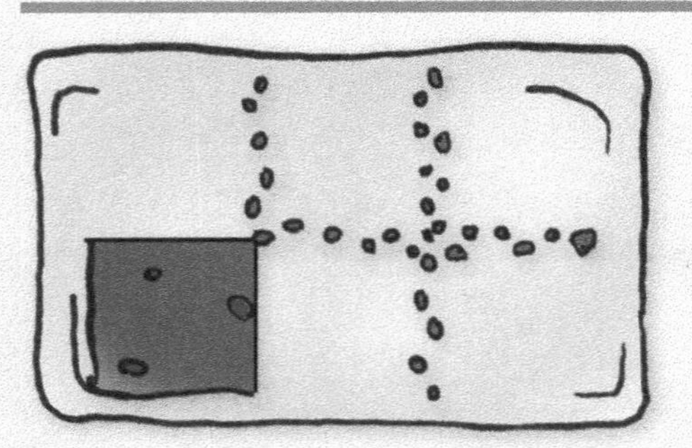

of the cake is left.

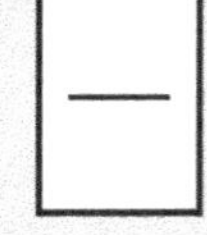

of the cake has been eaten.

See the Instructor Guide for directions.

	9	2	8
-	2	4	5

	8	7	2
-	6	0	9

	7	0	1
-	2	6	7

SPIN TO WIN!

906, 587, 850, 600, 703, 502

264, 158, 345, 407, 186, 319

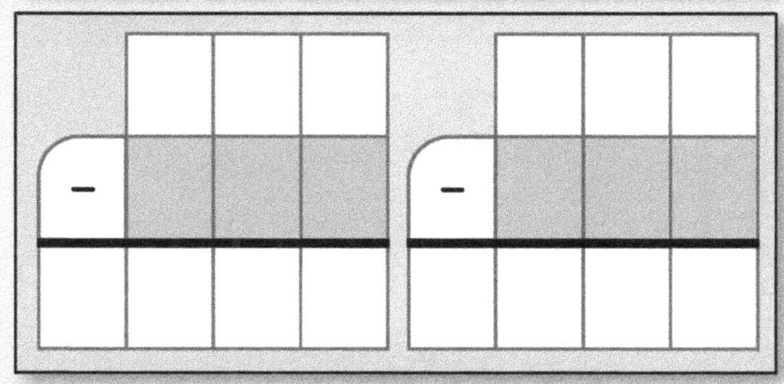

Complete.

1 week = ☐ days

1 day = ☐ hours

1 hour = ☐ minutes

1 minute = ☐ seconds

1 yard = ☐ feet

1 yard = ☐ inches

1 foot = ☐ inches

1 meter = ☐ centimeters

Complete.

400 + 500 = ☐	500 + 500 = ☐
400 + 50 = ☐	500 + 50 = ☐
400 + 5 = ☐	500 + 5 = ☐

Leila counted how many rainy days there were each month. Use her chart to complete the pictograph.

Month	Days
March	10
April	14
May	8

Rainy Days

March	💧💧💧💧💧
April	
May	

💧 = 2 rainy days

Use the chart to answer the questions.

How much more does a spiral slide cost than a regular slide?

$

How much more does a tire swing cost than a regular swing?

$

You have $300. You buy a climbing net. How much money do you have left?

$

A baby swing costs $116 less than a tire swing. How much does a baby swing cost?

$

Write the time.

Match the pairs that equal 1000.

900

500

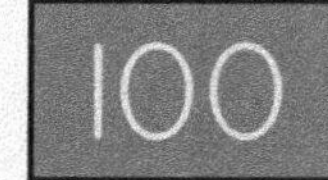

200

Circle the quadrilaterals. X the shapes that are not quadrilaterals.

Write the expanded form for each number.

352 =	671 =
499 =	908 =

Complete the circles with <, >, or =.

146 ◯ 140	964 ◯ 469	399 ◯ 400
200 ◯ 201	328 ◯ 519	602 ◯ 609
607 ◯ 670	564 ◯ 564	987 ◯ 978

Complete the sequences.

Complete.

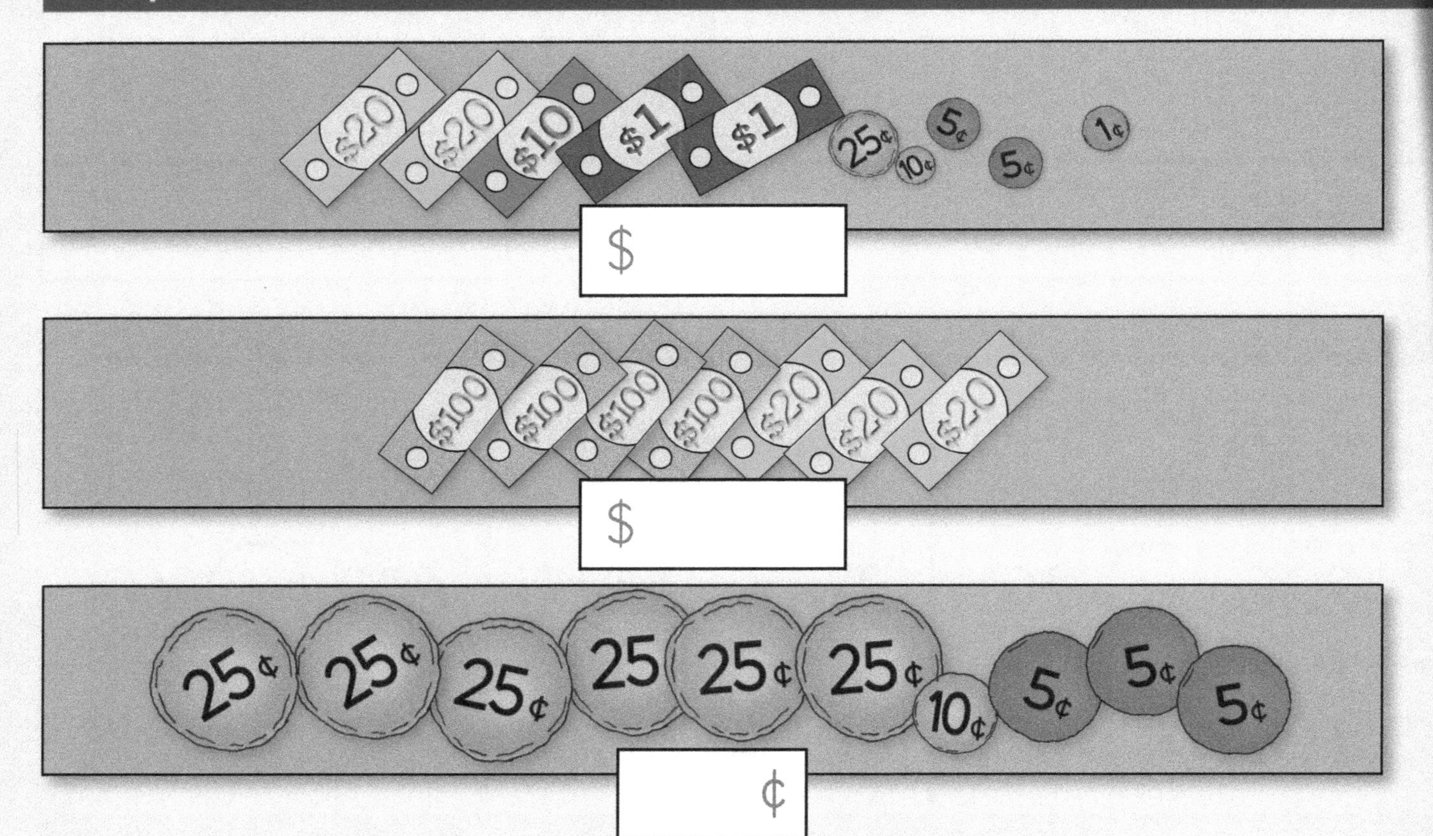

Color the even numbers yellow. Color the odd numbers red.

Complete.

	3	7	2
+	4	5	6

	6	0	8
+	2	4	8

	4	9	3
+	3	6	7

	6	8	4
-	2	3	5

	7	5	3
-	4	8	8

	8	0	9
-	2	5	4

Match.

352+2 ····	354	384-60
200+300	364	600-100
300+100	324	564-200
304+20	400	358-4
264+100	500	800-400

Aaron made a sketch about his family's summer road trip. Use his sketch to answer the questions.

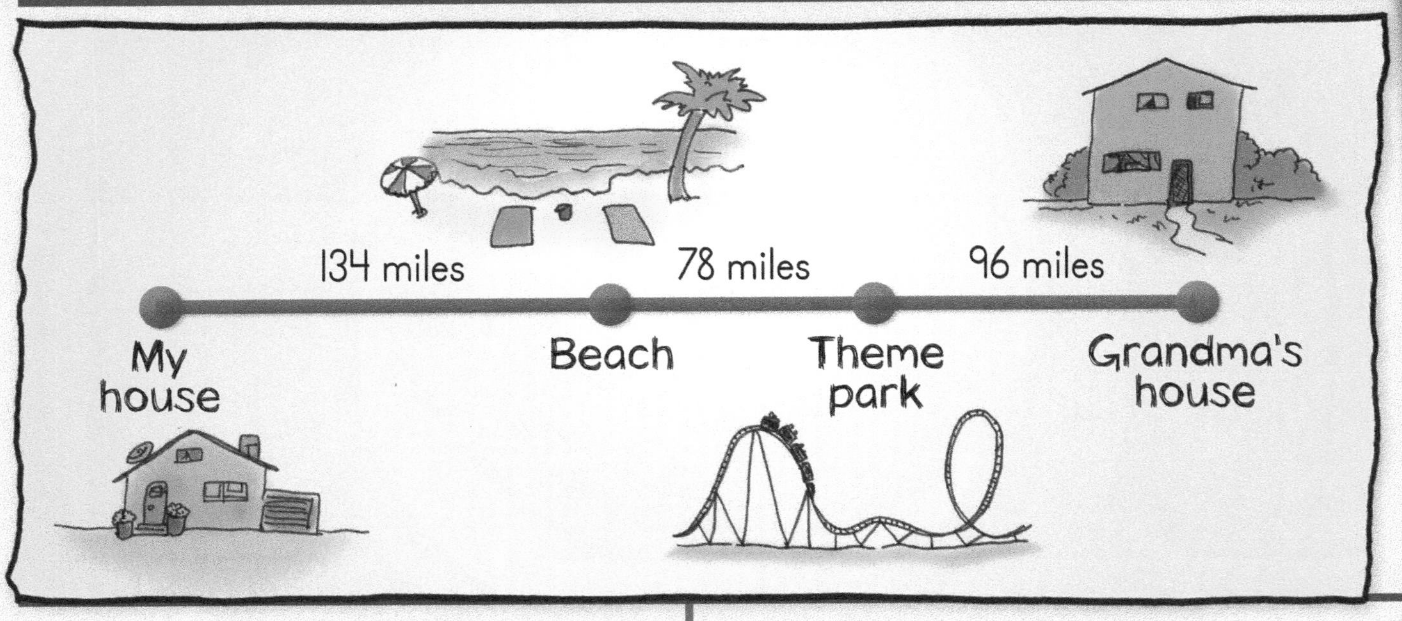

How far is it from Aaron's house to the theme park?

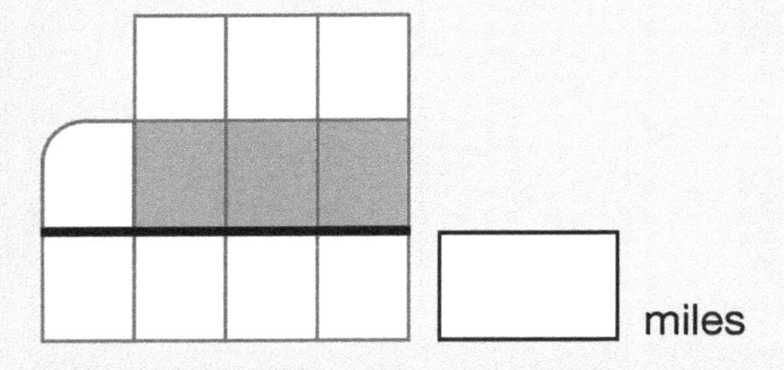

How much longer is the distance from Aaron's house to the beach than the distance from the beach to the theme park?

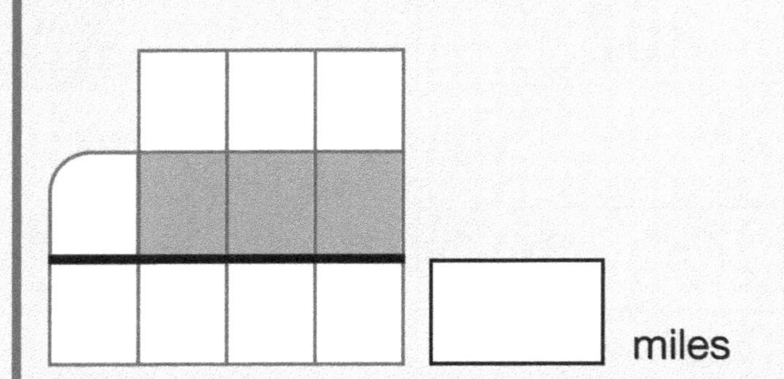

How much shorter is the distance from the beach to the theme park than the distance from the theme park to Grandma's house?

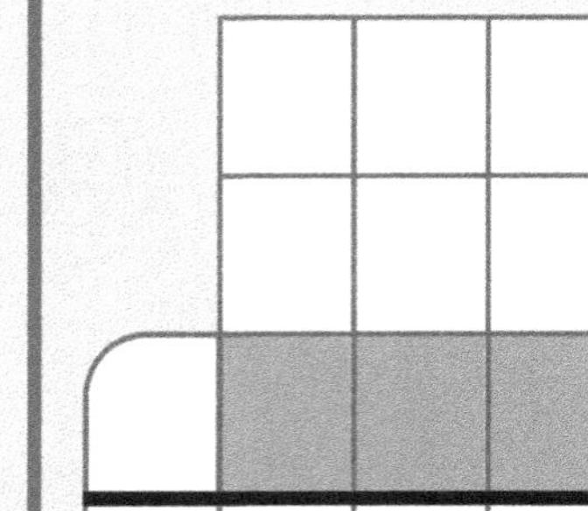

How far is it from Aaron's house to Grandma's house?

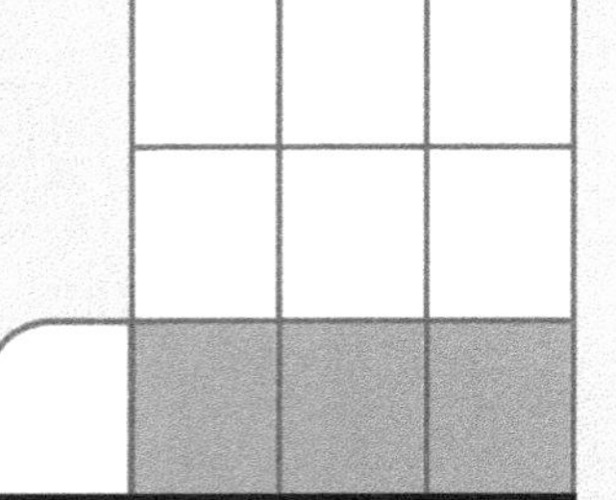

Write a fraction for the purple part of each shape.

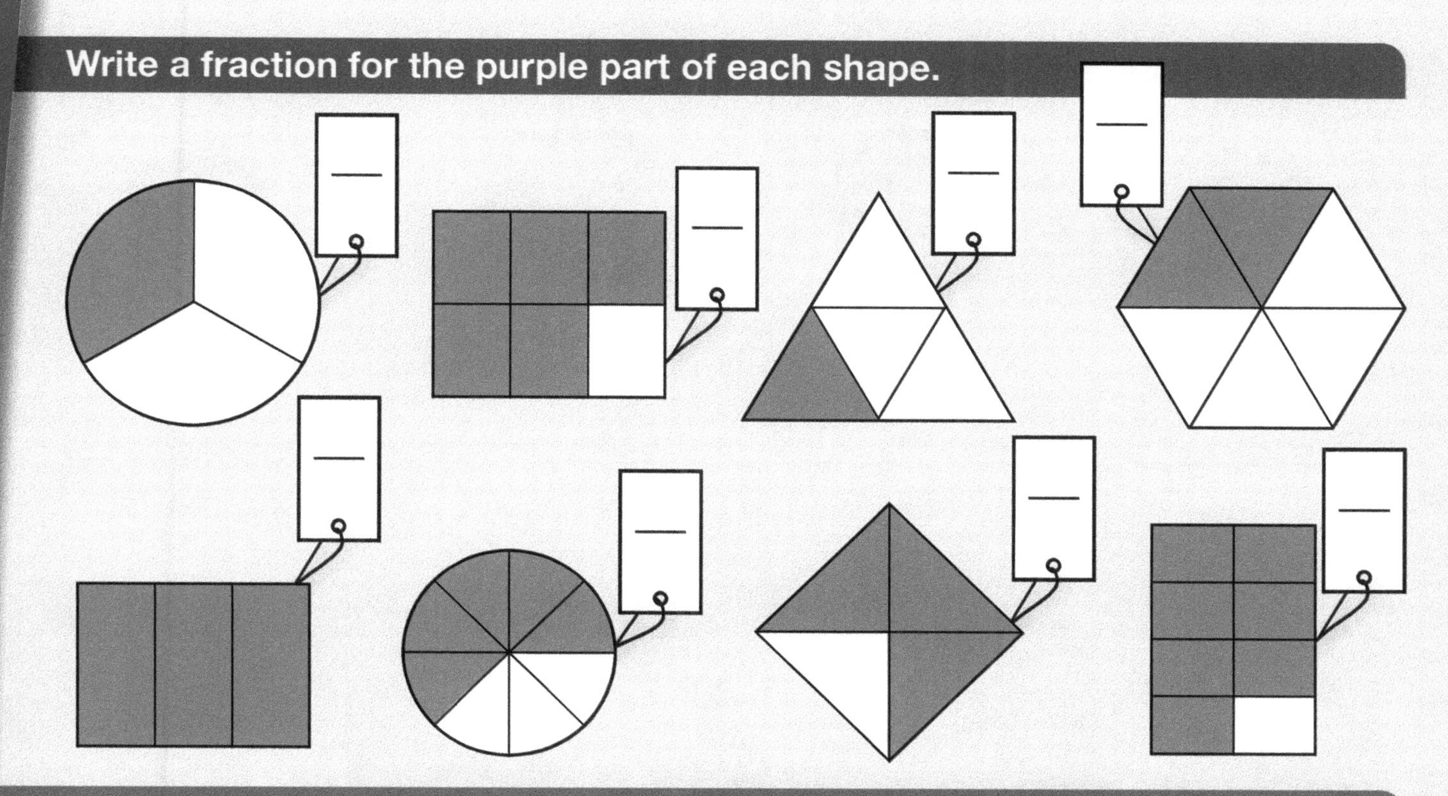

Circle the more sensible measurement.

Width of a butterfly

7 centimeters | 7 meters

Length of a spade

4 inches | 4 feet

Length of a hiking trail

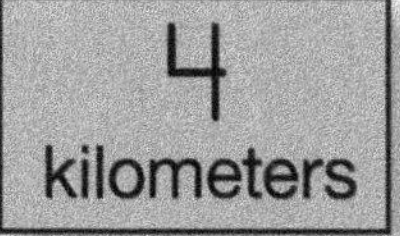

4 meters | 4 kilometers

Write the time.

Match each shape to its name.

Octagon

Hexagon

Pentagon

Quadrilateral

Match each shape to its name.

Cube

Rectangular prism

Cone

Cylinder

Sphere

Use a ruler to measure the lines.

inches

inches

centimeters

Complete each sentence.

My favorite math activity this year was

The most interesting thing I learned in math this year was

I worked hard to learn

Next year in math, I hope to learn

Draw a picture of your favorite math activity from this year.

CONGRATULATIONS!

Presented to

____

for successfully completing

Second Grade Math with Confidence

____________________ ____________________

Date Signature